OBJECTIVE RELIGION

Volume Two
Problems, Prosociality, Progress

Byron R. Johnson
Editor

BAYLOR UNIVERSITY PRESS
BAYLOR INSTITUTE FOR STUDIES OF RELIGION

© 2022 by Baylor University Press
Waco, Texas 76798

All Rights Reserved. No part of this publication may be reproduced, stored in a retrieval system, or transmitted, in any form or by any means, electronic, mechanical, photocopying, recording, or otherwise, without the prior permission in writing of Baylor University Press.

Cover and book design by Kasey McBeath
Typeset by Scribe Inc.

This project was made possible by funding from the Baylor Institute for Studies of Religion, Baylor University.

Paperback ISBN: 978-1-4813-1365-0
Printed case ISBN: 978-1-4813-1771-9

Library of Congress Control Number: 2022940216

About Baylor Institute for Studies of Religion

Launched in August 2004, the Baylor Institute for Studies of Religion (ISR) exists to initiate, support, and conduct research on religion, involving scholars and projects spanning the intellectual spectrum: history, psychology, sociology, economics, anthropology, political science, philosophy, epidemiology, theology, and religious studies. Our mandate extends to all religions, everywhere, and throughout history. It also embraces the study of religious effects on such things as prosocial behavior, family life, population health, economic development, and social conflict. While always striving for appropriate scientific objectivity, our scholars treat religion with the respect that sacred matters require and deserve.

About the *Interdisciplinary Journal for Research on Religion*

The *Interdisciplinary Journal for Research on Religion* (IJRR) was founded in 2005, in order to publish very high quality, original research on religion by scholars, regardless of their field of specialization. Unfortunate accidents of history separated the social sciences into an archipelago of fields and departments. Efforts to break through these artificial barriers by publishing interdisciplinary journals have been hindered because these publications have conferred less prestige to authors than have the best journals focused on a single field. Consequently, some of the most important articles published by the specialty journals are difficult for nonspecialists even to be aware of, let alone appreciate fully, while interdisciplinary journals have lacked the space needed to include the additional explanations, definitions, and context to make many important articles fully accessible to nonspecialists. IJRR was launched to eliminate these barriers and has helped to create a vehicle to catalyze an international community of scholars to conduct, publish, and disseminate cutting-edge research on religion and spirituality in the world.

CONTENTS

List of Tables and Figures	vii
Foreword	xiii
Jeff Levin	
Introduction	1
I Volunteerism	**3**
1 Religion and Volunteering in Four Sub-Saharan African Countries	9
Meredith J. Greif, Amy Adamczyk, and Jacob Felson	
2 Religion and Philanthropic Giving and Volunteering: Building Blocks for Civic Responsibility	39
Stephen V. Monsma	
3 Religious Motivations and Social Service Volunteers: The Interaction of Differing Religious Motivations, Satisfaction, and Repeat Volunteering	71
Richard M. Clerkin and James E. Swiss	
4 Women Religious in a Changing Urban Landscape: The Work of Catholic Sisters in Metropolitan Cleveland	91
Robert L. Fischer and Jennifer Bartholomew	
II Social Capital	**109**
5 Religious Tradition and Involvement in Congregational Activities That Focus on the Community	117
Jennifer M. McClure	
6 God, Guts, and Glory: An Investigation of Relational Support Mechanisms for War Veterans Provided by Religious Communities	151
Terry Shoemaker	

7 The Impact of Church Attendance on the Decline in
   Female Happiness in the United States   173
      G. Alexander Ross

8 The Socioeconomic Contribution of Religion to
   American Society: An Empirical Analysis   209
      Brian J. Grim and Melissa E. Grim

III Addressing Social Problems   **247**

9 Religion, Intact Families, and the Achievement Gap   251
      William H. Jeynes

10 Religion and Academic Achievement among Adolescents   277
      Benjamin McKune and John P. Hoffmann

11 The Faith Factor and Prisoner Reentry   299
      Byron R. Johnson

12 Does Change in Teenage Religiosity Predict Change in
   Marijuana Use over Time?   321
      Scott A. Desmond, George Kikuchi, and Kristen Budd

13 Religiosity as a Buffer in the Association between Economic
   Disadvantage and Violence   353
      Cassady Pitt and Alfred DeMaris

Contributors   381

LIST OF TABLES AND FIGURES

Table 1-1: Descriptive Statistics for Variables Included in the Analysis ($N = 6,175$)   19

Table 1-2: Logistic Regression Analysis of the Influence of Gender and Religion on Caregiver Volunteering   21

Table 1-3: Logistic Regression Analysis of the Influence of Gender and Religion on Political Volunteering   23

Table 1-4: Logistic Regression Analysis of the Influence of the Interaction between Gender and Religion on Caregiver Volunteering   25

Table 1-5: Logistic Regression Analysis of the Influence of the Interaction between Gender and Religion on Political Volunteering   26

Table 1-6: Logistic Regression Analysis of the Influence of the Interaction between Nation and Religion on Caregiver Volunteering   28

Table 1-7: Logistic Regression Analysis of the Influence of the Interaction between Nation and Religion on Political Volunteering   30

Table 2-1: Percent of Respondents Giving to Religious and Nonreligious Causes by Religious Salience, Level of Traditional Christian Beliefs, and Level of Private Religious Practices   50

Table 2-2: Percent of Respondents Volunteering, by Religious Salience, Level of Traditional Christian Beliefs, and Level of Private Religious Practices   51

Table 2-3: Percent of Respondents Giving to Religious Causes, by Religious Tradition and Level of Attendance at Religious Services   55

Table 2-4: Percent of Respondents Giving to Nonreligious Causes, by Religious Tradition and Level of Attendance at Religious Services — 57

Table 2-5: Percent of Respondents Volunteering for Religious Causes, by Religious Tradition and Level of Attendance at Religious Services — 58

Table 2-6: Percent of Respondents Volunteering for Nonreligious Causes, by Religious Tradition and Level of Attendance at Religious Services — 59

Table 2-7: Percentages of Respondents Voting and Not Voting, by Giving and Volunteering to Religious and Nonreligious Causes — 61

Table 2-8: Percentages of Respondents with High and Low Political Involvement, by Giving to and Volunteering for Religious and Nonreligious Causes — 64

Table 2-9: Political Involvement, by Church Attendance and Whether or Not Respondents Had Given or Volunteered to Religious and Nonreligious Causes (percent voting or ranking high in political involvement, Pew IV data) — 65

Table 3-1: Volunteer Motivation by Age — 76

Table 3-2: Volunteer Motivation by Gender — 77

Table 3-3: Volunteer Motivation by Religion — 77

Table 3-4: Type of Religious Motivation by Age — 79

Table 3-5: Type of Religious Motivation by First-Time Volunteer Status — 79

Table 3-6: Type of Religious Motivation by Faith Tradition — 80

Table 3-7: Logistic Regression of Satisfaction with Religious Outcomes for Youths and Adults — 82

Table 3-8: Logistic Regression of Overall Satisfaction for Youths and Adults — 83

Figure 3-1: Predicted Probability of Adult Returners and First-Timers Volunteering with the Same Nonprofit Organization Next Year — 85

Table 3-9: Logistic Regression of Likelihood to Volunteer within the Next Year — 86

Figure 4-1: Population Trends in Cuyahoga County — 93

Table 4-1: Religious Orders of Respondents — 95

Figure 4-2: Women Religious in Cuyahoga County — 96

Table 4-2: Primary Ministries of Women Religious	97
Table 4-3: Size and Scope of Ministries	98
Table 4-4: Target Service Populations of Ministries	100
Table 4-5: Potential Benefits of Collaboration	101
Figure 4-3: Ministries with Succession/Strategic Plans	102
Table 5-1: Descriptive Statistics	131
Table 5-2: Multilevel Logistic Regressions Predicting Involvement in Two Types of Congregational Activities That Focus on the Community	133
Figure 5-1: Predicted Probabilities for Involvement in Different Combinations of Congregational Activities That Focus on the Community	136
Table 5-3: Multilevel Multinomial Regression Predicting Involvement in Different Combinations of Congregational Activities That Focus on the Community	137
Figure 7-1: Change in Happiness among U.S. Women and Men, 1972–2008	177
Table 7-1: Trends in Happiness, United States, 1972–2008, GSS	179
Table 7-2: Church Attendance by Sex, GSS, 1972–2008	180
Table 7-3: General Happiness by Church Attendance, Women and Men	181
Figure 7-2: Estimates of the Probability of Church Attendance during the Week, by Sex	185
Table 7-4: Trends in Happiness with Church Attendance as Added Control	186
Table 7-5: Trends in Happiness for Each of Four Levels of Church Attendance	189
Table 7-1A: Trends in Happiness, United States, 1972–2008, GSS; Ordered Probit Results for All Variables	196
Table 7-4A: Trends in Happiness with Church Attendance as Added Control; Results for All Variables	198
Table 7-5A: Trends in Happiness for Each of Four Levels of Church Attendance; Results for All Variables	204
Table 8-1: Annual Tuition Payments to Faith-Based Higher Educational Institutions (Estimate)	213
Table 8-2: Annual Tuition Payments to Faith-Based Elementary Schools (Estimate)	213

x   List of Tables and Figures

Table 8-3: Annual Tuition Payments to Faith-Based Secondary
    Schools (Estimate) 214
Table 8-4: Annual Operating Revenues to Major Faith-Based
    Health Care Systems (Estimate, $Billions) 215
Table 8-5: Nationally Representative Data on Activities of U.S.
    Congregations (Multiple Faiths), ordered by amount or
    frequency of occurrence 218
Table 8-6: Annual Operating Revenues of Major Faith-Based
    Charities (Estimate, $Billions) 219
Table 8-7: Revenues of Faith-Based Media (Estimate, $Billions) ... 222
Table 8-8: Traditional Kosher and Halal Food Sales
    (Estimate, $Billions) 222
Table 8-9: Annual Revenue of U.S. Religious Organizations
    (Estimate, $Billions) 223
Table 8-10: Total Money Spent on Social Programs ($Billions) 224
Table 8-11: Nationally Representative Data on Activities of U.S.
    Congregations (Multiple Faiths), ordered by amount or
    frequency of occurrence 226
Figure 8-1: Religious Congregations' Value to U.S. Society
    ($418.9 billion, annually) 235
Table 8-12: Religion-Based Companies (Estimate, $Billions, 2014) ... 237
Table 8-13: Annual Socioeconomic Contribution of Religious
    Organizations to U.S. Society (Estimate, $Billions) ... 239
Table 8-14: Income of Religiously Affiliated (77.2% of population) ... 241
Table 9-1: Effects (in Percentage Score Increases) on the Academic
    Achievement of Twelfth-Grade Children by SES Quartile
    (NELS Dataset: $N = 20{,}706$) 257
Table 9-2: Effects (in Percentage Score Increases) on the Academic
    Achievement of Twelfth-Grade Children by Race (NELS
    Dataset: $N = 20{,}706$) 258
Table 9-3: Meta-Analysis Advantage for Low-SES Children
    Attending Religious Schools versus Their Counterparts in
    Public Schools by Level of Schooling 259
Table 9-4: Effects (in Standard Deviation Units) of Religious
    Schools versus Nonreligious Schools on the Five School
    Variables for the Twelfth Grade (1992) ($N = 18{,}726$) ... 262
Table 9-5: Rank Order of Learning Habits in Which Religious
    School Students Enjoy the Largest Advantage over Public

School Students and Learning Habits Most Closely Associated with High Academic Achievement	263
Table 9-6: Effects (in Standard Deviation Units) on Academic Achievement for Twelfth-Grade (1992) Black and Hispanic Children from a "More Traditional" Background versus White Children, Using the SES Model ($N = 24{,}599$)	267
Table 10-1: Regression Coefficients for Religiosity Predicting Academic Achievement (Partial Model), Add Health, 1994–1996	287
Table 10-2: Regression Coefficients for Religiosity Predicting Academic Achievement (Full Model), Add Health, 1994–1996	287
Table 10-3: Religious Homogamy and Academic Achievement (Partial Model), Add Health, 1994–1996	288
Table 10-4: Religious Homogamy and Academic Achievement (Full Model), Add Health, 1994–1996	288
Figure 10-1: Predicted Average Grades, by Parent and Adolescent Religiosity	290
Figure 11-1: Prisoner Reentry Initiative (PRI) Grants	311
Table 12-1: Descriptive Statistics for Marijuana Use, Religiosity, and Control Variables	331
Figure 12-1: Unconditional Latent Growth Curve Model for Marijuana Use	334
Table 12-2: Latent Growth Curve Model of Marijuana Use with Predictors	337
Figure 12-2: Religiosity and Trajectories of Marijuana Use	340
Figure 12-3: Dual-Trajectory Model of Religiosity and Marijuana Use	342
Table 12-3: Dual-Trajectory Model of Religiosity and Marijuana Use	346
Table 13-1: Descriptive Statistics	367
Table 13-2: Tobit Regression Coefficient Estimates (Standard Errors) for Models of Economic Disadvantage, Religiosity, and Violence	369

FOREWORD

Prosocial behavior is the phrase generally designated by social scientists to refer to actions devoted to benefiting other people. This meta-construct is of relatively recent vintage, a bit over three decades old by now, and it covers a large swath of psychosocial constructs and areas of research. Especially prominent are research programs in criminology, family studies, and community sociology, as well as studies of currently popular subjects such as altruism, happiness, and human flourishing. Research into patterns, determinants, and outcomes of prosocial behavior was and is motivated by a desire to encourage social and behavioral scientists to focus not just on the prevalence and predictors of social problems or pathologies, but on positive states and behaviors. The latter are not just the flip side of the former, but rather have their own theoretical bases and their own antecedents, and require their own conceptual models. Prosocial behavior, accordingly, is thus akin to other salutarily oriented meta-constructs such as subjective well-being and positive psychology, which, too, have experienced an uptick of attention from social researchers and psychologists over the past three decades.

Since the 1990s, as with well-being and positive psychology, studies have increasingly and consistently pointed to the domain of religiousness, spirituality, and faith as a principal source of determinants of prosocial behavior. People of faith, on average and across populations, tend to be happier and less depressed, to have more stable marriages, to be more charitable and altruistic, to have more traits indicative of psychological adjustment, and to be more law abiding. It is in the field of criminology, in my opinion, that the linkage between religion and prosocial behavior is most overt. To quote the title of a recent book on the subject, "More God, less crime."

The author of that book, my colleague Dr. Byron Johnson, is widely recognized as the most prominent researcher on religion within the field of criminology. But, more significantly, he is a leading voice in the larger field of prosocial behavior who has been calling attention to the mounting evidence that faith matters when it comes to generous other-regarding behavior. Religious faith is, of course, hardly a necessary condition when it comes to acting in ways that benefit others—compassionate other-regarding people are found across religious affiliations and faith identities, including "none of the above." But still, empirical research shows, on the whole and across populations there is a significant and meaningful association between the earnest practice of a life of faith and the practice of behavior in service to our brothers and sisters. Faith matters for the myriad categories of psychosocial outcomes noted above, as well as for other major outcomes included among the chapters in this marvelous book.

Indeed, *Objective Religion: Problems, Prosociality, Progress* is a veritable sourcebook on the subject of religion and prosocial behavior, and promises to be a generational benchmark on this vitally important yet underinvestigated topic. It may be a bit much to state that this will be the first and last word on this subject, but for the time being I suspect that this may well be the case. In my opinion, this collection of papers will be an important touchstone for scholars seeking to understand the impact and sweeping contributions of personal and communal religiousness on compassionate other-regarding behavior. It must be a source of great pride to Dr. Johnson, I am sure, that these papers are culled from the archives of the *Interdisciplinary Journal for Research on Religion*, which is edited out of the Baylor Institute for Studies of Religion (ISR), of which Johnson is the founding director.

The present book is the second of a planned three-volume series drawing on articles published in the *Journal*. All of us at Baylor and affiliated at ISR are excited to make these papers available to a wider audience. Admittedly, we have an "evangelistic" sense, as researchers, about sharing research findings pointing to religion as a salient determinant of salutary or positive psychosocial, political, economic, and cultural outcomes or markers. For decades, the magnitude of this literature has been something of a dirty little secret in the social sciences, widely overlooked or scorned, despite a growing body of basic and applied research studies providing empirical confirmation dating back, depending upon the field of study, to the 1950s. I can relate to this in my own professional discipline of epidemiology: thousands of published studies on religion and health date back over a century, yet these basic data remain largely unknown, or, where recently discovered, are thought to be surprising or unprecedented. As with the findings on religion in epidemiology and medicine, the findings on religion and prosocial behavior are hardly surprising, so long as one does not have an intrinsically jaundiced view of religion, and they are hardly new.

No matter the history of research on religion and prosocial behavior, as with the history of social research on religion in general, with publication of this important book the world of the social sciences no longer has a valid excuse for ignoring this subject. As the reader will discover, dimensions of religious identity or expression are salient determinants, on the whole, of a host of positive social, behavioral, and interpersonal outcomes. It is my sincere hope—my prayer—that *Objective Religion: Problems, Prosociality, Progress* will be a game-changer for the social sciences, and a blessing for researchers in this field, both raising the profile of their work and encouraging a new generation of scholars and social scientists to follow suit.

Jeff Levin, Ph.D., M.P.H.
Waco, Texas

Introduction

The Gallup World Poll has been tracking global data on religion for more than a decade, documenting that the vast majority of the world's population identifies with a religious tradition and considers religion to be an important part of life. But beyond people indicating religion is important, is there data demonstrating the impact, if any, of religion on the human condition?

There are now thousands of peer-reviewed publications linking religion to various aspects of mental and physical health, as well as other salutary outcomes, including lower crime and deviance, less substance abuse, and offender rehabilitation. For example, participation in religious communities and activities is associated with greater longevity, less depression, less suicide, less smoking, less substance abuse, better cancer and cardiovascular disease survival, less divorce, greater social support, greater meaning and purpose in life, greater life satisfaction, more charitable giving, more volunteering, more helping of others, greater civic engagement, and human flourishing. In fact, religious affiliation also helps people moderate their subjective well-being over the boom and bust of a business cycle.

And yet, in light of the mounting body of empirical evidence that religion is associated with well-being and human flourishing, it seems not even religious people are aware of or regularly acknowledge the beneficial impact of religion. Consider for a moment the field of criminology and its primary focus on antisocial behavior—with almost no attention given to prosocial activities. That is, criminologists ask why people commit crimes; they rarely ask why people do, or do not do, good deeds. Stated differently, criminologists largely overlook the other half of human behavior. And the same can be said for other academic disciplines. For example, why do so many people generously give money to help those in need? Or, why do most of the people reared in "bad" neighborhoods turn out not only to be law-abiding but to be good citizens? Indeed, how are people transformed from antisocial patterns of behavior to positive patterns? The papers in this volume examine the role of religion in promoting prosocial behavior. The role of religiosity in guiding individual behavior, as well as the role of faith-based groups and organizations in fostering prosocial activities is an important and yet understudied topic.

In order to address this oversight, Baylor University Press and Baylor's Institute for Studies of Religion have combined forces to publish select articles appearing in the *Interdisciplinary Journal for Research on Religion* (IJRR). Rodney Stark, Distinguished Professor of the Social Sciences at Baylor University and the founding editor of IJRR, had observed decades of bias within the academy toward studies of religion and thus believed it was necessary to launch an interdisciplinary journal that would publish high-quality articles on the long-neglected topic of religion. More than fifteen years after the founding of IJRR, it is more obvious than ever that Stark was right. The collection of papers in this volume helps to highlight this overlooked area.

This new book highlights select publications appearing in IJRR that not only document the pervasiveness of religion, but demonstrate the many complex ways faith, spirituality, and religious matters are consequential for individuals as well as for societies from every part of the world. Though religion remains woefully under-researched by scholars, this volume seeks to provide another platform to correct this oversight by advancing our understanding of religion, religious beliefs and practices, and spirituality, and thereby to enhance the trajectory of future studies of religion across the disciplines.

I
Volunteerism

We know that many Americans volunteer and that volunteers make critical contributions to American civil society. For example, volunteers provide a host of community services that the formal sector is either unwilling or unable to effectively provide, such as remedial education, sporting and recreational programs, medical and health services, mentoring of at-risk youth, shelters for the homeless, substance abuse counseling, educational programs for prisoners, and prisoner reentry initiatives.

According to a study by the Corporation for National and Community Service (CNCS), more Americans than ever are volunteering.[1] The 2018 *Volunteering in America* study found that more than seventy-seven million adults volunteered their time through an organization in the previous year. In total, Americans volunteered nearly 6.9 billion hours, worth an estimated $167 billion in economic value.[2] These extraordinary figures do not even account for the millions of Americans—some 43 percent—who voluntarily serve and support friends and family, or more than half of American adults (51 percent) who do favors for their neighbors; what might be called acts of "informal volunteering." The contribution volunteers make to civil society, civic engagement, and volunteerism in the United States is profound.[3] The nonprofit sector, which relies heavily on volunteers as a

---

1 *2018 Volunteering in America*. Corporation for National and Community Service. Washington, DC.
2 This figure is based on the Independent Sector's estimate of the average value of a volunteer hour for 2017.
3 Putnam, Robert D., and Lewis M. Feldstein. 2003. *Better Together: Restoring the American Community*. New York: Simon & Schuster.

strategic resource, has become increasingly important in the engagement of local communities. This is particularly the case in the human services sector, which relies heavily on the support of volunteers to fill the gaps in federal, state, and local funding. In sum, volunteers provide a staggering economic benefit to American society.

In addition, the contribution of volunteering goes beyond the value of services provided. Volunteering has been linked with the formation of social capital—social connections that help to build trust and collective action within the community.[4] Robert Putnam argues that a community that is more connected is likely to have a greater level of trust and reciprocity among its citizens, leading to a more cohesive and stable society with economic as well as social benefits.[5] For example, high levels of connectivity and trust can reduce transaction costs, improve information flows, and enhance workplace cooperation.[6]

Putnam concludes that strong communities are characterized by a high degree of trustworthiness and concern for the well-being of others. Perhaps more than anyone else, Putnam would be central to popularizing the term *social capital*, which succinctly captures the essence of such communities.[7] In towns and cities with high degrees of social capital, residents get to know their neighbors and build mutually reinforcing relationships with them. Putnam also noted that people in communities with strong social trust tend to be more engaged in civic activities and to volunteer their time at relatively high rates, which happens to benefit those they serve, as well as inspiring this same kind of generosity in the behavior of others.

Volunteering and expressions of concern for others clearly promote the common good. Volunteering not only benefits the community being served in tangible ways, but greatly enhances mutual social trust. It is also the case that volunteering benefits the volunteers in ways that one might not expect. A new study of thirteen thousand older adults with eight years of data on each participant found that volunteering in 2010 was related to subsequent

---

4 Putnam, Robert D. 1995. "Bowling Alone: America's Declining Social Capital." *The Journal of Democracy* 6: 65–78.
5 Putnam, Robert D. 2000. *Bowling Alone: The Collapse and Revival of American Community*. New York: Simon & Schuster.
6 Productivity Commission. 2003. "Social Capital: Reviewing the Concept and Its Policy Implications." Research Paper. AusInfo, Canberra.
7 Putnam 2000. Putnam and Feldstein 2003.

health and well-being in 2014, controlling for health and well-being outcomes in 2006, along with a vast range of social, demographic, and behavioral characteristics.[8] Study participants who volunteered at least two hours per week subsequently had higher levels of happiness, optimism, and purpose in life, and more contact with friends; they also had lower levels of depressive symptoms, hopelessness, and loneliness, fewer perceived physical discomforts and disabilities, and more physical activity. They were also notably less likely to die in the four-year follow-up period.

But what factors predict the likelihood that one will volunteer in the first place? As it turns out, religion is considered to be one of the key predictors of volunteer participation, both in religious as well as secular organizations. Numerous studies have documented a positive relationship between various measures of religion as an independent variable and social and civic outcomes such as philanthropic giving, community group membership, and volunteering.[9] Indeed, the more religious people are, the more likely they are to volunteer.[10]

Increased religious belief and attendance are both associated with greater service to others in a study examining religion and volunteering throughout adulthood.[11] This study offers longitudinal evidence that religious motivation, attendance, and involvement matter to increased volunteering behavior over time. Moreover, higher levels of religious belief made it more likely that individuals would volunteer in religious institutions.

8   Kim, Eric S., Ashley V. Whillans, Matthew T. Lee, Ying Chen, and Tyler J. VanderWeele. 2020. "Volunteering and Subsequent Health and Well-Being in Older Adults: An Outcome-Wide Longitudinal Approach." *American Journal of Preventive Medicine* 59: 176–86.
9   Lam, Pui-Yan. 2002. "As the Flocks Gather: How Religion Affects Voluntary Association Participation." *Journal for the Scientific Study of Religion* 41: 405–22. Lam, Pui-Yan. 2006. "Religion and Civic Culture: A Cross-National Study of Voluntary Association Membership." *Journal for the Scientific Study of Religion* 45: 177–93; Wuthnow, Robert. 1991. *Acts of Compassion: Caring for Others and Helping Ourselves*. Princeton, NJ: Princeton University Press. Putnam, Robert D., and David E. Campbell. 2010. *American Grace: How Religion Divides and Unites Us*. New York: Simon & Schuster.
10 Hustinx, Lesley, Johan von Essen, Jacques Haers, and Sara Mels. 2014. *Religion and Volunteering: Complex, Contested, and Ambiguous Relationships*. New York: Springer.
11 Johnston, Joseph B. 2013. "Religion and Volunteering over the Adult Life Course." *Journal for the Scientific Study of Religion* 52: 733–52.

Thus, volunteering in religious institutions increased the chances that people would move on to other forms of volunteering.[12]

Americans who volunteer for religious groups are two or three times as likely to also volunteer for secular groups as those who do not volunteer for religious groups, according to the Faith Matters surveys led by Robert Putnam of Harvard University and David Campbell of the University of Notre Dame. In their book, *American Grace: How Religion Divides and Unites Us*, they note:

> Religiously observant Americans are more generous with time and treasure than demographically similar secular Americans . . . This is true for secular causes (especially help to the needy, the elderly and young people) as well as for purely religious causes. It is true even for most random acts of kindness. (453)

A major reason cited by Putnam and Campbell and other researchers for the heightened volunteerism of religious individuals is the social networks that people form at houses of worship. Churches, synagogues, and mosques are places that encourage volunteerism and other-mindedness, and expose individuals to religious as well as secular opportunities for service that create social bonds, making it more likely individuals will respond to requests to volunteer. Indeed, these ties can extend beyond houses of worship. For example, there is empirical evidence that strong ties to people who are highly active within a congregation increases the likelihood that nonreligious people will be encouraged to volunteer.[13]

Religion can be seen as a catalyst that stimulates or generates volunteers who act out of a concern for the welfare of others. For example, when people attend religious congregations they tend to get connected to different social networks. Classes, retreats, small groups, mission trips, church-sponsored volunteer work, or any number of related group functions connect people to multiple networks of social support that have the potential to be meaningful. Research documents that social support

---

12 Johnston 2013.
13 Merino, Stephen M. 2013. "Religious Social Networks and Volunteering: Examining Recruitment via Close Ties." *Review of Religious Research* 55: 509–27. Lim, Chaeyoon, and Carol Ann MacGregor. 2012. "Religion and Volunteering in Context: Disentangling the Contextual Effects of Religion on Voluntary Behavior." *American Sociological Review* 77: 747–79.

in congregations has been linked to better coping skills,[14] increased life expectancy,[15] stress reduction,[16] and better self-reported health.[17]

People with religious affiliations are more satisfied with their lives mainly because they attend religious services more frequently and build social networks with people who share their faith and religious experience, thus building a strong sense of belonging to a community of religious faith.[18] So significant are faith-based networks, Putnam argues, that they generate unique effects that cannot be explained in any other way. The articles in this section shed light on the connection between various aspects of religion and religious affiliation and volunteerism in America.

---

14 Krause, Neal. 2009. "Church-Based Volunteering, Providing Informal Support at Church, and Self-Rated Health in Late Life." *Journal of Aging and Health* 21: 63–84.
15 Brown, Stephanie L., Randolph M. Nesse, Amiram D. Vinokur, and Dylan M. Smith. 2003. "Providing Social Support May Be More Beneficial Than Receiving It: Results from a Prospective Study of Mortality." *Psychological Science* 14: 320–27. Krause, Neal. 2006a. "Church-Based Social Support and Mortality." *Journal of Gerontology: Social Sciences* 61: S140–46.
16 Krause, Neal. 2006b. "Exploring the Stress-Buffering Effects of Church-Based Social Support and Secular Social Support on Health in Late Life." *Journal of Gerontology: Social Sciences* 61: S35–43.
17 Krause 2009.
18 Putnam and Campbell 2010.

1

Religion and Volunteering in Four Sub-Saharan African Countries

Meredith J. Greif | Amy Adamczyk | Jacob Felson

Around the world, people face poverty, disease, and malnutrition, and these problems are particularly concentrated in sub-Saharan Africa. HIV/AIDS continues to end lives while nations struggle to treat the infected and limit the spread of the disease. Many sub-Saharan African nations are increasingly relying on volunteers to care for HIV/AIDS-infected patients as they strive to survive and meet basic needs. In the meantime, gains are being made in health care and human rights at the hands of volunteer activists. In these regions where people experience powerful individual and structural obstacles to meeting their own needs, it is valuable to understand why many people volunteer as caregivers and activists in settings where they may suffer infection, emotional trauma, and even punitive measures. A clearer understanding of factors that encourage caregiving and political volunteering can facilitate successful recruitment of much-needed volunteers in sub-Saharan Africa.

One important factor motivating volunteering is religiosity. While religiosity has been discussed as a factor contributing to activism and volunteering, few studies have identified the specific religious attitudes and behaviors that spur voluntary labor. The overwhelming majority of people in sub-Saharan Africa pray regularly, attend church, and think that religion is very important (Pew Forum on Religion & Public Life 2010). This suggests that a critical mass of religious adherents exists that could be organized to improve the quality of life in the region.

However, patterns of volunteering and activism may depend on gender and can in turn affect gender dynamics in the region. Gender inequalities in sub-Saharan African societies limit women's social, political, and economic advancement as well as their agency in making sexual decisions that limit their exposure to diseases such as HIV. Since these inequalities permeate nearly all aspects of social life, we consider whether caregiver volunteering (which is frequently considered less prestigious) and political volunteering (traditionally associated with greater prestige and mobility into leadership roles) vary by gender. Moreover, we examine whether associations with religious institutions that reinforce traditional gender inequalities contribute to gendered patterns of civic engagement. Using the 2000 World Values Survey, this article examines which aspects of religion motivate health and political civic engagement in sub-Saharan Africa and explores whether these effects are conditioned by gender.

Civic Engagement in Sub-Saharan Africa

Civic engagement, that is, individuals' connections and interactions within their communities, can bring about vital changes that improve the quality of fellow residents' lives (Driskell, Embry, and Lyon 2008). There is an urgent need to improve the quality of life in sub-Saharan Africa. Across the region, approximately one in twenty adults is infected with HIV (UNAIDS 2009), and in several nations in the region, as many as one in four adults is infected with HIV (UNAIDS 2009). According to estimates from the World Bank, over 40 percent of sub-Saharan Africans live on less than $1 a day, and another 30 percent subsist on amounts that average between $1 and $2 a day (Chen and Ravallion 2004; Sachs 2005). Residents also struggle with other critical illnesses and conditions, including malaria, tuberculosis, and malnutrition, while poverty, inequality, unemployment, illiteracy, homelessness, civil rights abuse, and political corruption erode residents' quality of life (Mmatli 2008; United Nations Development Programme 2010). While solutions to these issues may ultimately depend on changes in governmental and economic infrastructure, citizens have sought and achieved improvements through volunteering for health- and justice-based organizations (Ampofo 2008; Robins 2006).

In sub-Saharan Africa, volunteer work has resulted in vital gains in the health care arena. Given the scarcity of doctors, nurses, hospitals, equipment, and other health-related resources, volunteer caregiving has become crucial for people who suffer from HIV and other common ailments (McCoy et al. 2005; Ogden, Esim, and Grown 2006). Caregivers assist sick people—who often could not afford adequate care even if it were available—by administering medical treatment and pain relief, helping with hygiene and household chores, and making referrals for professional medical help (Homan and Searle 2005).

As well as offering medical care, volunteer caregivers provide emotional support and can relieve the isolation that HIV-infected individuals experience because of their inability to work or travel, the stigma associated with the disease, and the difficulties they face in forming romantic relationships without spreading the disease (Ogden, Esim, and Grown 2006). Furthermore, volunteers can ease the temporal, emotional, and financial burdens shouldered by families with sick members (Akintola 2004; Kipp et al. 2006; Rugalema 2000). By freeing sick people's family members to generate income in the paid economy and to attend school, volunteer caregivers can prevent disadvantaged households from falling deeper into poverty and contribute to the overall productivity of the region (Ogden, Esim, and Grown 2006; Skovdal et al. 2009).

Volunteers have also spearheaded social reforms in numerous sub-Saharan African countries. Such changes have involved transitioning to democracy; enacting fairer tax laws; rallying for the release of imprisoned human rights activists; enhancing women's rights to trade, own land, and inherit property; and protecting women from domestic violence (Ampofo 2008; Klopp and Zuern 2007; Tripp 2001). Many steps remain before an acceptable standard of living and equality of rights exist for all sub-Saharan Africans, and political activism will remain essential to this process.

Religion and Civic Engagement

Despite the toll it takes on time and energy and the associated risks of danger, grief, and guilt from being unable to help those who are dying (Akintola 2008; de Figueiredo and Turato 2001), civic engagement remains high in a number of sub-Saharan African countries (Ruiter and De Graaf 2006). A host of social, cultural, economic, and political factors have been linked to volunteering and civic engagement, including religiosity (Bekkers 2001; McPherson and Rotolo 1996; Popielarz 1999; Wilson 2000). Researchers have found that religiously involved individuals are more likely than nonreligious people to donate their time to helping others. However, the majority of this research has been done in the United

States and other developed nations (Becker and Dhingra 2001; Lam 2002, 2006; Wilson and Janoski 1995). To date, few quantitative studies have been done in sub-Saharan Africa, in part because the data are particularly difficult to obtain. In one of the few cross-national studies of religion and volunteering, Ruiter and De Graaf (2006) found that rates of volunteering were higher in more devout nations. They also found that the effects of religious service attendance on volunteering were much weaker in more religious nations than in more secular nations. This raises the question of whether within-country variation in religiosity matters in more devout nations. Ruiter and De Graaf did not examine private forms of religious devotion such as prayer, so it is unclear whether such aspects of religiosity shape volunteering in devout regions such as those in sub-Saharan Africa. The study also did not distinguish between different types of volunteering, so the prevalence of health-related or political volunteering cannot be determined from their study.

Few researchers have examined which dimensions of religion are most likely to motivate unpaid organizational involvement (for an exception, see Lam 2002), though there is reason to believe that different aspects of religion (e.g., private religious devotion, active religious service attendance) may be more likely than others to shape involvement in volunteer health and political organizations. In this study, we focus on four key dimensions of religiosity: religious importance, private religious devotion, religious participation, and time spent socializing with fellow congregants.

Because the sacred texts of nearly all major religions encourage altruistic behavior, people who see their religion as important and spend time meditating or praying may be more inclined to follow the precepts of their faith and donate their time to helping others. While the private dimension of religiosity has been relatively unexplored in the research on membership in voluntary organizations and voluntary participation, a number of studies have found that personal religious importance is associated with a range of attitudes (Adamczyk and Pitt 2009; Finke and Adamczyk 2008) and behaviors (Adamczyk and Felson 2006; Adamczyk and Palmer 2008). These ideas lead to this set of hypotheses:

> *Hypothesis 1*: As religious importance increases, people will be more likely to participate in volunteer health and political organizations.
>
> *Hypothesis 2*: As the frequency of prayer increases, people will be more likely to participate in volunteer health and political organizations.

Service attendance has also been examined as a predictor of civic engagement (Becker and Dhingra 2001; Beyerlein and Chaves 2003; Beyerlein and Hipp 2006; Ruiter and De Graaf 2006; Verba, Schlozman, and Brady 1995; Wilson and Musick 1997). Service attendance can reinforce religious precepts, and clergy members and religious leaders may encourage civic engagement. Furthermore, churchgoers' participation may be enhanced by exposure to information about volunteering as well as by social pressure from others to volunteer (Musick, Wilson, and Bynum 2000; Ruiter and De Graaf 2006). Informal activities with friends from one's religious group could similarly shape the likelihood of involvement in a volunteer organization. Informal social opportunities can encourage bonding, solidarity, and obligation for reciprocity, leading to greater desire to volunteer and a sense of obligation to do so when an opportunity is presented (Beyerlein and Hipp 2006). Volunteering with friends could also make the activity more enjoyable. These ideas lead to the next two hypotheses:

> *Hypothesis 3*: Formal service attendance will increase participation in volunteer health and political organizations.
>
> *Hypothesis 4*: Informal church activities, namely, socializing with members of one's congregation, will increase participation in volunteer health and political organizations.

Gender, Religion, and Civic Engagement

Men and women may differ in their likelihood of volunteering for health and political organizations, as the activities and skills associated with both types of volunteering may be considered "gendered." In most regions of the world, the burdens of caring for both ill and healthy family members fall disproportionately on the shoulders of women (Akintola 2004; Orner 2006; UNAIDS 2008), and activities that are considered "women's work" are frequently undervalued. While some scholars suggest that women engage in caregiving activities more often because they inherently feel a greater responsibility to people in need (Gilligan 1982; Karniol, Grosz, and Schorr 2003), women may also do so as a result of being socialized into attitudes and skills that enhance their role as caregivers. Men's gender roles, by contrast, are more often associated with leadership and power and tend to be more publicly visible. We would therefore expect men to be more involved in volunteering on behalf of others' well-being by participating in activities such as organizing rallies and protests, speaking with political leaders, and directing others (Manning 2010; Rotolo and Wilson 2007). These suppositions lead to the following hypotheses:

> *Hypothesis 5a*: Women will be more likely than men to engage in health volunteering.
>
> *Hypothesis 5b*: Men will be more likely than women to engage in political volunteering.

The influence of religiosity on health and political volunteering may depend on gender. Historically, dominant religions have embraced traditional gender roles and have excluded women from holding high positions (Read 2003). These dominant gender norms, as well as a lack of female role models who have significant authority within the church, may encourage women to seek out less prestigious caregiving roles and avoid more commanding ones even outside of church activities. Direct requests to engage in a volunteer activity are one of the strongest predictors of volunteering (Paik and Navarre-Jackson 2011), so informal interactions with church members who embrace church gender norms and shape their own volunteer activities accordingly should also result in gendered recruitment. These same dynamics should encourage the channeling of male coaffiliates into more prestigious and public political volunteering, resulting in the following hypothesis:

> *Hypothesis 6*: The effect of religiosity on both caregiver volunteering and political volunteering will be conditioned by gender.

This gendered context extends beyond the church, as sub-Saharan Africa is characterized by deeply entrenched inequality that limits women's social, political, and economic advancement. Thus these congregational gender dynamics coexist with and reinforce patterns at the national level. This can maintain women's lower status in the region by limiting the types of activities and skills that would facilitate their transition into opportunities that involve leadership, decision making, and legislation on women's behalf. Thus gendered patterns of volunteering can have implications for gender inequality in sub-Saharan Africa.

In sum, this study seeks to unravel the relationship between religiosity and two distinct types of civic engagement in sub-Saharan Africa, both of which have powerful consequences for the vitality of the region. Gender norms that are reinforced by both church and state can affect volunteering patterns in ways that affect not only the direct beneficiaries of such activism, but also the volunteers themselves.

Data

To examine these relationships, the analysis relies on cross-sectional data from the 2001 World Values Survey (WVS). The WVS was designed to enable comparisons of values and norms on a wide variety of topics across nations and over time (Inglehart and Baker 2000). Beginning in 1981 with surveys in eight nations, the WVS has expanded over four subsequent waves to include surveys in fifty-seven nations. The current study relies on data from the 2001 WVS, as this is the only available survey year that includes information about the religion and volunteering activities of sub-Saharan African residents. The current analysis uses data from the four sub-Saharan African countries that asked residents about volunteering: South Africa, Zimbabwe, Tanzania, and Uganda.

Dependent Variables

The current study examines two outcomes: caregiver volunteering and political volunteering. Caregiver volunteering was coded as a dichotomous variable. Respondents were coded as having engaged in caregiver volunteering if they reported membership in or unpaid work for organizations concerned with health or organizations that, in the words of the survey question, provided "social services for elderly, handicapped or deprived people."

Political volunteering was also coded as a dichotomous variable. Respondents were coded as having engaged in political volunteering if they reported membership in or unpaid work for organizations involving: "political parties or groups," "local political action on issues like poverty, employment, housing, racial equality," "Third world development or human rights," "conservation, the environment, ecology, animal rights," or a "peace movement."

Independent Variables

We examined four measures of religiosity: frequency of attending religious services, frequency of socializing with others from their house of worship, self-reported religious importance, and frequency of prayer. For brevity, we refer to these measures as service attendance, religious socializing, religious importance, and prayer. Service attendance and religious socializing capture the more social aspects of religiosity, while religious importance and prayer capture interior aspects of religiosity.

Religious importance was based on the following question: "For each of the following aspects, indicate how important it is in your life." One of these aspects was religion, and responses ranged from "very important" = 1 to "not at all important" = 4. Frequency of prayer was measured with the question "How often do you pray to God outside of religious services?" Responses ranged from "never" = 1 to "every day" = 7. Religious service attendance was measured with the question "Apart from weddings, funerals and christenings, about how often do you attend religious services these days?" Responses ranged from "never or practically never" = 1 to "more than once a week" = 8. Religious socializing was measured in terms of how often respondents reported "spend[ing] time with people at [their] church, mosque or synagogue." Responses ranged from "not at all" = 1 to "weekly" = 4.

Control Variables

We controlled for several variables that previous research found to be related to both religion and volunteering. These variables include marital status, number of children in the household, age of respondent, level of education, financial satisfaction, work status, and self-reported health. Research has found that married people are more likely to volunteer (Wilson 2000) and are also more likely to attend religious services (Thornton, Axinn, and Hill 1992) in the United States. Therefore we controlled for marital status with two indicator variables, one for respondents who were currently married and one for respondents who were divorced, separated, or widowed. The reference category is "never married." We controlled for number of children, since it is positively related to both volunteering (Wilson and Musick 1997) and religiosity of the mother (Hayford and Morgan 2008; Norris and Inglehart 2004). The number of children is assessed with a single question that asks respondents how many children they have had, where eight is the maximum. Studies have found curvilinear relationships between age and volunteering (Ruiter and De Graaf 2006) and between age and religiosity (Argue, Johnson, and White 1999); hence we controlled for years of age. Research has also uncovered that education is positively associated with religious service attendance (Glaeser and Sacerdote 2008) and with volunteering (Ruiter and De Graaf 2006). We controlled for education using a question that asks respondents, "What is the highest educational level that you have attained?" Response categories range from "incomplete primary education" = 1 to "college degree" = 8. Intermediate categories include "completed primary school," "some technical secondary," "completed technical secondary," "some preparatory secondary," "completed preparatory secondary," and "some university."

Since previous studies found that employment status is related to volunteering (Wilson 2000), we also controlled for employment. Employment status is measured as a set of dummy variables representing people who worked full-time for pay, worked part-time for pay, were self-employed, were retired, worked as a housewife, or were students. Unemployed is the reference category.

People who are more comfortable with their financial condition may be more likely to devote time to religious activities as well as to volunteering. Therefore, we controlled for a measure of financial satisfaction. Financial satisfaction is based on answers to the question "How satisfied are you with the financial situation of your household?" Responses ranged from "dissatisfied" = 1 to "satisfied" = 10.

Scholars have also found that respondents who are ill themselves or suspect that they may have HIV/AIDS may be more likely to volunteer (Rödlach 2009). Therefore we controlled for self-reported health. Respondents were asked, "All in all, how would you describe your state of health these days?" Response categories were reverse coded so that the highest category, "4," indicates "very good" and the lowest category, "1," indicates "poor."

Finally, to account for covariation between the religion variables and the key outcome variables that are the result of different country contexts, we included a set of dummy variables for country of residence. We created indicator variables for Tanzania, Uganda, and Zimbabwe. South Africa is the reference group.

Analysis

We used logistic regression to examine the influence of religion and gender on the odds of caregiver volunteering and political volunteering. The analysis began by examining the influences of gender and of each of the religiosity variables on caregiver volunteering. Since the measures of religiosity are moderately correlated with each other, we examined the influence of each of them on caregiver volunteering separately. In the final model, we included all of the religion variables together with the full range of control variables to determine which, if any, predict caregiver volunteering independently of the others. We repeated the same steps for political volunteering.

We also ran models testing the interactions between each type of religiosity and gender and between each type of religiosity and each nation. We tested these interactions in two different ways to avoid bias. Interaction effects in logistic regressions can be biased if residual variance in the outcome variable differs across values of one of the independent variables comprising the interaction (Williams 2009). For example, it is possible there is more heterogeneity in the causal processes of volunteering among men than among women or vice versa. It is also possible that the causal processes of volunteering are more heterogeneous in some countries than in others. One way to avoid such bias is to estimate generalized logistic models (Williams 2009), which allow residual variance to be modeled. We estimated generalized logistic models to verify the significance of interactions uncovered in our logistic regression models. When logistic regression models yielded significant interactions between religiosity and gender, we checked whether these interactions remained significant in models in which residual variance was permitted to vary by gender. When logistic regression models yielded significant interactions between religiosity and nation, we checked whether those interactions remained significant in models in which residual variance was permitted to vary by nation.

All analyses were weighted so that each nation's share of our sample matched the nation's proportion of the total population of the four nations. For example, 16 percent of our sample was Ugandan, but 21 percent of the population from the four nations in our sample is Ugandan. Hence, respondents from Uganda were weighted by a factor equal to 21 percent divided by 16 percent. Respondents from the other three nations in the sample were weighted similarly.

Although less than 1 percent of information was missing from our data, listwise deletion would have reduced the sample by approximately 8.5 percent. For this reason, we opted to handle missing data via multiple imputation techniques, which take full advantage of the available data and avoid some of the bias in standard errors that can accompany listwise deletion (Allison 2001).[1] On the basis of the other variables that were included in the analysis, missing values were imputed for twenty

---

[1] Missing data were imputed by using the procedure written by Royston (2009) based on a technique outlined in van Buuren, Boshuizen, and Knook (1999).

1 | Religion and Volunteering in Four Sub-Saharan African Countries

datasets, and the parameter estimates were averages of regression coefficients produced through the "mi estimate" command in the statistical computing program, Stata. Standard errors from the multiple imputation process were calculated to reflect the uncertainty that is generated through simulated data. The final sample size consisted of 6,175 respondents.

Results

Table 1-1 presents descriptive statistics. Twenty-five percent of the sample engaged in caregiver volunteering, and 30 percent of the sample volunteered for political causes. Respondents indicated a strong sense of religious importance (3.70 on a scale of 1 to 4); the frequencies of prayer, service attendance, and religious socializing were also high.

Table 1-1: Descriptive Statistics for Variables Included in the Analysis ($N = 6,175$)

Variable	Mean	Standard Deviation	Minimum	Maximum
Dependent Variables				
Political volunteering	0.30	0.46	0	1
Caregiver volunteering	0.25	0.43	0	1
Key Independent Variables				
Religious importance	3.70	0.65	1	4
Frequency of prayer	6.20	1.60	1	7
Service attendance	5.50	1.70	1	7
Religious socializing	3.20	1.10	1	4
Female	0.48	0.50	0	1
Control Variables				
Currently married (reference)	0.55	0.50	0	1
Divorced, separated or widowed	0.10	0.30	0	1
Never married	0.35	0.48	0	1
Number of children	2.20	2.20	0	8

(*continued*)

Table 1-1: Descriptive Statistics for Variables Included in the Analysis ($N = 6{,}175$) (*continued*)

Variable	Mean	Standard Deviation	Minimum	Maximum
Control Variables				
Age in years	36.00	14.00	15	98
Level of education	4.00	1.90	1	8
Financially satisfied	4.40	2.90	1	10
Employed full-time (reference)	0.32	0.47	0	1
Employed part-time	0.06	0.24	0	1
Self-employed	0.14	0.35	0	1
Retired	0.06	0.23	0	1
Housewife	0.09	0.28	0	1
Student	0.10	0.30	0	1
Unemployed	0.22	0.41	0	1
Self-reported health	3.00	0.86	1	4

Cases are weighted proportionally to the national population.

Table 1-2 presents findings regarding the influence of religion on caregiver volunteering. Model 1 in Table 1-2 examines the influence of gender while controlling for all nonreligious variables and shows that the odds of doing caregiver volunteering are 17 percent higher for women than for men. Models 2 through 5 test the effects of each of the four measures of religiosity while controlling for all other nonreligious variables. Three out of four measures of religiosity are statistically significant in these models, showing that caregiver volunteering is higher among respondents who find religion important, pray frequently, and socialize with coaffiliates. Model 6 includes all four measures of religiosity together with control variables; despite moderate to high intercorrelations among the religion variables (ranging from 0.37 to 0.57), religious socializing remains statistically significant. We also note that the magnitude of the coefficient for gender is only slightly lower in Model 6 than in Model 1, suggesting that religiosity does not explain women's role as caregivers.

Table 1-2: Logistic Regression Analysis of the Influence of Gender and Religion on Caregiver Volunteering

	Model 1	Model 2	Model 3	Model 4	Model 5	Model 6
Key Independent Variables						
Female	1.17*	1.14+	1.14+	1.15+	1.16+	1.14+
Religious importance		1.16*				1.06
Frequency of prayer			1.07**			1.04
Service attendance				1.04+		0.97
Religious socializing					1.17***	1.16***
Control Variables						
Currently married	ref.	ref.	ref.	ref.	ref.	ref.
Formerly married	1.06	1.08	1.08	1.08	1.08	1.08
Never married	0.86	0.86	0.86	0.86	0.86	0.85
Number of children	0.95*	0.95*	0.95*	0.95*	0.95*	0.95*
Age in years	1.01*	1.01*	1.01*	1.01*	1.01*	1.01*
Level of education	1.08***	1.08***	1.08***	1.08***	1.08***	1.08***
Financially satisfied	1.01	1.01	1.01	1.01	1.01	1.01
Full-time	ref.	ref.	ref.	ref.	ref.	ref.
Part-time	1.28+	1.29+	1.29+	1.29+	1.29+	1.29+
Self-employed	1.02	1.02	1.03	1.02	1.01	1.01
Retired	1.31	1.31	1.30	1.31	1.30	1.29
Housewife	0.69*	0.69*	0.69*	0.69*	0.69*	0.69*

(continued)

Table 1-2: Logistic Regression Analysis of the Influence of Gender and Religion on Caregiver Volunteering (*continued*)

	Model 1	Model 2	Model 3	Model 4	Model 5	Model 6
Control Variables						
Student	0.85	0.85	0.85	0.84	0.83	0.84
Unemployed	0.95	0.95	0.96	0.95	0.94	0.96
Self-reported health	0.92+	0.92+	0.92+	0.92+	0.92+	0.92+
South Africa	ref.	ref.	ref.	ref.	ref.	ref.
Tanzania	6.04***	5.90***	5.86***	5.83***	5.66***	5.67***
Uganda	2.26***	2.25***	2.24***	2.20***	2.21***	2.24***
Zimbabwe	1.12	1.11	1.12	1.10	1.05	1.06
Constant	0.10***	0.06***	0.07***	0.08***	0.06***	0.05***
Observations	6,175	6,175	6,175	6,175	6,175	6,175

Exponentiated coefficients are shown. Cases are weighted proportionally to the national population.
+$p < 0.10$; *$p < 0.05$; **$p < 0.01$; ***$p < 0.001$.

Table 1-3 presents results from logistic regressions of political volunteering on measures of gender and religiosity. Model 1 demonstrates that, in contrast to findings regarding caregiver volunteering, women are less likely than men to donate their time to political causes. Models 2 through 5 estimate the effects of each measure of religiosity in turn. Here, only the effect of religious socializing is significant. In Model 6 of Table 1-3, which includes all religiosity variables as well as gender and other control variables, we see that all four religion variables emerge as significant predictors of political volunteering. The effects of religious socializing and frequency of prayer remain positive, while the effects of religious importance and service attendance are negative.

We suggested that religiosity and gender may interact, in that engagement in religious institutions that have presented obstacles to women's social equality may heighten women's engagement in lower-esteemed caregiving and weaken their involvement in political activities that are related to status and leadership. Tables 1-4 and 1-5 address these hypotheses. Table 1-4 examines whether gender conditions the effects of religiosity on

1 | Religion and Volunteering in Four Sub-Saharan African Countries

Table 1-3: Logistic Regression Analysis of the Influence of Gender and Religion on Political Volunteering

	Model 1	Model 2	Model 3	Model 4	Model 5	Model 6
Key Independent Variables						
Female	0.66***	0.67***	0.65***	0.66***	0.65***	0.67***
Religious importance		0.94				0.86**
Frequency of prayer			1.04+			1.06*
Service attendance				0.98		0.91***
Religious socializing					1.15***	1.23***
Control Variables						
Currently married	ref.	ref.	ref.	ref.	ref.	ref.
Formerly married	0.90	0.89	0.90	0.89	0.91	0.88
Never married	0.84+	0.84+	0.85+	0.84+	0.84+	0.83+
Number of children	1.00	1.00	1.00	1.00	1.00	1.00
Age in years	1.00	1.00	1.00	1.00	1.00	1.00
Level of education	1.07***	1.07***	1.07***	1.07***	1.07***	1.07***
Financially satisfied	0.98+	0.98+	0.98+	0.98+	0.98+	0.98+
Full-time	ref.	ref.	ref.	ref.	ref.	ref.
Part-time	1.16	1.16	1.16	1.16	1.16	1.16
Self-employed	1.09	1.09	1.10	1.10	1.08	1.08
Retired	0.92	0.93	0.92	0.93	0.91	0.91

(*continued*)

Table 1-3: Logistic Regression Analysis of the Influence of Gender and Religion on Political Volunteering (*continued*)

	Model 1	Model 2	Model 3	Model 4	Model 5	Model 6
Control Variables						
Housewife	0.86	0.86	0.85	0.85	0.86	0.85
Student	0.77+	0.77+	0.77+	0.77+	0.75*	0.77+
Unemployed	0.82*	0.82*	0.82*	0.82*	0.81*	0.82*
Self-reported health	0.91*	0.91*	0.91*	0.91*	0.90*	0.91*
South Africa	ref.	ref.	ref.	ref.	ref.	ref.
Tanzania	4.70***	4.76***	4.60***	4.79***	4.40***	4.66***
Uganda	1.63***	1.63***	1.61***	1.65***	1.58***	1.66***
Zimbabwe	0.69**	0.69**	0.69**	0.70**	0.65***	0.66***
Constant	0.31***	0.38***	0.26***	0.33***	0.22***	0.32***
Observations	6175	6175	6175	6175	6175	6175

Exponentiated coefficients are shown. Cases are weighted proportionally to the national population.
+$p < 0.10$; *$p < 0.05$; **$p < 0.01$; ***$p < 0.001$.

caregiver volunteering, and the findings do not support this hypothesis. Table 1-5, however, uncovers evidence that the effect of religious socializing on political volunteering depends on gender. Model 4 in Table 1-5 suggests that religious socializing heightens political engagement only among women.

Given the unique political and social dynamics among the four countries examined, we ran additional analyses to ascertain whether the influence of religiosity differed across countries. Table 1-6 indicates some cross-national variations in the influence of religion on caregiver volunteering. There is a consistent pattern suggesting that the effects of all aspects of religiosity on caregiver volunteering are higher in South Africa than in any other nation. However, differences in the effects of religiosity across nations are significant in only two of the twelve comparisons that were made.

Table 1-7 presents models of interaction effects of religiosity by nation on political volunteering. There is little evidence of systematic differences
(text continues on page 32 below)

Table 1-4: Logistic Regression Analysis of the Influence of the Interaction between Gender and Religion on Caregiver Volunteering

	Model 1	Model 2	Model 3	Model 4
Key Independent Variables				
Female	1.02	0.95	1.05	1.06
Religious importance	1.15+			
Frequency of prayer		1.06*		
Service attendance			1.03	
Religious socializing				1.16**
Interactions between Religion and Gender				
Female × religious importance	1.03			
Female × prayer		1.03		
Female × service attendance			1.02	
Female × religious socializing				1.03
Control Variables				
Currently married	ref.	ref.	ref.	ref.
Formerly married	1.08	1.07	1.08	1.08
Never married	0.86	0.86	0.86	0.86
Number of children	0.95*	0.95*	0.95*	0.95*
Age in years	1.01*	1.01*	1.01*	1.01*
Level of education	1.08***	1.08***	1.08***	1.08***
Financially satisfied	1.01	1.01	1.01	1.01
Full-time	ref.	ref.	ref.	ref.
Part-time	1.29+	1.29+	1.29+	1.29+
Self-employed	1.02	1.03	1.02	1.01
Retired	1.31	1.30	1.31	1.30
Housewife	0.69*	0.68*	0.69*	0.69*
Student	0.85	0.86	0.84	0.83

(*continued*)

Table 1-4: Logistic Regression Analysis of the Influence of the Interaction between Gender and Religion on Caregiver Volunteering (*continued*)

	Model 1	Model 2	Model 3	Model 4
Control Variables				
Unemployed	0.95	0.96	0.95	0.95
Self-reported health	0.92+	0.92+	0.92+	0.92+
South Africa	ref.	ref.	ref.	ref.
Tanzania	5.91***	5.88***	5.84***	5.67***
Uganda	2.25***	2.25***	2.20***	2.22***
Zimbabwe	1.11	1.12	1.10	1.05
Constant	0.06***	0.07***	0.09***	0.07***
Observations	6175	6175	6175	6175

Exponentiated coefficients are shown. Cases are weighted proportionally to the national population.
+$p < 0.10$; *$p < 0.05$; **$p < 0.01$; ***$p < 0.001$.

Table 1-5: Logistic Regression Analysis of the Influence of the Interaction between Gender and Religion on Political Volunteering

	Model 1	Model 2	Model 3	Model 4
Key Independent Variables				
Female	0.79	0.72	0.66+	0.32***
Religious importance	0.95			
Frequency of prayer		1.04		
Service attendance			0.98	
Religious socializing				1.05
Interactions between Religion and Gender				
Female × religious importance	0.96			
Female × prayer		0.98		
Female × service attendance			1.00	
Female × religious socializing				1.24***a

(*continued*)

Table 1-5: Logistic Regression Analysis of the Influence of the Interaction between Gender and Religion on Political Volunteering (*continued*)

	Model 1	Model 2	Model 3	Model 4
Control Variables				
Currently married	ref.	ref.	ref.	ref.
Formerly married	0.89	0.91	0.89	0.89
Never married	0.84+	0.85+	0.84+	0.84+
Number of children	1.00	1.00	1.00	1.00
Age in years	1.00	1.00	1.00	1.00
Level of education	1.07***	1.07***	1.07***	1.07***
Financially satisfied	0.98+	0.98+	0.98+	0.98+
Full time	ref.	ref.	ref.	ref.
Part time	1.16	1.16	1.16	1.16
Self-employed	1.09	1.10	1.10	1.08
Retired	0.93	0.92	0.93	0.92
Housewife	0.86	0.85	0.85	0.86
Student	0.77+	0.77+	0.77+	0.76*
Unemployed	0.81*	0.82*	0.82*	0.82*
Self-reported health	0.91*	0.91*	0.91*	0.90*
South Africa	ref.	ref.	ref.	ref.
Tanzania	4.75***	4.60***	4.79***	4.49***
Uganda	1.63***	1.61***	1.65***	1.64***
Zimbabwe	0.69**	0.69**	0.70**	0.65***
Constant	0.36**	0.25***	0.33***	0.28***
Observations	6175	6175	6175	6175

Exponentiated coefficients are shown. Cases are weighted proportionally to the national population.
+$p < 0.10$; *$p < 0.05$; **$p < 0.01$; ***$p < 0.001$.
[a] Interaction term was significant in a generalized logistic regression model in which residual variance was permitted to vary by gender.

Table 1-6: Logistic Regression Analysis of the Influence of the Interaction between Nation and Religion on Caregiver Volunteering

	Model 1 Importance	Model 2 Prayer	Model 3 Attendance	Model 4 Socializing
Nations				
South Africa	ref.	ref.	ref.	ref.
Tanzania	14.18***	10.05***	20.26***	11.72***
Uganda	5.54**	4.75***	7.13***	2.44**
Zimbabwe	2.38	1.72	1.88+	1.67
Key Religion Variables				
Religious importance	1.36***			
Frequency of prayer		1.14***		
Service attendance			1.19***	
Religious socializing				1.30***
Nation by Religion Interactions				
Tanzania × religious importance	0.79			
Uganda × religious importance	0.78			
Zimbabwe × religious importance	0.81			
Tanzania × prayer		0.92		
Uganda × prayer		0.89+		
Zimbabwe × prayer		0.93		
Tanzania × service attendance			0.80***[b]	
Uganda × service attendance			0.81**[a]	
Zimbabwe × service attendance			0.90	
Tanzania × religious socializing				0.80**[a]

(*continued*)

Table 1-6: Logistic Regression Analysis of the Influence of the Interaction between Nation and Religion on Caregiver Volunteering (*continued*)

	Model 1 Importance	Model 2 Prayer	Model 3 Attendance	Model 4 Socializing
Nation by Religion Interactions				
Uganda × religious socializing				0.96
Zimbabwe × religious socializing				0.86
Control Variables				
Female	1.14⁺	1.13	1.14⁺	1.16⁺
Currently married	ref.	ref.	ref.	ref.
Formerly married	1.08	1.07	1.07	1.08
Never married	0.86	0.86	0.87	0.86
Number of children	0.95*	0.95*	0.95*	0.95*
Age in years	1.01*	1.01*	1.01*	1.01*
Level of education	1.08***	1.08***	1.08***	1.08***
Financially satisfied	1.01	1.01	1.01	1.01
Full-time	ref.	ref.	ref.	ref.
Part-time	1.28⁺	1.27	1.27	1.29⁺
Self-employed	1.02	1.02	1.01	1.01
Retired	1.30	1.29	1.26	1.29
Housewife	0.69*	0.68*	0.68**	0.68*
Student	0.85	0.85	0.84	0.83
Unemployed	0.94	0.95	0.94	0.95
Self-reported health	0.92⁺	0.92⁺	0.92⁺	0.92*
Constant	0.03***	0.05***	0.04***	0.05***
Observations	6175	6175	6175	6175

Exponentiated coefficients are shown. Cases are weighted proportionally to the national population.
⁺$p < 0.10$; *$p < 0.05$; **$p < 0.01$; ***$p < 0.001$.
[a] Interaction term was significant in a generalized logistic regression model in which residual variance was permitted to vary by nation.
[b] Interaction term was *not* significant in a generalized logistic regression model in which residual variance was permitted to vary by nation.

Table 1-7: Logistic Regression Analysis of the Influence of the Interaction between Nation and Religion on Political Volunteering

	Model 1 Importance	Model 2 Prayer	Model 3 Attendance	Model 4 Socializing
Nations				
South Africa	ref.	ref.	ref.	ref.
Tanzania	4.61**	2.59*	8.02***	3.34***
Uganda	6.09***	2.73**	4.04***	1.12
Zimbabwe	0.82	0.80	0.91	0.85
Key Religion Variables				
Religious importance	1.03			
Frequency of prayer		1.03		
Service attendance			1.04	
Religious socializing				1.09*
Nation by Religion Interactions				
Tanzania × religious importance	1.00			
Uganda × religious importance	0.69**a			
Zimbabwe × religious importance	0.95			
Tanzania × prayer		1.09		
Uganda × prayer		0.92		
Zimbabwe × prayer		0.98		
Tanzania × service attendance			0.91*b	
Uganda × service attendance			0.85**a	
Zimbabwe × service attendance			0.95	
Tanzania × religious socializing				1.09

(continued)

1 | Religion and Volunteering in Four Sub-Saharan African Countries

Table 1-7: Logistic Regression Analysis of the Influence of the Interaction between Nation and Religion on Political Volunteering (*continued*)

	Model 1 Importance	Model 2 Prayer	Model 3 Attendance	Model 4 Socializing
Nation by Religion Interactions				
Uganda × religious socializing				1.12
Zimbabwe × religious socializing				0.93
Control Variables				
Female	0.66***	0.65***	0.66***	0.66***
Currently married	ref.	ref.	ref.	ref.
Formerly married	0.89	0.90	0.89	0.91
Never married	0.84+	0.84+	0.84+	0.84+
Number of children	1.00	1.00	1.00	1.00
Age in years	1.00	1.00	1.00	1.00
Level of education	1.07***	1.07***	1.07***	1.07***
Financially satisfied	0.98+	0.98+	0.98+	0.98+
Full-time	ref.	ref.	ref.	ref.
Part-time	1.15	1.15	1.15	1.17
Self-employed	1.08	1.09	1.08	1.08
Retired	0.92	0.91	0.90	0.92
Housewife	0.85	0.85	0.84	0.86
Student	0.77+	0.77+	0.77+	0.75*
Unemployed	0.81*	0.82*	0.81*	0.82*
Self-reported health	0.91*	0.91*	0.91*	0.90*
Constant	0.28***	0.27***	0.25***	0.25***
Observations	6175	6175	6175	6175

Exponentiated coefficients are shown. Cases are weighted proportionally to the national population.

$^+ p < 0.10$; $^* p < 0.05$; $^{**} p < 0.01$; $^{***} p < 0.001$.

[a] Interaction term was significant in a generalized logistic regression model in which residual variance was permitted to vary by nation.

[b] Interaction term was *not* significant in a generalized logistic regression model in which residual variance was permitted to vary by nation.

in the effects of various aspects of religiosity across nations. Only two of twelve interactions are significant in both the logistic regression models and the generalized logistic regression models. The effects of religious importance and service attendance on political activism are weaker in Uganda than in South Africa. Although there is a significant interaction between service attendance and an indicator for Tanzania, this interaction did not remain significant in a model that permitted heterogeneity of residual variance across nations.

Conclusion

This study examined the influence of religion on both caregiving and political volunteering in four sub-Saharan African countries. We explored whether there are unrealized opportunities to engage citizens' energy and skills for helping other residents in need and found support for our first four hypotheses when predicting caregiver volunteering, with a particularly robust effect of religious socializing. Findings also indicated that aspects of religion affected political volunteering, as individuals who prayed regularly and socialized with coaffiliates donated more time to political causes, though attending services and affirming the importance of religion lowered activism.

Overall, religious socializing exerted the most consistent effect on both types of volunteering, suggesting that religiosity best translates into caregiving and activist endeavors when the religiosity is informal and is experienced in a communal way. The effects of service attendance and prayer on volunteering may be relatively weak because ritualistic religious behaviors may be performed without the attachment of significant meaning and would not necessarily produce outcomes encouraged by the particular religion or church. Religious socializing likely heightens caregiver volunteering in a variety of ways. Socializing with fellow congregants may heighten awareness of both expectations about altruism and opportunities for volunteering. Given the importance of the social component of religion in motivating people to volunteer, it may be worthwhile to consider whether the social dynamics of religious congregations could be replicated by secular groups that are interested in boosting voluntary involvement.

A number of factors could contribute to the dampening effects of religious importance and church attendance on political engagement. Christianity, which is the dominant religion in these four nations, puts a strong emphasis on helping people who are sick. Christianity also encourages people to help others who are poor and in need, but it does not provide a lot of direction for how helping others should be manifested and whether involvement in political organizations would be the best way to help people. Additionally, some political movements encourage ideas and perspectives (e.g., Marxism) that may be at odds with Christianity. Finally, involvement in political volunteering may involve some of the same types of activities as involvement in formal religious activities does. For example, political volunteering may include attending organized meetings at which individuals listen to a speaker; this is similar to attending religious services at which congregants listen to a preacher. People might not want to increase the amount of time they spend on similar types of activities. As a result, those who attend religious services may be less likely to participate in political volunteering.

We also found support for Hypotheses 5a and 5b, as women are more likely than men to engage in caregiver volunteering, whereas men are more likely than women to engage in political volunteering. These findings have implications for gender dynamics because they reduce women's chances of obtaining higher offices that would facilitate advocacy and policymaking on behalf of women's status in the social, economic, and health spheres. The relationship between women's social status and their volunteer opportunities was not given sufficient attention in prior research, suggesting a greater need for future studies surrounding this topic. There was also evidence to suggest a gender-related conditioning effect, whereby religious socializing enhanced political activism among women. Since political and cultural norms likely contribute to women's diminished political activism in sub-Saharan Africa, women's political engagement may particularly benefit from the trust, shared norms, and information shared among religious coaffiliates.

We found some evidence that the effects of religiosity on caregiver volunteering were more powerful in South Africa than in Tanzania, Uganda, and Zimbabwe. These differences could arise from the fact that high levels of religiosity are normative in all of the nations we examined except South Africa. In each nation aside from South Africa, a majority of people reported socializing with fellow religious congregants. Among the four nations that we examined, service attendance was lowest in South Africa. Where levels of religious commitment are normative, social life may be dominated by religious institutions. In such environments, commitment to a religious community may reflect a bond to the community in general rather than a connection to specifically religious elements. By contrast, in South Africa, where religiosity is relatively less common, religious involvement may be more a matter of individual choice than a social obligation and therefore may reflect deeper, more heartfelt religious commitment. This could explain why various measures of religiosity appear more strongly related to caregiver volunteering in South Africa than in the other nations in our sample.

The data have some weaknesses that merit discussion. One of the biggest challenges for the current study is that the data are cross-sectional, making it difficult to establish the correct causal ordering between religion and volunteering. Our study posits that religion leads to volunteering. In South Africa, Zimbabwe, Tanzania, and Uganda, residents report very high levels of religious involvement and importance. By contrast, a minority of people participate in caregiver or political volunteering. It is possible that volunteering engenders religiosity in people who might otherwise be secular by putting them in contact with religious leaders and with programs sponsored by religious organizations. Very few longitudinal studies have been done in sub-Saharan Africa, and we do not know of any that include measures of volunteering and religion. Our hope is that future longitudinal studies done in sub-Saharan Africa will include questions about religion and volunteering so that we can empirically unravel the correct causal ordering.

Researchers have long suggested that more religious people are more likely than others to donate their time and energy to causes in which they believe, but few researchers have disentangled the effects of specific aspects of religiosity on volunteering as we have done here. Religion plays a highly significant role in the lives of the vast majority of people living in sub-Saharan Africa, and our results suggest that religiosity—particularly when social in nature—may be an especially valuable resource to enhance the well-being of community members in need.

References

Adamczyk, Amy, and Jacob Felson. 2006. "Friends' Religiosity and First Sex." *Social Science Research* 35: 924–47.

Adamczyk, Amy, and Ian Palmer. 2008. "Religion and Initiation into Marijuana Use: The Deterring Role of Religious Friends." *Journal of Drug Issues* 38: 717–41.

Adamczyk, Amy, and Cassady Pitt. 2009. "Shaping Attitudes about Homosexuality: The Role of Religion and Cultural Context." *Social Science Research* 38: 338–51.

Akintola, Olagoke. 2004. "A Gendered Analysis of the Burden of Care on Family and Volunteer Caregivers in Uganda and South Africa." Research Report, Health Economics and HIV/AIDS Research Division. Durban, South Africa: University of KwaZulu-Natal.

Akintola, Olagoke. 2008. "Defying All Odds: Coping with the Challenges of Volunteer Caregiving for Patients with AIDS in South Africa." *Journal of Advanced Nursing* 63: 357–65.

Allison, Paul D. 2001. *Missing Data*. Thousand Oaks, CA: Sage.

Ampofo, Adomako. 2008. "Collective Activism: The Domestic Violence Bill Becoming Law in Ghana." *African and Asian Studies* 7: 395–421.

Argue, Amy, David Johnson, and Lynn White. 1999. "Age and Religiosity: Evidence from a Three-Wave Panel Analysis." *Journal for the Scientific Study of Religion* 38: 423–35.

Becker, Penny, and Pawan Dhingra. 2001. "Religious Involvement and Volunteering: Implications for Civil Society." *Sociology of Religion* 62: 315–35.

Bekkers, Rene. 2001. "Participation in Voluntary Associations: Resources, Personality, or Both." Paper presented at the Fifth Conference of the European Sociological Association. Helsinki, Finland, August.

Beyerlein, Kraig, and Mark Chaves. 2003. "The Political Activities of Religious Congregations in the United States." *Journal for the Scientific Study of Religion* 42: 229–46.

Beyerlein, Kraig, and John Hipp. 2006. "From Pews to Participation: The Effect of Congregation Activity and Context on Bridging Civic Engagement." *Social Problems* 53: 97–117.

Chen, Shaohua, and Martin Ravallion. 2004. "How Have the World's Poorest Fared Since the Early 1980s?" *The World Bank Research Observer* 19: 141–69.

de Figueiredo, Rosely M., and Egberto Turato. 2001. "Needs for Assistance and Emotional Aspects of Caregiving Reported by AIDS Patient Caregivers in a Day-Care Unit in Brazil." *Issues in Mental Health Nursing* 22: 633–43.

Driskell, Robyn, Elizabeth Embry, and Larry Lyon. 2008. "Faith and Politics: The Influence of Religious Beliefs on Political Participation." *Social Science Quarterly* 89: 294–314.

Finke, Roger, and Amy Adamczyk. 2008. "Cross-National Moral Beliefs: The Influence of National Religious Context." *Sociological Quarterly* 49: 615–50.

Gilligan, Carol. 1982. *In a Different Voice: Psychological Theory and Women's Development*. Cambridge, MA: Harvard University Press.

Glaeser, Edward, and Bruce Sacerdote. 2008. "Education and Religion." *Journal of Human Capital* 2: 188–215.

Hayford, Sarah R., and S. Philip Morgan. 2008. "Religiosity and Fertility in the United States: The Role of Fertility Intentions." *Social Forces: A Scientific Medium of Social Study and Interpretation* 86: 1163–88.

Homan, Rick, and Catherine Searle. 2005. *Exploring the Role of Family Caregivers and Home-Based Care Programs in Meeting the Needs of People Living with HIV/AIDS*. Horizons Research Update. Johannesburg, South Africa: Population Council.

Inglehart, Ronald, and Wayne E. Baker. 2000. "Modernization, Cultural Change, and the Persistence of Traditional Values." *American Sociological Review* 65: 19–51.

Karniol, Rachel, Efrat Grosz, and Irit Schorr. 2003. "Caring, Gender Role Orientation, and Volunteering." *Sex Roles* 49: 11–19.

Kipp, Walter, Thomas Matukala Nkosi, Lory Laing, and Gian S. Jhangri. 2006. "Care Burden and Self-Reported Health Status of Informal Women Caregivers of HIV/AIDS Patients in Kinshasa, Democratic Republic of Congo." *AIDS Care* 18: 694–97.

Klopp, Jacqueline M., and Elke Zuern. 2007. "The Politics of Violence in Democratization: Lessons from Kenya and South Africa." *Comparative Politics* 39: 127–46.

Lam, Pui-Yan. 2002. "As the Flocks Gather: How Religion Affects Voluntary Association Participation." *Journal for the Scientific Study of Religion* 41: 405–22.

Lam, Pui-Yan. 2006. "Religion and Civic Culture: A Cross-National Study of Voluntary Association Membership." *Journal for the Scientific Study of Religion* 45: 177–93.

Manning, Lydia. 2010. "Gender and Religious Differences Associated with Volunteering in Later Life." *Journal of Women & Aging* 22: 125–35.

McCoy, David, Mickey Chopra, Rene Loewenson, Jean-Marion Aitken, Thalabe Ngulube, Adamson Muula, Sunanda Ray, Tendayi Kureyi, Petrida Ijumba, and Mike Rowson. 2005. "Expanding Access to Antiretroviral Therapy in Sub-Saharan Africa: Avoiding the Pitfalls and Dangers, Capitalizing on the Opportunities." *American Journal of Public Health* 95: 18–22.

McPherson, J. Miller, and Thomas Rotolo. 1996. "Testing a Dynamic Model of Social Composition: Diversity and Change in Voluntary Groups." *American Sociological Review* 61: 179–202.

Mmatli, Tlamelo. 2008. "Political Activism as a Social Work Strategy in Africa." *International Social Work* 51: 297–310.

Musick, Marc A., John Wilson, and William B. Bynum, Jr. 2000. "Race and Formal Volunteering: The Differential Effects of Class and Religion." *Social Forces* 78: 1539–70.

Norris, Pippa, and Ronald Inglehart. 2004. *Sacred and Secular: Religion and Politics Worldwide*. New York: Cambridge University Press.

Ogden, Jessica, Simel Esim, and Caren Grown. 2006. "Expanding the Care Continuum for HIV/AIDS: Bringing Carers into Focus." *Health Policy and Planning* 21: 333–42.

Orner, Phyllis. 2006. "Psychosocial Impacts on Caregivers of People Living with AIDS." *AIDS Care* 18: 236–40.
Paik, Anthony, and Layana Navarre-Jackson. 2010. "Social Networks, Recruitment, and Volunteering: Are Social Capital Effects Conditional on Recruitment?" *Nonprofit and Voluntary Sector Quarterly* 40: 476–96.
Pew Forum on Religion & Public Life. 2010. "Tolerance and Tension: Islam and Christianity in Sub-Saharan Africa." Washington, DC: Pew Research Center. Available at http://pewforum.org/about-the-project-islam-and-christianity-in-sub-saharan-africa.aspx.
Popielarz, Pamela. 1999. "(In)Voluntary Association." *Gender & Society* 13: 234–50.
Read, Jen'nan Ghazal. 2003. "The Sources of Gender Role Attitudes among Christian and Muslim Arab-American Women." *Sociology of Religion* 64: 207–22.
Robins, Steven. 2006. "From 'Rights' to 'Ritual': AIDS Activism in South Africa." *American Anthropologist* 108: 312–23.
Rödlach, Alexander. 2009. "Home-Based Care for People Living with AIDS in Zimbabwe: Voluntary Caregivers' Motivations and Concerns." *African Journal of AIDS Research* 8: 423–31.
Rotolo, Thomas, and John Wilson. 2007. "Sex Segregation in Volunteer Work." *Sociological Quarterly* 48: 559–85.
Royston, Patrick. 2009. "Multiple Imputation of Missing Values: Further Update of Ice, with an Emphasis on Categorical Variables." *Stata Journal* 9: 466–77.
Rugalema, Gabriel. 2000. "Coping or Struggling? A Journey into the Impact of HIV/AIDS in Southern Africa." *Review of African Political Economy* 27: 537–45.
Ruiter, Stijn, and Nan Dirk De Graaf. 2006. "National Context, Religiosity, and Volunteering: Results from 53 Countries." *American Sociological Review* 71: 191–210.
Sachs, Jeffrey. 2005. *The End of Poverty: Economic Possibilities for Our Time*. New York: Penguin.
Skovdal, Morten, Vincent Ogutu, Cellestine Aoro, and Catherine Campbell. 2009. "Young Carers as Social Actors: Coping Strategies of Children Caring for Ailing or Ageing Guardians in Western Kenya." *Social Science & Medicine* 69: 587–95.
Thornton, Arland, William G. Axinn, and Daniel H. Hill. 1992. "Reciprocal Effects of Religiosity, Cohabitation, and Marriage." *American Journal of Sociology* 98: 628–51.
Tripp, Aili Mari. 2001. "The New Political Activism in Africa." *Journal of Democracy* 12: 141–55.
UNAIDS. 2008. *Report on the Global HIV/AIDS Epidemic 2008*. Geneva, Switzerland: UNAIDS.
UNAIDS. 2009. *AIDS Epidemic Update: December 2009*. Geneva, Switzerland: UNAIDS.

United Nations Development Programme. 2010. *Human Development Report.* New York: Oxford University Press.

van Buuren, S., H. C. Boshuizen, and D. L. Knook. 1999. "Multiple Imputation of Missing Blood Pressure Covariates in Survival Analysis." *Statistics in Medicine* 18: 681–94.

Verba, Sidney, Kay Schlozman, and Henry Brady. 1995. *Voice and Equality: Civic Voluntarism in American Politics.* Cambridge, MA: Harvard University Press.

Williams, Richard. 2009. "Using Heterogeneous Choice Models to Compare Logit and Probit Coefficients across Groups." *Sociological Methods and Research* 37: 531–49.

Wilson, John. 2000. "Volunteering." *Annual Review of Sociology* 26: 215–40.

Wilson, John, and Thomas Janoski. 1995. "The Contribution of Religion to Volunteer Work." *Sociology of Religion* 56: 137–52.

Wilson, John, and Marc Musick. 1997. "Who Cares? Toward an Integrated Theory of Volunteer Work." *American Sociological Review* 62: 694–713.

2

Religion and Philanthropic Giving and Volunteering

Building Blocks for Civic Responsibility

Stephen V. Monsma

Civic responsibility plays a huge role in the success of a constitutional democracy such as that of the United States. By civic responsibility, I mean a combination of behaviors, skills, and virtues that are manifested by citizens who are active, involved, contributing members of their community and society. Included in this combination are an ingrained acceptance of a shared or communal accountability for the common, or public, good of one's community and society; giving to and volunteering for organizations that contribute to the welfare of one's community; possessing a sense of social trust; and practicing honesty in one's dealings with others. One key aspect of civic responsibility is responsible citizenship. The responsible citizen votes in elections; is informed about candidates, officeholders, and public issues; and in other ways contributes to the political process.

It is hard to exaggerate the importance of responsible citizenship—as well as the broader concept of civic responsibility—for a healthy, well-functioning democratic society. Many scholars, in many different ways, have made this point (Eberly 1995; Verba, Schlozman, and Brady 1995; Wilson 1985, 1993). Others have made the equally crucial point of the importance of religion in American society: "People gather for many reasons and in many places, but no voluntary or cultural institution in American society gathers more people more regularly than religious congregations" (Chaves 2004: 1). Given the importance of religion in

American life and the importance of the existence of a sense of civic responsibility for a healthy, democratic polity, the conjunction of religion and civic responsibility has been explored by many scholars (e.g., Brooks 2003, 2006; Nemeth and Luidens 2003; Regnerus, Smith, and Sikkink 1998; Wuthnow 1990). Nevertheless, a survey of previous studies in the area illuminates how many issues have not been studied.

This article focuses on the conjunction of religion and giving money and volunteering time to nonprofit, community-building associations. Giving and volunteering intersect with civic responsibility in at least two ways. First, they themselves constitute behavior in keeping with the ideal of civic responsibility. They involve contributing scarce resources (time or money) to help one's community and fellow human beings. Second, individuals who give and volunteer may also fulfill other facets of civic responsibility, including responsible citizenship, since all these facets involve looking beyond one's personal, immediate context and contributing to one's broader community. More specifically, this article has three goals: to systematize the many findings of previous studies of religion and philanthropic giving and volunteering, to contribute to the theoretical understanding of the role religion plays in philanthropic giving and volunteering, and to relate the conjunction of religion and philanthropic giving and volunteering to a polity marked by democratic norms.

Findings and Theoretical Insights from Previous Studies

Anyone who wants to understand the relationship between religion and giving and volunteering faces a buzzing confusion of previously published studies. The first task therefore is to systematize the findings and theoretical insights from the many studies of religion and philanthropic volunteering and giving. Doing so will clarify what we do and do not know and will help us to focus on key remaining questions. I have organized the differing conceptualizations of religion used by researchers in terms of belonging, behavior, and belief. Belonging refers simply to membership in a religious congregation. Behavior consists of any number of religiously oriented activities, such as attending religious services, engaging in prayer, and reading the Bible or other devotional literature. Belief denotes professed religious beliefs.

Convergent Findings

Giving to Charitable Organizations. The most consistently reported finding regarding religion and giving is that individuals who are religious are more likely to give money to charitable organizations and to give more money than those who are not religious. Among the religious, people who are more religious give and give more than those who are less religious. This pattern holds whether one considers financial gifts to all charitable organizations, only to religious organizations, or only to secular organizations. This also holds true whether religion is measured in terms of religious belonging (Hodgkinson, Weitzman, and Kirsch 1990: 103, 107; Nemeth and Luidens 2003) or in terms of religious behavior, particularly church attendance (Brooks 2003; Hodgkinson et al. 1996: 4–91, 4–93; Regnerus, Smith, and Sikkink 1998).

Volunteering for Charitable Organizations. Researchers have also found that giving and volunteering go together: People who give tend to be the same people who volunteer, and those who volunteer tend to be the same people who give (Hodgkinson, Weitzman, and Kirsch 1990: 102ff; Putnam 2000: 118). Therefore in considering volunteering, many of the patterns resemble those of giving to charities. But there are some variations.

Virtually all researchers agree that individuals who are members of religious congregations volunteer their time more frequently to charitable organizations and volunteer more hours than do those who are not members of religious congregations. While Hodgkinson and her associates (1990: 102) found that members of religious congregations volunteer more than nonmembers do, most studies of religion and volunteering look beyond belonging to a religious congregation to note attendance at religious worship services and its relationship to volunteering. Here too there is near-unanimous agreement; as with giving, the behavior pattern of regular attendance at religious services is related to higher levels of volunteering (e.g., Brooks 2003; Campbell and Yonish 2003; Hodgkinson et al. 1996). Brooks (2003: 43) reports that regular church attendees "volunteer an average of 12 times per year, while secular people volunteer an average of 5.8 times," a difference that persisted even after controlling for a number of demographic characteristics. Many other studies have produced similar findings (Campbell and Yonish 2003; Park and Smith 2000; Wuthnow 1999: 351; 2004: 103).

In summary, previous studies on the relationship between religion and philanthropic giving and volunteering are in agreement on the following points:

1. Members of religious congregations give and give larger amounts to charities, whether religious or secular, than do nonmembers.
2. Regular attendees at religious worship services give and give larger amounts to charities, whether religious or secular, than do those who rarely, if ever, attend religious worship services.
3. Members of religious congregations volunteer and volunteer more hours to charitable organizations than do nonmembers.
4. Regular attendees at worship services volunteer and volunteer more hours to charitable organizations than do those who rarely, if ever, attend religious services.

Divergent Findings

Despite the consistent confirmation of these four patterns, earlier studies have produced conflicting answers to three other questions: (1) Do more highly religious people volunteer for nonreligious, secular organizations at higher rates than do less religious people? (2) Why do religiously involved people tend to give and to volunteer more than irreligious people do? (3) Do people from certain religious traditions tend to give or volunteer more than do people from other religious traditions? The last two of these questions move us into explanatory issues and thus raise theoretical questions concerning why religious people tend to give and volunteer more than nonreligious people do.

The first area in which studies have obtained different results concerns the relationship between religious involvement and volunteering for secular charitable programs. Some findings are clear. People who are religious volunteer more than do those who are irreligious, and people who are religious—not surprisingly—volunteer more for religious organizations. Ambiguities arise, however, in regard to whether or not people who are religious volunteer more for secular organizations than do the irreligious. Here, things become complex. Brooks (2003: 43) found that 60 percent of highly religious people volunteered for nonreligious causes, while only 39 percent of irreligious people did so, even when controlling for basic demographic variables. Campbell and Yonish (2003: 102) found that individuals who did not attend church averaged only 2.56 hours of volunteering a month for nonreligious causes, while those who attended church weekly averaged 5.33 hours of volunteering for nonreligious causes.

Park and Smith (2000), however, found that regular church attendance decreased volunteering for non-church-related causes, although they found that other forms of church activity increased volunteering for non-church-related causes. Lam (2002) also found that regular church attendance decreased volunteering for nonreligious causes, albeit to only a small degree. He and others theorized that churches to some degree compete for their members' time. Thus as a member spends time in church activities—as indicated by weekly church attendance—less time is available for that person to volunteer in extra-church causes. Nevertheless, the relationship between religious involvement and volunteering for nonreligious organizations remains murky.

The second question on which previous studies have reached divergent conclusions is crucial: Why do religiously involved people tend to give and to volunteer more than irreligious people do? Previous studies have raised two key theoretical explanations to account for this phenomenon. One explanation is the social network theory (Becker and Dhingra 2001: 316; Wilson and Janoski 1995: 138). It suggests that being deeply religious and the attendant involvement in a religious congregation mean that one is involved in social networks outside of one's immediate family and circle of friends. As one's experience extends into the broader community and as one is drawn into a wider social network—whether rooted in religious or secular involvements—one is stimulated to give and volunteer. These social networks work to increase giving and volunteering in two ways: by exposing individuals to broader needs in their communities and by increasing the likelihood that one will be exposed to efforts to recruit one to give or volunteer.

There is some empirical evidence in support of this theory. Putnam (2000: 120) found that members of religious congregations were more likely to give and to give more than nonmembers, as have others. But he also found that an even higher percentage of members of secular organizations gave to charities than did members of religious organizations and that they tended to give larger amounts. Putnam (2000: 119) also reports that in a comparison of people who attended church at least monthly with those who attended club meetings at least monthly, club attendees volunteered more than did church attendees. Moreover, these two types of involvements reinforced each other: people who attended both church and clubs volunteered the most, and those who attended neither church nor clubs volunteered the least.

Campbell and Yonish (2003: 103–5) compared people who attend church weekly with those who attend secular organizations weekly and found that both attendance patterns were significantly related to volunteering in both religious and nonreligious organizations. As one would expect, church attendance was more strongly related to religious volunteering, and attending secular organizations was more strongly related to nonreligious volunteering. Both types of attendance were significantly related to both. This led the authors to conclude that being part of a church community "does not have appreciably different effects from that found within secular voluntary associations, at least in regards to voluntarism" (Campbell and Yonish 2003: 105).

Some studies have focused on how church-based social networks act as recruitment grounds. Campbell and Yonish (2003: 95), for example, found that people who had volunteered for nonreligious causes most frequently cited church and family settings as the places where they had been recruited to volunteer, rather than in either work or membership organizations. Similarly, Park and Smith (2000: 282) found that respondents who were significantly more likely to volunteer reported having many Christian friends and relatives.

In short, social networks that enmesh religiously active individuals—whether by acting as a recruiting ground or by increasing one's exposure to community needs—might explain their higher levels of giving and volunteering.

A second theory that seeks to explain increased volunteering and giving by religious people focuses on the content of their religious beliefs. Since Christianity, Judaism, and Islam all teach the responsibility of the believer to help those in need, it may be religious beliefs themselves that lead to increased giving and volunteering. This is the religious belief theory (Wuthnow 1990: 7–9).

There is also some empirical evidence in support of this theory. Hodgkinson and her colleagues found that individuals who had as a personal goal "making a strong commitment to a religious life" gave and volunteered in a much higher proportion than did those who had other types of personal goals (Hodgkinson, Weitzman, and Kirsch 1990: 109). Wuthnow (2004: 103) found that people who reported daily Bible reading, prayer, or meditation also volunteered for charity or social service programs to a greater extent than those who did not. For example, he found that 31 percent of people who read the Bible "nearly every day" volunteered, while only 13 percent of those who read the Bible less often had done so (Wuthnow 2004: 103). Another study found that "the devotional dimension of religiosity, measured by frequency of prayer and religious reading, does have a significant positive influence on voluntary association participation" (Lam 2002: 420). These studies suggest private devotional activities—which do not involve people in social networks—might increase volunteering. Also supporting this view is the finding that respondents who indicated spiritual growth as being extremely or very important to them were more than twice as likely to volunteer as were those who indicated that spiritual growth was less important (Wuthnow 2004: 103).

In short, there are studies that lend support to the religious belief theory by showing a relationship between religious beliefs and private religious behaviors and philanthropic giving and volunteering. Both the social network and the religious belief theories need to be subjected to further testing.

The third question that has produced inconsistent answers concerns whether or not people in certain religious traditions give and volunteer at higher levels than do those in other traditions. Studies that have examined this question compared giving and volunteering by evangelical Protestants, Mainline Protestants, Catholics, and, in some cases, Jews and Black Protestants. Resultant findings have been inconsistent—in fact, they have been all over the map. Some studies have found no relationship between denominational allegiance and levels of volunteering and giving. Becker and Dhingra (2001: 326) found "no effect of denomination or religious conservatism on volunteering." Campbell and Yonish (2003: 98) found that once they took church attendance levels into account, the religious tradition of individuals had no predictive power for volunteering. Lam (2002: 415) concluded that his "study reveals no significant differences among liberal, moderate, and conservative Protestants in voluntary association involvement," while Wilson and Janoski (1995) report almost no denominational differences in volunteering.

Other studies report differences in giving and volunteering by religious tradition, but their findings do not agree on which religious traditions give and volunteer more than other traditions. Wuthnow (1990: 345), for example, found that "mainline Protestants are more likely than evangelicals to say they are currently involved in charity or social service activities, to have donated time in the past year to a voluntary organization, and to have worked on a community service project." Similarly, Schwadel (2005) found that members of conservative, or evangelical, Protestant congregations belonged to fewer nonchurch organizations than did members of other, less theologically conservative congregations, though it should be noted that Schwadel considered only membership in secular organizations, not levels of volunteering.

Yet other studies report differences in giving and volunteering by religious tradition but with the more theologically conservative, or evangelical, Protestants giving or volunteering at higher levels than other Christian traditions. In a recent study, Wuthnow (2004: 103) found that 26 percent of evangelical Protestants had volunteered in the previous year, while about 20 percent of Mainline Protestants and Catholics had done so. Similarly, Regnerus, Smith, and Sikkink (1998: 9) concluded, "Among Christians, it appears that evangelical Protestants are mildly distinguishable from other Protestants and Catholics in a positive direction" in their giving to antipoverty agencies. The relationship between philanthropic giving and volunteering and religious traditions remains a puzzle.

Unexplored Questions

Numerous studies of the relationship between religion and giving or volunteering have left several key issues largely unexplored. Here I outline four of them.

First, earlier studies have not made a clear distinction between giving or volunteering for one's local congregation in its core religious activities and rituals and giving or volunteering for one's own congregation or other religiously based organizations in programs that offer services to the broader community. The former includes activities such as giving to the church's budget, singing in a church choir, and ushering at religious services. The latter includes working at a congregation's food bank, tutoring children at a church-sponsored after-school program, and giving to a faith-based shelter for abused spouses. This is a crucial question. Whether or not the patterns earlier studies found in regard to religious giving and volunteering hold up when religious giving and volunteering is limited to religiously based programs and activities involving community service and help needs to be considered.

A second unexplored question deals with the relationship between individual religious beliefs and giving and volunteering. Previously published studies have not explored the impact religious beliefs have on giving and volunteering. Finding answers to this question will throw light on the unresolved question of the competing social network and religious belief theories.

A third largely unexplored question is the relationship between giving and volunteering and religiously motivated behavior that is private and personal (such as devotional Bible reading and private prayer) rather than public and social (such as attendance at worship services). Finding answers to this question will also throw light on the unresolved question of the competing social network and religious belief theories. If private religious behavior is related to increased giving and volunteering, support would be given to the religious belief theory over the social network theory, owing to the private, personal nature of such activities.

A fourth unanswered question asks what the relationship is between philanthropic giving and volunteering and other aspects of civic responsibility. Do people who give and volunteer exhibit more characteristics denoting a sense of civic responsibility? Are they more likely to vote and stay informed on the issues of the day? These questions ask whether giving and volunteering stand largely by themselves as actions we all admire. Or are they expressions of deeper underlying attitudes and values that take expression as other forms of behavior crucial to a democratic polity? Are they indeed building blocks of civic responsibility—and its subset, responsible citizenship?

Breaking New Ground: Exploring Inconsistent Findings and Unasked Questions

This section makes use of several existing datasets to explore these questions on which findings either are in disagreement or have not been adequately addressed.

Does Social Network Theory or Religious Belief Theory Better Explain Giving and Volunteering?

As was noted earlier, previous studies have given some support to both the social network and the religious belief theories of why religious individuals are more likely to give and volunteer than less religious individuals are. Christianity clearly teaches the importance of giving to and helping those who are in need. Thus it is appropriate to hypothesize that if religious beliefs are driving increased giving and volunteering, Christians who report that their religious faith plays an important role in their lives, who accept the traditional teachings of Christianity, and who engage in private religious practices—that is, people who are especially religious in a traditionally Christian sense—will be especially prone to give to and volunteer for charitable organizations. According to this hypothesis, church attendance and its resulting social network are not the key factors in giving and volunteering, but church attendance is an indicator of high religiosity. It is the religiosity that drives the giving and volunteering. The alternative hypothesis—one for which we have seen that there is also support—is that religious beliefs are not the motivator for people who are more highly religious to give and volunteer more than the nonreligious. Instead, it is the broader perspectives and wider social networks resulting from one's religious involvements that are the key factors. According to this hypothesis, activity in nonreligious organizations is as likely to lead to giving and volunteering as is religious activity.

To shed light on these competing explanations, I made use of two national survey datasets that measured the variables of giving, volunteering, and religiosity (the 2000 Pew IV study of Religion and American Public Life and the 1998 General Social Survey).[1] Both datasets contain information on the respondents' giving and volunteering for traditional social service programs for the needy, homeless, or elderly as well as for community recreational or arts and cultural programs. To focus on giving and volunteering that was of a clearly philanthropic nature, I excluded giving and volunteering for political causes and for religious congregations in their core religious practices and rituals. In what I report below, giving to or volunteering for "religious causes" includes only giving to or volunteering for church-sponsored or otherwise faith-based community

---

[1] I used a total of four national survey datasets in this article: the 1998 General Social Survey (www.thearda.com/Archive/Files/Descriptions/GSS1998.asp, principal investigators: James Allen Davis and Tom W. Smith); the 1996 God and Society in North America survey, using only the U.S. respondents (www.thearda.com/Archive/Files/Descriptions/QUEENS.asp, principal investigators: Angus Reid Group at Queen's University and the Institute for the Study of American Evangelicals—John Green, James L. Guth, Lyman Kellstedt, and Corwin Smidt); the 2000 Social Capital Community Benchmark Survey of the Saguaro Seminar (www.thearda.com/Archive/Files/Descriptions/SCCBS.asp, principal investigator: Robert Putman); and the 2000 Pew IV survey (see Guth et al. 2002, especially footnote 12). The first three of these surveys were downloaded from the Association of Religion Data Archives (www.thearda.com).

service programs. The Pew survey on both giving and volunteering and the General Social Survey on giving carefully distinguished between giving or volunteering for religious community service programs and giving or volunteering to one's church as church. However, in regard to volunteering, the General Social Survey asked only about volunteering for "religious and church-related activities." Thus among its volunteers, there are some people who volunteered for their churches' core religious activities. In regard to the Pew survey on both giving and volunteering and the General Social Survey on giving, I am confident that the "religious cause" category does not include giving or volunteering for one's local congregation in its core religious practices and rituals.

In all of the following analyses, I considered a respondent as having given or volunteered if the person reported giving or volunteering at all. I did not take into account the amount of money given or the amount of time volunteered.

First, I considered the question of whether or not people for whom religion has a high salience in their lives, who hold to traditional Christian beliefs, and who engage in private devotional activities apart from public religious services give and volunteer more than do those with opposite characteristics. I derived the salience measure from one to four items that asked respondents about the importance of religion in their lives and the extent to which they look to religion or God for guidance and help. The measure of traditional beliefs consisted of four to six items that asked respondents about such beliefs as the divinity of Jesus, the inspiration of the Bible, the existence of heaven, and whether all religions are equally good and true. The measure of private devotional activities consisted of two to four items that asked respondents about their activities in praying and Bible reading outside formal religious services.

The basic results appear in Tables 2-1 and 2-2. In regard to giving (Table 2-1), both surveys reveal that a significantly higher percentage of people marked by high levels of religiosity—measured by religious salience, traditional religious beliefs, and private religious practices—were more likely to give to religiously sponsored community causes than were those who exhibited low levels of religiosity. In terms of giving to nonreligious community causes, people who scored high and low in religiosity were giving at roughly the same level. Among the Pew respondents, those who were low in religious salience and private religious practices were actually significantly more likely to give than those
(text continues on page 52 below)

Table 2-1: Percent of Respondents Giving to Religious and Nonreligious Causes by Religious Salience, Level of Traditional Christian Beliefs, and Level of Private Religious Practices

	Pew IV	GSS 1998
Gave to religious causes:[a]		
High religious salience	56%[b]	49%[b]
Low religious salience	12%[b]	17%[b]
Gave to nonreligious causes:		
High religious salience	53%[c]	60%
Low religious salience	59%[c]	57%
Gave to religious causes:[a]		
High traditional beliefs	54%[b]	48%[b]
Low traditional beliefs	23%[b]	24%[b]
Gave to nonreligious causes:		
High traditional beliefs	54%	65%
Low traditional beliefs	62%	63%
Gave to religious causes:[a]		
High private practices	62%[b]	48%[b]
Low private practices	17%[b]	20%[b]
Gave to nonreligious causes:		
High private practices	52%[c]	63%[c]
Low private practices	58%[c]	54%[c]

Note: The table presents only the findings for those who scored high or low in the three measures of religiosity; those falling into the medium category are not presented here. In almost all cases, they fell in between the high and low categories in giving.
[a] For the Pew IV survey, religious causes consist only of community service programs with a religious nature or sponsorship. For the 1998 General Social Survey, religious causes consist of giving to "religious organizations, programs or causes" other than the respondent's own congregation.
[b] Significant at the 0.001 level.
[c] Significant at the 0.01 level.

2 | Religion and Philanthropic Giving and Volunteering

Table 2-2: Percent of Respondents Volunteering, by Religious Salience, Level of Traditional Christian Beliefs, and Level of Private Religious Practices

	Pew IV	GSS 1998
Volunteered for religious causes:[a]		
High religious salience	52%[b]	62%[b]
Low religious salience	13%[b]	13%[b]
Volunteered for nonreligious causes:		
High religious salience	56%[b]	58%[b]
Low religious salience	65%[b]	43%[b]
Volunteered for religious causes:[a]		
High traditional beliefs	48%[b]	53%[b]
Low traditional beliefs	20%[b]	18%[b]
Volunteered for nonreligious causes:		
High traditional beliefs	59%[c]	53%
Low traditional beliefs	71%[c]	52%
Volunteered for religious causes:[a]		
High private practices	59%[b]	64%[b]
Low private practices	17%[b]	15%[b]
Volunteered for nonreligious causes:		
High private practices	57%	63%[b]
Low private practices	61%	41%[b]

Note: The table presents only the findings for those who scored high or low in the three measures of religiosity; those falling into the medium category are not presented here. In almost all cases, they fell in between the high and low categories in volunteering.

[a] For the Pew IV survey, religious causes consist only of community service programs with a religious nature or sponsorship. For the 1998 General Social Survey, religious causes consist of giving to "religious organizations, programs or causes" other than the respondent's own congregation.
[b] Significant at the 0.001 level.
[c] Significant at the 0.01 level.

who were high in those religious measures. The General Social Survey respondents produced the opposite result in regard to private religious practices: those who ranked high were significantly more likely to give to nonreligious causes. Clearly, however, the more religious individuals were giving to nonreligious community service programs at much higher rates than those at which less religious individuals were giving to religious community service programs.

In regard to volunteering (Table 2-2), much the same pattern held. Respondents who scored high in religiosity—whether in terms of religious salience, traditional beliefs, or private religious practices—volunteered in significantly higher proportions for religious programs than did those who scored low in religiosity.

As with giving, the pattern in volunteering for nonreligious causes was mixed. The low-religiosity Pew respondents tended to volunteer for nonreligious causes in higher proportions than did the high-religiosity respondents, significantly so in terms of religious salience and traditional beliefs. But the respondents from the General Social Survey who ranked high in religious salience or private religious practices volunteered at significantly higher levels than did those ranking low. As with giving, the religious are much more likely to volunteer for nonreligious causes, than are the less religious to volunteer for religious causes.

In summary, earlier studies found that members of religious congregations and those who attend church regularly are more likely to give and to volunteer than are those who are not members or do not attend regularly, except in regard to volunteering for secular causes, for which the evidence has been mixed. I found that people for whom religion is highly salient in their lives, who hold more traditional Christian beliefs, and who engage in private religious practices also give and volunteer for religiously sponsored community-serving causes more than do those for whom religion is not salient, hold less traditional beliefs, and tend not to engage in private religious practices. In other words, when one focuses on religious programs of a community-serving nature (as distinct from core religious activities and rituals) and when one goes beyond attendance at religious services to take into account other measures of religiosity, the pattern holds by which the more religious give and volunteer for religious causes at a much higher rate than do the less religious.

The differences in the case of giving to and volunteering for secularly sponsored community-serving causes were mixed, especially between the two different surveys. Clarifying this relationship will have to await further research.

However, this does not yet deal with the question of whether the social network theory or the religious belief theory better explains the patterns found in Tables 2-1 and 2-2. Some insight into this question can be gained by introducing church attendance into the findings of Tables 2-1 and 2-2. I divided the respondents in each of the cells into those who attended church at least weekly and those who attended less than monthly. Doing so revealed, first, that church attendance is more strongly related to giving and volunteering than is each of the three measures of religiosity reported in Tables 2-1 and 2-2. Respondents who were high in church attendance and low in one of the other three measures of religiosity were more likely to give or volunteer than were those who were low in church attendance and high in one of the other measures of religiosity. There were twenty-four possible combinations: the three measures of religiosity, times two for giving or volunteering, times two for religious or nonreligious causes, times two for the two studies. In five of these twenty-four combinations, the differences between the high and low church attendees were very small: only one to five percentage points separated them. In the other nineteen combinations, there were differences of over five percentage points in giving or volunteering between the high and low attendees. And in fourteen of these, respondents who were high on church attendance and low on one of the other measures of religiosity were more likely to give or volunteer than were those who were low on church attendance and high in one of the other measures of religiosity. In only five cases did a higher percentage of respondents who were high one of the measures of religiosity and low on church attendance give or volunteer at a higher rate than did those who were high on church attendance and low on one of the other religiosity measures.

A second pattern revealed by this analysis is that in most cases, those who were high on both church attendance and one of the other three measures of religiosity gave or volunteered at higher levels than did those who ranked high only on church attendance or only on one of the other three religiosity measures. Respondents who ranked low on both church attendance and one of the other three measures of religiosity gave or volunteered at lower levels than did those who ranked low only on church attendance or one of the other three measures of religiosity.

The conclusion I reach from these two patterns is that church attendance—with its associated integration into a social network—and individuals' more personal, internalized religious beliefs both motivate giving and volunteering. I found support for both the social network and the religious belief theories, but the former proved to be a stronger factor than the latter.

Is Religious Tradition Related to Giving and Volunteering?

I noted earlier that previous studies reported wildly varying results on the question of whether or not the adherents of certain religious traditions give or volunteer in higher proportions than do the adherents of other religious traditions. The patterns that I uncovered by the use of two different datasets shed additional light on this question, although they are not fully consistent.

In regard to giving, varying results emerged according to whether the giving was for a religious cause or a secular cause. (Recall that I excluded religious congregations in their worship and religious rituals from religiously based causes. The term *religiously based causes* refers to social or community services that are sponsored by religious bodies or that have a religious component.) Table 2-3 shows that in both surveys, the irreligious, or secular, respondents were the least likely to give to religiously based community service programs. In the columns labeled "All," only about 15 percent of the secular respondents reported doing so, while 30–50 percent of the five religious traditions did so. The Mainline Protestants were the most likely to give, followed very closely by the evangelical and Black Protestants. Catholics and Jews were somewhat less likely to give. These differences were statistically significant.

For the four Christian traditions, I also looked at giving patterns divided by respondents who attended religious services weekly or more and those who attended less than monthly. In both surveys and all four religious traditions, respondents who attended religious services regularly were more likely to give than those who did not. This is not surprising; it is in line with other of my findings and those of earlier studies.

The differences between high and low church attendees *within* a religious tradition tended to be greater than the differences *among* the religious traditions. The differences were statistically significant, except in the case of Black Protestants in the General Social Survey. This supports the

Table 2-3: Percent of Respondents Giving to Religious Causes, by Religious Tradition and Level of Attendance at Religious Services

	Pew IV	GSS 1998
Evangelical		
High Attendance	59%[b]	51%[b]
Low Attendance	25%[b]	31%[b]
All	46%[a]	40%[a]
Mainline Protestant		
High Attendance	72%[b]	63%[b]
Low Attendance	25%[b]	30%[b]
All	48%[a]	44%[a]
Black Protestant		
High Attendance	65%[b]	32%
Low Attendance	10%[b]	27%
All	48%[a]	31%[a]
Catholic		
High Attendance	53%[b]	50%[b]
Low Attendance	24%[b]	24%[b]
All	38%[a]	34%[a]
Jewish		
All	29%[a]	50%[a]
Secular		
All	15%[a]	16%[a]

Note: For both surveys, religious causes were determined in the same way as for Table 2-1. The table presents only the findings for those who scored high or low in attendance at religious services; those falling into the medium category are not presented here. Those who reported attending services weekly or more were put in the high-attendance category, and those who reported attending services less than monthly were put into the low-attendance category. The distinction among the six religious traditions was made on a combination of self-reported denominational affiliation (or lack of any affiliation) and reported religious beliefs. All Jewish and secular respondents were considered together, owing to the very small numbers in the high-attendance category.
[a] Significant at the 0.001 level, based on all of the adherents of the six religious traditions without regard to church attendance.
[b] Significant at the 0.001 level, based on the attendance levels of each religious tradition taken separately.

social network theory for the conjunction of religiosity and philanthropic giving. Church attendance and its associated integration into a social network had a stronger influence than did the differing beliefs emphasized by the various religious traditions.

Table 2-4 reports giving to nonreligious, or secular, community service programs. Here, the patterns are not consistent. The General Social Survey secular respondents were less likely to give than were the respondents from any of the five religious traditions, while the Pew secular respondents gave at higher rate than the respondents from three of the five religious traditions. Adding to the puzzle, in both cases, the differences were statistically significant. In both surveys, the Jews and Mainline Protestants were the most likely to give to nonreligious programs. The evangelicals, Black Protestants, and Catholics were less likely to give than were the Mainline Protestants and Jews. In short, the differences in giving to religious causes between the high and low attendees largely disappeared in regard to nonreligious causes.

Overall, these findings in regard to giving and religious traditions demonstrate, first, the motivating power of religion, as mentioned elsewhere in this article. People who are affiliated with a religious tradition are, as a rule, more likely to give than those who are not, a pattern that was clear in the case of religiously based services. Second, the Mainline Protestants were among those most likely to give, whether to a religious or to a secular cause, although the differences between them and the other religious traditions were usually small. By a number of measures, evangelical Protestants were almost as likely to give, despite their reputation for being inward looking and concerned with individual salvation, not social causes. This may be due to evangelicals being less inward looking than is sometimes claimed or to the power of church attendance and the resulting integration into a social network. This latter conclusion is supported by the fact, noted earlier, than the differences in giving were greater between high and low attendees within a tradition than among the different traditions.

Tables 2-5 and 2-6 report my findings in regard to volunteering by religious tradition and level of church attendance. In regard to volunteering for religious causes (Table 2-5), Black Protestants tended to volunteer the most, followed closely by Mainline Protestants and evangelicals.

(text continues on page 60 below)

Table 2-4: Percent of Respondents Giving to Nonreligious Causes, by Religious Tradition and Level of Attendance at Religious Services

	Pew IV	GSS 1998
Evangelical		
High Attendance	51%[c]	70%
Low Attendance	55%[c]	63%
All	54%[a]	66%[a]
Mainline Protestant		
High Attendance	59%	74%
Low Attendance	61%	71%
All	60%[a]	74%[a]
Black Protestant		
High Attendance	48%	46%
Low Attendance	48%	44%
All	49%[a]	50%[a]
Catholic		
High Attendance	54%	77%[b]
Low Attendance	57%	51%
All	56%[a]	60%[a]
Jewish		
All	65%[a]	85%[a]
Secular		
All	59%[a]	47%[a]

Note: For both surveys, religious causes were determined in the same way as they were for Table 2-1. High and low church attendance and the various religious traditions were determined in the same way as they were in Table 2-3.
[a] Significant at the 0.001 level, based on all of the adherents of the six religious traditions without regard to church attendance.
[b] Significant at the 0.001 level based on attendance levels of each religious tradition taken separately.
[c] Significant at the 0.05 level based on attendance levels of each religious tradition taken separately.

Table 2-5: Percent of Respondents Volunteering for Religious Causes, by Religious Tradition and Level of Attendance at Religious Services

	Pew IV	GSS 1998
Evangelical		
High Attendance	54%[b]	81%[b]
Low Attendance	25%[b]	12%[b]
All	42%[a]	49%[a]
Mainline Protestant		
High Attendance	67%[b]	84%[b]
Low Attendance	23%[b]	11%[b]
All	43%[a]	38%[a]
Black Protestant		
High Attendance	65%[b]	82%[b]
Low Attendance	21%[b]	33%[b]
All	50%[a]	57%[a]
Catholic		
High Attendance	42%[b]	53%[b]
Low Attendance	20%[b]	9%[b]
All	31%[a]	28%[a]
Jewish		
All	28%[a]	45%[a]
Secular		
All	17%[a]	9%[a]

Note: For both surveys, religious causes were determined in the same way as they were in Table 2-1. High and low church attendance and the various religious traditions were determined in the same way as they were in Table 2-3.

[a] Significant at the 0.001 level, based on all of the adherents of the six religious traditions without regard to church attendance.

[b] Significant at the 0.001 level, based on the attendance levels of each religious tradition taken separately.

Table 2-6: Percent of Respondents Volunteering for Nonreligious Causes, by Religious Tradition and Level of Attendance at Religious Services

	Pew IV	GSS 1998	God and Society
Evangelical			
High Attendance	54%	63%[b]	52%[b]
Low Attendance	56%	32%[b]	25%[b]
All	56%[a]	51%[a]	43%
Mainline Protestant			
High Attendance	68%	73%[b]	60%[b]
Low Attendance	65%	43%[b]	34%[b]
All	66%[a]	56%[a]	48%
Black Protestant			
High Attendance	56%	68%	49%[c]
Low Attendance	59%	59%	23%[c]
All	57%[a]	63%[a]	36%
Catholic			
High Attendance	56%	54%[d]	51%[b]
Low Attendance	61%	38%[d]	29%[b]
All	60%[a]	44%[a]	43%
Jewish			
All	57%[a]	55%[a]	46%
Secular			
All	60%[a]	44%[a]	40%

Note: High and low church attendance and the various religious traditions were determined in the same way as they were in Table 2-3.

[a] Significant at the 0.001 level, based on all of the adherents of the six religious traditions without regard to church attendance.

[b] Significant at the 0.001 level, based on attendance levels of each religious tradition taken separately.

[c] Significant at the 0.01 level, based on attendance levels of each religious tradition taken separately.

[d] Significant at the 0.05 level, based on attendance levels of each religious tradition taken separately.

In the General Social Survey, Jews also ranked high in volunteering. As with giving, the secularists had the lowest levels of volunteering. Most striking, however, is the size of the differences between the high church attendees and the low attendees. People who attended church weekly or more volunteered at a much higher rate than did those who rarely attended. This was the case within all four religious traditions to an even greater extent than is seen in giving to religious causes. This pattern adds support to the social network theory.

In the case of volunteering for nonreligious community causes, I was able to use, in addition to the Pew survey and the General Social Survey, data from the 1996 God and Society in North America survey, since it also clearly asked about volunteering for nonreligious causes. Table 2-6 shows there were no clear patterns by religious tradition. Although there were significant differences between the Pew survey and the General Social Survey, no one tradition was consistently higher or lower in such volunteering. Differences persisted, however, between those who attended church regularly and those who did not in the General Social Survey and the God and Society survey. In both surveys, respondents who attended regularly were more likely to volunteer for secular causes than those who did not attend regularly. This again demonstrates the motivating power of religion, even when it comes to volunteering for secular programs. It also adds support to the social network theory.

Relating Giving and Volunteering to Other Measures of Civic Responsibility

Giving to or volunteering for organizations that actively serve community needs is one way for people to fulfill the norms of civic responsibility. But giving and volunteering—and their links to religiosity—may indicate a more general sense of civic responsibility. Thus giving and volunteering may have significance beyond their immediate effect. In this section, I explore the relationship between philanthropic giving and volunteering and several other measures of civic responsibility.

One key aspect of civic responsibility that was outlined at the beginning of this article is responsible citizenship, which includes such traits as voting in elections and being informed on public issues. I used four measures to identify people who fulfill the ideal of responsible citizenship:

2 | Religion and Philanthropic Giving and Volunteering

Table 2-7: Percentages of Respondents Voting and Not Voting, by Giving and Volunteering to Religious and Nonreligious Causes

	General Social Survey, 1998[a]			Pew IV[b]		
	Percent Voting	Percent Not Voting	N	Percent Voting	Percent Not Voting	N
If gave, religious causes:						
Yes	71%[c]	16%[c]	452	49%[c]	24%[c]	1248
No	60%[c]	28%[c]	783	36%[c]	37%[c]	2015
If gave, nonreligious causes:						
Yes	70%[c]	17%[c]	787	47%[c]	25%[c]	1832
No	55%[c]	34%[c]	448	33%[c]	41%[c]	1430
If volunteered, religious causes:						
Yes	73%[c]	17%[c]	386	45%[c]	27%[c]	1170
No	59%[c]	27%[c]	658	38%[c]	34%[c]	2092
If volunteered, nonreligious causes:						
Yes	73%[c]	17%[c]	531	45%[c]	28%[c]	1942
No	56%[c]	30%[c]	507	38%[c]	34%[c]	1338

[a] Percent voting were those who reported that they had voted in both the 1992 and 1996 presidential elections; percent not voting were those who reported that they had voted in neither of these elections. Those who had voted in one election but not the other were excluded from this analysis.

[b] Percent voting were those who reported they had voted in both the 1996 presidential election and the 1998 congressional election; percent not voting were those who reported they had voted in neither of these elections. Those who had voted in one election but not the other were excluded from this analysis.

[c] Significant at the 0.001 level.

voting, political activities other than voting, regular newspaper reading, and knowing one's U.S. Senators. I found that respondents who had given or volunteered ranked higher in these four measures of active citizenship than did those who had not given or volunteered. In regard to voting, Table 2-7 shows that the respondents who gave or volunteered were also more likely to have voted. In both surveys used in the analysis, respondents who gave or volunteered—whether for a religious or a secular cause—were more likely to vote than were those who had not given or volunteered. There were no exceptions, and the differences were clear and significant, not small or marginal.

In studying political activities other than voting, I was able to use, in addition to the Pew survey and the God and Society survey, data from the 2000 Social Capital Community Benchmark Survey of the Saguaro Seminar. Table 2-8 (see below) shows that on the basis of a number of possible political activities other than voting—attending political meetings, contacting public officials, and working or contributing to a party or candidate—respondents who had given or volunteered were much more likely to be politically involved than were those who had not given or volunteered. This pattern was significant and consistent across the three studies for respondents who had given or volunteered for either a religious or nonreligious cause.

In regard to newspaper reading, the General Social Survey found that of respondents who had given to a religious cause, 51 percent reported reading a newspaper on a daily basis, and only 13 percent reported reading a newspaper less than once a week, while only 39 percent of those who had not given reported reading a newspaper daily, and 24 percent reported reading one less than once a week. Similarly, of respondents who had given to nonreligious causes, 48 percent reported reading a newspaper daily, and 15 percent reported reading a newspaper less than weekly. In contrast, of the nongivers, 35 percent reported reading a newspaper daily, and 28 percent reported less than weekly reading. I found similar patterns in regard to volunteering.

In regard to political knowledge, the Saguaro survey asked the respondents to name their two U.S. Senators. I found that respondents who had given to or volunteered for nonreligious community causes were more likely to know the names of their Senators than were those who had not given. Of respondents who had given to nonreligious causes,

47 percent could name one or both of their Senators, and 53 could name neither; of those who had not given to nonreligious causes, only 26 percent could name one or both of their Senators, and 74 could name neither. Of respondents who had volunteered for a nonreligious cause, 48 percent knew the names of one or both of their Senators, and 52 percent knew neither, while 38 percent of those who had not volunteered knew one or both Senators' names, and 62 percent knew neither. However, when it came to giving for religious causes, the differences were small or inconsistent.

This leaves the question of whether or not the respondents who were givers or volunteers *and* who were marked by other characteristics of responsible citizenship also tended to be more religious than did those who were not givers or volunteers or who were not marked by other characteristics of responsible citizenship. Table 2-9 (see below), based on data from the Pew survey, addresses this question. It considers both voting and the other marks of political involvement on which Table 2-8 is based. Voting, other forms of political involvement, philanthropic giving and volunteering, and religiosity as measured by church attendance all tend to go together. If we look at giving first, the highest levels of voting and other forms of political involvement were among those respondents who had given *and* attended church on a weekly basis. The lowest levels of voting and other forms of political involvement were found among those respondents who had not given and who attended church less than monthly. The pattern was the same in the case of volunteering, except that those respondents who had failed to volunteer for any religious cause were not the lowest in voting and other forms of political involvement (and they tied with those who were low in church attendance and had volunteered).

In short, individuals who fulfill the marks of civic responsibility by giving and volunteering for causes that meet community needs also tend to meet the civic responsibility norms for responsible citizenship by voting, taking part in the political process, reading newspapers, and knowing the names of their Senators. Also, there is evidence indicating that among people who give and volunteer, those who are regular church attendees are the most likely to meet the norms of responsible citizenship.

(text continues on page 67 below)

Table 2-8: Percentages of Respondents with High and Low Political Involvement, by Giving to and Volunteering for Religious and Nonreligious Causes

	Pew IV			Saguaro			God and Society		
	Percent High	Percent Low	N	Percent High	Percent Low	N	Percent High	Percent Low	N
If gave, religious causes:									
Yes	16%[a]	45%[a]	1440	32%[a]	37%[a]	1800	NA	NA	NA
No	10%[a]	56%[a]	2273	18%[a]	56%[a]	738	NA	NA	NA
If gave, nonreligious causes:									
Yes	16%[a]	44%[a]	2083	36%[a]	32%[a]	1690	NA	NA	NA
No	8%[a]	61%[a]	1628	14%[a]	62%[a]	934	NA	NA	NA
If volunteered, religious causes:									
Yes	15%[a]	47%[a]	1328	NA	NA	NA	59%[a]	12%[a]	817
No	11%[a]	54%[a]	2385	NA	NA	NA	33%[a]	37%[a]	2193
If volunteered, nonreligious causes:									
Yes	15%[a]	45%[a]	2218	44%[a]	21%[a]	1467	62%[a]	12%[a]	1303
No	8%[a]	61%[a]	1514	13%[a]	54%[a]	180	23%[a]	45%[a]	1707

Note: The levels of political activity were based on a series of questions (five in the case of Pew IV and four in the other two studies) the three studies asked concerning whether or not the respondents had engaged in such political activities as attending a political or civic meeting, contacting a political official, working for a candidate or party, or participating in a demonstration or protest. Those who had taken part in two or more of these were put in the "high" category, and those who had taken part in none of these were put in the "low" category. It should be noted that the Saguaro survey in terms of giving to religious causes and the God and Society survey in terms of volunteering for religious causes did not clearly distinguish between community-serving religious causes and core religious activities and rituals.

[a] Significant at the 0.001 level.

Table 2-9: Political Involvement, by Church Attendance and Whether or Not Respondents Had Given or Volunteered to Religious and Nonreligious Causes (percent voting or ranking high in political involvement, Pew IV data)

	Percent with a High Level of Voting[a]		Percent with a High Level of Political Involvement[b]	
	High Church Attendance	Low Church Attendance	High Church Attendance	Low Church Attendance
If gave, religious causes:				
Yes	54%	35%	16%	13%
	(N = 522)	(N = 265)	(N = 918)	(N = 300)
No	39%	33%	10%	9%
	(N = 522)	(N = 1125)	(N = 610)	(N = 1254)
If gave, nonreligious causes:				
Yes	55%	41%	18%	13%
	(N = 680)	(N = 581)	(N = 801)	(N = 905)
No	40%	24%	9%	6%
	(N = 625)	(N = 807)	(N = 725)	(N = 650)
				(continued)

Table 2-9: Political Involvement, by Church Attendance and Whether or Not Respondents Had Given or Volunteered to Religious and Nonreligious Causes (percent voting or ranking high in political involvement, Pew IV data) (continued)

	Percent with a High Level of Voting[a]		Percent with a High Level of Political Involvement[b]	
	High Church Attendance	Low Church Attendance	High Church Attendance	Low Church Attendance
If volunteered, religious causes:				
Yes	51%	33%	16%	10%
	(N = 715)	(N = 271)	(N = 830)	(N = 300)
No	44%	34%	11%	10%
	(N = 591)	(N = 1118)	(N = 698)	(N = 1254)
If volunteered, nonreligious causes:				
Yes	53%	38%	19%	12%
	(N = 730)	(N = 846)	(N = 872)	(N = 945)
No	42%	28%	8%	7%
	(N = 580)	(N = 553)	(N = 662)	(N = 619)

[a] The percentages are the percent of respondents who reported having voted in both the 1992 and 1996 presidential elections out of the total number of high or low church attendees who had reported either giving or volunteering or not doing so.

[b] The percentages are the percent of the respondents who reported having taken part in three or more political activities besides voting out of the total number of high or low church attendees who had reported either giving or volunteering or not doing so.

Summary and Observations

This study yields seven key results concerning civic responsibility and religion:

1. There is a relationship between religiosity and giving to and volunteering for religious causes, even when religious congregations in their core religious services and rituals are eliminated.

2. There is a relationship between giving to and volunteering for religiously based, community-serving causes and marks of religiosity other than church attendance (the measure on which earlier studies focused). People who rank high in religious salience, in traditional religious beliefs, and in private religious practices were found to give and volunteer more for religiously based community-service causes than did their counterparts who ranked low on those variables.

3. There is no clear relationship between giving to and volunteering for secular community causes and the marks of religiosity noted in point 2.

4. Church attendance and the associated integration into a social network and internalized religious beliefs are both related to giving and volunteering, but the former is more strongly related than is the latter.

5. Adherents of certain religious traditions tend to give or volunteer at higher levels than do those of other traditions. However, the patterns vary for giving or volunteering and in relation to religiously or secularly based programs. Adherents of all of the five religious traditions studied gave to and volunteered for religiously based causes more than did the secular respondents. The surveys varied on whether or not the adherents of the five religious traditions gave to or volunteered for nonreligious causes more than the secular respondents did. The surveys agree that religious respondents gave to and volunteered for nonreligious causes at higher levels than those at which nonreligious respondents gave to or volunteered for religious causes.

6. Among the religious traditions, Mainline Protestants had a slight tendency to rank higher in giving and volunteering than did the adherents of the four other religious traditions. However, evangelical Protestants, Black Protestants, and Jews sometimes ranked almost as high as or higher than Mainline Protestants, depending on whether giving or volunteering was being considered and on whether the giving or volunteering was for a religiously based or a secularly based cause.

7. Philanthropic giving and volunteering, religiosity, and the marks of civic responsibility I have termed *responsible citizenship* are all related. Givers and volunteers rank higher in voting, other political activities, newspaper reading, and political knowledge. Among people who give and volunteer, a higher level of religiosity is related to increased voting and other political involvements.

These findings reveal that religiously committed people who give and volunteer are also active citizens. As such, they may constitute the chief exemplars of civic responsibility. Those who, by several measures, are religiously active and committed are the citizens who are likeliest to give to and volunteer for religiously based community causes. Moreover, they give and volunteer to about the same extent as the irreligious respondents do to secularly based community causes. In addition, the highly religious respondents were much more likely to give to or volunteer for secularly based causes than the secular respondents were to support religiously based community causes. Giving and volunteering are related to other aspects of civic responsibility, such as being politically involved and aware. This is especially true of people who give and volunteer and are also religiously involved.

There is an irony here. Emerging from the Enlightenment era—with its reaction against the religious wars of Europe—was the idea that religion was dangerous for democracy. Even today, the Supreme Court regularly warns against "religious divisiveness." In 2002, Justice Stephen Breyer wrote of the need "for protecting the Nation's social fabric from religious conflict" (2002: 717). Chief Justice Warren Burger once declared that "political division along religious lines was one of the principal evils against which the First Amendment was intended to protect" (1971: 622). Ted Jelen and Clyde Wilcox report that some 75 percent of people included in an elite survey believe that evangelicals and the religious right are a threat to democracy (1995: 46).

Since deeply religious people believe that they know the truth, it is often argued, their minds will be closed to discussion and accommodation. It is thus presumed that rational secularists are the natural and best carriers of the democratic tradition. Being unfettered by a faith-based religious tradition and otherworldly values and aspirations, they presumably are inclined toward making this world a better place—and toward doing so in a moderate, rational, open manner. Thus they ought to be the backbone of a free, democratic society.

This study seriously challenges such conventional wisdom. In fact, it is the religious among us, not the irreligious, who are more likely to give to and volunteer for community causes. And people who give and volunteer tend to vote and in other ways to be politically informed and active. Even evangelical Protestants—whose growing influence some social critics characterize as a threat to normal democratic processes—are more likely to give and volunteer than are the irreligious. As a rule, religionists live out more facets of civic responsibility than do the irreligious.

References

Becker, Penny, and Pawan Dhingra. 2001. "Religious Involvement and Volunteering: Implications for Civil Society." *Sociology of Religion* 62: 315–35.

Breyer, Stephen. 2002. Dissenting opinion in *Zelman v. Simmons-Harris*, 536 U.S. 639.

Brooks, Arthur C. 2003. "Religious Faith and Charitable Giving." *Policy Review* 121: 39–50.

Brooks, Arthur C. 2006. *Who Really Cares? The Surprising Truth about Compassionate Conservatism*. New York: Basic Books.

Burger, Warren. 1971. Majority opinion in *Lemon v. Kurtzman*, 403 U.S. 602.

Campbell, David E., and Steven J. Yonish. 2003. "Religion and Volunteering in America." In *Religion as Social Capital: Producing the Common Good*, edited by Corwin Smidt, 87–106. Waco, TX: Baylor University Press.

Chaves, Mark. 2004. *Congregations in America*. Cambridge, MA: Harvard University Press.

Eberly, Don E. 1995. *The Content of America's Character: Recovering Civic Virtue*. Lanham, MD: Madison Books.

Guth, James L., Lyman A. Kellstedt, John C. Green, and Corwin E. Smidt. 2002. "A Distant Thunder? Religious Mobilization in the 2000 Election." In *Interest Group Politics*, edited by Allan J. Ciglar and Burdett A. Loomis, 161–84. Washington, DC: CQ Press.

Hodgkinson, Virginia A., Murray S. Weitzman, Eric A. Crutchfield, Aaron J. Heffron, and Arthur D. Kirsch. 1996. *Giving and Volunteering in the United States*. Washington, DC: Independent Sector.

Hodgkinson, Virginia A., Murray S. Weitzman, and Arthur D. Kirsch. 1990. "From Commitment to Action: How Religious Involvement Affects Giving and Volunteering." In *Faith and Philanthropy in America: Exploring the Role of Religion in America's Voluntary Sector*, edited by Robert Wuthnow and Virginia A. Hodgkinson, 93–114. San Francisco: Jossey-Bass.

Jelen, Ted G., and Clyde Wilcox. 1995. *Public Attitudes toward Church and State*. Armonk, NY: M.E. Sharpe.

Lam, Pui-Yan. 2002. "As the Flocks Gather: How Religion Affects Voluntary Association Participation." *Journal for the Scientific Study of Religion* 41: 405–22.

Nemeth, Roger J., and Donald A. Luidens. 2003. "The Religious Basis of Charitable Giving in America: A Social Capital Perspective." In *Religion as Social Capital: Producing the Common Good*, edited by Corwin Smidt, 107–20. Waco, TX: Baylor University Press.

Park, Jerry Z., and Christian Smith. 2000. "'To Whom Much Has Been Given . . .': Religious Capital and Community Voluntarism among Churchgoing Protestants." *Journal for the Scientific Study of Religion* 39: 272–86.

Putnam, Robert D. 2000. *Bowling Alone: The Collapse and Revival of American Community*. New York: Touchstone.

Regnerus, Mark D., Christian Smith, and David Sikkink. 1998. "Who Gives to the Poor? The Influence of Religious Tradition and Political Location on the Personal Generosity of Americans towards the Poor." *Journal for the Scientific Study of Religion* 37: 481–93.

Schwadel, Philip. 2005. "Individual, Congregational, and Denominational Effects on Church Members' Civic Participation." *Journal for the Scientific Study of Religion* 44: 159–71.

Verba, Sidney, Kay Lehman Schlozman, and Henry E. Brady. 1995. *Voice and Equality: Civic Voluntarism in American Politics*. Cambridge, MA: Harvard University Press.

Wilson, James Q. 1985. "The Rediscovery of Character: Private Virtue and Public Policy." *The Public Interest* 81: 3–16.

Wilson, James Q. 1993. *The Moral Sense*. New York: Free Press.

Wilson, John, and Thomas Janoski. 1995. "The Contribution of Religion to Volunteer Work." *Sociology of Religion* 56: 137–52.

Wuthnow, Robert. 1990. "Religion and the Voluntary Spirit in the United States: Mapping the Terrain." In *Faith and Philanthropy in America: Exploring the Role of Religion in America's Voluntary Sector*, edited by Robert Wuthnow and Virginia A. Hodgkinson, 3–21. San Francisco: Jossey-Bass.

Wuthnow, Robert. 1999. "Mobilizing Civic Engagement: The Changing Impact of Religious Involvement." In *Civic Engagement in American Democracy*, edited by Theda Skocpol and Morris P. Fiorina, 331–63. Washington, DC: Brookings.

Wuthnow, Robert. 2004. *Saving America? Faith-Based Services and the Future of Civil Society*. Princeton, NJ: Princeton University Press.

3

Religious Motivations and Social Service Volunteers

The Interaction of Differing Religious Motivations, Satisfaction, and Repeat Volunteering

Richard M. Clerkin | James E. Swiss

Faith-based organizations are playing an increasingly important role in the delivery of social services in the United States, and many of these organizations rely heavily on volunteers (President's Advisory Council on Faith-Based and Neighborhood Partnerships, 2010). Previous research has established that religious commitment is a strong predictor of volunteerism (Campbell and Yonish 2003; Caputo 2009; Cnaan, Kasternakis, and Wineburg, 1999; Perry et al. 2008; Ruiter and De Graaf 2006). However, relatively little is known about how differing types of religious motivations interact with the volunteer experience to determine volunteer satisfaction and willingness to volunteer again.

As Eisenstein (2006) demonstrates, religious motivation is distinct from traditional religiousness. In this study, we seek to move beyond traditional measures of religiosity to understand better the role of religious motivations in volunteering. We examine the motivations of a sample of religiously committed volunteers, looking at how different religious motivations lead to differing evaluations of the volunteer experience and to different levels of willingness to volunteer again. Since almost all of the volunteers (96 percent) indicated a Christian religious affiliation, we were able to analyze differences within a religiously committed group.

We analyzed a group of youth volunteers and a group of adult volunteers for a Christian nonprofit organization who participated in a week-long project repairing housing in Appalachia. At the end of their week, the volunteers completed a survey that asked about their religious background, their motivations for volunteering, and their overall evaluation of the volunteer experience. Because religious organizations play such an important part in the nonprofit sector and because religious people represent a disproportionately large share of all volunteers, the role of religion in motivating volunteerism is an important issue to be investigated.

Evidence suggests that religious individuals volunteer more than nonreligious individuals do for two reasons: because of their religious beliefs and because their church participation provides a social network that encourages volunteering (Monsma 2007). Even in the context of this faith-related association, individuals can have both religious and secular motivations to volunteer. We will examine three broad questions:

1. What are the differences between individuals who volunteer primarily for secular reasons and those who volunteer primarily for religious reasons?

2. For individuals who volunteer primarily for religious reasons, what aspects of their faith or belief seem to be the most important motivators? The positive relationship between religious commitment and volunteerism has been widely noted. Nonetheless, there has been relatively little research on what specific aspects of religious faith are most important in motivating religiously committed people to volunteer.

3. Do volunteers who differ in their level or type of religious motivation also differ in their satisfaction with the volunteer experience and does the difference in motivation affect their willingness to volunteer again? We measured respondents' satisfaction with their religious growth during the week of volunteering and their satisfaction with the overall volunteer experience to explore whether different religious motivations (and therefore different expectations about the volunteer week) affected the respondents' expressed willingness to volunteer again.

Literature Review: Religion and Volunteering

In 2011, 27 percent of American adults (64.3 million people age sixteen years and older) engaged in formal volunteering, and more than one-third (35 percent) of this volunteering took place in religious organizations. Similar proportions hold true for teenagers (4.4 million sixteen- to nineteen-year-olds); 26 percent volunteered, and 31 percent of this volunteering took place in religious organizations (Corporation for National and Community Service 2012). These substantial figures understate the importance of religion in volunteerism, because studies show that religiosity increases all types of volunteerism, including volunteer work for nonreligious organizations (Monsma 2007; Wilson and Musick 1997).

Volunteer Motivations

Research consistently shows that when all else is held constant, more highly religious people—whether measured by religious salience, traditional beliefs, or attendance—volunteer more than less religious people do (Campbell and Yonish 2003; Monsma 2007). Research also indicates that the positive relationship between religiosity and volunteering has two causes: religious motivations and social motivations. Religious motivations may be connected to religious services and religious readings, which consistently reinforce the message that God wants all people to help others (Houston and Cartwright 2007). Social motivations are seen in the finding that individuals with larger social networks belong to more associations and volunteer at a greater rate than do individuals with smaller social networks (Becker and Dhingra 2001; McPherson, Popielarz, and Drobnic 1992; Smidt 2003). This pattern holds whether the social network springs from a church or from a bowling league (Putnam 2001; Putnam and Campbell 2012).

Comparing Youth and Adult Religious Volunteering

Only a few studies have looked at youth volunteering and religiosity. Gibson (2008) found that volunteer patterns for adults and teens were similar and that highly religious teens (measured either by church attendance or by professed beliefs) were more likely to volunteer. Caputo (2009) looked at thirteen- to seventeen-year-olds and also found religious participation to be a strong predictor of social volunteerism. These two studies suggest that the link between increased religiosity and increased volunteerism holds for both adolescents and adults.

Religious Denominations and Volunteering

Several researchers have examined whether volunteer behavior differs by religion. Caputo (2009) found no major differences in willingness to volunteer. Rigney, Matz, and Abney (2004) note that some observers have suggested that Catholics may have a different volunteer motivation, but they too found no major difference by denomination in willingness to volunteer. Although Loveland, Jones-Stater, and Park (2008) found differences in number of memberships in civic organizations by Christian religious tradition among individuals who attend services infrequently, Mainline Protestants belonging to more civic organizations than Black Protestants or Catholics do, the differences virtually disappeared among frequent attenders.

Data and Methods

The respondents for our survey were members of church youth groups and their adult chaperones who were drawn from across the eastern third of the United States. The youth and adult volunteers worked side by side during a week-long service project rehabilitating housing in Appalachia. During the summer of 2011, both youth and adult volunteers completed an exit survey at the end of their week of service.

The housing rehabilitation program is conducted in twenty-nine centers located in four Appalachian states for eight weeks each summer. The centers conducted two types of exit surveys, one that focused on issues of center management and one that focused on issues of motivations to volunteer. Half the centers administered the management survey one week while the other half administered the motivation survey; the following week, they switched. In total, we collected 5,192 motivation surveys. Because we wanted to examine the motivations of adults and youths separately, we discarded 603 surveys that lacked clear age information and surveys that had been filled out by individuals aged eighteen to twenty-two years, an age group that could not be clearly characterized as adult or youth. This left 4,589 respondents, comprising 2,697 (65 percent) youths age fourteen to eighteen years and 1,622 (35 percent) adults.

Findings

Secular Motivations versus Religious Motivations

Respondents were asked to agree or disagree, on a five-point Likert scale, with statements about their motives for volunteering. All volunteers expressed both religious and secular motivations for volunteering.

Previous studies have suggested that religious individuals are more likely to volunteer, both for strictly religious reasons and for church-based social reasons. There is little evidence about which motivation predominates. In the one major study of the question, Monsma (2007) compared religious motives to "social network" motivation, a broader measure than our measure of church-based friendships. He found that both religious and social network motivations are important predictors of volunteering but that the social network motivation is stronger.

We examined whether volunteers have primarily friendship-based social motivations, which would lead them to say they volunteered because their (church-based) friends volunteered, or primarily religious motivations, which would lead them to say they volunteered for reasons of God or faith. The responses indicate that social motivations play a part for some volunteers but that religious motivations are considerably stronger than friendship-based social motivations.

Average Motivations. Among youths, the statement "I volunteer because it makes me feel closer to God" had an average score of 4.3 on a five-point scale, and the statement "I volunteer because my faith encourages me to do so" had an average score of 4.0. By contrast, the main social motivator average was much lower for youths: volunteering "because my friends volunteer" had an average score of 3.4. Another secular motivator, résumé building, averaged only 3.1 points.

For adults, the disparity between religious and friendship motivations was even higher. Adults scored the "faith encourages me" and "feel closer to God" reasons for volunteering similarly, at 4.4 points. The influence of friends who volunteer scored lower than was the case for youths, at 2.7 points; neutral and negative responses accordingly outweighed positive ones on the Likert scale. As might be expected in an older group, résumé building averaged a very low 1.9 points.

Motivational Differences by Group. We created three categories of primary motivations by summing each respondent's score on two secular motivations ("I volunteer because it looks good on my résumé" and "I volunteer because my friends volunteer") and subtracting the result from the sum of two religious motivations ("I volunteer because it makes me feel closer to God" and "I volunteer because my faith encourages me to do so"). If the sum was negative, we categorized the respondent's motivation as primarily secular (about 12 percent of the sample). If the sum was zero, we categorized the respondent as having equal secular and religious motivation (about 14 percent of the sample). Finally, if the sum was positive, we categorized the respondent's motivation as primarily religious (about 73 percent of the sample). While the sample as a whole was more religiously than secularly motivated, we did find differences in motivation by age, gender, previous volunteer experience with this nonprofit organization, and religious faith tradition. We explore these differences below.

Adults (93 percent) were much more likely to be religiously motivated than were youths (63 percent), as Table 3-1 shows. The balance of youth volunteers was fairly evenly split between being secularly motivated (18 percent) and having equal secular and religious motivations (18 percent). Although the 36 percent of youths who were equally or secularly motivated represent a minority, it seems a notably large minority for church-group youths who have volunteered for an explicitly religious nonprofit organization.

As Table 3-2 indicates, females (76 percent) were slightly more likely to be primarily religiously motivated than were males (71 percent). This finding is in accord with earlier studies, which indicated that women are more likely to be religious and to volunteer.

Secular and religious motivations differed somewhat by the respondent's faith tradition. As might be expected, non-Christians (69 percent) were more likely than any other group to report primarily secular motivations. Among the religiously affiliated, Catholic respondents (17 percent) were the most likely to report predominantly secular motivations, followed by the group of self-characterized other Christians (12 percent). Evangelical (7 percent) and Protestant (6 percent) volunteers, by contrast, were least likely to cite primarily secular motivations and were correspondingly most likely (82 percent of each group) to report primarily religious motivation.

Table 3-1: Volunteer Motivation by Age

Religious Motivations	Adults	Youths	Total
Greater secular motivation	1.20%	18.05%	12.12%
Equal secular and religious motivation	6.01%	18.45%	14.07%
Greater religious motivation	92.79%	63.49%	73.81%
Total	100%	100%	100%
Observations	1,497	2,753	4,250

Note: $\chi^2 = 446.60$; $p < 0.001$.

Table 3-2: Volunteer Motivation by Gender

Religious Motivations	Male	Female	Total
Greater secular motivation	13.39%	11.52%	12.45%
Equal secular and religious motivation	15.98%	12.95%	14.45%
Greater religious motivation	70.63%	75.52%	73.10%
Total	100%	100%	100%
Observations	1,927	1,961	3,888

Note: $\chi^2 = 12.07$; $p = 0.002$.

Table 3-3: Volunteer Motivation by Religion

Religious Motivations	Protestant	Evangelical	Catholic	Other Christian	Non-Christian	Total
Greater secular motivation	6.38%	7.09%	16.86%	11.55%	68.75%	11.81%
Equal secular and religious motivation	11.81%	11.35%	16.20%	16.06%	18.06%	14.00%
Greater religious motivation	81.80%	81.56%	66.94%	72.39%	13.19%	74.19%
Total	100%	100%	100%	100%	100%	100%
Observations	1,896	141	611	13	144	4,056

Note: $\chi^2 = 566.31$; $p < 0.001$.

Looking Deeper into Religious Motivation: Which Aspects of Belief Are the Prime Motivators?

As we noted earlier, studies have shown that religious beliefs are an important motivator of volunteerism, but the studies did not examine what specific aspects of those religious beliefs produce the increased volunteerism. We examined the underlying components of this religious motivation through two items on the survey: "I volunteer because it makes me feel closer to God" and "I volunteer because my faith encourages me to do so." The first item attempts to capture an internal, personal religious motivation to volunteer. The second item attempts to capture an external, institutional religious motivation to volunteer.

Because we want to understand what drives religiously motivated individuals, in this section we will examine only the subgroup of respondents who reported being religiously motivated rather than primarily secularly motivated. This removes approximately six hundred volunteers, discussed in the preceding section, who were more motivated by friendship or résumé building. These dropped cases represent roughly 12 percent of the respondents.

As might be expected, of the remaining group of volunteers, a large majority expressed both types of religious motivations to volunteer. More than 83 percent of the respondents somewhat agreed or agreed with the statement that they volunteer to feel closer to God, and 75 percent somewhat agreed or agreed with the statement that they volunteer because their faith encourages them to do so. Nonetheless, there was substantial variation in the intensity ("somewhat agree" versus "agree") with which respondents endorsed these motivations.

To determine group-based differences in religious motivation, we took the responses for the "feel closer to God" motivation and subtracted the responses for "because my faith encourages me." The higher the resulting number, the more the respondent is motivated by internal (personal) religious motives rather than externally guided (institutional) religious motives. Roughly 61 percent of the sample had equal personal and institutional religious motivations for volunteering, about 27 percent had greater personal religious motivations, and the remaining 12 percent had greater institutional religious motivations.

The responses indicated no difference by gender between volunteers who were institutionally motivated ("my faith") and those whose religious motivations were more internal and personal ("feel closer to

God"). However, we did find differences by age, by whether the respondent had volunteered with this nonprofit organization before, and by religious faith tradition.

As Table 3-4 shows, youths (33 percent) were considerably more likely than adults (20 percent) to be personally religiously motivated. Because the psychological development literature often characterizes adolescence as involving a search for autonomy and personal identity, it is not surprising that more youths than adults would express an individualistic motivation.

Table 3-4: Type of Religious Motivation by Age

Religious Motivations	Adults	Youths	Total
Institutional	12.81%	10.18%	11.35%
Equal institutional and personal	66.88%	56.64%	61.17%
Personal	20.30%	33.18%	27.48%
Total	100%	100%	100%
Observations	1,389	1,748	3,137

Note: $\chi^2 = 64.7234; p < 0.001$.

When we examined different religious motivations by whether the respondent had volunteered with this nonprofit organization previously, we found that a greater proportion of first-time volunteers (32 percent) than repeat volunteers (24 percent) were personally religiously motivated, as Table 3-5 shows. This pattern is similar for adults and youths.

Finally, we found differences in religious motivations for volunteering by faith tradition. As Table 3-6 shows, Catholics (34 percent) and other Christians (32 percent) were more likely to report personal religious motivation than were Protestants (24 percent) and, somewhat

Table 3-5: Type of Religious Motivation by First-Time Volunteer Status

Religious Motivations	Repeater	First Time	Total
Institutional	10.33%	11.74%	10.97%
Equal institutional and personal	65.99%	56.42%	61.63%
Personal	23.68%	31.84%	27.40%
Total	100%	100%	100%
Observations	1,626	1,363	2,989

Note: $\chi^2 = 30.3924; p < 0.001$.

Table 3-6: Type of Religious Motivation by Faith Tradition

Type of Religious Motivation	Protestant	Evangelical	Catholic	Other Christian	Non-Christian	Total
Institutional	11.54%	18.26%	10.02%	9.51%	26.32%	11.07%
Equal institutional and personal	64.73%	67.83%	56.48%	58.47%	31.58%	61.62%
Personal	23.73%	13.91%	33.50%	32.02%	42.11%	27.32%
Total	100%	100%	100%	100%	100%	100%
Observations	1,551	115	409	915	19	3,009

Note: $\chi^2 = 566.3077$; $p < 0.001$.

surprisingly, evangelicals (14 percent). By contrast, evangelicals (18 percent) were more likely to report being institutionally religiously motivated than were Protestants (12 percent), Catholics (10 percent), and other Christians (10 percent).[1]

In comparison to the other denominations, the religious motivations of the Catholic volunteers were driven less by the guidance of their faith and more by personal religious considerations. This seems to contradict the hypothesis of Tropman (1995), who postulated a Catholic ethic that emphasized community and community service, in contrast to the more individualistic ethic of many Protestant denominations, a hypothesis that is partially supported by a panel study (Wilson and Janoski 1995). However, our findings are in accord with the empirical findings of Caputo (2009) and Rigney, Matz, and Abney (2004).

Because evangelical denominations often emphasize the individual's personal connection to God, it is somewhat surprising that evangelicals were the least likely to report that they were motivated by the desire to "feel closer to God."

The Effect of Different Motivations on Satisfaction with Religious Outcomes

Do volunteers with different motivations also differ in their satisfaction with the volunteer experience? We considered several measures of satisfaction. In this section, we explore the volunteers' satisfaction with

---

[1] Because only nineteen non-Christians were members of this subgroup, their percentage breakdowns are not meaningful.

specific religious outcomes. In the next section, we will look at how their overall satisfaction with the volunteer experience and their willingness to volunteer again were affected both by their motivations for volunteering and by the success of the organization in meeting their most important religious expectations.

We asked volunteers about the degree to which their specific religious motivations for volunteering had been fulfilled. In particular, we asked them to specify the extent to which they agreed with two religious evaluation statements: "I am satisfied with the opportunity [this program] has given me to deepen my faith" and "Because of this experience I feel closer to God."

The majority of respondents agreed or somewhat agreed with both statements, but there were notable differences between groups. Because the answers skewed positively, we treated agreement with the two religious statements as dichotomous variables (i.e., "agree" versus all other answers). We constructed a variable to measure the extent of religious motivation ("feel closer to God" motivation plus faith-based motivation minus two times friendship motivation). We then used logistic regression to look at how well strong religious motivations predicted satisfaction with the two religious evaluation measures (whether the experience deepened the respondent's faith and, separately, whether it helped the respondent to feel closer to God). We ran these models separately for youths and adults.

As Table 3-7 indicates, there was a clear positive relationship between being more religiously than secularly motivated and being satisfied with both religious outcomes. However, two groups particularly deviated from the volunteer norm: religiously motivated evangelical adults and first-time volunteers (youths and adults) were considerably less satisfied with their religious outcomes than were other volunteers. Although the reason for the relative dissatisfaction of evangelical adults is not clear, the relative dissatisfaction of the most religious first-time volunteers seems intuitively plausible. First-time volunteers overall are unlikely to be as positive as repeat volunteers because some first-timers discover that the program is not what they expected or hoped. By contrast, repeat volunteers are a self-selected group who liked the program enough in the past that they chose to return this year.

The Effect of Different Religious Motivations on Overall Satisfaction

In addition to examining respondents' satisfaction with the religious outcomes of the program, we captured their overall level of satisfaction. Overall satisfaction was measured through responses to the survey item "I

Table 3-7: Logistic Regression of Satisfaction with Religious Outcomes for Youths and Adults

Variables	Model 1: Youth Deepen Faith	Model 2: Youth Closer to God	Model 3: Adult Deepen Faith	Model 4: Adult Closer to God
Religious minus friends motivation	1.18*** (10.49)	1.23*** (12.23)	1.05** (2.27)	1.09*** (4.07)
Evangelical Protestant	1.24 (0.76)	1.26 (0.79)	0.55** (−2.14)	0.65 (−1.48)
Catholic	1.29 (1.89)	1.37** (2.30)	1.48 (1.85)	1.10 (0.48)
Other Christian	1.07 (0.65)	1.24** (2.03)	1.00 (−0.03)	1.30 (1.51)
Non-Christian	0.62 (−1.78)	0.12*** (−4.06)	0.49 (−1.28)	0.17** (−2.23)
Female	1.05 (0.56)	1.03 (0.33)	1.60*** (3.77)	1.47** (3.01)
Involved with youth group	1.25*** (5.94)	1.44*** (9.19)	1.31*** (4.51)	1.40*** (5.47)
First-time volunteer	0.84** (−1.96)	0.90 (−1.08)	0.65*** (−3.33)	0.76** (−2.08)
Constant	0.50*** (−3.84)	0.22*** (−7.79)	0.41** (−3.18)	0.29*** (−4.34)
Observations	2,341	2,342	1,226	1,228

Note: z-statistics are in parentheses.
*** $p < 0.001$; ** $p < 0.01$; * $p < 0.05$.

am satisfied with my overall experience with [this program]." Once again, we divided the variable between the highest rating ("agree") and all other responses. In general, respondents were very satisfied with their experience, but the more religiously motivated individuals were much more satisfied than were the secularly motivated ones. Table 3-8 lists specific elements of satisfaction and how well they predict overall satisfaction. Satisfaction with strengthening the faith was a particularly strong predictor of overall satisfaction for both youths and adults. However, a large halo effect suggests that satisfaction with many aspects of the experience similarly predicted overall satisfaction. Accordingly, we looked next at a measure of a higher, more demanding level of satisfaction: willingness to volunteer again.

Table 3-8: Logistic Regression of Overall Satisfaction for Youths and Adults

Variables	Model 5: Youths	Model 6: Adults
Outcome: closer to God	1.23**	1.37**
	(2.91)	(2.62)
Outcome: deepen faith	1.33***	1.85***
	(3.75)	(4.12)
Outcome: service to people in need	2.25***	3.03***
	(6.38)	(5.31)
Outcome: food	1.06	1.14
	(1.24)	(1.86)
Outcome: evening gathering	1.77***	2.06***
	(9.16)	(6.82)
Outcome: supply delivery	1.39***	2.79***
	(6.01)	(10.74)
Evangelical Protestant	0.59	0.80
	(−1.63)	(−0.60)
Catholic	1.37	2.49**
	(1.83)	(3.13)
Other Christian	1.06	1.28
	(0.44)	(1.13)
Non-Christian	3.42***	3.93
	(3.91)	(1.61)
Female	1.00	0.91
	(−0.03)	(−0.55)
Church involvement	1.05	0.99
	(0.92)	(−0.14)
First-time volunteer	0.92	1.03
	(−0.71)	(0.15)
Constant	0.00***	0.00***
	(−12.87)	(−14.15)
Observations	2,320	1,237

Note: z-statistics are in parentheses.
*** $p < 0.001$; ** $p < 0.01$; * $p < 0.05$.

Fulfilled Religious Motivations and Willingness to Volunteer Again

Measuring Fulfilled Motivators. Drawing on the functional model for volunteering that was first developed by Clary and Snyder (1991), we hypothesized that a strong predictor of willingness to volunteer again is how well the strongest religious motivations are met. This model suggests that if an individual's primary motives for volunteering are fulfilled by the volunteer experience, the likelihood that the individual will continue to volunteer will increase (McBride and Lee 2012; Stukas et al. 2009).

To construct a variable that measures both the intensity of an individual's specific motivator and the individual's level of satisfaction with how well that motivator was fulfilled, we multiplied the level of a motivation by how well the volunteer indicated that it was met.[2] For example, if a volunteer gave the highest rating (5 on a five-point scale) to "feel closer to God" as the reason for volunteering and then indicated the highest level of satisfaction (5) on the item about how well the experience brought the individual closer to God, the value for the fulfilled motivator variable is 25 (5 × 5). We constructed a similar "fulfilled motivator" faith variable by multiplying the responses on the item measuring faith as a motivator and the item measuring how well the week strengthened the respondent's faith.

Measuring Willingness to Volunteer Again. We measured two forms of willingness to volunteer again: willingness to volunteer for this organization next year and willingness to volunteer for this or other social service nonprofit organizations next year. In looking at youths' willingness to volunteer for this specific organization next year, we began by counting all youths who positively responded to the statement "I want to volunteer for [this organization] next year." Because high school seniors "age out" and are ineligible to participate as youth volunteers in this program next year, we also included all positive responses to a separate question that asked whether the youth was interested in serving as a summer staff member in this program next year. For adults, we determined willingness to volunteer for this organization again by counting all affirmative responses to the same primary statement ("I want to volunteer with [this organization] next year") plus all positive responses to a statement about volunteering for this organization's separate adult program.

---

2 Similar scales were first developed by Stukas and colleagues (2009).

For both youths and adults, we operationalized their willingness to volunteer for other social services by positive responses to the statement "I will seek opportunities to volunteer with other social service projects in the next year."

Results. As Table 3-9 shows, the "fulfilled motivator" variables do predict willingness to volunteer again, both overall and—a bit more strongly—for this specific organization. Adults and youths are generally similar in their willingness to volunteer again; other group differences for the most part reflect expected patterns.

For example, adult evangelicals were more negative in their responses than other volunteers, as were first-timers. In addition, most studies have shown female volunteers to be more religious, and our results also show that fulfilled religious motivators for women were particularly likely to produce a greater willingness to volunteer for all types of social projects.

Figure 3-1 shows how the probability of volunteering again changes as religious fulfillment increases. Greater motivational fulfillment consistently leads to higher levels of volunteering again, but there are some differences between first-time volunteers and returners.

Figure 3-1: Predicted Probability of Adult Returners and First-Timers Volunteering with the Same Nonprofit Organization Next Year

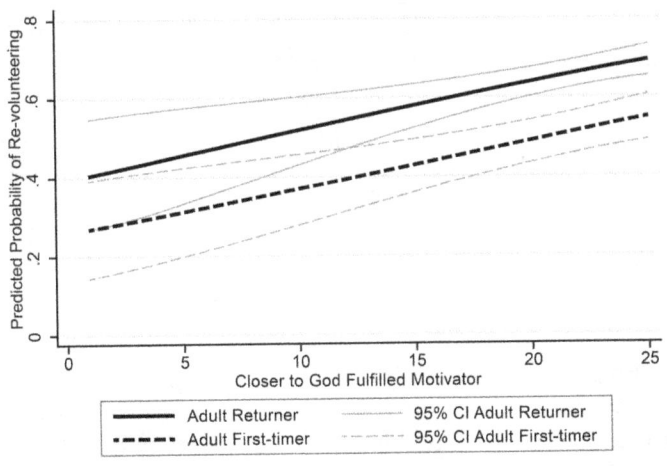

Table 3-9: Logistic Regression of Likelihood to Volunteer within the Next Year

Variables	Model 7: Youth Same Nonprofit	Model 8: Youth All Nonprofits	Model 9: Adults Same Nonprofit	Model 10: Adults All Nonprofits
Closer to God motivation × evaluation	1.04*** (3.29)	1.04*** (3.55)	1.05*** (3.38)	1.05** (3.05)
Faith motivation × evaluation	1.04*** (3.51)	1.04** (2.77)	1.07*** (4.43)	1.06*** (3.41)
Evangelical Protestant	0.66 (−1.41)	0.53 (−1.81)	0.62 (−1.61)	0.50** (−2.25)
Catholic	1.11 (0.67)	0.90 (−0.62)	1.37 (1.46)	1.22 (0.85)
Other Christian	1.29** (2.05)	0.95 (−0.38)	1.20 (1.09)	1.03 (0.18)
Non-Christian	1.78** (2.25)	1.64 (1.78)	1.29 (0.41)	3.32** (2.06)
Female	1.40** (3.23)	1.97*** (5.48)	0.93 (−0.58)	1.47** (2.66)
Involved with youth group	1.22*** (4.62)	1.38*** (6.43)	1.16** (2.32)	1.42*** (5.12)
First-time volunteer	0.48*** (−6.81)	0.54*** (−4.81)	0.54*** (−4.70)	0.60*** (−3.54)
Constant	0.52** (−2.93)	0.51** (−2.72)	0.09*** (−6.86)	0.09*** (−6.61)
Observations	2,364	2,367	1,235	1,239

Note: z-statistics are in parentheses.
*** $p < 0.001$; ** $p < 0.01$; * $p < 0.05$.

It is not possible to say whether the probability of volunteering again differs for the two groups at lower levels of fulfilled motivation because the confidence intervals overlap. However, by roughly fulfillment level 12, we can say that fulfilled religious motivators have a larger impact on returners than on first-timers. This suggests that nonprofit agencies cannot take their returners for granted and must ensure that their volunteers' faith motivators are fulfilled each time they return. Although Figure 3-1 is based on the responses of adults and on "deepen my faith" as the motive, very similar patterns are found for "feel closer to God" motivators and—a bit more strongly—for youths.

Implications for Faith-Based Social Service Agencies

This study's results suggest a number of practical implications for volunteer recruitment and retention in faith-based nonprofit organizations. Because youths are much more likely than adults to cite social motivations along with religious ones, volunteer recruiters should focus on multiple incentives when recruiting youths. Although first-time volunteers were more religiously motivated (and less socially motivated) than returners, they were also more dissatisfied and less likely—even when their religious motivators were fulfilled—to say they would volunteer again. These characteristics suggest that recruiters should recognize that first-time volunteers need a great deal of guidance and attention throughout their initial volunteer experience. The findings also suggest that recruiters for religious nonprofit organizations will find that repeat volunteers and strongly religious women are their most reliable recruits because these individuals are most likely to be satisfied with their experience and to volunteer again.

Summary and Conclusion

Religious individuals represent a disproportionately large share of volunteers for all nonprofit organizations. Therefore, there are both theoretical and practical advantages in better understanding religion-based motivations for volunteering and how these motivations affect satisfaction with the volunteer experience.

The survey results from more than four thousand volunteers for a Christian nonprofit organization suggest that some volunteers are primarily motivated by secular incentives (friendships or résumé building) but that most volunteers are primarily motivated by religious incentives. However, there are clear subgroup differences, religious motivations being much stronger for adults than for youth volunteers and slightly stronger for female and Protestant volunteers.

In addition to the differences between secular and religious motivations for volunteering, we found differences within the religiously motivated group. For individuals who are primarily motivated by religious incentives, volunteering is driven both by personal religious reasons (to feel closer to God) and by institutional religious reasons (to follow the guidance of one's faith). However, personal religious motivations are considerably more important (and institutional ones correspondingly less important) to youth volunteers, first-time volunteers, and Catholic volunteers. Somewhat surprisingly, evangelical volunteers are less likely than volunteers from other religious traditions to be motivated by the desire to "feel closer to God."

Religious motivation affects volunteers' overall satisfaction and their willingness to volunteer again. In particular, religiously motivated individuals are more satisfied than are secularly motivated individuals, and those with strong religious motivations who believed that the volunteer week fulfilled their specific religious needs are the most willing to volunteer again.

These findings help to illuminate the components of religious motivation for volunteering, showing that young, Catholic, and first-time volunteers responded more to personal than to faith-based religious motivations. These results highlight the need to continue to move beyond measures of religiosity in studying volunteering to look at different types of religious motivations to volunteer. The findings also support the functional model of volunteering because whether the volunteer's most intense religious motivators were fulfilled was a strong predictor of willingness to volunteer again. Future research can build on these initial findings by developing a more complete set of religious motivations for volunteering and by exploring the effect of these motivations on volunteer satisfaction (and willingness to volunteer again) in other types of nonprofit organizations.

References

Becker, Penny Edgell, and Pawan H. Dhingra. 2001. "Religious Involvement and Volunteering: Implications for Civil Society." *Sociology of Religion* 62: 315–35.

Campbell, David E., and Steven J. Yonish. 2003. "Religion and Volunteering in America." In *Religion as Social Capital: Producing the Common Good*, edited by Corwin Smidt, 87–106. Waco, TX: Baylor University Press.

Caputo, Richard K. 2009. "Religious Capital and Intergenerational Transmission of Volunteering as Correlates of Civic Engagement." *Nonprofit and Voluntary Sector Quarterly* 38: 983–1002.

Clary, E. Gil, and Mark Snyder. 1991. "A Functional Analysis of Altruism and Prosocial Behavior: The Case of Volunteerism." In *Prosocial Behavior*, edited by Margaret S. Clark, 119–48. Review of Personality and Social Psychology 12. Newbury Park, CA: Sage.

Cnaan, Ram A., Amy Kasternakis, and Robert J. Wineburg. 1999. "Religious People, Religious Congregations, and Volunteerism in Human Services: Is There a Link?" *Nonprofit and Voluntary Sector Quarterly* 22: 33–51.

Corporation for National and Community Service. 2012. "Volunteering and Civic Life in America." Available at www.volunteeringinamerica.gov.

Eisenstein, Marie A. 2006. "Religious Motivation versus Traditional Religiousness: Bridging the Gap between Religion and Politics and the Psychology of Religion." *Interdisciplinary Journal for Research on Religion* 2: 1–30.

Gibson, Troy. 2008. "Religion and Civic Engagement among America's Youth." *The Social Science Journal* 45: 504–14.

Houston, David J., and Katherine E. Cartwright. 2007. "Spirituality and Public Service." *Public Administration Review* 67: 88–102.

Loveland, Matthew T., Keely Jones-Stater, and Jerry Z. Park. 2008. "Religion and the Logic of the Civic Sphere: Religious Tradition, Religious Practice, and Voluntary Association." *Interdisciplinary Journal for Research on Religion* 4: 1–26.

McBride, Amanda Moore, and YungSoo Lee. 2012. "Institutional Predictors of Volunteer Retention: The Case of AmeriCorps National Service." *Administration and Society* 44: 343–66.

McPherson, J. Miller, Pamela A. Popielarz, and Sonja Drobnic. 1992. "Social Networks and Organizational Dynamics." *American Sociological Review* 57: 53–70.

Monsma, Stephen V. 2007. "Religion and Philanthropic Giving and Volunteering: Building Blocks for Civic Responsibility." *Interdisciplinary Journal for Research on Religion* 3: 1–28.

Perry, James L., Jeffrey L. Brudney, David Coursey, and Laura Littlepage. 2008. "What Drives Morally Committed Citizens? A Study of the Antecedents of Public Service Motivation." *Public Administration Review* 68: 445–58.

President's Advisory Council on Faith-Based and Neighborhood Partnerships. 2010. "A New Era of Partnerships: Report of Recommendations to the President." Washington, DC: White House Office of Faith-Based and Neighborhood Partnerships. Available at https://obamawhitehouse.archives.gov/sites/default/files/microsites/ofbnp-council-final-report.pdf.

Putnam, Robert D. 2001. *Bowling Alone: The Collapse and Revival of American Community*. New York: Touchstone Books.

Putnam, Robert D., and David E. Campbell. 2012. *American Grace: How Religion Divides and Unites Us*. New York: Simon & Schuster.

Rigney, Daniel, Jerome Matz, S.M., and Armando J. Abney. 2004. "Is There a Catholic Sharing Ethic? A Research Note." *Sociology of Religion* 65: 155–65.

Ruiter, Stijn, and Nan Dirk De Graaf. 2006. "National Context, Religiosity, and Volunteering: Results from 53 Countries." *American Sociological Review* 71, 191–210.

Smidt, Corwin. 2003. *Religion as Social Capital: Producing the Common Good.* Waco, TX: Baylor University Press.

Stukas, Arthur A., Keilah A. Worth, E. Gil Clary, and Mark Snyder. 2009. "The Matching of Motivations to Affordances in the Volunteer Environment: An Index for Assessing the Impact of Multiple Matches on Volunteer Outcomes." *Nonprofit and Voluntary Sector Quarterly* 38: 5–28.

Tropman, John E. 1995. *The Catholic Ethic in American Society: An Exploration of Values*. San Francisco, CA: Jossey-Bass.

Wilson, John, and Thomas Janoski. 1995. "The Contribution of Religion to Volunteer Work." *Sociology of Religion* 56: 137–52.

Wilson, John, and Marc Musick. 1997. "Who Cares? Toward an Integrated Theory of Volunteer Work." *American Sociological Review* 62: 694–713.

4

Women Religious in a Changing Urban Landscape

The Work of Catholic Sisters in Metropolitan Cleveland[1]

Robert L. Fischer | Jennifer Bartholomew

Since the arrival of the first Catholic Sisters in North America in 1727, these women religious have undertaken a dramatic breadth of service and ministry activities (McNamara 1998). Some 180,000 Sisters were in ministry in the United States by 1965, although four decades later, their numbers had fallen to approximately 57,000 (Center for Applied Research in the Apostolate 2010).[2] The work and contributions of Catholic Sisters in the United States have been detailed in numerous book-length accounts (see, for example, Fialka 2004; Kauffman 1995; Koehlinger 2007; Lewis and Appleby 2004; McCauley 2005; McNamara 1998; Munley 2002; Taylor 2007). These presentations often describe the distinctive role of Sisters in particular geographic areas and/or in categories of ministry (e.g., health care, ecology). Other authors have examined the religiosity of

---

1 This research was sponsored by the Sisters of Charity Foundation of Cleveland, specifically through its Collaboration for Ministry Initiative (CMI). With research, communications, conferences, and grants, CMI engages in collaborative efforts that strengthen the ministries of Catholic women religious in northeast Ohio. The authors wish to thank all the Catholic Sisters who took part in this study. The authors also wish to thank Mary Ann Murphy, OSU, an Ursuline Sister of Cleveland, who provided vital research support to this study, and Lynn Berner and Kathy Csank, who provided helpful feedback.
2 The number of women religious has declined in many Western nations, as a result of changing societal structures and other forces (Ebaugh, Lorence, and Chafetz 1996).

Sisters as well as the various roles they have taken on in religious and other contexts (Briody and Sullivan 1988; Juteau and Laurin 1986; Petersen and Takayama 1983; Wallace 1991; Wittberg 1989). The present study seeks to extend the knowledge base by documenting the ministries of Catholic Sisters from their own perspective and making observations about the nature and strengths of these ministries.

Research Context

Between 2006 and 2010, the Catholic Diocese of Cleveland engaged in a process of consolidating the number and distribution of parishes to reflect changing demographics in its eight-county region. The process ultimately resulted in a reduction in the total number of parishes by fifty (approximately one-quarter); many of the parishes that were closed were in Cleveland's inner city. In urban neighborhoods where churches have been anchor institutions and providers of critical services, the loss of these parishes created a potentially serious gap in the provision of services that help to maintain the residents' well-being. In anticipation of the impact of this wave of parish closures and consolidations, many women religious began to consider how they could respond to the needs of the communities that would be affected. While they generally knew many of the other Sisters working in these areas, data were needed to get a collective sense of where Sisters currently worked, which ministries might be at risk, and where they should focus their attention.

As part of this work, we undertook two data collection strategies: We completed an inventory of the assignments and ministries of women religious to assess the geographic distribution of sisters, and we conducted a survey of almost three hundred Catholic women religious in active ministry in the Cleveland region about the nature of their work and the impact of the forthcoming parish closures. This work is relevant to women religious and others looking for effective responses to shifting community realities.

The major objectives of the research were to develop a baseline assessment of the work of women religious in the region; solicit perspectives from women religious themselves about their challenges, needs, and vision; assess the strengths and opportunities for collaboration; and compile data that would illuminate the unique approach and spirit of women religious as conveyed in these ministries.

The focus of the study in the Cleveland, Ohio area highlights the economic and social realities of a region that has experienced decades of population loss and economic decline. In the latter half of the twentieth

Figure 4-1: Population Trends in Cuyahoga County

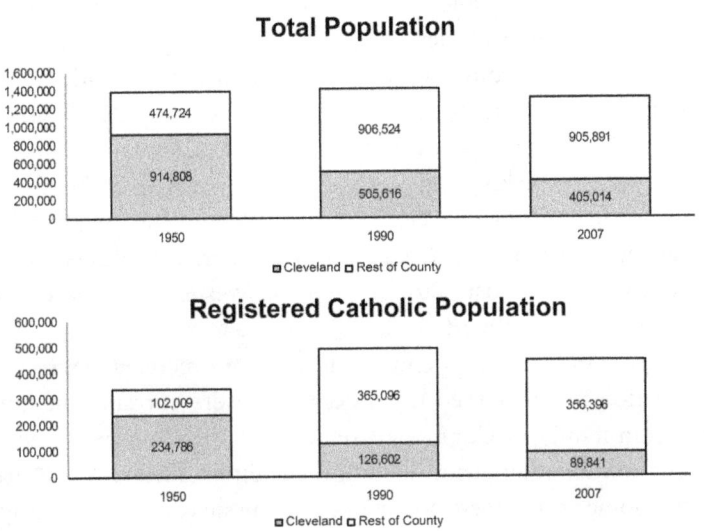

century, poverty in Cleveland increased and spread out from the center city. As people migrated to the inner- and outer-ring suburbs, an increasing proportion of poor families was left in the center city. In recent years, poverty has also increased in inner-ring suburbs. The Cleveland metropolitan area continues to be one of the most racially segregated cities in the United States, and the segregation and sprawl particularly disadvantage African American residents. Figure 4-1 shows that the shift in the Catholic population mirrors the trend in the total population over this period in that most now live outside the city of Cleveland.

Driven by population and fiscal realities, in 2006, the Catholic Diocese of Cleveland initiated a process of parish clustering among its 224 parishes, in which groups of parishes collaboratively developed recommendations for the diocese. The diocese announced a plan in March 2009 whereby twenty-nine parishes would close and forty-one parishes would be involved in eighteen mergers. The result of this was fifty fewer parishes operating in the diocese by June 30, 2010.[3]

3   On March 14, 2012, the Catholic Diocese of Cleveland announced that the Vatican had issued a reversal of the closings of thirteen of these parishes on the grounds that the bishop had not followed church law or procedures in his handling of the closures.

Methodology

We developed an inventory and conducted a survey of Sisters in ministry in Cuyahoga County, Ohio, the urban county that surrounds Cleveland. The survey combined a series of closed-ended and open-ended items and was adapted in part from a survey that was used in a key study conducted in South Carolina (Small and Csank 2009; Small et al. 2007). Given the multitude of religious orders that are active in the Cleveland region, a crucial step involved seeking and receiving an endorsement of the study from the Conference of Religious Leadership, a collaborative organization with representatives from the leadership of the majority of orders. The study was approved in August 2009 by the Case Western Reserve University Institutional Review Board.

To assess the impact of church closings and mergers, we sought for participation in the survey the Sisters who were currently in ministry in the community in Cuyahoga County. Although approximately 1,100 Catholic women religious resided in the eight counties of the Cleveland Diocese, some groups were not included in the survey effort. These groups were retired Sisters (397); administration, leadership, and support staff of the orders (141); and contemplative nuns (58). Among the remaining 514 Sisters, an estimated 70 percent, or 360, resided in Cuyahoga County (Diocese of Cleveland 2008).

Using congregational listings and public records and with the assistance of an Ursuline Sister of Cleveland, we compiled a listing of Sisters along with their ministry sites. Congregational leaders from each order reviewed the listings for accuracy. We distributed surveys in early September 2009 to approximately 288 Sisters, along with a stamped return envelope. In total, 164 usable surveys were returned (57 percent). It should be noted that in December 2008, the Vatican initiated an Apostolic Visitation of Institutes of Women Religious in the United States, involving nearly 400 U.S. religious congregations and approximately 59,000 practicing Catholic Sisters. A survey of major superiors of congregations was being done concurrently with our study, and this may have lessened Sisters' willingness to participate in our survey.

Findings

Women from fifteen religious orders participated in the survey. Over half the respondents were either Ursuline Sisters or Sisters of Notre Dame, reflecting the prevalence of Sisters from these orders in the population surveyed (see Table 4-1). The median age of respondents was sixty-four years, and 16 percent were seventy-five years old or older; the median age for all Sisters in the diocese is 72.5, so this somewhat younger group of respondents reflects their engagement in active ministry. Nearly half of respondents (46 percent) had begun their career in the ministry in northeast Ohio in 1964–1974, and overall, the median number of years of experience in their current ministry was nearly twenty. Over 80 percent of respondents held a graduate degree of some type, reflecting a highly educated group of professional women.

The survey results can be summarized according to a number of descriptive themes, as follows.

Table 4-1: Religious Orders of Respondents

Order of Women Religious	Survey Population	Total Responses
Ursuline Sisters of Cleveland	88	49
Sisters of Notre Dame	71	44
Congregation of Saint Joseph	25	14
Sisters of St. Joseph of the Third Order of St. Francis	24	12
Sisters of the Humility of Mary	15	10
Sisters of the Most Holy Trinity	12	3
Sisters of Charity of Cincinnati	12	10
Sisters of the Incarnate Word and Blessed Sacrament	11	6
Sisters of Charity of St. Augustine	10	5
Sisters of the Holy Spirit	7	5
Orders with smaller numbers of Sisters serving in the county[a]	13	6
Total	288	164

[a] Other orders include the Dominican Sisters of Peace; Sisters Servants of Mary Immaculate; Mercedarian Sisters of the Blessed Sacrament; Society of the Precious Blood; Sisters of the Holy Family of Nazareth; Sisters, Servants of the Immaculate Heart of Mary; and Sisters of Providence.

Presence in the Community

Nearly 60 percent of respondents resided in the geographic area where their primary ministry was located, and 88 percent of these Sisters believed that their physical presence in the geographic area was either extremely important or very important to their effectiveness in ministry. As one Sister noted, "The greatest challenge is to maintain groundedness in the face of overwhelming injustice." Figure 4-2 shows the geographic spread of Sisters across Cuyahoga County. In general, the Sisters' ministries were concentrated in areas of higher poverty, particularly in the City of Cleveland. In addition, there were many neighborhoods in which several different ministries operated in close proximity to one another.

Diversity of Ministries

The ministries that the respondents reported reflect the diversity of the work Sisters do and the charism that they and their order bring to ministry. When asked to name their primary ministry, nearly half of respondents (42 percent) identified an educational setting and role. Religious education in the parish setting was the primary ministry of an additional

Figure 4-2: Women Religious in Cuyahoga County

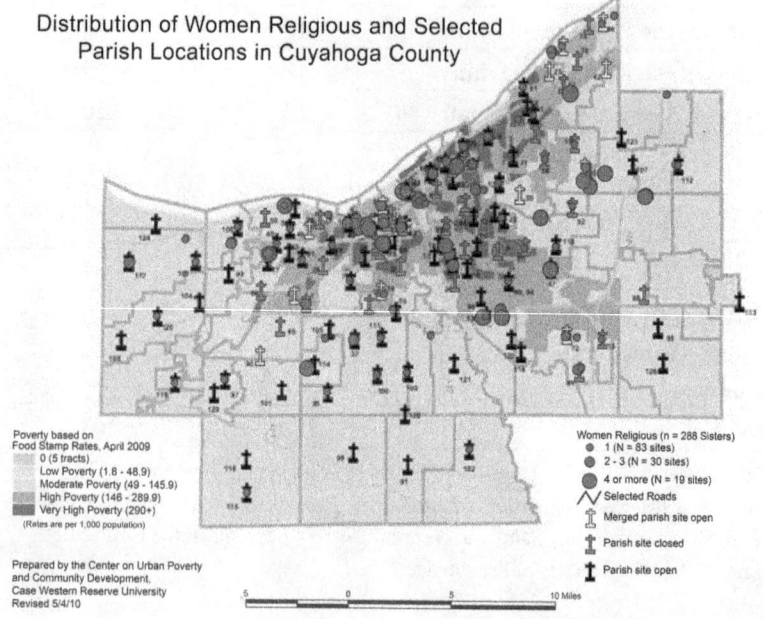

16 percent of respondents. Besides this majority in the area of education, Sisters are spread out over many fields (see Table 4-2).

This is, at best, a rough characterization of the ministry of Sisters, in part because many Sisters found the notion of identifying a "primary" ministry foreign to their way of working.

Involvement in Multiple Ministries

Although the sample was designed to encompass employed Sisters, the survey did ask how many ministries a Sister worked in beyond her primary ministry, typically in a volunteer capacity. It is notable that 99 percent of respondents reported being involved in more than one ministry. More than half of respondents reported involvement in two ministries, one-quarter reported involvement in three ministries, and 13 percent reported four ministries. Sisters reported working an average of forty-one hours per week, but the range was seven to eighty hours of work weekly; 21 percent of Sisters worked fewer than thirty hours per week, 43 percent worked thirty to forty hours per week, and over one-third (37 percent) worked more than forty hours per week.

Table 4-2: Primary Ministries of Women Religious

Ministry Type	Percentage of Respondents
Education (preschool to postsecondary)	42
Religious education (e.g., Rite of Christian Initiation of Adults, Director of Religious Education, liturgy)	16
Social services	10
Administrative duties (e.g., diocesan)	7
Hospice and health care	6
Congregational support [a]	5
Counseling, family services, adult education	4
Retreat, spirituality, and intercessions	4
Other	5

[a] Defined as service to the religious order, such as caring for other Sisters or duties at the motherhouse. There was some overlap of responsibilities of this group and those of the administrative group that was not surveyed.

Site and Size of Ministries

Sisters reported that their ministries were housed at a diverse set of community sites, including parishes, churches, or schools (44 percent); sites operated by their order (17 percent); independent 501(c)(3) agency sites (12 percent); hospital or health care facilities (10 percent); college campuses (7 percent); diocesan offices (4 percent); and other sites (6 percent). Many hospitals, senior care facilities, and colleges are sponsored by orders of women religious, although they maintain separate 501(c)(3) status.

The ministries also varied substantially in regard to the numbers of people served annually (see Table 4-3). Overall, 19 percent of ministries served fewer than 100 people, 44 percent served 100 to 499, 12 percent served 500 to 999, and 25 percent served 1,000 or more. Nearly half the Sisters reported that in the preceding twelve months, their program had experienced an expansion (46 percent), and a similar number reported that the programs were about the same size (44 percent). Only 5 percent reported that their program had been reduced.

Funding of Ministries

Sisters' ministries received their funding from a great variety of sources. Financial data were provided by 59 percent of respondents (97). Half of the respondents were in a ministry that received 90 percent or more of its funding from a single source, and 88 percent were in a ministry that received 50 percent or more of its funding from a single source. The diocese or host parish or school and the Sister's order were the two largest sources of funding that were identified. Nearly one-third of the ministries were reported to be receiving governmental funding, although the vast majority of these were in school settings. Just over one-third of respondents

Table 4-3: Size and Scope of Ministries

	Median Number	Smallest	Largest
Full-time paid staff	8.5	63% served fewer than 20	8% served more than 100
Part-time paid staff	3.0	88% served fewer than 10	2% served more than 100
Volunteers	7.0	57% served fewer than 10	4% served more than 100

reported that their ministry had sought funding from a new source (39 percent), and approximately one-quarter of ministries had obtained funding from a new source (26 percent). Forty-three percent had not yet sought funding from new sources. Over half of the new funding that was sought was funding from charitable foundations.

People Served by Ministries

As to the characteristics of their targeted service population, respondents reported on the presence of general populations and special populations in the focus of their ministry (see Table 4-4). What is abundantly clear from these data is that, regardless of the population that a particular ministry's effort targeted, the population that was served routinely shows a greater degree of need than was anticipated. For example, although just over one-quarter of respondents reported that low-income families were their primary target population, 44 percent reported that low-income families were served by their ministry.

The beneficiaries of Sisters' ministries lived throughout the county, but among the top fifteen identified ZIP Codes served by ministries, nine were located in the city of Cleveland. These ministries served people from many faith traditions; 47 percent served mostly Catholics, 38 percent served mostly non-Catholics, 2 percent served those with no faith tradition, 6 percent of respondents did not know, and 7 percent did not respond.

Use of Collaboration

The survey asked Sisters about their ministry's collaboration with other entities, and 72 percent reported being engaged in collaboration of some kind. The term *collaboration* has a range of meanings but fundamentally reflects the act of working together. At a minimum, collaboration may reflect such activities as information sharing, referral of clients, and cooperative planning. Collaboration may also be much more substantive, including joint programs or shared staffing. Nearly half of Sisters' ministries were engaged with Sisters from other orders (45 percent) and with diocesan organizations (48 percent). To some extent, ministries were collaborating with nonprofit or governmental organizations (41 percent) and with faith-based organizations (34 percent). Among Sisters who reported collaboration, over two-thirds reported collaboration across two or more domains. This might reflect the multiple ministries in which Sisters are

Table 4-4: Target Service Populations of Ministries

Service Population	Percent Identifying as Their Primary Population	Percent Reporting That Ministry Serves This Population
General Populations		
Youth: grades K–8	35.4	47.0
Families	34.2	61.6
Seniors: General population	20.7	37.2
Single adults	20.1	35.4
Youth: grades 9–12	18.3	33.5
Infants, toddlers, preschoolers	15.9	29.9
Young adult: college age, 20s, and 30s	14.0	23.2
Special Populations		
Low-income families	27.4	44.5
Ill and the dying	15.2	26.2
Homeless or at-risk	12.8	26.8
Developmentally disabled	11.6	22.6
Drug/alcohol users	8.5	19.5
Victims of domestic violence	7.9	18.9
Former prisoners	7.3	14.6
Immigrants/refugees	6.1	13.4
Incarcerated	3.7	7.3

engaged, many in a volunteer capacity, beyond their primary ministry. Sisters see many benefits to collaboration (see Table 4-5), most frequently citing as benefits the increased ability to serve clients better; to participate in advocacy, awareness, and education; and to develop and operate joint programming.

One-third or fewer Sisters reported seeing benefits from collaboration in the areas of leveraging resources, recruiting volunteers, accessing

Table 4-5: Potential Benefits of Collaboration

Benefit Type	Percent Seeing as a Benefit
Serve clients better	66
Participate in advocacy, awareness, and education	54
Develop and operate joint programming	53
Assess community needs	40
Access new funding sources	38
Receive and make service referrals	36
Leverage resources	34
Recruit volunteers	33
Access complementary skills/knowledge	30
Engage in peer learning	28
Obtain in-kind donations	21

complementary skills or knowledge, peer learning, and obtaining in-kind donations.

Long-Term Ministry Planning

Sisters were asked about plans for sustaining their primary ministry and their own personal ministry plans. Although fewer than one-third reported having a succession plan in place, nearly half reported that there was someone to take the Sister's place should she be absent from the ministry (see Figure 4-3). In addition, nearly one-half reported having a strategic plan for the ministry. Approximately 20 percent reported having a nonprofit in the community that was committed to sustaining the ministry, though many of these were specific funders that were willing to fund the activities. The future sustainability of the ministry is, in part, dependent on the willingness of other institutional partners to take on the ministerial work after the Sister has transitioned from her role.

Individual Concerns and Plans for the Future

When asked whether they were worried about the future of their primary ministry, more than one-third of respondents were "not at all worried" (38 percent), almost half were "somewhat worried" (46 percent), 13 percent were "very worried," and 3 percent did not respond. The Sisters who

Figure 4-3: Ministries with Succession/Strategic Plans

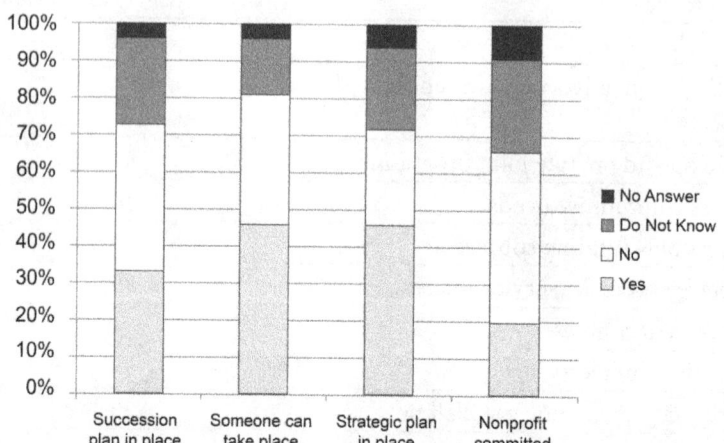

reported not being worried were disproportionately in ministries located at sites operated by religious orders or health care facilities. Sisters who were most worried were located at parish, church, or school sites. In regard to their own ministry plans, one-third of Sisters reported that they planned to continue for up to three years in their current ministry, 25 percent reported planning to continue for four to six years, and 37 percent were planning to continue for seven years or longer. One Sister's sentiments reflected those of many respondents: "as long as able, healthy, God permits." Asked what they would do if they were to leave their current ministry, nearly one-half of respondents (46 percent) said that they would seek another ministry in the region, 18 percent would not, and 34 percent were unsure.

Ministries Need Resources

A clear tension is evident in the necessity to balance the desire to serve people who are in need with the financial requirements of the ministry (and the order), given that the income of Sisters supports the overall needs of the order. The primary identified requirements related to financial stability and to the tension and time associated with the process of seeking and securing funding. As was mentioned above, fewer than 40 percent of respondents' ministries had sought new funding, though the majority of those that did seek new funding received it. A significant number of Sisters (60 of 122) saw funding as the primary challenge. The tension was noted by one Sister, who described it as "balancing the need to bring in income as a member of a congregation with call to work with low income folks who cannot afford to pay full fee for service." In addition to funding, respondents suggested that networking and connecting with other funding sources, including corporations, individuals, and foundations would be helpful (twenty-eight respondents indicated that this type of training and assistance was important).

Managing in a Shifting Environment

Looking to the future, respondents indicated a continuing commitment to neighborhood or community unity, service, and social justice; however, an almost equal number of respondents indicated that they envisioned substantive changes in their particular ministry arenas (i.e., liturgical, pastoral, parish, or vocational ministries). The shifting environment was of great concern to respondents, second only to funding in importance. Naturally, those with concerns for their ministries (close to 59 percent) were more commonly in parish and school sites, where the greatest changes were expected because of the parish reconfiguration in the diocese. Furthermore, 64 percent of respondents were between sixty and seventy-four years old, and many respondents had been active in ministry for over forty years. Long-term planning related to staff transitions to ensure the stability of current ministries is appropriate. This is particularly challenging in the context of declining vocations to religious life, which suggests that laypeople may need to transition into roles formerly held by Sisters. However, the respondents' comments suggest that Sisters are still very future-oriented, as conveyed in one Sister's reminder that "the harvest will be great, though the laborers are few." Approximately 45 percent of respondents indicated that there would be someone in line to take their place if they were absent from their primary ministry, but fewer than one-third of Sisters reported that a formal succession plan was in place for their ministry.

Supporting the Work of Women Religious

Sisters shared a range of ideas about how their work could be enhanced as well as specific challenges that they encountered.

Collaboration as a Vehicle to Enhance Ministries

Over 118 survey respondents (72 percent) indicated that their primary ministry engaged in joint programming or some other type of collaboration. Collaboration was noted to be a valuable resource for ministry, with 100 respondents indicating that it leads to better services. While the majority of respondents already embraced collaboration, the high value placed on collaboration indicates that more work could be done. Such efforts could be directed especially to areas of shared organizational needs among ministries (e.g., fundraising, communications) and to connecting ministries in a particular neighborhood.

Support for Specific Groups or Ministry Types

Throughout the survey, several groupings of primary ministries surfaced as perhaps warranting special attention. These ministries are highlighted either because of their predominance (such as education) or because of an elevated level of need: seniors (especially the homebound), young adults, individuals who have lost faith during the process of parish reconfiguration, families with school-age children, and immigrants. One Sister called for "[g]reater training and outreach programs for the parishes, especially since most cluster plans have a commitment to greater outreach to the poor. More events, activities that address systemic change."

Education, both inside and outside the classroom, emerged as an important substantive domain; specifically, at least sixty-nine respondents reported a primary ministry in K–12, postsecondary, or out-of-school-time education fields. Additionally, seven respondents indicated that they worked primarily with day care, early childhood, or early intervention initiatives. Also, when respondents were asked to select their ministry's target groups, the categories of families, infants/toddlers/preschoolers, youth K–8, youth 9–12, and youth college age were selected 193 times. Many of these groups are found in areas hit hardest by the diocesan reconfiguration. Collaborative efforts could address specific at-risk groups (homebound seniors, immigrants, young adults, etc.) or at-risk ministries in the education field (i.e., schools in or near clustered parishes).

The Challenge of the Smaller Ministry

Small ministries, those with nineteen or fewer full-time employees, accounted for almost 63 percent of respondents (83 of 132 individuals responding). Furthermore, 38 percent of respondents with knowledge of budgets and operating costs indicated that their primary ministry's budget was under $250,000; interestingly, this was almost equal to number of respondents who indicated an annual budget of $1 million or more. The small ministries are more likely to need development in many areas, such as succession, strategic planning, and funding. However, they also enable Sisters to work with the clients in a special way: holistically, present, and with time for listening and reflection. As Sisters are drawn to smaller-scale ministries, some efforts aimed at increasing organizational capacity could be specifically geared to the needs of the smaller organization.

The Geography of Need

Ministries identified in our survey heavily targeted poor neighborhoods, and nine of the top fifteen client ZIP Codes served by ministries were located in the city of Cleveland, where poverty rates are highest and most concentrated. Sisters have considerable experience and commitment to neighborhoods in the city of Cleveland. Sisters expressed interest in receiving technical assistance in the area of monitoring and sharing changes in community demographics and needs, particularly in neighborhoods where many Sisters are working in different though related fields (e.g., education and social services). Similarly, Sisters saw benefit in conferences and meetings that assist in connecting women religious to other nonprofits, stakeholders, and neighborhood representatives in these neighborhoods. Services and supports such as these, though available to nonprofits and human service providers, are often not well suited to the particular needs of Sisters and their ministries.

Faith as the Core of Ministry

Ninety percent of the Sisters who responded to the survey believed that faith plays a significant role in the effectiveness of their work. One Sister put it simply: "Faith is at the core of what we do." The few who did not indicate that faith plays a significant role generally cited legal restrictions on the expression of faith in their work as the reason. Their comments reveal different ways in which faith played a role in the effectiveness of their programming. For most, their life choice to serve as a religious woman made self-evident the role of faith in their work. One Sister commented, "For most of my clients, God is with them by the mere fact that 'Sister' is there." Other Sisters distinguished between their personal ministry and the program ministry in which they had a role. In this case, though faith may be at the core of all they do, Sisters saw a less overt role of faith in some service settings. Sisters' ministries are clearly infused with faith. How does that affect their approach to service in education, health, social service, or other areas? How does it affect their adaptability to change, or personal sustainability in a given ministry? How is funding secured for spiritually based ministries? The role of faith in service deserves further attention.

Conclusion

The ministries of women religious have served untold numbers of individuals and families in the United States for almost three hundred years, yet there has been little systematic collection of data on the nature and scope of these ministries. Efforts to extend and support the work of women religious can be effectively informed not only by a better understanding of these ministries, but also through the insights that women religious can offer from their years of experience. Our study has shown that nearly all the Sisters are engaged in multiple ministries and that the majority of Sisters work nearly full-time or more than full-time in their ministry efforts. The ministries of women religious, regardless of the identified primary target populations, tend to serve populations with greater levels of disadvantage. Sisters serve in communities of great need and believe that their presence in these communities is central to their effectiveness in ministry. Sisters' ministries tend to rely heavily on a limited number of funding streams, often only a single source. In terms of sustainability, one-half to two-thirds of these ministries are reported not to have an articulated plan for carrying forward the work beyond the tenure of the current Sister. Collectively, these characteristics depict an array of human services that often operate with very limited capacity and could well be in jeopardy when the Sister moves on from her current role. Strategies to address this situation include success and transition planning, fund development, and the effective use of collaboration to sustain ministries.

References

Briody, Elizabeth K., and Teresa A. Sullivan. 1988. "Sisters at Work: Career and Community Changes." *Work and Occupations* 15: 313–33.

Center for Applied Research in the Apostolate. 2010. "Frequently Requested Church Statistics." Washington, DC: Georgetown University. Retrieved on October 20, 2010.

Diocese of Cleveland. 2008. *Communities of Women Religious: Statistical Data for 2007–2008*. Cleveland, OH: Diocese of Cleveland.

Ebaugh, Helen Rose, Jon Lorence, and Janet Saltzman Chafetz. 1996. "The Growth and Decline of the Population of Catholic Nuns Cross-Nationally, 1960–1990: A Case of Secularization as Social Structural Change." *Journal for the Scientific Study of Religion* 35: 171–83.

Fialka, John J. 2004. *Sisters: Catholic Nuns and the Making of America*. New York: St. Martin's Griffin.

Juteau, Danielle, and Nicole Laurin. 1986. "Nuns in the Labor Force: A Neglected Contribution." *Gender Issues* 6: 75–87.

Kauffman, Christopher J. 1995. *Ministry and Meaning: A Religious History of Catholic Health Care in the United States*. New York: Crossroad.

Koehlinger, Amy L. 2007. *The New Nuns: Racial Justice and Religious Reform in the 1960s*. Cambridge, MA: Harvard University Press.

Lewis, Helen M., and Monica Appleby. 2004. *Mountain Sisters: From Convent to Community in Appalachia*. Lexington: University Press of Kentucky.

McCauley, Bernadette. 2005. *Who Shall Take Care of Our Sick? Roman Catholic Sisters and the Development of Catholic Hospitals in New York City*. Baltimore: Johns Hopkins University Press.

McNamara, Jo Ann Kay. 1998. *Sisters in Arms: Catholic Nuns through Two Millennia*. Cambridge, MA: Harvard University Press.

Munley, Anne. 2002. *Carriers of the Story*. Silver Spring, MD: Leadership Conference of Women Religious.

Petersen, Larry R., and K. Peter Takayama. 1983. "Local-Cosmopolitan Theory and Religiosity among Catholic Nuns and Brothers." *Journal for the Scientific Study of Religion* 22: 303–15.

Small, M., and K. Csank. 2009. "The Continuing Legacy of Ministries of Catholic Women Religious in South Carolina: Five Year Report of the Collaboration in Ministry Initiative." Columbia: Sisters of Charity Foundation of South Carolina.

Small, M., K. Csank, J. Ott, and R. Wills. 2007. "Ministries of Catholic Women Religious in South Carolina: A Report on the Collaboration in Ministry Initiative." Columbia: Sisters of Charity Foundation of South Carolina.

Taylor, Sarah McFarland. 2007. *Green Sisters: A Spiritual Ecology*. Cambridge, MA: Harvard University Press.

Wallace, Ruth A. 1991. "Women Administrators of Priestless Parishes: Constraints and Opportunities." *Review of Religious Research* 32: 289–304.

Wittberg, Patricia. 1989. "Non-Ordained Workers in the Catholic Church: Power and Mobility among American Nuns." *Journal for the Scientific Study of Religion* 28: 148–61.

II
Social Capital

James Coleman was an American sociologist who was interested in the interaction between different types of capital, namely human, physical, and social capital. Coleman linked the social actions of individuals with the rational ideas of economists.[1] He saw social capital as essentially residing in the social structure of relationships among people.[2] Coleman argued that social capital was a public good where the actions of individuals benefit the whole. Therefore, Coleman conceptualized social capital as a collective asset of the group.[3] For Coleman, individuals engage in social interactions, relationships, and networks for as long as the benefits persist. This logic stems from rational choice theory, which seeks to explain human behavior through rationality. These rational actions are set in a particular social context accounting for not only the actions of individuals, but also the development of social organizations.[4]

In this sense, social capital is both a private and a public good benefiting everyone in the group, not only those who invest in organizing the associations or networks, but those who are passive beneficiaries as a result of being in the group. For example, everyone in a neighborhood benefits when a neighborhood watch group forms to help lower the local crime

---

1 Coleman, James S. 1988. "Social Capital in the Creation of Human Capital." *American Journal of Sociology* 94: S95.
2 Coleman, James S. 1986. "Social Theory, Social Research, and a Theory of Action." *American Journal of Sociology* 91: 1309–35.
3 Coleman, James S. 1987. "Norms as Social Capital." In *Economic Imperialism: The Economic Approach Applied outside the Field of Economics*, edited by Gerard Radnitzky and Peter Bernholz, 133–55. New York: Paragon House.
4 Coleman 1988.

rate, even those people who never personally participate. Direct contributions by actors will benefit the whole, not just the individual. Consequently, strong families or communities accrue from strong social bonding among members.[5] Coleman was so convinced of these effects that he treated social capital as almost universally productive. Indeed, one can make the argument that social capital allows people to achieve particular ends that would have been impossible without it.[6]

A number of scholars from different disciplines would also weigh in on the significance of social capital. In *The Handbook of Social Psychology*, C. Daniel Batson explains that prosocial behaviors refer to "a broad range of actions intended to benefit one or more people other than oneself—behaviors such as helping, comforting, sharing and cooperation."[7] Prosocial behavior is characterized by a concern for the rights, feelings, and welfare of other people. Behaviors that can be described as prosocial include not just feeling empathy and concern for others, but actually behaving in ways that help or benefit other people. Thus, prosocial behaviors are those intended to help other people.

The term *prosocial behavior* originated during the 1970s, and one can argue that it was introduced by social scientists as an antonym for the term *anti-social behavior*. But in recent years the term has come to mean far more than the opposite of antisocial behavior. I have argued that the field of criminology has been preoccupied with only "half" of a field.[8] Its general focus has largely been limited to understanding antisocial behavior, with almost no attention given to prosocial activities. That is, criminologists tend to ask why people commit crimes; they rarely ask why people do good deeds. Rather than neglecting "half" of human behavior, I think criminologists should also be interested in studying a number of important questions that focus on positive and prosocial factors. For example, positive criminology is interested in understanding: 1) Why do the vast majority of Americans choose to obey rather than break laws? 2) Why do most of the people reared in disadvantaged neighborhoods turn out not

---

5   Coleman, James S. 1990. *Foundations of Social Theory*. Cambridge, MA: Harvard University Press.
6   Coleman 1990.
7   Batson, C. Daniel. 2012. "A History of Prosocial Behavior Research." In *Handbook of the History of Social Psychology*, edited by Arie W. Kruglanski and Wolfgang Stroebe, 243–64. Washington, DC: Psychology Press.
8   Johnson, Byron R. 2011. *More God, Less Crime: Why Religion Matters and How It Could Matter More*. West Conshohocken, PA: Templeton Press.

only to be law-abiding but to be good citizens? 3) How is it that offenders who previously exhibited antisocial patterns of behavior can undergo transformations that result in consistent patterns of positive behavior, accountability, and other-mindedness? 4) What is the role of religion in guiding individual behavior in positive ways and the role of faith-based groups and organizations in fostering prosocial activities?

Indeed, we need to fully understand what role religion plays in the expression and modeling of prosocial behavior. The motivation for organized prosocial helping behaviors can often be traced to religious practice. The world's three primary monotheistic traditions—Islam, Judaism, and Christianity—teach that helping the less fortunate is a religious obligation. The compulsory alms tax, or zakat, is one of the five pillars of Islam. There are also numerous examples of God commanding Jews to aid the poor throughout the Old Testament. In the parable of the "Good Samaritan," Jesus instructs his disciples to follow the example of the good neighbor who aided a poor beaten man previously ignored by other passersby, including a priest. The emphasis on giving and helping within the Judeo-Christian religions is a primary reason prosocial behavior is considered a social norm in Western culture.[9] The concept of prosocial behavior and its psychological and sociological foundations is extremely important in furthering research and practice in a number of fields, including education, social work, criminal justice, and law.

Involvement in religious practices and related activities can foster the development of and integration into personal networks that provide both social and emotional support.[10] When such personal networks overlap with other networks, it is reasonable to expect these networks will not

9 Stark, Rodney. 2014. *How the West Won: The Neglected Story of the Triumph of Modernity*. Wilmington, DE: ISI Books. Stark, Rodney. 1997. *The Rise of Christianity: How the Obscure, Marginal Jesus Movement Became the Dominant Religious Force in the Western World in a Few Centuries*. Princeton, NJ: Princeton University Press. Wilken, Robert Louis. 2019. *Liberty in the Things of God: The Christian Origins of Religious Freedom*. New Haven, CT: Yale University Press.
10 Jang, Sung Joon, and Byron R. Johnson 2004. "Explaining Religious Effects on Distress among African Americans." *Journal for the Scientific Study of Religion* 43: 239–60. Johnson, Byron R., David B. Larson, Spencer De Li, and Sung Joon Jang. 2000. "Escaping from the Crime of Inner Cities: Church Attendance and Religious Salience among Disadvantaged Youth." *Justice Quarterly* 17: 377–91. Johnson, Byron R., Sung Joon Jang, Spencer De Li, and David Larson. 2000. "The 'Invisible Institution' and Black Youth Crime: The Church as an Agency of Local Social Control." *Journal of Youth and Adolescence* 29: 479–98. Putnam, Robert D.

only constrain illegal behavior but may also protect one from the effects of living in disadvantaged areas.[11] In other words, an individual's integration into a community-based religious network actually weakens the effects of other factors that might otherwise influence deviant behavior. Thus, religious networks can buffer or shield one from the harmful effects of negative influences.[12]

It makes sense, therefore, that those who regularly attend church and participate in religious activities would be more likely to internalize values modeled and taught in such settings. These faith-filled networks may encourage appropriate behavior as well as emphasize concern for others' welfare. Such processes can contribute to the acquisition of positive attributes that give those attending a greater sense of empathy toward others, which in turn makes them less likely to commit acts that harm others. Perhaps this influence is why research confirms that religiosity can help people to be resilient even in the midst of poverty, unemployment, or other social ills.[13] Churches and communities of faith provide instruction and the teaching of religious beliefs and values that, if internalized, may help individuals make good decisions.

This influence may explain why church-attending youth from disadvantaged communities are less likely to use illicit drugs than youth from suburban communities who attend church less frequently or not at all.[14] In a similar vein, preliminary research has examined intergenerational religious influence and finds parental religious devotion is a protective factor

   and David E. Campbell. 2010. *American Grace: How Religion Divides and Unites Us*. New York: Simon & Schuster.
11 Krohn, Marvin D., and Terence P. Thornberry. 1993. "Network Theory: A Model for Understanding Drug Abuse among African-American and Hispanic Youth." In *Drug Abuse among Minority Youth: Advances in Research and Methodology*, edited by Mario De La Rosa and Juan-Luis Recio-Adrados, pp. 1931–1936. NIDA Research Monograph 130. U.S. Department of Health and Human Services.
12 Johnson, Byron R. 2006. *Objective Hope—Assessing the Effectiveness of Religion and Faith-Based Organizations: A Systematic Review of the Literature*. Institute for Studies of Religion, Baylor University. Johnson, Byron R. 2006. *The Great Escape: How Religion Alters the Delinquent Behavior of High-Risk Adolescents*. Institute for Studies of Religion, Baylor University.
13 Johnson 2011.
14 Johnson, Byron R., and Marc Siegel. 2006. *The Role of African-American Churches in Reducing Crime among Black Youth*. Philadelphia: Center for Research on Religion and Urban Civil Society Address Leadership Hall. Republished in 2008 by the Institute for Studies of Religion, Baylor University.

for crime.[15] Taken together, these findings suggest that the effect of church attendance is compelling in and of itself. Either through the networks of support they provide, the learning of self-control through the teaching of religious moral beliefs, or the condemning of inappropriate behavior, regular church attendance may foster each of these possibilities.

Over the last several decades scholars have produced an impressive body of evidence that has helped to highlight the many ways in which religious participation is linked to religious practices and beliefs that are consequential for a variety of important outcomes. These include overall flourishing and well-being,[16] social integration and support,[17] delivery of social services to disadvantaged populations,[18] mental and physical health,[19] forgiveness,[20] voluntary activities,[21] crime

---

15 Regnerus, Mark D. 2003. "Linked Lives, Faith, and Behavior: Intergenerational Religious Influence on Adolescent Delinquency." *Journal for the Scientific Study of Religion* 42: 189–203. Petts, Richard J. 2009. "Trajectories of Religious Participation from Adolescence to Young Adulthood." *Journal for the Scientific Study of Religion* 48: 552–71.

16 VanderWeele, Tyler J. 2017. "On the Promotion of Human Flourishing." *Proceedings of the National Academy of Sciences* 114: 8148–56. Makridis, Christos. 2019. "Human Flourishing and Religious Liberty: Evidence from over 150 Countries, 2006–2018." *SSRN*. https://papers.ssrn.com/sol3/papers.cfm?abstract_id=3472793.

17 Lim, Chaeyoon, and Robert D. Putnam. 2010. "Religion, Social Networks, and Life Satisfaction." *American Sociological Review* 75: 914–33. https://doi.org/10.1177/0003122410386686. McClure, Jennifer M. 2013. "Sources of Social Support: Examining Congregational Involvement, Private Devotional Activities, and Congregational Context." *Journal for the Scientific Study of Religion* 52: 698–712.

18 Cnaan, Ram A. 2008. *The Invisible Caring Hand: American Congregations and the Provision of Welfare.* New York: NYU Press. Johnson, Byron R., and William H. Wubbenhorst. 2017. "Assessing the Faith-Based Response to Homelessness in America: Findings from Eleven Cities." Program on Prosocial Behavior, Baylor University.

19 Koenig, Harold G. 2015. "Religion, Spirituality, and Health: A Review and Update." *Advances in Mind-Body Medicine* 29: 19–26; Rosmarin, David H., and Harold G. Koenig. 2020. *Handbook of Spirituality, Religion, and Mental Health.* 2nd ed. Academic Press.

20 McCullough, Michael E., Giacomo Bono, and Lindsey M. Root. 2005. "Religion and Forgiveness." In *Handbook of the Psychology of Religion and Spirituality*, edited by Raymond F. Paloutzian and Crystal L. Park, 394–411. New York: Guilford. McCullough, Michael E. 2008. *Beyond Revenge: The Evolution of the Forgiveness Instinct.* San Francisco: Jossey-Bass.

21 Lam, Pui-Yan. 2002. "As the Flocks Gather: How Religion Affects Voluntary Association Participation." *Journal for the Scientific Study of Religion* 41: 405–22.

reduction,[22] prisoner rehabilitation,[23] family relations,[24] substance use/abuse,[25] sobriety,[26] health care utilization,[27] coping strategies for stressful conditions,[28] and even longevity/mortality.[29] Thus, efforts to restrict religious freedom will unnecessarily curtail the effort of

---

Wilson, John, and Marc Musick. 1997. "Who Cares? Toward an Integrated Theory of Volunteer Work." *American Sociological Review* 62: 694–713.

22 Johnson 2011. Kelly, P. Elizabeth, Joshua R. Polanin, Sung Joon Jang, and Byron R. Johnson. 2015. "Religion, Delinquency, and Drug Use: A Meta-Analysis." *Criminal Justice Review* 40: 505–23.

23 Hallett, Michael, Joshua Hays, Byron R. Johnson, Sung Joon Jang, and Grant Duwe. 2016. *The Angola Prison Seminary: Effects of Faith-Based Ministry on Identity Transformation, Desistance, and Rehabilitation.* New York: Routledge. https://doi.org/10.4324/9781315648309.

24 Edgell, Penny. 2013. *Religion and Family in a Changing Society.* Princeton, NJ: Princeton University Press. Mahoney, Annette, Kenneth I. Pargament, Aaron Murray-Swank, and Nichole Murray-Swank. 2003. "Religion and the Sanctification of Family Relationships." *Review of Religious Research* 44: 220–36.

25 Bahr, Stephen J., and John P. Hoffmann. 2008. "Religiosity, Peers, and Adolescent Drug Use." *Journal of Drug Issues* 38: 743–69; Bahr, Stephen J., and John P. Hoffmann. 2010. "Parenting Style, Religiosity, Peers, and Adolescent Heavy Drinking." *Journal of Studies on Alcohol and Drugs* 71: 539–43.

26 Lee, Matthew T., Maria E. Pagano, Byron R. Johnson, Stephen G. Post, George S. Leibowitz, and Matthew Dudash. 2017. "From Defiance to Reliance: Spiritual Virtue as a Pathway towards Desistence, Humility, and Recovery among Juvenile Offenders." *Spirituality in Clinical Practice* 4: 161–75.

27 Benjamins, Maureen Reindl, and Carolyn Brown. 2004. "Religion and Preventative Health Care Utilization among the Elderly. *Social Science & Medicine* 58: 109–18.

28 Ellison, Christopher G., and Andrea K. Henderson. 2011. "Religion and Mental Health: Through the Lens of the Stress Process." In *Toward a Sociological Theory of Religion and Health*, edited by Anthony Blasi, 11–44. Leiden: Brill. Makridis, Christos, Byron R. Johnson, and Harold G. Koenig. 2020. "Does Religious Affiliation Protect People's Well-Being? Evidence from the Great Recession after Correcting for Selection Effects." *SSRN*. https://papers.ssrn.com/sol3/papers.cfm?abstract_id=3429422. Park, Crystal L. 2005. "Religion as a Meaning-Making Framework in Coping with Life Stress." *Journal of Social Issues* 61: 707–29.

29 Hummer, Robert A., Richard G. Rogers, Charles B. Nam, and Christopher G. Ellison. 1999. "Religious Involvement and US Adult Mortality." *Demography* 36: 273–85; VanderWeele, Tyler J., Jeffrey Yu, Yvette C. Cozier, Lauren Wise, M. Austin Argentieri, Lynn Rosenberg, Julie R. Palmer, and Alexandra E. Shields. 2017. "Attendance at Religious Services, Prayer, Religious Coping, and Religious/Spiritual Identity as Predictors of All-Cause Mortality in the Black Women's Health Study." *American Journal of Epidemiology* 185: 515–22.

faith-motivated volunteers, lessen acts of service, reduce social capital, and come with a staggering cost to society.

We live in an age when discussions about inequality and discrimination and the need to correct injustice in all its manifestations are clearly front and center in contemporary society. Examples of injustice receive ample attention—and it is good that they do. Receiving far less attention, however, is the empirical evidence documenting that many people are working diligently in an effort to remedy many of the injustices and social problems found in our society. It is one thing to complain about injustice, inequality, or various social problems, it is quite another to intentionally work to reduce or even eliminate these problems. Stated differently, there are those who spend a great deal of time *looking* for justice, while there are others who spend a great deal of time actively and quietly *doing* justice. Oswald Chambers provides a critical insight when it comes to the issue of justice. He argues that people who *look* for justice can easily become sidetracked by any number of distractions. He goes on to invoke the teaching of Jesus from the Sermon on the Mount, suggesting a better way of correcting injustice is to simply give or do justice at every opportunity. Chambers puts it this way—"Never look for justice in this world, but never cease to give it."[30] One can make a compelling argument that this is the very essence of what countless individuals—often motivated by faith—do each day without fanfare.

Research is beginning to help us understand the importance of religious beliefs and practices not only as protective factors in buffering individuals from harmful outcomes, but as mechanisms that promote beneficial and prosocial outcomes. This salutary relationship is not simply a function of religion's constraining element or what it discourages—harmful behavior—but also through what it encourages—promoting other-minded behaviors that can enhance purpose, well-being, and human flourishing. Simply put, these faith-infused networks of support—in and of themselves—are powerful independent predictors of beneficial outcomes.[31] The following chapters examine the many consequential ways in which religion is linked to prosocial behavior.

---

30 Chambers, Oswald. 2017. *My Utmost for His Highest*. Classic Edition. Grand Rapids: Our Daily Bread Publishing. See June 27th entry.
31 Lim and Putnam 2009.

5

Religious Tradition and Involvement in Congregational Activities That Focus on the Community[1]

Jennifer M. McClure

Research on community involvement underscores the importance of religion. Despite a near consensus that religious people are more likely to be involved in the community than are nonreligious people (Beyerlein and Hipp 2006; Driskell, Lyon, and Embry 2008; Putnam 2000; Putnam and Campbell 2010), there is little research concerning why some religious people are involved in the community while other religious people are not (for notable exceptions, see Park and Smith 2000; Schwadel 2005). In this article, I address that question by exploring whether some attenders of religious congregations are more likely than other attenders to engage in a unique form of community involvement: participating in congregational activities that focus on the community.

These congregational activities can take two different forms. Some of the activities concern community service, social justice, and advocacy, such as serving meals at a soup kitchen or homeless shelter, providing cash assistance for impoverished families, offering after-school programs for neighborhood children, and advocating for a living wage for low-income workers (Cnaan 2002). On the other hand, congregational activities can focus on evangelism and outreach, building relationships

---

1 The data used in this project are publicly available through the Association of Religion Data Archives (www.theARDA.com). The author would like to thank Roger Finke, Diane Felmlee, David Johnson, Eric Plutzer, and Christine Bucior for their assistance in the development of this article.

and even serving in the community to encourage people to join a religious group (Dunn 2012; Wilson and Janoski 1995). Because these two types of community involvement are commonly contrasted in the literature on religion and community involvement (Beyerlein and Hipp 2006; Kanagy 1992; Schwadel 2005; Wilson and Janoski 1995), in this article I examine attenders' involvement in each of these types of congregational activities. I also describe how involvement in each of these types of activities varies among different religious groups or traditions.

This study contributes to the literature on religion and community involvement in a number of ways. First, whereas other studies have focused on describing how religious people are more likely than nonreligious people to be involved in the community (Beyerlein and Hipp 2006; Driskell, Lyon, and Embry 2008; Putnam 2000; Putnam and Campbell 2010), this study investigates why some attenders are involved in the community while others are not. By limiting the focus to attenders, I am able to examine involvement in specific congregational activities that focus on the community, which is not normally measured in surveys of the general American population. I also explore how congregational context—in this case, each congregation's religious group or tradition—relates to involvement in these activities because all of the attenders are connected to a religious congregation. Finally, I address whether the relationship between religious tradition and involvement in these activities is different from the relationship between religious tradition and involvement in other community organizations.

Religious Tradition and Community Involvement

The main approach that scholars use to study different religious groups is categorizing them into religious traditions on the basis of which denominations and groups have similar histories and theologies. The largest religious traditions in America are Mainline Protestants, Evangelical Protestants, Black Protestants, and Catholics (Steensland et al. 2000). Affiliation with these groups is related to religious beliefs and behaviors, and political and social attitudes (Steensland et al. 2000), and even involvement in community organizations (Beyerlein and Hipp 2006; Loveland, Jones-Stater, and Park 2008). Mainline Protestants have the most memberships in charitable organizations (Beyerlein and Hipp 2006), and Mainline Protestants, Black Protestants, and Catholics have more memberships in voluntary, community-based organizations than Evangelical Protestants

5 | Religious Tradition and Involvement in Congregational Activities

do. These studies argue that Evangelicals are less likely to be involved in community organizations because they are more concerned with evangelism (Beyerlein and Hipp 2006; Loveland, Jones-Stater, and Park 2008). In these ways, levels of community involvement differ between attenders from different religious traditions.

Looking More Closely at Religious Traditions

To understand the relationships that religious traditions have with community involvement, it is important to understand their historical foundations, theological orientations, and social ministry emphases. The religious traditions that I examine in this article include the three Protestant traditions that Brian Steensland and his colleagues (2000) identified (Mainline Protestants, Evangelical Protestants, and Black Protestants) and Roman Catholics.

Mainline Protestantism. Throughout American history, Mainline Protestants have enjoyed a privileged position in the religious landscape. This privilege began in the colonies as the Episcopalians and the Congregationalists (the predecessors of the United Church of Christ) were legally established in a number of American colonies (Melton 2009). Mainline denominations have relied on well-educated, seminary-trained clergy whose preaching is guided more by academic theology than by stirring up devotion or enthusiasm (Ahlstrom 2004). Yet the privileged position of Mainline Protestantism in American religion may be eroding, in part because of its declining membership (Chaves 2011; Finke and Stark 2005; Kelley 1972).

Mainline denominations' academic stance toward theology has resulted in a progressive approach to religion. These denominations have accommodated their theology to correspond with more modern philosophies, have focused on economic and social justice, and have allowed members to have a variety of personal beliefs (Steensland et al. 2000). Because of their theological heterogeneity, Mainline Protestant denominations have encouraged members to unite around a "social gospel" of political and social activism (Loveland, Jones-Stater, and Park 2008; Roof and McKinney 1987). Social gospel theology has two main aims: to make religion relevant to more modern social situations, such as poverty, racial issues, and the environment, and to engage middle-class congregations in addressing local and global social problems (Putnam 2000). This theology expresses optimism that "social problems [can] be solved" (Roof and McKinney 1987: 80) and has encouraged members to work together to reform society in such a way that it reflects Christian principles of "love, peace, and justice" (Beyerlein and Hipp 2006: 100). The social gospel framework provides much of the motivation for Mainline Protestants' charitable work in the community.

Mainline Protestant congregations are involved in a wide variety of civic and charitable activities. They are more likely to "participate in or support programs for battered women, abused children, pregnant teenagers, migrants or refuges, and foster care" as well as "day-care programs for the elderly, tutoring, international peace and economic development, adult education, and higher education" (Wilson and Janoski 1995: 138; cf. Hodgkinson, Weitzman, and Kirsch 1988). Attending a Mainline Protestant church is also more strongly related to developing civic skills, volunteering, and political participation than is attending a Catholic or Evangelical Protestant church (Wuthnow 1999). Even though membership in Mainline Protestant denominations is declining numerically (Finke and Stark 2005; Kelley 1972), these denominations remain very engaged and influential in social activism and public policy (Wuthnow and Evans 2002).

Evangelical Protestantism. Evangelical Protestantism developed through a series of revivals in the eighteenth and nineteenth centuries (Smith et al. 1998). Led by enthusiastic preachers such as George Whitefield and Charles Finney, these revivals focused on calling people to salvation and repentance (Balmer 2004). Evangelical churches, such as the early Methodists and the Baptists, spread more rapidly throughout the country than did Mainline Protestant churches because itinerant preachers would plant and oversee multiple churches and because, early on, it was easier for Evangelicals to recruit clergy, since their clergy were not seminary-trained (Finke and Stark 2005). The emotionalism of Evangelical revivals was opposed by Mainline clergy and denominations, but Evangelicals argued that faith was more important than theological training (Gaustad and Schmidt 2002). From its revivalist roots, Evangelical Protestantism has grown in the United States (Chaves 2011; Finke and Stark 2005; Kelley 1972).

Evangelical denominations rejected the more modern theologies of Mainline Protestants. Rather than accommodating to the broader culture, Evangelicals have emphasized the fundamentals of the faith (Steensland et al. 2000). Theologically, they focus on conversion and otherworldly teachings concerning salvation, repentance, heaven, and hell (Finke and Stark 2005; Schwadel 2005). Evangelicals encourage involvement within their own congregations and tend to discourage involvement in secular organizations or activities (Iannaccone 1994; Schwadel 2005; Steensland et al. 2000). Evangelical Protestantism can maintain these strong in-group social networks, strict adherence to beliefs, and high levels of commitment because it has a strong subcultural identity (Smith et al. 1998). Yet these very attributes that allow Evangelical churches to grow and to be strong (Kelley 1972; Iannaccone 1994) can limit involvement in the broader community (Putnam 2000; Schwadel 2005).

Evangelicals tend to focus more on serving within their congregations than on serving in the community (Schwadel 2005). They tend to volunteer within their own congregations, "teaching Sunday school, singing in choirs, or serving as ushers during religious services" (Beyerlein and Hipp 2006: 101). While this volunteering is very valuable to congregations (Hoge et al. 1998), it does not encourage broader engagement in the community (Putnam 2000). When Evangelicals are involved in the community, their activities focus on developing personal relationships or engaging in community outreach for the sake of evangelism (Beyerlein and Hipp 2006; Dunn 2012; Wilson and Janoski 1995). Evangelical Protestantism, in general, values evangelism more than volunteering in the broader community (Beyerlein and Hipp 2006; Emerson and Smith 2000; Wilson and Janoski 1995).

Black Protestantism. Black Protestantism developed in the United States as a tradition that is distinct from both Mainline Protestantism and Evangelical Protestantism (Steensland et al. 2000). During the eighteenth and nineteenth centuries, many Mainline and Evangelical Protestant denominations wanted to convert slaves to Christianity, and the Methodists and Baptists were the most successful in doing so, in part because they provided opportunities for African Americans to preach and to lead (Finke and Stark 2005). Owing to the continued marginalization of African Americans after the emancipation of slaves, many African Americans split from mainly white denominations and started their own denominations, such as the African Methodist Episcopal Church and the National Baptist Convention (Gaustad and Schmidt 2002; Roof and McKinney 1987). Black Protestant congregations remain a very important institution in African American communities because they provide institutional free space, a place of "refuge in a hostile white world" (Frazier 1974 [1963]: 50).

As a result of the marginalization and segregation of African Americans, Black Protestant denominations have unique theological emphases. More than other Protestant traditions, they emphasize freedom, justice, liberation, and deliverance (Beyerlein and Hipp 2006; Lincoln and Mamiya 1990; Roof and McKinney 1987). They also combine attributes of both Mainline Protestantism and Evangelical Protestantism. Black Protestants' high levels of attendance and very strong within-congregation ties resemble those of Evangelicals, but their emphasis on social justice is more similar to the social gospel that is promoted in Mainline Protestantism (Roof and McKinney 1987). Politically, Black Protestants are "liberal on most economic attitudes, such as those related to poverty and the redistribution of wealth" but "generally conservative on social and family issues" (Steensland et al. 2000: 294; cf. Lincoln and Mamiya 1990). Unlike Mainline Protestants, who focus on social issues, or Evangelical Protestants, who focus on the divine, Black Protestants maintain a balance between the social and the divine. They emphasize intimacy with God and then extend that intimacy to the people and community around them (Carter 1976; Costen 1993; Mattis and Jagers 2001; McKay 1989).

African American congregations have many connections to the wider community and provide "a structure that facilitates charity and civic engagement and cultivates human capital" (Loveland, Jones-Stater, and Park 2008: 8). They have helped to form banks and schools and to provide social and material support and artistic and cultural opportunities (Lincoln and Mamiya 1990). Compared to white congregations, Black congregations are more likely to be involved in civil rights activities and in helping the underprivileged (Chaves and Higgins 1992). As an institution that both mobilizes and supports African Americans, Black Protestantism encourages community involvement and helping others.

Roman Catholicism. Roman Catholicism has a tradition and history that are distinct from those of American Protestantism. Historically, many Catholics came to the United States as immigrants in the nineteenth century (Ahlstrom 2004). Many of these immigrants were only nominally Catholics; they rarely attended Mass, received the sacraments, or contributed financially to a parish (Finke and Stark 2005; Stark 1992). A number of Catholic orders undertook revivalistic campaigns to stir commitment among the new immigrants (Reid et al. 1990). Historically, because their religion was quite different from

American Protestantism, Catholics were "excluded from community institutions and civic organizations" (Loveland, Jones-Stater, and Park 2008: 7). In response, Catholics created separate social institutions that mirrored those around them, including schools, social services, professional organizations, and fraternal organizations (Finke and Stark 2005; McBride 1995; Ryan 1908). Over time, the Roman Catholic Church in the United States has transitioned "from being an immigrant church in ethnic enclaves" to adopting "middle class styles of worship and social interaction in the suburbs" (Neal 1990: 205–6).

Four traditional aspects of Catholic theology are authority, sin, ritual, and the miraculous. The authority of the Catholic Church and its leaders, especially the pope, is central in Catholic theology (Dolan 1992). Closely connected to authority is an emphasis on sin. Catholic theology frames sin as powerful, people as created in the image of God yet having sinful predispositions, and the church as "a necessary companion in this struggle" against sin (Dolan 1992: 226). Another important aspect of Catholicism is ritual. The main Catholic worship service, the Mass, is a commonly occurring liturgical ritual, and there are also rituals that serve as rites of passage, such as baptisms, confirmations, weddings, and funerals. Catholicism also values the miraculous, especially concerning holy people, such as saints, and holy objects, such as relics and holy water (Dolan 1992). Although contemporary American Catholics, on average, do not highly value the authority of the Catholic hierarchy or the Church's opposition to certain behaviors that it considers to be sins, such as homosexual acts and abortion, they do value Catholic rituals and sacraments as well as doctrines concerning the miraculous and saints (D'Antonio, Dillon, and Gautier 2013).

While these traditional emphases are primarily transcendent and focused on the divine, some Catholic observers have noticed a trend away from the transcendent toward the immanent and particularly toward social activism (Neal 1990). This emphasis has become more apparent since the Second Vatican Council, which called for a faith that "[penetrates] the believer's entire life, including its worldly dimensions, and [activates] him toward justice and love, especially regarding the needy" (Paul VI 1965: n. 21). With this shift toward more social theology, the Catholic Church has emphasized a preference toward the poor, opposing social and economic injustice, protecting human rights, and societal transformation (Haughey 1977; Neal 1990). Encyclicals by current and recent popes, including Pope John Paul II (1987) and Pope Francis (2013), have focused on social justice.

Catholicism not only has strong theological support for social activism and charity work, but also offers many charitable institutions through which Catholics can serve in the community. In the United States, Catholics developed many charitable institutions because they were excluded from more established Protestant organizations (Finke and Stark 2005). Through these institutions, such as Catholic Charities and the St. Vincent de Paul Society, Catholics can serve in the community.

Hypotheses

On the basis of how religious tradition relates to community involvement and the historical, theological, and social ministry emphases of each religious tradition, one can hypothesize how religious tradition may relate with involvement in congregational activities that focus on the community. Two such activities are examined in this chapter: (1) community service, social justice, or advocacy activities and (2) evangelism or outreach activities. The first two hypotheses that I examine concern whether attenders from specific religious traditions are more likely to participate in one activity or the other. Research discussed above suggests that Mainline Protestants, Black Protestants, and Catholics have higher levels of community involvement than do Evangelicals, who prefer evangelistic activities (Beyerlein and Hipp 2006; Wilson and Janoski 1995). These two hypotheses are as follows:

Hypothesis 1: Mainline Protestants, Black Protestants, and Catholics are more likely than Evangelical Protestants to participate in congregational community service, social justice, or advocacy activities.

Hypothesis 2: Mainline Protestants, Black Protestants, and Catholics are less likely than Evangelical Protestants to participate in congregational evangelism or outreach activities.

The next three hypotheses concern whether people from a certain religious tradition are more likely to participate in only a specific type of activity or in both types of activities. Given that Mainline Protestants and Catholics have strong social justice emphases (Neal 1990; Roof and McKinney 1987), they may be the most likely to participate in congregational community service, social justice, or advocacy activities only. Evangelical Protestants, by contrast, should be the most likely to participate only in congregational evangelistic or outreach activities (Beyerlein and Hipp 2006; Wilson and Janoski 1995). Black Protestants, who

5 | Religious Tradition and Involvement in Congregational Activities

incorporate aspects of Mainline and Evangelical traditions, may be the most likely to participate in both types of congregational activities (Lincoln and Mamiya 1990; Roof and McKinney 1987). These three hypotheses are as follows:

> *Hypothesis 3*: Mainline Protestants and Catholics are the most likely to participate only in congregational community service, social justice, or advocacy activities.
>
> *Hypothesis 4*: Evangelical Protestants are the most likely to participate only in congregational evangelism or outreach activities.
>
> *Hypothesis 5*: Black Protestants are the most likely to participate in both congregational community service, social justice, or advocacy activities and congregational evangelism or outreach activities.

Data and Methods

Data

In this article, I use data from the 2008/2009 U.S. Congregational Life Survey (USCLS) (Research Services, Presbyterian Church [U.S.A.] 2008/2009). The Presbyterian Church (U.S.A.) Research Services conducted this survey, and The Lilly Endowment, Inc., the Louisville Institute, and the Presbyterian Church (U.S.A.) funded it. The USCLS is ideal for my purposes because it includes data on both congregations and their attenders and because it has questions concerning involvement in congregational activities that focus on the community. Data were collected through self-administered questionnaires. Congregational data were collected through congregational profiles, which clergy members or lay leaders completed. Attenders completed questionnaires during services over a weekend of each congregation's choice. Because congregations collected data over only one weekend, regular attenders were more likely than less frequent attenders to take part in the survey. The sampling frame for the data collection was generated by Harris Interactive using hypernetwork sampling. The sampling frame includes the congregations that participated in the 2001 USCLS and additional congregations sampled by Harris Interactive, and it can be generalized to all U.S. congregations. About a quarter (26.3 percent) of the congregations that participated in the 2001 USCLS and that still existed participated in the 2008/2009 USCLS. Just over a tenth (11 percent) of the new congregations selected by Harris Interactive participated (Woolever and Bruce 2010).

The Sample

The sample of attenders that I utilized in this study was developed by starting with the cases that had both attender and congregational data. This criterion was important because some congregations submitted congregational data but did not survey their attenders, while other congregations surveyed their attenders but did not submit congregational data. There were 63,371 attenders from 250 congregations that met this criterion. I used two selection filters to focus the sample. The sample excludes attenders who were younger than eighteen years old and those who attended their congregation for less than a year. I used these selection filters to restrict the sample to adults and to increase the likelihood that the congregation that influenced the attender was the congregation that the respondent was currently attending. Because of the selection filters, the sample was reduced further to 53,473 attenders from 250 congregations.

The selection filters introduced a number of biases into the sample. The sample became, on average, older. The proportion of attenders who were involved in congregational evangelism or outreach activities increased, as did the proportion of attenders who were involved in congregational community service, social justice, and advocacy activities.

Compared to nationally representative surveys, the sample is highly religiously active. In the 2008 General Social Survey (National Opinion Research Center 2008), about a quarter of respondents attended religious services once a week or more, while 80 percent of the attenders in the sample attended services that frequently. This sample is beneficial because it allows scholars to begin to understand why some attenders participate in community-focused congregational activities while other attenders do not. However, the overall high level of some religiosity measures, such as attendance, is a weakness and results in lower variation in these variables.

Variables

Dependent Variables. This study has three dependent variables. The first measures involvement in congregational community service, social justice, or advocacy activities, represented by the question "Do you regularly take part in any activities of this congregation that reach out to the wider community (visitation, evangelism, outreach, community service, social justice)? In community service, social justice, or advocacy activities of this congregation." The responses are (0) No and (1) Yes. The second measure concerns involvement in congregational evangelism or outreach activities:

5 | Religious Tradition and Involvement in Congregational Activities

"Do you regularly take part in any activities of this congregation that reach out to the wider community (visitation, evangelism, outreach, community service, social justice)? In evangelism or outreach activities." The responses are (0) No and (1) Yes. These two variables are combined to create a third measure, in which the categories are (1) Involved in congregational community service, social justice, or advocacy activities ONLY; (2) Involved in congregational evangelism or outreach activities ONLY; (3) Involved in BOTH congregational community service, social justice, or advocacy activities AND congregational evangelism or outreach activities; and (4) Not involved in either type of congregational activity.

Independent Variable. The independent variable in this analysis is religious tradition, and it is coded according to Steensland and colleagues' (2000) RELTRAD scheme. The traditions included in this coding scheme are Mainline Protestants, Evangelical Protestants, Black Protestants,[2] Roman Catholics, and other religious traditions.[3] This variable is coded on the congregational level, based on each congregation's denomination.

Control Variables. The analyses also control for a number of attender and congregational characteristics that correlate with community involvement and congregational participation. Older people are more involved in community organizations, but women are less involved in them (Schwadel 2005). Higher levels of education and income are associated with being involved in more civic organizations (Schwadel 2005). African Americans are less likely than non-Hispanic whites to volunteer (Wilson 2000; Wilson and Musick 1997). Church attendance is related to volunteering and involvement in community organizations (Beyerlein and Hipp 2006; Wilson and Musick 1997). Attenders of larger congregations are also less likely to participate in congregational activities (Wilken 1971). Congregations differ in how many social service activities they offer (Chaves 2004), and people who attend congregations that offer more social service

---

2   The Black Protestant category includes two types of congregations: congregations in historically African American denominations, such as the National Baptist Convention and the National Missionary Baptist Convention, and Mainline and Evangelical Protestant congregations that have high percentages (75 percent or higher) of African American attenders.

3   For the 2008/2009 USCLS, the other traditions category includes Orthodox Christian, Unitarian Universalist, Jewish, and Latter-day Saint congregations. Because "other traditions" is a residual category that helps to retain cases in the analysis but does not have much substantive value (Steensland et al. 2000), its results are not discussed here.

activities may also be more likely to participate in congregational activities that focus on the community, owing to having more opportunities. On the attender level, the analyses control for respondents' age, gender, educational attainment, income, race, and frequency of attendance at worship services. On the congregational level, the analyses control for congregation size and the number of social service activities that congregations offer.

Attender control variables are measured in the following ways: Age is measured in years. Gender is a dichotomous variable: (0) Male and (1) Female. Educational attainment is measured with the following categories: (1) Less than high school diploma, (2) High school diploma, (3) Trade school or associate's degree, (4) Bachelor's degree, and (5) Graduate degree. Pre-tax income is measured through the following categories: (1) Less than $10,000, (2) $10,000 to $24,999, (3) $25,000 to $49,999, (4) $50,000 to $74,999, (5) $75,000 to $99,999, (6) $100,000 to $124,999, (7) $125,000 to $149,000, and (8) $150,000 or more. Race is measured through dummy variables for the following racial categories: African American, Asian, Hispanic, non-Hispanic white, other race. The other race category includes respondents who are multiracial. Frequency of attendance at worship services is measured through the following question: "How often do you go to worship services at this congregation?" Response categories are (1) Once a month or less, (2) Two to three times a month, (3) Once a week, and (4) More than once a week.

Congregational control variables are measured in the following ways: Congregational size is operationalized as the average weekly attendance for 2008 and is transformed by a natural log because of its positive skew. The total number of social service activities offered by each congregation was measured through responses to the following question: "In the past 12 months, did your congregation provide any of the following services for this congregation's members or for people in the community? (Mark all that apply.)" Congregations were given a list of twenty social service activities to which they could respond.[4]

---

[4] The complete list of social service activities was (1) housing for senior citizens (nursing homes, assisted living); (2) housing for other groups (crisis, youth shelters, homeless, students); (3) other senior citizen programs or assistance (Meals on Wheels, transportation); (4) prison or jail ministry; (5) care for persons with disabilities (skills training, respite care, home care); (6) counseling or support groups (marriage or bereavement counseling, parenting programs, women's groups);

Analytic Strategy

I tested the hypotheses for this study using multilevel models. Multilevel modeling is ideal to use because it allows scholars to examine both attender-level and congregational-level predictors and because it can adjust for the clustering of attenders within congregations. Each of the multilevel models used in this article has a random intercept, which allows the likelihood of participating in these congregational activities to vary among congregations. Congregational-level predictors are then used to predict each congregation's likelihood (Raudenbush and Bryk 2002). I used multilevel logistic regressions to test Hypotheses 1 and 2, and I used a multilevel multinomial regression to examine Hypotheses 3 through 5. The specific regression equations that I examined for this article are listed in Appendix A. In these analyses, I weighted the congregation-level data to make the data more closely resemble the population of American congregations.[5] I also used multiple imputation to address missing data (Allison 2002; Johnson and Young 2011).[6]

---

(7) substance abuse or 12-step recovery programs; (8) other programs for children and youth (job training, literacy program, scouting, sports); (9) programs or activities for college students; (10) emergency relief or material assistance (free meals, food, clothes for the needy); (11) financial literacy programs or other help with budgeting, debt management, or investing; (12) health-related programs and activities (blood drives, screenings, health education); (13) programs or services for persons with HIV or AIDS; (14) immigrant support activities (English as a second language, refugee support, interpreting service); (15) activities for unemployed people (preparation for job seeking, skills training); (16) voter registration or voter education; (17) community organizing or neighborhood action groups; (18) political or social justice activities (civil rights or human rights); (19) animal welfare or environmental activities; and (20) other welfare, community service, or social action activities not mentioned above.

5 The weight variable was calculated on the basis of each congregation's size, region of the United States, and denominational family.

6 HLM 6.0 can analyze multiply imputed data as long as imputed datasets were generated previously in another statistical program, such as Stata. For multiple imputation in two-level analyses, HLM uses one group-level dataset and multiple imputed individual-level datasets (Raudenbush et al. 2004). HLM 6.0 also requires that there be full group-level data, so the analytical sample was limited to attenders whose congregations had complete data (van Buuren 2011). Using Stata 13.1, I imputed ten datasets of data, the maximum number of datasets that HLM 6.0 can analyze, using chained equations. The requirement to have complete group-level data biases some of the data on congregational religious tradition. Before I restricted congregational data to only cases with complete data, 13 percent of congregations were Catholic, 26 percent were Evangelical Protestant, 48 percent

Results

Table 5-1 presents the descriptive statistics for the variables. Twenty percent of the attenders were involved in congregational community service, social justice, or advocacy activities, while 18 percent were involved in congregational evangelism or outreach activities. These data can also be examined through different combinations of these activities. About 14 percent of attenders participated in congregational community service, social justice, or advocacy activities only, while 12 percent participated in congregational evangelism or outreach activities only. About 6 percent participated in both types of activities, while over two-thirds of attenders (68 percent) did not participate in any congregational activities that focus on the community.[7] Half of the congregations in the study were Mainline Protestant, and about a quarter (26 percent) were Evangelical Protestant. Six percent were Black Protestant, 9 percent were Catholic, and 8 percent were from other traditions (Judaism, Orthodox Christianity, Unitarian-Universalism, and the Latter-day Saints). The average attender was in his or her mid-fifties. About 60 percent of the attenders were female. The average attender had a trade school or associate's degree and a pre-tax income of about $50,000 to $74,999. Three percent of the attenders were Asian, 6 percent were African American, 8 percent were Hispanic, 79 percent were non-Hispanic white, and 3 percent were of another race. The average attender attended worship services about once a week. For the congregational control variables, the average congregation had a weekly attendance of about two hundred in 2008, and congregations had, on average, four to five social service activities.

Table 5-2 presents the logistic regressions that analyze how different religious traditions relate to involvement in community-focused

---

were Mainline Protestant, 5 percent were Black Protestant, and 8 percent were from other traditions. After I applied this restriction, however, these percentages changed. Now, 9 percent of congregations are Catholic, 26 percent are Evangelical Protestant, 50 percent are Mainline Protestant, 6 percent are Black Protestant, and 8 percent are from other traditions. With this restriction, the percentages of congregations that are Mainline Protestant and Black Protestant increased, and the percentage of congregations that are Catholic decreased. Multiple imputation is beneficial, though, because it allows many cases to be retained in the analysis. Through using multiple imputation, I was able to analyze data from 46,514 attenders and 227 congregations; if this study were to use casewise deletion, I would be able to analyze data from only 37,960 attenders and 227 congregations.

7 These results are not presented in Table 5-1 but are available upon request.

Table 5-1: Descriptive Statistics

Variable	N	Mean	Standard Deviation	Minimum	Maximum
Involvement in Congregational Activities That Focus on the Community					
Community service, social justice, or advocacy activities	46,514	0.20	—	0	1
Evangelism or outreach activities	46,514	0.18	—	0	1
Congregational Religious Tradition					
Mainline Protestant	227	0.50	—	0	1
Evangelical Protestant	227	0.26	—	0	1
Black Protestant	227	0.06	—	0	1
Catholic	227	0.09	—	0	1
Other traditions	227	0.08	—	0	1
Attender Control Variables					
Age	44,358	55.74	16.92	18	100
Female	43,164	0.61	—	0	1
Education	44,731	3.22	1.23	1	5
Income	40,818	4.16	1.92	1	8
Asian	44,588	0.03	—	0	1
African American	44,588	0.06	—	0	1
Hispanic	44,588	0.08	—	0	1
White, non-Hispanic	44,588	0.79	—	0	1
Other race	44,588	0.03	—	0	1
Attendance	46,327	2.86	0.70	1	4

(*continued*)

Table 5-1: Descriptive Statistics (*continued*)

Variable	N	Mean	Standard Deviation	Minimum	Maximum
Congregational Control Variables					
Congregation size	227	207.72	380.76	15	10,000
Number of social service activities	227	4.67	2.94	0	18

Source: U.S. Congregational Life Survey, 2008/2009.

congregational activities. All of the variables are grand mean centered, and the constant is the odds of participating in a specific type of congregational activity that focuses on the community when all of the other variables are set to their means. The average respondent has a 0.39 odds (0.28 probability) of participating in congregational community service, social justice, or advocacy activities and a 0.26 odds (0.21 probability) of participating in congregational evangelism and outreach activities.

The first model that is presented in Table 5-2 examines involvement in congregational community service, social justice, or advocacy activities, the outcome for Hypothesis 1. The results indicate that Mainline Protestants are more likely than Evangelical Protestants to participate in these activities (OR = 1.57, $p < 0.05$), that Black Protestants are neither more nor less likely than Evangelical Protestants to participate in these activities (OR = 1.49, $p > 0.10$), and that Catholics are less likely than Evangelical Protestants to participate in these activities (OR = 0.43, $p < 0.001$). These results provide partial support for Hypothesis 1. Mainline Protestants are more likely than Evangelical Protestants to participate in congregational community service, social justice, or advocacy activities, but Black Protestants and Catholics are not more likely than Evangelical Protestants to do so.

The second model that is presented in Table 5-2 examines involvement in congregational evangelism or outreach activities, the outcome for Hypothesis 2. These results suggest that Mainline Protestants are neither more nor less likely than Evangelical Protestants to participate in these activities (OR = 1.13, $p > 0.10$), that Black Protestants are more likely than Evangelical Protestants to participate in these activities (OR = 1.71, $p < 0.05$), and that Catholics are neither more nor less likely than Evangelical

5 | Religious Tradition and Involvement in Congregational Activities

Table 5-2: Multilevel Logistic Regressions Predicting Involvement in Two Types of Congregational Activities That Focus on the Community

	Congregational Community Service, Social Justice, or Advocacy Activities		Congregational Evangelism or Outreach Activities	
Variable	Odds Ratio	t	Odds Ratio	t
Congregational Religious Tradition				
Evangelical Protestant (reference)	—	—	—	—
Mainline Protestant	1.57*	2.13	1.13	0.98
Black Protestant	1.49	1.15	1.71*	2.41
Catholic	0.43***	−5.34	0.97	−0.21
Other traditions	2.51**	3.63	0.32***	−5.76
Attender Characteristics				
Age	1.01***	3.67	<1.01**	2.77
Age squared	>0.99***	−5.14	>0.99***	−5.65
Female	1.17**	3.54	1.24***	5.07
Education	1.12***	5.78	1.08***	4.04
Income	1.04**	3.22	1.01	0.53
White, non-Hispanic (reference)	—	—	—	—
Asian	0.70*	−1.97	0.71+	−1.96
African American	1.09	0.55	0.91	−0.60
Hispanic	1.01	0.83	1.19	1.65
Other race	1.02	0.13	1.04	0.35
Attendance	2.08***	14.60	2.69***	25.38
Other Congregational Characteristics				
Congregation size (LN)	0.75**	−3.22	0.88+	−1.82

(continued)

Table 5-2: Multilevel Logistic Regressions Predicting Involvement in Two Types of Congregational Activities That Focus on the Community (*continued*)

Variable	Congregational Community Service, Social Justice, or Advocacy Activities		Congregational Evangelism or Outreach Activities	
	Odds Ratio	t	Odds Ratio	t
Other Congregational Characteristics				
Number of social service activities	1.07***	4.66	1.02	1.10
Constant	0.39***	−20.51	0.26***	−28.87

N = 46,514 for attenders and 227 for congregations.
+ $p < 0.10$; * $p < 0.05$; ** $p < 0.01$; *** $p < 0.001$.
Source: U.S. Congregational Life Survey, 2008/2009.

Protestants to participate in these activities (OR = 0.97, $p > 0.10$). These results do not support Hypothesis 2. Mainline Protestants, Black Protestants, and Catholics are not less likely than Evangelical Protestants to participate in congregational evangelism and outreach activities.

Figure 5-1 presents predicted probabilities for involvement in three different combinations of congregational activities that focus on the community: (1) community service, social justice, or advocacy activities only; (2) evangelism and outreach activities only; or (3) both. The predicted probabilities are based on the results of the multinomial regression presented in Table 5-3, and all of the control variables were set at their means to predict these probabilities.

The first graph presented in Figure 5-1 concerns involvement in congregational community service, social justice, or advocacy activities only, the outcome of Hypothesis 3. Mainline Protestants have the highest predicted probability of involvement (0.24), with Black Protestants close behind them (0.22). Evangelical Protestants have a probability of 0.18, and Catholics have the lowest probability (0.09). These results partially support Hypothesis 3, which posits that Mainline Protestants and Catholics would be the most likely to participate in congregational community

5 | Religious Tradition and Involvement in Congregational Activities

service, social justice, or advocacy activities only. Mainline Protestants are the most likely to do so, but Catholics are the least likely to do so.

The second graph presented in Figure 5-1 examines involvement in congregational evangelism and outreach activities only, the focus of Hypothesis 4. Black Protestants are the most likely to participate in these activities (0.19), followed by Catholics, who have a predicted probability of 0.16. Evangelical Protestants have a probability of 0.13, and Mainline Protestants have the lowest probability (0.12). These results do not support Hypothesis 4, which suggested that Evangelical Protestants would be the most likely to participate in evangelism and outreach activities only. In fact, Black Protestants and Catholics are more likely than Evangelicals to do so.

The third graph in Figure 5-1 pertains to involvement in both congregational community service, social justice, or advocacy activities and congregational evangelism or outreach activities. Black Protestants are the most likely to participate in both activities, with a probability of 0.12, followed by Mainline Protestants (0.10). Evangelical Protestants have a 0.07 probability, while Roman Catholics are the least likely to participate in both (0.03). These results support Hypothesis 5, which proposed that Black Protestants would be the most likely to participate in both types of activities.

A number of attender and congregational characteristics also relate to involvement in congregational activities that focus on the community (see Table 5-2). To simplify this discussion, I will not discuss nonsignificant results. For attender control variables, involvement in each activity increases with age until the early sixties[8] and then decreases with age. Females are more likely to participate in each of the activities, as are attenders with more education. Attenders with higher incomes are more likely to be involved in community service, social justice, and advocacy activities. The only significant finding in terms of race is that Asians are less likely than non-Hispanic whites to participate in each of the activities. People who attend worship services more frequently are more likely to participate in each of the activities. For congregational control variables, attenders of larger congregations are less likely to participate in each of the activities, and attenders of congregations who offer more social service

---

[8] The actual maximum occurs at age sixty-three for congregational community service, social justice, and advocacy activities and at age sixty for congregational evangelism or outreach activities.

Figure 5-1: Predicted Probabilities for Involvement in Different Combinations of Congregational Activities That Focus on the Community

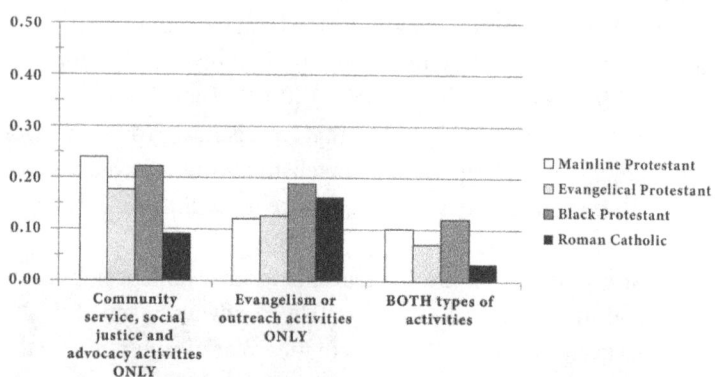

activities are more likely to participate in congregational community service, social justice, or advocacy activities.

Overall, these results provide mixed support for the hypotheses. Contrary to Hypothesis 1, which suggested that Mainline Protestants, Black Protestants, and Catholics would be more likely than Evangelical Protestants to participate in congregational community service, social justice, or advocacy activities, only Mainline Protestants were more likely than Evangelical Protestants to do so. While Hypothesis 2 posited that Evangelical Protestants would be more likely than Mainline Protestants, Black Protestants, and Catholics to participate in congregational evangelism or outreach activities, Black Protestants were more likely than Evangelical Protestants to do so, and Mainline Protestants and Catholics were just as likely as Evangelical Protestants to do so. Hypothesis 3 proposed that Mainline Protestants and Catholics would be the most likely to be involved in congregational community service, social justice, or advocacy activities only. Mainline Protestants were the most likely to do so, while Catholics were the least likely to do so. Even though Hypothesis 4 postulated that Evangelicals would be the most likely to participate in only congregational evangelism or outreach activities, Evangelicals were actually less likely than Black Protestants and Catholics to do so. Finally, Hypothesis 5 suggested that Black Protestants would be the most likely to be involved in both congregational community service, social justice, or advocacy activities and

(text continues on page 139 below)

Table 5-3: Multilevel Multinomial Regression Predicting Involvement in Different Combinations of Congregational Activities That Focus on the Community

	Congregational Community Service, Social Justice, or Advocacy Activities ONLY		Congregational Evangelism or Outreach Activities ONLY		BOTH Types of Congregational Community-Focused Activities	
	OR	t	OR	t	OR	t
Congregational Religious Tradition						
Evangelical Protestant (reference)	—	—	—	—	—	—
Mainline Protestant	1.58*	2.05	1.11	0.69	1.64*	2.31
Black Protestant	1.69	1.35	1.99*	2.54	2.29*	2.00
Catholic	0.45***	-4.77	1.12	0.65	0.39***	-3.69
Other traditions	2.72***	3.90	0.35*	-2.52	0.69	-0.94
Attender Characteristics						
Age	1.01**	2.94	<1.01*	2.18	1.01***	4.06
Age squared	>0.99**	-3.36	>0.99**	-3.64	>0.99***	-6.92
Female	1.16**	2.76	1.24***	4.58	1.38***	4.71
Education	1.13***	5.35	1.09***	4.11	1.16***	5.31
Income	1.05**	3.19	1.01	0.54	1.04+	1.87

(continued)

Table 5-3: Multilevel Multinomial Regression Predicting Involvement in Different Combinations of Congregational Activities That Focus on the Community (*continued*)

	Congregational Community Service, Social Justice, or Advocacy Activities ONLY		Congregational Evangelism or Outreach Activities ONLY		BOTH Types of Congregational Community-Focused Activities	
	OR	t	OR	t	OR	t
Attender Characteristics						
White, non-Hispanic (reference)	—	—	—	—	—	—
Asian	0.73+	−1.70	0.73+	−1.82	0.51+	−1.76
African American	1.19	1.06	1.01	0.04	0.85	−0.71
Hispanic	0.99	−0.03	1.19+	1.74	1.20	0.90
Other race	1.07	0.46	1.11	0.80	0.97	−0.12
Attendance	2.04***	14.65	2.71***	22.17	4.57***	17.10
Other Congregational Characteristics						
Congregation size (LN)	0.73**	−3.25	0.85*	−2.05	0.72**	−2.94
Number of social service activities	1.07***	4.58	1.02	0.92	1.08***	3.80
Constant	0.34***	−22.03	0.22***	−31.05	0.13***	−26.66

Note: Participating in neither of the types of activities is the reference category for the multinomial model.
N = 46,514 for attenders and 227 for congregations.
+ $p < 0.10$; * $p < 0.05$; ** $p < 0.01$; *** $p < 0.001$.
Source: U.S. Congregational Life Survey, 2008/2009.

congregational evangelism and outreach activities, and it was supported. In summary, there is full support for Hypothesis 5, partial support for Hypotheses 1 and 3, and no support for Hypotheses 2 and 4.

Discussion

This study has explored how involvement in congregational activities that focus on the community differs among religious traditions. The analyses provide four main findings: (1) Mainline Protestants are very likely to be involved in congregational community service, social justice, or advocacy activities; (2) Evangelical Protestants are not the most likely to participate in congregational evangelism or outreach activities; (3) Black Protestants are likely to participate in both congregational community service, social justice, or advocacy activities and congregational evangelism or outreach activities; and (4) Catholics are not very likely to be involved in congregational community service, social justice, or advocacy activities. These findings are beneficial for understanding three things: why some attenders of religious congregations are involved in the community while other attenders are not, the role that congregational context and activities have in promoting community involvement, and whether the relationship between religious tradition and involvement in these activities differs from the relationship between religious tradition and involvement in other community organizations.

Of the religious traditions studied in this chapter, Mainline Protestants are the most likely to engage in congregational community service, social justice, and advocacy activities. These activities are an important form of community involvement in Mainline Protestantism, and Mainline Protestants' social gospel theology likely encourages attenders to engage in these activities. Consistent with this theology, many Mainline Protestant congregations and attenders emphasize social and economic justice and the importance of broad social awareness, concern, and activism (Roof and McKinney 1987; Steensland et al. 2000). Social gospel theology provides a strong motivation for Mainline Protestants to be involved in the community, and their involvement in these congregational activities is no surprise, given their extensive engagement in other community organizations (Beyerlein and Hipp 2006; Loveland, Jones-Stater, and Park 2008).

Evangelical Protestants are not highly involved in either of the congregational activities examined, whether they pertained to community service, social justice, and advocacy or evangelism and outreach. These activities are not as likely to promote community involvement among Evangelicals as they are in other religious traditions; this is likely due to the strong norms of intracongregational involvement in Evangelical Protestant congregations (Beyerlein and Hipp 2006; Iannaccone 1994; Schwadel 2005). While Evangelicals' low level of involvement in congregational community service, social justice, or advocacy activities corresponds with the results of other studies that found that Evangelicals are not as likely to be involved in community organizations (Beyerlein and Hipp 2006; Loveland, Jones-Stater, and Park 2008), the low level of Evangelical involvement in congregational evangelism or outreach activities is surprising (Emerson and Smith 2000; Smith et al. 1998). Indeed, many studies explain Evangelicals' lower levels of involvement in community organizations by citing Evangelicals' focus on evangelism (Beyerlein and Hipp 2006; Schwadel 2005; Wilson and Janoski 1995). Yet this finding may be the result of how Evangelicals are encouraged to engage in evangelism. Evangelicals often use a personal influence strategy, seeking to bring someone to salvation through a personal relationship. This strategy is highly individualistic, and evangelism in Evangelical Protestantism may be more likely to occur in one-on-one relationships than in congregational activities (Smith et al. 1998). Although Evangelical Protestants are not as likely to be involved in congregational evangelism and outreach activities as was expected, these results may reflect an evangelism strategy that many Evangelical Protestants use.

Of the four religious traditions studied in this chapter, Black Protestants have the highest levels of involvement in congregational activities that focus on the community. Both congregational community service, social justice, or advocacy activities and congregational evangelism or outreach activities encourage community involvement among Black Protestants. Black Protestants may be active in both serving the community and evangelism because they value having intimacy with God and extending it to others (Carter 1976; Costen 1993; Mattis and Jagers 2001; McKay 1989). Not only do Black Protestants offer this intimacy with God through evangelism by encouraging other people to develop a relationship with God, but they also embody this intimacy through serving people in the community. Of all of the religious traditions, Black Protestants are the most active in congregational activities that focus on the community, regardless of whether the activities pertain to community service or evangelism, and this corresponds with other studies that document Black

5 | Religious Tradition and Involvement in Congregational Activities

Protestants' high levels of involvement in community organizations (Beyerlein and Hipp 2006; Loveland, Jones-Stater, and Park 2008: 14).

The most perplexing result in this chapter concerns Catholics. Catholics are not very likely to participate in congregational community service, social justice, or advocacy activities, even though past research indicates that they are active volunteers (Putnam 2000; Wilson and Janoski 1995) and that they are likely to be involved in community organizations (Beyerlein and Hipp 2006; Loveland, Jones-Stater, and Park 2008). While Catholics have a strong tradition of social teachings (Haughey 1977; Neal 1990), it seems unlikely that these teachings would encourage involvement in community organizations but not in congregational community service, social justice, and advocacy activities. This unexpected finding may be tied to the unique history of Catholicism in the United States. Because Catholics were historically excluded from many social institutions, they created their own schools, universities, hospitals, and charitable organizations (Finke and Stark 2005; Loveland, Jones-Stater, and Park 2008). These Catholic charitable institutions, such as Catholic Charities and the Society of St. Vincent de Paul, provide Catholics with many opportunities for volunteering and community involvement that are not directly through their parishes. Catholics may engage in the community more through these institutions than they do through parish activities.

In summary, this article demonstrates that religious tradition matters for understanding why some attenders of religious congregations are more likely than other attenders to be involved in two types of congregational activities: (1) community service, social justice, or advocacy activities and (2) evangelism or outreach activities. Congregations can use these activities to promote community involvement among attenders, but attenders' involvement in these activities varies by religious tradition, possibly due to the emphases of different religious traditions. Some of the findings correspond with previous research on religious tradition and community involvement, while other findings are surprising. Mainline Protestants' and Black Protestants' high likelihoods of involvement in congregational activities that focus on community are consistent with their active involvement in community organizations (Beyerlein and Hipp 2006; Loveland, Jones-Stater, and Park 2008). There are unexpected findings, however, concerning Evangelical Protestants and Catholics. Evangelicals are not very likely to be involved in congregational evangelism or outreach activities, and this result is likely due to an individualistic evangelism strategy that Evangelicals use (Smith et al. 1998). Catholics are not very likely to be involved in parish community service, social justice, and advocacy activities, and this finding is likely a consequence of parishioners' involvement in other Catholic charitable organizations (Finke and Stark 2005). Religious tradition matters for understanding why some attenders are involved in these congregational activities that focus on the community while other attenders are not, but religious tradition does not always relate with involvement in these activities in a way that is similar to how it relates with involvement in community organizations.

Conclusion

Although this study begins to examine congregational activities that focus on the community, a number of questions about these activities remain. First, what other personal characteristics of attenders and aspects of congregational life help to explain why some attenders participate in these activities while others do not? Second, since community involvement is a key predictor of prosocial behavior (Putnam 2000; Wang and Graddy 2008), does involvement in these activities predict other forms of prosocial behavior, such as charitable giving and providing social support? Answering these questions will add to scholars' understanding of how congregations can promote community involvement and prosocial behavior among attenders.

This study has two major limitations. The first limitation concerns the two types of community-focused congregational activities that I examine: congregational community service, social justice, and advocacy activities and congregational evangelism or outreach activities. There is a fine line between community service and outreach, which are separated into different variables in the 2008/2009 USCLS. Community service focuses on improving the community, while outreach involves community-oriented activity for the sake of evangelism (Beyerlein and Hipp 2006; Dunn 2012; Kanagy 1992). Since these distinctions were not explained in the questionnaire, some respondents may have been confused by the terms, and there may be some error in the results. The second major limitation is that the analyses do not control for general sociability, a key predictor of involvement in religious congregations (Bradley 1995; Ellison and George 1994) and in the community (Putnam 2000). If general sociability had been measured for all of the attenders in the USCLS[9] and if it had been

---

9 Unfortunately, the 2008/2009 USCLS measured this concept for only 1.4 percent of attenders.

included in this study's statistical models, I might have obtained different results and come to different conclusions.

In this article, I aim to explore how religion relates to community involvement by examining how involvement in two types of congregational activities—community service, social justice, and advocacy activities and evangelism or outreach activities—varies among religious traditions in a sample of attenders of religious congregations. By limiting the focus to attenders of religious congregations, this study contributes to the literature on religion and community involvement in three ways. First, it explores why some attenders are more likely than other attenders to be involved in the community. Second, it addresses how congregational context and activities can promote community involvement. Third, it examines a unique form of community involvement that is not measured in surveys of American adults—involvement in congregational activities that focus on the community—and suggests that religious tradition's relationship with it is in some ways similar to and in other ways different from what previous studies have indicated about the relationship between religious tradition and involvement in community organizations.

References

Ahlstrom, Sydney E. 2004. *A Religious History of the American People*. 2nd ed. New Haven, CT: Yale University Press.

Allison, Paul D. 2002. *Missing Data*. Thousand Oaks, CA: Sage.

Balmer, Randall. 2004. *Encyclopedia of Evangelicalism: Revised and Expanded*. Waco, TX: Baylor University Press.

Beyerlein, Kraig, and John R. Hipp. 2006. "From Pews to Participation: The Effect of Congregation Activity and Context on Bridging Civic Engagement." *Social Problems* 53: 97–117.

Bradley, Don E. 1995. "Religious Involvement and Social Resources: Evidence from the Data Set 'Americans' Changing Lives.'" *Journal for the Scientific Study of Religion* 34: 259–67.

Carter, Harold A. 1976. *The Prayer Tradition of Black People*. Valley Forge, PA: Judson Press.

Chaves, Mark. 2004. *Congregations in America*. Cambridge, MA: Harvard University Press.

Chaves, Mark. 2011. *American Religion: Contemporary Trends*. Princeton, NJ: Princeton University Press.

Chaves, Mark, and Lynn M. Higgins. 1992. "Comparing the Community Involvement of Black and White Congregations." *Journal for the Scientific Study of Religion* 31: 425–40.

Cnaan, Ram. 2002. *The Invisible Caring Hand: American Congregations and the Provision of Welfare*. New York: NYU Press.

Costen, Melva W. 1993. *African American Christian Worship*. Nashville, TN: Abingdon.

D'Antonio, William V., Michele Dillon, and Mary L. Gautier. 2013. *American Catholics in Transition*. Lanham, MD: Rowman & Littlefield.

Dolan, Jay P. 1992. *The American Catholic Experience: A History from Colonial Times to the Present*. Notre Dame, IN: University of Notre Dame Press.

Driskell, Robyn L., Larry Lyon, and Elizabeth Embry. 2008. "Civic Engagement and Religious Activities: Examining the Influence of Religious Tradition and Participation." *Sociological Spectrum* 28: 578–601.

Dunn, Joshua. 2012. "Who Governs in God's City?" *Society* 49: 24–32.

Ellison, Christopher G., and Linda K. George. 1994. "Religious Involvement, Social Ties, and Social Support in a Southeastern Community." *Journal for the Scientific Study of Religion* 33: 46–61.

Emerson, Michael O., and Christian Smith. 2000. *Divided by Faith: Evangelical Religion and the Problem of Race in America*. New York: Oxford University Press.

Finke, Roger, and Rodney Stark. 2005. *The Churching of America 1776–2005: Winners and Losers in Our Religious Economy*. New Brunswick, NJ: Rutgers University Press.

Francis. 2013. *Evangelii Gaudium (Joy of the Gospel)*. Vatican City: Vatican Press. Available at www.vatican.va/evangelii-gaudium/en/index.html.

Frazier, E. Franklin. 1974 [1963]. *The Negro Church in America*. New York: Schocken Books.

Gaustad, Edwin, and Leigh Schmidt. 2002. *The Religious History of America: The Heart of the American Story from Colonial Times to Today*. New York: HarperCollins.

Haughey, John C. 1977. *The Faith That Does Justice: Examining the Christian Sources for Social Change*. New York: Paulist Press.

Hodgkinson, Virginia Ann, Murray S. Weitzman, and Arthur D. Kirsch. 1988. *From Belief to Commitment: The Activities and Finances of Religious Congregations in the United States*. Washington, DC: The Independent Sector.

Hoge, Dean R., Charles Zech, Patrick McNamara, and Michael J. Donahue. 1998. "The Value of Volunteers as Resources for Congregations." *Journal for the Scientific Study of Religion* 37: 470–80.

Iannaccone, Laurence R. 1994. "Why Strict Churches Are Strong." *American Journal of Sociology* 99: 1180–1211.

John Paul II. 1987. *Sollicitudo Rei Socialis (On Social Concerns)*. Vatican City: Libreria Editrice Vaticana. Available at www.vatican.va/holy_father/john_paul_ii/encyclicals/documents/hf_jp-ii_enc_30121987_sollicitudo-rei-socialis_en.html.

5 | Religious Tradition and Involvement in Congregational Activities

Johnson, David R., and Rebekah Young. 2011. "Toward Best Practices in Analyzing Datasets with Missing Data: Comparisons and Recommendations." *Journal of Marriage and the Family* 73: 926–45.

Kanagy, Conrad L. 1992. "Social Action, Evangelism, and Ecumenism: The Impact of Community, Theological, and Church Structural Variables." *Review of Religious Research* 34: 34–50.

Kelley, Dean M. 1972. *Why Conservative Churches Are Growing: A Study in Sociology of Religion*. New York: Harper & Row.

Lincoln, C. Eric, and Lawrence H. Mamiya. 1990. *The Black Church in the African American Experience*. Durham, NC: Duke University Press.

Loveland, Matthew T., Keely Jones-Stater, and Jerry Z. Park. 2008. "Religion and the Logic of the Civic Sphere: Religious Tradition, Religious Practice, and the Voluntary Association." *Interdisciplinary Journal for Research on Religion* 4: 1–26.

Mattis, Jacqueline S., and Robert J. Jagers. 2001. "A Relational Framework for the Study of Religiosity and Spirituality in the Lives of African Americans." *Journal of Community Psychology* 29: 519–39.

McBride, Richard P., ed. 1995. *The HarperCollins Encyclopedia of Catholicism*. New York: HarperCollins.

McKay, Nellie Y. 1989. "Nineteenth-Century Black Women's Spiritual Autobiographies: Religious Faith and Self-Empowerment." In *Interpreting Women's Lives: Feminist Theory and Personal Narrative*, edited by Personal Narratives Group, 139–54. Bloomington: Indiana University Press.

Melton, J. Gordon. 2009. *Melton's Encyclopedia of American Religions*. 8th ed. Farmington Hills, MI: Gale.

National Opinion Research Center. 2008. *General Social Survey 2008 Cross-section and Panel Combined*. Chicago: National Opinion Research Center [producer]. University Park, PA: The Association of Religion Data Archives [distributor].

Neal, Marie Augusta. 1990. "Faith and Social Ministry: A Catholic Perspective." In *Faith and Social Ministry: Ten Christian Perspectives*, edited by James D. Davidson, C. Lincoln Johnson, and Alan K. Mock, 205–26. Chicago: Loyola University Press.

Park, Jerry Z., and Christian Smith. 2000. "'To Whom Much Has Been Given . . .': Religious Capital and Community Voluntarism among Churchgoing Protestants." *Journal for the Scientific Study of Religion* 39: 272–86.

Paul VI. 1965. *Gaudium et Spes (Pastoral Constitution on the Church in the Modern World)*. Vatican City: Libreria Editrice Vaticana. Available at www.vatican.va/archive/hist_councils/ii_vatican_council/documents/vat-ii_cons_19651207_gaudium-et-spes_en.html.

Putnam, Robert D. 2000. *Bowling Alone: The Collapse and Revival of American Community*. New York: Simon & Schuster.

Putnam, Robert D., and David E. Campbell. 2010. *American Grace: How Religion Divides and Unites Us*. New York: Simon & Schuster.

Raudenbush, Stephen W., and Anthony S. Bryk. 2002. *Hierarchical Linear Models: Applications and Data Analysis Methods.* Thousand Oaks, CA: Sage.

Raudenbush, Stephen W., Anthony S. Bryk, Yuk Fai Cheong, Richard Congdon, and Mathilda du Toit. 2004. *HLM 6: Hierarchical Linear and Nonlinear Modeling.* Lincolnwood, IL: Scientific Software International.

Reid, Daniel G., Robert D. Linder, Bruce L. Shelley, and Harry S. Stout, eds. 1990. *Dictionary of Christianity in America.* Downers Grove, IL: InterVarsity Press.

Research Services, Presbyterian Church (U.S.A.). 2008/2009. *U.S. Congregational Life Survey, Wave 2, Fall 2008/Spring 2009.* Louisville: Research Services, Presbyterian Church (U.S.A.) [producer]. University Park, PA: The Association of Religion Data Archives [distributor].

Roof, Wade Clark, and William McKinney. 1987. *American Mainline Religion: Its Changing Shape and Future.* New Brunswick, NJ: Rutgers University Press.

Ryan, John A. 1908. "Charity and Charities." In *The Catholic Encyclopedia.* New York: Robert Appleton. Available at www.newadvent.org/cathen/03592a.htm.

Schwadel, Philip. 2005. "Individual, Congregational, and Denominational Effects on Church Members' Civic Participation." *Journal for the Scientific Study of Religion* 44: 159–71.

Smith, Christian, with Michael Emerson, Sally Gallagher, Paul Kennedy, and David Sikkink. 1998. *American Evangelicalism: Embattled and Thriving.* Chicago: University of Chicago Press.

Stark, Rodney. 1992. "Do Catholic Societies Really Exist?" *Rationality and Society* 4: 261–71.

Steensland, Brian, Jerry Z. Park, Mark D. Regnerus, Lynn D. Robinson, W. Bradford Wilcox, and Robert D. Woodberry. 2000. "The Measure of American Religion: Toward Improving the State of the Art." *Social Forces* 79: 291–318.

van Buuren, Stef. 2011. "Multiple Imputation of Missing Data." In *Handbook of Advanced Multilevel Analysis*, edited by Joop J. Hox and J. Kyle Roberts, 173–96. New York: Taylor & Francis Group.

Wang, Lili, and Elizabeth Graddy. 2008. "Social Capital, Volunteering, and Charitable Giving." *Voluntas* 19: 23–42.

Wilken, Paul H. 1971. "Size of Organizations and Member Participation in Church Congregations." *Administrative Science Quarterly* 16: 173–79.

Wilson, John. 2000. "Volunteering." *Annual Review of Sociology* 26: 215–40.

Wilson, John, and Thomas Janoski. 1995. "The Contribution of Religion to Volunteer Work." *Sociology of Religion* 56: 137–52.

Wilson, John, and Marc A. Musick. 1997. "Who Cares? Toward an Integrated Theory of Volunteer Work." *American Sociological Review* 62: 694–713.

Woolever, Cynthia, and Deborah Bruce. 2010. *A Field Guide to U.S. Congregations: Who's Going Where and Why.* 2nd ed. Louisville: Westminster John Knox Press.

Wuthnow, Robert. 1999. "Mobilizing Civic Engagement: The Changing Impact of Religious Involvement." In *Civic Engagement in American Democracy*, edited by T. Skocpol and M. Fiorina, 331–63. Washington, DC: Brookings Institution Press.

Wuthnow, Robert, and John H. Evans, eds. 2002. *The Quiet Hand of God: Faith-Based Activism and the Public Role of Mainline Protestantism*. Berkeley: University of California Press.

Appendix A: Multilevel Model Equations

The multilevel logistic regression for testing Hypothesis 1 is as follows:

$$Prob(community\ service/social\ justice/advocacy = 1|\beta) = \varphi$$

$$Log\left[\frac{\varphi}{(1-\varphi)}\right] = \eta$$

$$\eta = \beta_0 + \beta_1 * age + \beta_2 * age\ squared + \beta_3 * female + \beta_4 * education + \beta_5 * income + \beta_6 * Asian + \beta_7 * African\ American + \beta_8 * Hispanic + \beta_9 * Other\ Race + \beta_{10} * attendance$$

$$\beta_0 = \gamma_{00} + \gamma_{01} * Mainline\ Protestant + \gamma_{02} * Black\ Protestant + \gamma_{03} * Catholic + \gamma_{04} * Other\ Traditions + \gamma_{05} * Congregation\ Size\ (LN) + \gamma_{06} * Number\ of\ Social\ Service\ Activities + \upsilon_0$$

$$For\ all\ i\ from\ 1\ ...\ 10, \quad \beta_i = \gamma_{i0}$$

The multilevel logistic regression for testing Hypothesis 2 is as follows:

$$Prob(evangelism/outreach = 1|\beta) = \varphi$$

$$Log\left[\frac{\varphi}{(1-\varphi)}\right] = \eta$$

$$\eta = \beta_0 + \beta_1 * age + \beta_2 * age\ squared + \beta_3 * female + \beta_4 * education + \beta_5 * income + \beta_6 * Asian + \beta_7 * African\ American + \beta_8 * Hispanic + \beta_9 * Other\ Race + \beta_{10} * attendance$$

$$\beta_0 = \gamma_{00} + \gamma_{01} * Mainline\ Protestant + \gamma_{02} * Black\ Protestant + \gamma_{03} * Catholic + \gamma_{04} * Other\ Traditions + \gamma_{05} * Congregation\ Size\ (LN) + \gamma_{06} * Number\ of\ Social\ Service\ Activities + \upsilon_0$$

$$For\ all\ i\ from\ 1\ ...\ 10, \quad \beta_i = \gamma_{i0}$$

5 | Religious Tradition and Involvement in Congregational Activities

Multilevel multinomial regression for testing Hypotheses 3-5 is as follows:

$Prob(congregational\ community\ activities\ =$
$Only\ community\ service/social\ justice/advocacy\ |\beta) = P(1)$

$Prob(congregational\ community\ activities\ =$
$Only\ evangelism/outreach\ |\beta) = P(2)$

$Prob(congregational\ community\ activities\ =\ Both|\beta) = P(3)$

$Prob(congregational\ community\ activities\ =\ None|\beta) = P(4)$
$= 1 - P(1) - P(2) - P(3)$

$Log\left[\dfrac{P(1)}{P(4)}\right] = \beta_{0(1)} + \beta_{1(1)} * age + \beta_{2(1)} * age\ squared + \beta_{3(1)}$
$* female + \beta_{4(1)} * education + \beta_{5(1)} * income + \beta_{6(1)}$
$* Asian + \beta_{7(1)} * African\ American + \beta_{8(1)} * Hispanic$
$+ \beta_{9(1)} * Other\ Race + \beta_{10(1)} * attendance$

$Log\left[\dfrac{P(2)}{P(4)}\right] = \beta_{0(2)} + \beta_{1(2)} * age + \beta_{2(2)} * age\ squared + \beta_{3(2)}$
$* female + \beta_{4(2)} * education + \beta_{5(2)} * income + \beta_{6(2)}$
$* Asian + \beta_{7(2)} * African\ American + \beta_{8(2)} * Hispanic$
$+ \beta_{9(2)} * Other\ Race + \beta_{10(2)} * attendance$

$Log\left[\dfrac{P(3)}{P(4)}\right] = \beta_{0(3)} + \beta_{1(3)} * age + \beta_{2(3)} * age\ squared + \beta_{3(3)}$
$* female + \beta_{4(3)} * education + \beta_{5(3)} * income + \beta_{6(3)}$
$* Asian + \beta_{7(3)} * African\ American + \beta_{8(3)} * Hispanic$
$+ \beta_{9(3)} * Other\ Race + \beta_{10(3)} * attendance$

$\beta_{0(1)} = \gamma_{00(1)} + \gamma_{01(1)} * Mainline\ Protestant + \gamma_{02(1)}$
$* Black\ Protestant + \gamma_{03(1)} * Catholic + \gamma_{04(1)}$
$* Other\ Traditions + \gamma_{05(1)} * Congregation\ Size\ (LN)$
$+ \gamma_{06(1)} * Number\ of\ Social\ Service\ Activities + \upsilon_{0(1)}$
For all i from 1 ... 10, $\beta_{i(1)} = \gamma_{i0(1)}$

$\beta_{0(2)} = \gamma_{00(2)} + \gamma_{01(2)} * Mainline\ Protestant + \gamma_{02(2)}$
$* Black\ Protestant + \gamma_{03(2)} * Catholic + \gamma_{04(2)}$
$* Other\ Traditions + \gamma_{05(2)} * Congregation\ Size\ (LN)$
$+ \gamma_{06(2)} * Number\ of\ Social\ Service\ Activities + \upsilon_{0(2)}$
For all i from 1 ... 10, $\beta_{i(2)} = \gamma_{i0(2)}$

$\beta_{0(3)} = \gamma_{00(3)} + \gamma_{01(3)} * Mainline\ Protestant + \gamma_{02(3)}$
$* Black\ Protestant + \gamma_{03(3)} * Catholic + \gamma_{04(3)}$
$* Other\ Traditions + \gamma_{05(3)} * Congregation\ Size\ (LN)$
$+ \gamma_{06(3)} * Number\ of\ Social\ Service\ Activities + \upsilon_{0(3)}$
For all i from 1 ... 10, $\beta_{i(3)} = \gamma_{i0(3)}$

6

God, Guts, and Glory

An Investigation of Relational Support Mechanisms for War Veterans Provided by Religious Communities[1]

Terry Shoemaker

"I'm a Christian and thou shall not kill. But if I am put in a position where it is me or somebody else, I feel like God is on my side and whatever I have to do ... I have to do." This is how Chris, a soldier in the first Persian Gulf War, expressed his position during my last interview session with him.[2] Chris was taking part in a research project being conducted to discover the mechanisms of support provided to veterans by religious communities. He was not unique in his sentiments. In fact, in long interview sessions with several soldiers, I recorded similar ideas repeatedly. Indeed, when discussing their return from participating in war, the interviewees made consistent connections between church, faith, spiritual support, and their own well-being. In addition, the Christian soldiers expressed a deep appreciation for their faith-based communities' role in their lives before, during, and after their military deployment.

The goal of this article is to examine the mechanisms by which spiritual support has been provided to a sample of Christian soldiers in the U.S. Army who have returned from combat zones. Although a general scholarly consensus has formed regarding the positive relationship between religiosity and subjective well-being, little research has been conducted

---

1   Jeff Samuels, Brittany Ryan, and Jennifer Shoemaker provided valuable assistance in completing this research.
2   Chris is not the actual name of the interviewee. All names in this article have been modified for participants' anonymity.

allowing religious subjects to describe in their own words the mechanisms by which religious organizations provide support during stressful periods in their lives. For this research, I conducted qualitative interviews with several self-identified Christian soldiers who have been active in combat zones. The goal of the interviews was to discover the modes of support provided by their respective churches. Literature discussing the relationship between religious participation and well-being supports my finding that for the soldiers who were interviewed, congregational support fills a pivotal role by creating divine associations of symbols and rhetoric; enabling an emphasis on the masculine, warrior portions of hagiographic resources (e.g., the Bible) for soldiers to mimic; and promoting mutually beneficial protective services. Each of these resources allows soldiers to legitimate their combat experiences while reintegrating into U.S. society.

Background and Literature

Extensive literature has been published linking participation in religious organizations and subjective well-being (for a summary, see Koenig, McCullough, and Larson 2001). A broad range of scholarship in fields including sociology, psychology, and the epidemiology of religion has indicated that perceptions of well-being may increase when a subject participates in religious rituals or holds strongly to a religious belief system (Campbell, Yoon, and Johnstone 2008; Krause 2002, 2003, 2009; Levin 2001). As this literature has developed, different indicators of religiosity and well-being have been discussed. These discussions have led to the development of numerous specific research projects on the topic. For instance, various ways of measuring religiosity have included participation levels (Schumaker 1992), forgiveness (McCullough, Pargament, and Thoresen 2000), and prayer (Levin and Taylor 1997), to name but a few. Additionally, many of the research projects focus on specific subgroups, such as denominational affiliation (Ellison et al. 2008) or age and race (Krause 2002).

Several scholars have approached this issue by using psychological analyses, which have suggested that religious organizations and religiosity serve as a stress buffer. "The stress-buffering hypothesis implies that religion has stronger positive effects on the well-being of individuals facing high levels of stress" (Dezutter et al. 2010: 508). Other researchers have credited religious organizations with providing social networks, informational and material support, and problem-solving assistance for helping individuals to cope with stress (Maton 1989). In addition, religious organizations offer opportunities for people with similar values to interact, and they promote fundamental social norms such as family structures; both of these aspects of organized religion reaffirm the value of members' lifestyles (Ellison 1991; Krause et al. 2001).

Other scholars suggest that religion provides well-being because of perceived divine interactions. This theory proposes that devotees who retain a "sense of trust in God, believe that God is in control in their lives, believe that God knows what is best for them, and believe that God ultimately ensures they will get what they need" display higher levels of subjective well-being (Krause 2002: 335). Other researchers credit the certainty of divine guidance with "enhancing perceived well-being by deepening the sense of orderliness and predictability of events and by investing problematic situations with new religious meanings" (Ellison 1991: 81). Melvin Pollner theorized that subjects build relationships with a "divine other" in much the same way in which they construct relationships with family members and coworkers. He referred to this relationship with the "divine other" as the most pervasive in U.S. society and asserted that it was "related substantially to several dimensions of well-being and satisfaction" (Pollner 1989: 102).

There seems to be a general academic consensus in regard to the correlation between enhanced well-being and religiosity.[3] In an attempt to discover the processes of church support, B. Gail Frankel Perry conducted some of the first interviews with devotees of a specific religious tradition, namely, Christianity. After several interviews with self-identified Christians, she concluded that churches provide spiritual support through an integrative function of community, an assurance of peace, well-formed meaning systems, and a regulative function of behavioral constraints (Perry 1998). She stated that churches provide mechanisms that enhance congregant welfare that are centered on a concept of peace through an understanding of both the Old and New Testaments.

Method

Like Perry's analysis, my research is not concerned with the theoretical debates but rather focuses more narrowly on identifying the practices of Christian churches from members' perspectives. Instead of discovering formal, spiritual support provided by local churches through interviewing

---

3   Not everyone agrees that the relationship between religious participation and well-being is positive (e.g., see Sloan 2006).

the leadership (ministers, elders, priests, etc.), I employed a bottom-up process of interviewing church members who were also soldiers who had been previously deployed into active combat duty. Several community-based research projects as well as ethnographic research have utilized a bottom-up process. For instance, Karen Curtis (1999) suggests that more bottom-up ethnographies could have positive impacts on global poverty and welfare policies. Application of this approach can provide insights from individuals who are clients or recipients of services. In my research, a bottom-up approach discovered the perceptions of congregational support that Christian soldiers maintain that they receive.

Many soldiers have difficult postwar experiences because of the psychological, social, and psychiatric toll of war. A 2007 study found that 62 percent of returning service members received various mental health care treatments, 27 percent consumed alcohol at dangerous levels, and 6 percent were diagnosed with post-traumatic stress disorder (Erbes et al. 2009). The experience of war and the effects on soldiers' mental health can produce stress-inducing challenges in reintegration into nonmilitary employment and family life, thus making the soldiers valuable subjects in regard to accessing the mechanisms of spiritual support.

Methodologically, I used qualitative interviews to gather data and analytical conclusions. Steinar Kvale (1996: 30, 31) defined qualitative interviews as seeking "to describe the meanings of central themes in the life world of the subjects." He noted that informal (and, at times, formal) interviews allowed subjects to give their own perspective in their own words. In addition, I used a technique of semistructured interviews during the interview process. Schensul, Schensul, and LeCompte (1999: 149) defined semistructured interviews as interviews that

> combine the flexibility of the unstructured, open-ended interview with the directionality and agenda of the survey instrument to produce focused, qualitative, textual data at the factor level. The questions on a semi-structured interview guide are pre-formulated, but the answers to those questions are open-ended, they can be fully expanded at the discretion of the interviewer and the interviewee, and can be enhanced by probes.

I was able to use this technique in my research because of the soldiers' willingness to participate and full disclosure. Each interview was conducted privately and was recorded. All respondents were informed that their real names, the names of their churches, and any other identifiers would not be disclosed in this article.

I conducted a total of seven interviews. Four of the interviewees were soldiers who had been deployed to Iraq or Afghanistan and self-identified as Christian. I conducted another interview with a soldier who self-identified as Christian but, because of health issues, had never been deployed. I also interviewed a member of the ROTC at a local university who self-identified as Christian; this young man will serve four to eight years in the military after he has earned his bachelor's degree. The seventh interviewee was a National Guardsman who had been deployed to Iraq but self-identified as an atheist. All the interviewees were Caucasian and male.[4] All were twenty-two to twenty-eight years of age except Chris, who served in the first Persian Gulf War at the age of forty and is now close to sixty years old. The individuals who self-identified as Christian were members of different Christian denominations: Southern Baptist, Independent Baptist, Free Will Baptist, Church of Christ, Presbyterian, and nondenominational affiliation.

Before conducting this research, I had previously become acquainted with two of the interviewees, Kenneth and Jackson. Two others volunteered in response to an announcement to a university class stating that research was being conducted pertaining to Christians who had a record of war deployment and military experience. After I interviewed these two, they supplied names of others to possibly interview. Out of this pool of names, I randomly selected other military personnel.

As an aside, I was not rejected by any of the men whom I approached and requested to interview. In fact, I had to turn some interviewees away because of the time constraints of the project. This is a very revealing characteristic of the soldiers. During the interviews, I had to ask very few questions. In essence, I discovered that the soldiers were seeking opportunities to discuss their experiences in war and military service. In fact, two of the soldiers revealed that they were attending support groups just to have an audience to whom they could tell their stories. Several thanked me for the opportunity to share their military experiences and were openly disappointed when I informed them that aliases would be used in the final product. Some suggested that the interview had been cathartic.

---

4   It would be interesting to conduct more interviews with minority military personnel (e.g., African American, Latino, and female soldiers). However, the time constraints of the project did not permit me to conduct such interviews.

Overall, the interviewed soldiers were confident and calm. Several explained that they had never been confronted or critiqued about their participation in war. None of the Christian soldiers worried about their souls in the afterlife, they identified no tension between being a Christian and being a soldier, and all of them felt secure that their military actions were justified. As a matter of fact, all the interviewees except for Jackson, who identified as an atheist, were extremely proud of both their military service and their faith organizations.[5] As one soldier said, "Force was always authorized and for a just cause. I don't feel in a sense that I did anything wrong. Or did anything that God wouldn't like or disapprove of."

As I conducted interviews with these soldiers, their words recalled many personal memories. In full disclosure, I should note that I was in the military during the Persian Gulf War in the early 1990s. I was never deployed into combat duty; however, I did serve as an assistant chaplain, officially known as a Religious Program Specialist. My previous experience in the military allowed me to understand much of the military terminology that the interviewees used and created an immediate social bond, allowing the soldiers to openly discuss their experiences.

When I began this research, I assumed that churches provided institution-wide celebrations or recognition services for each of their members who were in military service upon the member's deployment and homecoming. I had hoped to get the details of these events as a legitimizing process for military service by religious congregants. Instead, I discovered that my assumption was incorrect. Only one soldier stated that he had been publicly recognized at a central Sunday service. This was especially moving for this soldier because his church (Church of Christ) prohibits applauding within its services.[6] He stated that he had one memory as a young boy of his church congregation breaking normative practices and applauding for a man who happened to be an older World War II veteran. It was very encouraging to him that upon his return, he too was the recipient of applause by his church. The other soldiers stated that they

---

5   Neal Krause (2009) noted the connection between self-esteem and religious practice. Although his research did not employ psychological analysis, all of the self-identified Christians whom I interviewed seemed to have an acute awareness that they were divinely valued.
6   Southern Churches of Christ promote a worship that abides by the New Testament commandment to "make a joyful noise with your heart" during worship services. This prescription is interpreted to mean that musical instruments, which include applauding, are prohibited.

were allowed to speak at a less-attended Bible study or evening worship service throughout the week but never during the main Sunday service.

Instead of an institutional-wide celebration or recognition, I found that the faith-based organizations' role in disseminating support for soldiers is less formal, more individualized, and relational. For instance, all the respondents stated that they received an abundance of individual encouragement from their church communities.[7] In this regard, one soldier described his church as "loving all over" him. Additionally, each soldier confirmed previous research indicating that religious organizations function as social networks and support. But the interviewed soldiers revealed very specific mechanisms of spiritual support provided for military personnel during their deployment and return.

Supplying Gifts of Divine Associations

"They just wanted to kill something," Chris told me about the other members of his unit as we sat on a comfortable couch in his church's youth room. The room was quiet, and Chris held his small terrier in his lap as he recalled his experiences in the first Persian Gulf War in 1991. Now close to sixty years old, Chris had no problems relaying several stories, and he was a great storyteller. He continued:

> We had these guys and they had their flak jackets on. And we had an artist in the group and he'd paint "One Shot, One Kill." They just wanted to kill something. So we come into this town and this ol' dog was chewing on this dead Iraqi body. I mean that wasn't funny, but . . . we just stopped there and the commander said, "That's not right. Somebody shoot that dog." I bet eighty people opened up with M16s and there was nothing left of that dog. I mean, there were pieces of that dog just flying everywhere. He [the commander] finally got them to stop [shooting] and he said, "My fault. Next time, we'll have a sharpshooter do this."

Chris laughed hysterically as he remembered this story.

---

7 The lack of institution-wide recognition could be due to the controversial nature of the war in Iraq. The Pew Research Center (2008) noted that by the fifth year, that is, 2008, only 38 percent of those surveyed supported the war. This number was down from 72 percent support in March 2003. Many of the soldiers whom I interviewed were deployed in 2009. It would be interesting to know whether there were more institution-wide celebrations and recognitions during the early years of the war in Iraq.

The first Persian Gulf War, also known as Operation Desert Storm, symbolically lasted a total of one hundred hours. In 1990, Iraqi troops moved into Kuwait when a conflict arose over oil production. The United Nations attempted a diplomatic resolution to solve the conflict. When this resolution failed, economic sanctions soon followed. However, Iraq refused to withdraw its troops from Kuwait by the officially mandated deadline of January 15, 1991, so the United States assembled a coalition of thirty-four countries to start air campaigns on January 17. Iraq quickly found that they were no match for the American-assembled convoy. In a little over a month, all Iraqi forces had been expelled from Kuwait.

When Iraq invaded Kuwait in 1990, Chris was one day away from retirement. He had registered for the National Guard on December 4, 1970, when he was twenty years old. Having served almost exactly twenty years, he was told on December 3, 1990, that all military retirements had been halted and he was going to be deployed to Iraq. So at age forty, Chris found himself in Iraq in charge of seventy soldiers, a compilation of three units, who were attempting to catch the lead convoy of Iraqi attackers. But his unit never caught up to any actual fighting. As Chris explained, "We hauled ammunition across the desert and never saw anything."

At the very end of the interview, I asked Chris whether there was anything else that he could recall that he thought would be beneficial for me to know about his experience. Again he mentioned the artist in his group, but this time his reflection was serious:

> I wish you could see some of the Easter pictures that I have. I still have some [of the pictures]. This artist in our company could paint anything. [The soldiers] had built this berm around the back and they filled sandbags and made seats out of them for Easter sunrise service. They built three crosses and put them up. Then he [the artist] painted rocks with our unit crest on it. It's beautiful. There were some guys who got some really good [pictures] of the sunrise coming up over that berm with the crosses right there. We had such a good chaplain over there [in Iraq].

In response to his mention of the crosses that were built, I pressed Chris to further explain what the crosses and paintings meant to him. He stated, "It was like God was sitting there beside of me with his arm around me saying, 'Chris, it's going to be alright. I'm going to take care of you.' From that night on, I wasn't scared." In essence, the crosses, the painting, and the sunrise provided a divine assurance that safety and protection were being provided. The connection between the three crosses and the company insignia was obvious to Chris: it symbolized divine purpose and protection. It is also interesting to note that Chris referred to the pictures that he had kept. The very act of storing the photos of the Easter morning in Iraq demonstrates the continued value he attributed to the photos. Finally, at the end of the story, it is the chaplain, the religious figure of the story, who is given credit for the construction of the symbolic Easter site.

Like Chris, other soldiers described objects that they considered sacred from which they derived guidance and strength. Some talked about a cross necklace or a religious tattoo that kept them focused and calm during their war deployment. Others referred to a church bulletin that they had received in the mail. Each of these bulletins included a list of all their home church activities as well as a prayer listing that included the soldiers' names. Two of the soldiers stated that they held onto those bulletins because it was proof that people were praying for them back home.

Even Jackson, the self-described atheist, had an interesting story about a religious object that had been sent to him through the mail:

> I got prayed for a lot by my friend. One of my best friends from scouts, he actually sent me a Bible. I did read a couple of the passages that he underlined for me. It was comforting. I don't have strong beliefs, but it did help—the fact that he did that for me. I mean, he bought that Bible for me and wrote in it.

For this atheist, the gift of a religious object during war deployment, in this case a Bible, provided comfort. I continued to question Jackson about the Bible verses. He stated that he could not remember any of the verses that were underlined but assured me that he would bring me the Bible for my inspection. He clarified that it was not necessarily the Bible itself that he so valued, but rather its association with someone back home who was thinking about him. He also noted that the friend who sent him the Bible was currently a traveling evangelist.

It is interesting to note that in the case of the constructed Easter scene and the gift Bible, the items were given by a chaplain or evangelist, the items provided solace, and all of the items were maintained. The items themselves became a source of spiritual support, which offered immense comfort in a highly stressful experience. And just as each object communicated to the soldiers that they were highly valued by their loved ones and by a divine being, the objects became a symbol of that value and gained immeasurable worth. Additionally, the gifts of divine association were offered personally versus institutionally, which contributed to the impact of the symbol.

In addition to associating certain symbols with the divine, the Christian soldiers employed a rhetoric that was closely associated with scripture. All the Christian soldiers used words such as *service, mission,* and *calling* throughout the interview process. In fact, sometimes it was difficult to discern whether the soldiers were speaking of their religious journey or their war experiences.

Sociologist E. L. Idler conducted a study concerning the correlation of well-being and religious involvement of an elderly population. She discovered the same emphasis on religious symbols by her respondents that I found in interviewing the soldiers. Idler (1987: 229) described religious symbols as "a unique system of symbols . . . a consistent body of knowledge and a set of meanings that allow individuals to make sense of and cope with their experience." B. Gail Frankel Perry also noted that symbols were of great importance to those whom she interviewed. She stated that the "symbols associated with the practice of Christianity and with church life—Scripture, prayer, and Communion—appear to be important contributors to well-being" (Perry 1998: 131).

Anthropologist Justin McDaniel noted a strong emphasis on protective amulets for a distinctly different religious group: Thai Buddhists. McDaniel (2011: 208) suggested that the amulets are more than just protective:

> Amulets create communities and texts. The wonderings, reflections, and visualizations that take place while looking at an image . . . generate questions that can be posed to texts or help individuals develop new beliefs. The conversations that take place over the trading of amulets can be seen as emerging doctrine.

Although McDaniel's work was conducted in a different context than mine, his insight into the emerging doctrines and creation of communities by way of amulets seems applicable to the soldiers as well. For the soldiers whom I interviewed, the symbols given by their spiritual leaders were transferred from a familiar space (home) to an unfamiliar space (a war zone), resulting in a magnification in importance and value that continues to this day. The objects supplied by religious associates provided comfort, served as coping mechanisms, and created communal identities.

Hagiographical Mimesis

In 2005, Jason celebrated his twenty-first birthday in Iraq. He was deployed for a mission that he referred to as "CSI: Iraq." In essence, he was part of a unit that investigated battle scenes in the aftermath of combat in an attempt to uncover any forensic evidence that might be useful. His group "put on gloves . . . and looked for video materials, ID making materials, weapons, and fingerprints by doing biometrics." They were conducting field research on a war that had started two years earlier.

The second Persian Gulf War, also known as Operation Iraqi Freedom, was initiated when the United States and the United Kingdom accused then Iraqi President Saddam Hussein of possessing weapons of mass destruction. Although the military campaign was not as brief as the first Persian Gulf War, the coalition forces of the United States, the United Kingdom, and others countries did quickly end Hussein's reign. However, meeting other objectives, such as establishing a more democratic government, proved to be a difficult task. U.S. soldiers continued to stay in Iraq, hoping to find former government leaders, securing the state, and attempting to assist in setting up a stable government that would be able to defend itself. The war was officially declared over in December 2011, and the last U.S. troops left Iraq on December 18, 2011.

In the midst of the post-invasion turmoil, Jason found himself and his Marine unit conducting forensic investigations in Iraq. Jason had volunteered to be deployed even though he was assigned to a nondeployable unit. He is a self-described quiet guy who does not like to be the center of attention and had grown up attending a small Church of Christ congregation. During the interview, however, he talked quickly and energetically about his military experience. One of the first statements he made when I asked him to tell me about himself was "I'm glad that I could serve my country and be proud of my actions."

When I asked Jason whether he had ever been confronted about identifying as a Christian and participating in war, he answered:

> The Bible says "Thou shall not kill." [And some people ask,] How can you do that? But I look at it in the sense that God commanded people to kill. God had armies that he helped win . . . God gave Samson the strength to pull pillars down and he killed a lot of people. God also gave him strength to kill thousands of men with the jawbone of an ox.

Jason started by stating the most obvious commandment in the Bible that can be applied to war: the Hebrew proscription against murder. However, he renegotiated this command by referencing a specific destructive command found in the book of Judges. The story of Samson's feats is familiar even to many people outside of the Abrahamic traditions. The Bible story recounts God's selection of Samson at an early age to lead the Israelites from under Philistine oppression. Samson was given extraordinary strength but was also explicitly commanded not to drink alcohol, cut his hair, or come into contact with a corpse. The story continues with Samson killing a lion with his bare hands, catching three hundred foxes, and reportedly killing one thousand men with the jawbone of a donkey. Eventually, Samson was defeated through the wiles of a woman who tricked him into revealing his secrets and then, while Samson was asleep, cut his hair, thus taking away his superhuman abilities. Because Samson's strength had been reduced to average, he was captured and imprisoned. Eventually, God gave Samson one last burst of energy to escape by pushing down the supporting pillars of a building, causing it to collapse, killing him and those who had imprisoned him.

Like Jason, most of the other Christian soldiers whom I interviewed made references to biblical figures without being prompted. The references were always to male characters found in the Christian Old Testament and involved obeying divine commandments. For instance, another soldier referenced the story of Jonah and the whale, which provided association and understanding for his own military experience.

Larry was a member of the U.S. Army stationed in California. He was part of the Airborne Infantry, a specialized group of paratroopers. Larry enlisted in 2005 and had high hopes of being deployed to Iraq. However, he was diagnosed with a severe medical issue that rendered him unable to complete his military commitment. He therefore was assigned desk duty. Because of his medical issue, inability to be deployed, and assignment at a desk, Larry fell into a deep depression that resulted in alcohol abuse. He told me that he knew the abuse was wrong because he had been raised in church; however, in his words, he was "running from God." Larry repeatedly talked about being obedient to God and following the divine commands. Toward the end of his interview, Larry referred to the story of Jonah:

> I kind of look at my life as Jonah and the whale. When Jonah had a calling on his life to go preach to the Ninevites, and he was disobedient to God and he didn't want to go. So he ran from God. And when he

ran from God, the waves started to roar and his life was being turned upside down on this boat. And it's kind of how my life was too. It was crazy though when Jonah finally gave in, he went to the Gentiles on the boat and said, "Hey, the waves will stop if you throw me over. This is my fault." So the Gentiles threw him overboard and all of a sudden the Gentiles started praising God because of it.

Larry associated much of his failure with being disobedient to God, like Jonah. Additionally, Larry attributed much of his present success to giving up his own desires and following God's plan for his life (like Jonah's eventual success).

It was with the story of the masculine, violent, and divinely inspired Samson that Jason aligned himself. The connections that Jason could make for his own life and those of other soldiers are not difficult to ascertain. This association permitted Jason to have a superhuman view of himself as a warrior of God, attribute any success to God who gave the abilities in the first place, and provide a divine calling for the task to be completed. For Larry, the story of Jonah reassured him that God accepts failures, that God's message needs to be proclaimed, and that his own life is valuable as long as he follows God's commands. The stories provided these men with a divine narrative to mimic and a heroic figure with whom to associate. When the soldiers identified with individual characters in the Old Testament—in contrast to Jesus in the New Testament, whom Christians proclaim to emulate—they also anticipated that their future lives would continue to be divinely navigated.

The divine interventions that were expressed through the hagiographical mimesis are not uncommon for religious people. Religious texts have the potential to enhance well-being, but not simply because the texts are "replete with guidance on how to deal with stressful situations" (Krause et al. 2001: 642). The daily guidance is definitely available for devotees, and many people utilize scriptures in this manner. I would suggest that a deeper relational bond is occurring between a devotee and the religious text and that this bond grants the text the ability to legitimate actions and provide comfort. Additional research noted that religious individuals "may resolve problematic situations more easily by defining them in terms of a biblical figure's plight and by considering their own personal conditions from the vantage point of the 'God-role'" (Ellison 1991: 81). Owe Wikstrom (1987: 392) detailed this relational, hagiographic mimesis:

> In the Christian tradition, one finds a lot of scenes in the Bible, where persons are described as living in interaction with God. In all of these human scenes, "The other" (God or Christ) is a counterpart. And, as God in the Bible is described and experienced as the God of history, he deals with man in this world and interacts with him in ordinary occurrences and events. [This] is seen as a sign from or an activity on the part of God, and is not attributed as nothing but an accident, or merely occasional, chance or fate.

In essence, soldiers found comfort, enhanced their own well-being, and legitimated their combat experiences by associating themselves with ancient religious characters. For many of the soldiers whom I interviewed, associations with the Old Testament God figure were pronounced. Many of these soldiers considered the God figure in the Old Testament to be the ultimate warrior and understood themselves as simply being utilized by this divine soldier.

Several scholars (e.g., Elisha 2004; Malley 2004; Watt 2002) have suggested that there is a uniquely strong relationship between Christians and texts. Brian Malley (2004: 1) stated that for Christians, the Bible has achieved "a certain timelessness, a kind of superhistorical status, such that [Christians] continue to read, recite, and expound as part of social life. Such texts are 'living and active.'" Susan Friend Harding (2000) noted specifically that evangelicals and fundamentalists utilize the stories of the Old Testament to justify their actions. One of the main arguments of Harding's work is the idea that conservative Christians are continually struggling to self-identify to those whom they perceive as outsiders. Harding posits that Christians continually reinterpret their motives, history, and plans during their lives by associating with biblical stories and characters. James Bielo (2009: 50) summarized this thought succinctly:

> Evangelicals assert an extremely close relationship between text and action. In other words, their logics for decision making—from everyday ethics to political voting, financial giving, and volunteering—are figured in biblical terms . . . Evangelicals' use of scripture to guide action is not completely uniform and typically takes shape in ad hoc and selective ways. Still, much of what Evangelicals do is presented and justified with explicit references to scripture.

Indeed, most of the soldiers whom I interviewed embedded their war experiences in an Old Testament story or interpreted it through reference to a specific biblical figure without being specifically prompted to do so.

In essence, emphasizing particular Old Testament stories created a relational, liturgical resource for the soldier to utilize.

The Old Testament stories that were referenced have been told repeatedly to the children of Christian devotees during Sunday school, at summer camps, and in other children's educational programs. All the Christian soldiers whom I interviewed had attended churches from a young age and were active in their church's educational programs. In fact, Bible studies or weekly Sunday Schools are a very important form of institutional programming provided by churches. It is estimated that over thirty million Protestants in the United States attend small group studies every week, and "Bible study contends strongly for being the most consequential form of religious practice to the ever-evolving contours of American Evangelicalism" (Bielo 2009: 3). The relationship with the biblical text as an ultimate authority supplies masculine, heroic Old Testament stories, which provide spiritual, social, and psychological support for military personnel.

Mutually Beneficial Roles of Protector

Allen is a Southern Baptist who grew up in church. He had been active in Sunday school, youth ministry, and then college ministry when he signed up for the U.S. Army. Since his youth, he had had a strong desire to be in the military. While in high school, he was a committed participant in the ROTC program on campus. In 2009, he was deployed to Iraq. I asked him whether he had ever received any critique for his love of the military and being a Christian. He replied:

> The Bible says that shepherds have to defend their flock. . . . One of the reasons that I feel so strongly about this is that one of the ministers at [Allen's church] is retired military. He did twelve years enlisted duty as an enlisted tank crewman. He got out, went to seminary, and became a chaplain. He was my mentor for the longest time and I asked him this question [about being a Christian and participating in the military and war] early on. He [said], "Big picture, we are the shepherds and we have to defend the flock. You live in America, and you want the freedom to worship freely unlike other countries who can't. You want to defend that. You want to defend what you love."

Allen had taken the idea of being a shepherd and applied it to his entire life. Numerous times, Allen referred to himself as a shepherd fulfilling his calling by serving in the military and the church. His mentor was an associate minister at his church. Allen explained that his mentor specifically "gave" Allen the Old Testament reference Psalm 144:1-2, which states:

> Praise be to the LORD my Rock, who trains my hands for war, my fingers for battle. He is my loving God and my fortress, my stronghold and my deliverer, my shield, in whom I take refuge, who subdues peoples under me.

The psalm continues with verses extolling God to "send forth lightning and scatter the enemy; shoot your arrows and rout them." Allen stated that his minister *gave* him the verses, as if the minister possessed the verses. Maybe another way of stating it is to say that the minister transferred the protective power of the verses to Allen.[8] Allen told me that he now *carries* these verses with him wherever he goes.

But it is not only the soldiers who feel like shepherds or protectors of the flock. Chris described his church's dedication to the care of his family while he was in Iraq:

> We were in the process of changing churches and we just started coming [to his current church]. . . . [My wife] had joined the church, but I hadn't. So when I left I was not a member [of the church]. But I had been here long enough that the church had really taken me in. The great part about it was that while I was gone [the church members] took care of [my wife and son] just like they had known them their entire lives. They were very good folks. [Chris lists several church members by name here.] . . . When I came

---

8   Indeed, many religious leaders are put into a precarious situation when it comes to devotees' participation in war. How does a minister offer support and comfort but also disavow the potential murder of other human beings? Some people have suggested that religious participants are in complete violation of scriptural prescriptions when they enter combat duty; however, instead of asking how Christians justify war, one must answer how Christians understand their military actions. This is not unique to Christianity. Daniel Kent noted that Buddhist monks of Sri Lanka have also been in this situation: "A preacher does not want to encourage soldiers to kill; on the other hand, he does not want soldiers to have any doubts that might put them in danger. At the same time, these monks hope that the soldiers to whom they preach will go into battle with selfless intentions. Rather than fighting for money or out of personal hatred, the monks urge the soldiers to adopt selfless intentions, such as the intention to protect the innocent and defenseless" (Kent 2010: 173). Like the monks, Christian ministers offer comfort and support to their own devotees. In addition, they offer soldiers a transcendental way of understanding their own actions.

back I was invited to speak at one of the [weekly Bible studies], and they let me tell my story. I told them that I really appreciated everything that they did for [my wife and son] while I was gone, and that I will be joining the church next Sunday. That's when I joined the church. They took care of my family while I was gone and I knew that this was the place to be.

Almost twenty years after this event, Chris is still an active member of his church. In fact, all the Christian soldiers conveyed an idea that the church's commitment to taking care of their families during their deployments had a huge impact on their continued commitment to the church. Jason explained that several of the men of his church made sure that his parents' yard was mowed, and other members continually stopped by to offer encouraging words. Allen noted that several of the women in his church offered his mother the spiritual encouragement that she needed while he was deployed. In essence, while each of the soldiers was deployed, the church members took on the role of protector of the soldier's family.

Several of the soldiers used phrases such as "fighting for God and my country" or "protecting my church and my country." Two insights can be gained from the construction of these phrases. First, the soldiers' statements demonstrated a keen understanding of their role as protector at both micro and macro levels. Just as the soldiers were fighting for national issues, they also acknowledged their service to their religious group. Second, each of these soldiers mentioned their religious commitment first in their statement. This is not uncommon for American Christians. A recently conducted Pew Research poll found that many American Christians self-identify first in terms of religious identity rather than their national identity (Pew Research Center 2012). The importance of religious identity and religious communities enhances the perception that Christian soldiers are defending their local congregations as well as a transcendent purpose.

Previous research has acknowledged that "people are motivated to form and maintain interpersonal bonds" (Baumeister and Leary 1995: 497). This position has prompted many scholars to analyze the effect of religious interpersonal bonds as they relate to well-being, coping, and social support (Ellison and George 1994; Krause et al. 2001). The social support provided by coreligionists may offer some devotees "affirmation that their conduct and perceptions concerning daily events and community affairs are reasonable and appropriate" (Ellison and George 1994: 48). The interviews that I conducted for this research yielded a unique form of social support disseminated relationally to deployed military personnel.

The interviews demonstrate an unofficial relational contract between the soldier and the religious community to provide mutually beneficial services of protection. Instinctively, members of the soldier's religious community take on the responsibility of support for the soldier's family and loved ones while the soldier is perceived as taking on the role of protector for the religious community. Again, the soldiers noted the congregational support versus formal, institutional support. This aspect of the church and deployed soldier's relationship has not been researched. Hence the specific impact and effects of mutual protecting roles between congregations and deployed soldiers should be further researched to discover the sociological and psychological benefits for subjective well-being.

Conclusion

A couple of weeks after I conducted my last interview session, I reconnected unintentionally with Jackson, the self-declared atheist. We both happened to be attending the same event, and he inquired about my research. I expressed many of the ideas of relational support that I was discovering as I listened to my recorded interviews. Jackson simply nodded and stated that he was envious of the congregational support. He reminded me that he was extremely frustrated during his short deployment to Iraq, and he noted that he could have benefited from what the churches had provided for other soldiers.

Jackson was not alone in his frequent periods of frustration during his deployment in Iraq and Afghanistan. For instance, Allen described some of his frustrations while he was deployed in Iraq:

> There were times that I was angry at the people, the culture, the rules that we had to follow, the whole situation. It wasn't done the way that it could have been done better.... I didn't lose my faith, but I questioned it a lot. I think that the big kicker for that was when they turned the chapel that we had on our operating base into a housing facility for the some of the local Iraqis to live in. So we didn't really have a chapel for a while and it was the final straw. I was mad at everyone involved with that.

In fact, all the soldiers that I interviewed expressed several frustrations with their military experience. However, the Christian soldiers whom I interviewed seemed to exude a confidence that trumped their frustrations.

Many of the soldiers carried with them symbols as reminders of their military duty. For example, Allen has since had Psalm 144 tattooed on his back. Likewise, Jason has "USMC" (United States Marine Corps) tattooed on his arm. Larry carries his Bible everywhere that he goes, and Chris carries a photo of three crosses in his wallet at all times. The religious symbols remind the soldiers of their military service to their country but also reinforce the idea that they participated in a divine service as well. As Allen told me, "God has given people the ability to train me and other Christians in how to defend themselves, their friends in arms, and the country that they love."

In addition, each of the men discovered legitimation from the retelling of certain biblical narratives. Violent stories, such as those of Samson and Jonah, as well as Psalm 144, assure the soldiers that their actions are justified by their country, their church, and ultimately the God they serve. Many of the men whom I interviewed now teach and preach to young people at their own churches and parachurch organizations (e.g., campus ministries). They are continuing a legacy by emphasizing the same stories that have reassured them to the next generation.

The Christian soldiers will not soon forget the care and protection afforded to their family members in their absence. All of these soldiers maintain a high level of appreciation for the service that members of their religious communities provided during their deployment. In fact, all still attend the same churches they did before they were deployed. The mutual roles of protector forge deep and long-lasting relationships, which reinforces the necessity for the religious organization. As Jason stated, "All the close calls [near-death war experiences] does reaffirm my church participation. I do try my best now to make it to church and I feel that God realizes that. I feel that [God] knows that I give it my max effort."

Kenneth Maton's research delineated four distinct aspects of religious support: spiritual coping (prayer), spiritual support (perceived comfort from God), congregational coping (rituals), and congregational support (support from fellow congregants). He found that for people in high-stress situations, "church attendance was not significantly related to well-being; nor, for example might doctrinal orthodoxy ... necessarily be expected to be related to well-being for high life stress subsamples" (Maton 1989: 320). Instead, it was "extensive small-group structures and widespread member involvement" that was of great importance for providing support (Maton 1989: 321). Indeed, the congregational support that is provided to military personnel deployed in combat zones is overwhelmingly provided by individual members of the congregation and not necessarily formally by the institution. Also, congregational support provides an opportunity for Christian devotees to develop their own agency as ministers and protectors.

Rates of suicide and post-traumatic stress disorder (PTSD) are increasing among military personnel in the United States. Figures released for the first six months of 2012 confirmed that more military personnel had committed suicide than had been killed on the battlefield (Williams 2012). Specifically, 2012 witnessed an 18 percent increase in military suicides compared to the same period in 2011. Also on the increase were combat-related PTSD diagnoses. Of the two million deployed military personnel who seek medical attention, it is estimated that over 56 percent are diagnosed with multiple mental disorders, of which PTSD is prevalent (Kaiser 2012). PTSD can lead to relational, substance abuse, and financial problems. At a time when soldiers are returning home from combat deployment, the necessity of relational support services provided by local religious organizations should be given more attention. The role of religious organizations in assimilating and reintegrating combat duty soldiers into U.S. society could prove extremely essential for the well-being of numerous military personnel and their families.

References

Baumeister, Roy, and Mark Leary. 1995. "The Need to Belong: Desire for Interpersonal Attachments as a Fundamental Human Motivation." *Psychological Bulletin* 117: 497–529.

Bielo, James. 2009. *Words upon the Word: An Ethnography of Evangelical Group Bible Study*. New York: NYU Press.

Campbell, James, Dong Phil Yoon, and Brick Johnstone. 2008. "Determining Relationships between Physical Health and Spiritual Experience, Religious Practices, and Congregational Support in a Heterogeneous Medical Sample." *Journal of Religious Health* 49: 3–17.

Curtis, Karen. 1999. "'Bottom-up' Poverty and Welfare Policy Discourse: Ethnography to the Rescue?" *Urban Anthropology Studies of Cultural Systems and World Economic Development* 28: 103–40.

Dezutter, Jessie, Koen Luyckx, Linda A. Robertson, and Dirk Hutsebaut. 2010. "Life Satisfaction in Chronic Pain Patients: The Stress-Buffering Role of the Centrality of Religion." *Journal for the Scientific Study of Religion* 49: 507–16.

Elisha, Omri. 2004. "Sins of Our Soccer Moms: Servant Evangelism and the Spiritual Injuries of Class." In *Local Actions: Cultural Activism, Power, and Public Life in America*, edited by Melissa Checker and Maggie Fishman, 136–58. New York: Columbia University Press.

Ellison, Christopher. 1991. "Religious Involvement and Subjective Well-Being." *Journal of Health and Social Behavior* 32: 80–99.
Ellison, Christopher, and Linda George. 1994. "Religious Involvement, Social Ties, and Social Support in a Southeastern Community." *Journal for the Scientific Study of Religion* 33: 46–61.
Ellison, Christopher, Jinwoo Lee, Maureen Benjamins, Neal Krause, Daniel Ryan, and John Marcum. 2008. "Congregational Support Networks, Health Beliefs, and Annual Medical Exams: Findings from a Nationwide Sample of Presbyterians." *Review of Religious Research* 50: 176–93.
Erbes, C., J. Westermeyer, B. Engdahl, and E. Johnsen. 2009. "Post-Traumatic Stress Disorder and Service Utilization in a Sample of Service Members from Iraq and Afghanistan." *Military Medicine* 172: 359–63.
Harding, Susan Friend. 2000. *The Book of Jerry Falwell: Fundamentalist Language and Politics*. Princeton, NJ: Princeton University Press.
Idler, Ellen L. 1987. "Religious Involvement and the Health of the Elderly: Some Hypotheses and an Initial Test." *Social Forces* 66: 226–38.
Kaiser, Dakota J. 2012. "Combat Related Post Traumatic Stress Disorder in Veterans of Operation Enduring Freedom and Operation Iraqi Freedom: A Review of the Literature." *Graduate Journal of Counseling Psychology* 3(1): Article 5. Available at http://epublications.marquette.edu/gjcp/vol3/iss1/5.
Kent, Daniel. 2010. "Onward Buddhist Soldiers: Preaching to the Sri Lankan Army." In *Buddhist Warfare*, edited by Michael K. Jerryson and Mark Juergensmeyer, 157–78. New York: Oxford University Press.
Koenig, Harold G., Michael E. McCullough, and David B. Larson. 2001. *Handbook of Religion and Health*. New York: Oxford University Press.
Krause, Neal. 2002. "Church-Based Social Support and Health in Old Age: Exploring Variations by Race." *Journal of Gerontology* 57B: S332–47.
Krause, Neal. 2003. "Religious Meaning and Subjective Well-Being in Late Life." *Journal of Gerontology* 58B: S160–70.
Krause, Neal. 2009. "Church-Based Social Relationships and Change in Self-Esteem over Time." *Journal for the Scientific Study of Religion* 48: 756–73.
Krause, Neal, Christopher Ellison, Benjamin Shaw, John Marcum, and Jason Boardman. 2001. "Church-Based Social Support and Religious Coping." *Journal for the Scientific Study of Religion* 40: 637–56.
Kvale, Steinar. 1996. *InterViews: An Introduction to Qualitative Research Interviewing*. Thousand Oaks, CA: Sage.
Levin, Jeffrey. 2001. "God, Love, and Health: Findings from a Clinical Study." *Review of Religious Research* 42: 277–93.
Levin, Jeffrey, and R. Taylor. 1997. "Age Differences in Patterns and Correlates of the Frequency of Prayer." *The Gerontologist* 37: 75–88.
Malley, Brian. 2004. *How the Bible Works: An Anthropological Study of Evangelical Biblicism*. Walnut Creek, CA: AltaMira Press.

Maton, Kenneth. 1989. "The Stress-Buffering Role of Spiritual Support: Cross-Sectional and Prospective Investigations." *Journal for the Scientific Study of Religion* 28: 310–23.

McCullough, Michael, Kenneth Pargament, and Carl Thoresen. 2000. *Forgiveness: Theory, Research, and Practice*. New York: Guilford Press.

McDaniel, Justin. 2011. *The Lovelorn Ghost and the Magical Monk: Practicing Buddhism in Modern Thailand*. New York: Columbia University Press.

Perry, B. Gail Frankel. 1998. "The Relationship between Faith and Well-Being." *Journal of Religion and Health* 37: 125–36.

Pew Research Center. 2008. "Public Attitudes toward the War in Iraq: 2003–2008." Available at http://pewresearch.org/pubs/770/iraq-war-five-year-anniversary.

Pew Research Center. 2012. "The American-Western European Values Gap: American Exceptionalism Subsides." Available at http://www.pewglobal.org/2011/11/17/the-american-western-european-values-gap/?src=prc-headline.

Pollner, Melvin. 1989. "Divine Relations, Social Relations, and Well-Being." *Journal of Health and Social Behavior* 30: 92–104.

Schensul, Stephen L., Jean J. Schensul, and Margaret Diane LeCompte. 1999. *Essential Ethnographic Methods: Observations, Interviews, and Questionnaires*. Walnut Creek, CA: AltaMira Press.

Schumaker, John, ed. 1992. *Religion and Mental Health*. New York: Oxford University Press.

Sloan, Richard P. 2006. *Blind Faith: The Unholy Alliance of Religion and Medicine*. New York: St. Martin's.

Watt, David Harrington. 2002. *Bible-Carrying Christians: Conservative Protestants and Social Power*. Oxford: Oxford University Press.

Wikstrom, Owe. 1987. "Attribution, Roles and Religion: A Theoretical Analysis of Sundén's Role Theory of Religion and Attributional Approach to Religion Experience." *Journal for the Scientific Study of Religion* 26: 390–400.

Williams, Timothy. 2012. "Suicides Outpacing War Deaths for Troops." *The New York Times*, June 8. Available at http://www.nytimes.com/2012/06/09/us/suicides-eclipse-war-deaths-for-us-troops.html?_r=0.

7

The Impact of Church Attendance on the Decline in Female Happiness in the United States

G. Alexander Ross

"We all certainly desire to live happily," wrote St. Augustine of Hippo late in the fourth century (Augustine 1983). This is still true in the twenty-first century, though few of us examine happiness with Augustine's philosophical depth. We suppose that we are happier today than the people of the fourth century were, because we make the assumption that societal advances bring us more happiness. So it surprises us when, as social conditions improve, we do not become happier.

Such a finding serves as the basis for what two researchers have described as the "paradox of declining female happiness" in the United States (Stevenson and Wolfers 2009). Although objective indicators suggest that the past few decades have brought improvement to the lives of American women, Stevenson and Wolfers present a variety of measures of subjective well-being showing that over that time, "women's happiness has declined both absolutely and relative to men" (2009: 190).

Many economic and educational indicators demonstrate improved conditions for women relative to men. Wages, labor force participation, and occupational distribution among women over the past few decades have grown closer to levels that are characteristic of men (Blau 1998; Lee and Mather 2008). Educational outcomes have also improved dramatically for women; for example, by 1980, the number of women attending colleges had surpassed male attendance, and the trend has continued (Freeman 2004; Snyder, Dillow, and Hoffman 2009).

Yet these and other social changes have entailed costs as well as benefits. Women's greater participation in the economy and in education often conflicts with the traditional roles of wife and mother that remain attractive to women. These new expectations that women can "do it all" have resulted in increased stress and physical and emotional exhaustion (Soares, Grossi, and Sundin 2007). They have also introduced further ambiguity about the role of women in society and have often compromised the social integration of the families, communities, and associations to which women belong (Putnam 2000). This combination of uncertain expectations and weakened social ties has long been recognized as a threat to the well-being of the human person (Durkheim 1951).

A variable of considerable relevance to these social changes, one that Stevenson and Wolfers did not include in their analysis, is church attendance. Research has shown that American women are more likely than men to attend church regularly, suggesting that this is a more important activity in women's lives than it is in the lives of men. Regular church attendance offers protection against both the anomic and egoistic tendencies in modern society that can undermine one's sense of well-being. In this social context, traditional beliefs and values centered on transcendent truths are honored and reinforced, providing a source of meaning and purpose that helps churchgoers to face the stresses of everyday living and contributes to a positive evaluation of life. Although religious institutions have not been immune to the modernizing forces that have undermined many traditional beliefs and practices, the more successful churches do appear to attract people because of their ability to satisfy this need for transcendent meaning (Stark and Smith 2010).

Regular attendance at a service of religious worship also provides opportunities to build social relationships around the common pursuit of subjectively important otherworldly goals. Church attendance inhibits social isolation, which, the literature shows, is a strong contributor to unhappiness (Baumeister and Leary 1995: 510). Membership and attendance at church functions offer women not only opportunities for interaction but also assistance in some of the responsibilities of child-rearing. Furthermore, for Christians and those of some other faiths, the interpersonal contact facilitated by regular church attendance is not only with other people, but also with a loving God.

As we would expect, the literature does find that church attendance is positively associated with self-reported happiness (Green and Elliott 2010;

Lewis and Cruise 2006; Stark and Meier 2008). Yet while attending church may offer some antidote to the harmful effects of social changes over the past few decades, church attendance itself appears to have declined in the United States over this period, although it might have stabilized in the last decade or two (Miller and Nakamura 1996; Presser and Chaves 2007). The simultaneous declines in church attendance and happiness among women suggest that there could be a significant association between the two.

The hypothesis guiding this research is that the decline in female happiness over the past three and a half decades is in part a result of the drop in regular church attendance, an activity that normally supports the meanings and purposes of people's lives, helping to sustain in them a positive and hopeful perspective. In this study, I will first seek to replicate the analysis of Stevenson and Wolfers that shows a decline in happiness among women over the past three and half decades. I will then examine church attendance as a factor that may help to account for this decline in women's happiness during this period.

Methods

The data used in the present study are drawn from the comprehensive file of the General Social Survey (GSS) for the years 1972–2008 (Davis and Smith 2009). Stevenson and Wolfers used the same data source, although the latest year available at the time of their research was 2006.

While the literature contains a variety of measures of happiness (Diener 2000; Lewis and Cruise 2006), I measure happiness in this study with the GSS variable HAPPY, a simple three-category self-report of trait happiness, the same item that Stevenson and Wolfers used. The question is worded identically in all years of the GSS: "Taken all together, how would you say things are these days—would you say that you are very happy, pretty happy, or not too happy?" For the purposes of this study, I reversed the original codes given to the answers, so "very happy" is coded as 3, "pretty happy" as 2, and "not too happy" as 1. This results in a simple ordinal measure in which higher values indicate greater self-reported happiness.

For time-series data, it is important to maintain stability in measurement in order to gauge actual change rather than variation in the measuring instrument. In the case of the variable HAPPY, some inadvertent measurement variation did occur in the GSS (Smith 1985, 1990). In all years other than 1972, a question on marital happiness (HAPMAR) preceded HAPPY. Furthermore, in every year other than 1972 and 1985, HAPPY was preceded by a five-item satisfaction scale. Testing done at the GSS found evidence that scores on personal happiness are significantly higher for married people when preceded by an item on marital happiness and significantly lower for all respondents when not preceded by the five-item satisfaction scale (Smith 1990). Following the advice of Smith and the procedure used by Stevenson and Wolfers (2008, 2009), I adjusted the data for these variations by modifying the GSS sampling weights in the dataset.[1]

I made two other adjustments to the dataset that followed the procedure of Stevenson and Wolfers. In 1982 and 1987, the GSS oversampled the Black population; and in 2006 and 2008, interviews in Spanish were offered. In my dataset, I dropped the 1982 and 1987 Black oversamples; I also dropped the 2006 and 2008 interviews that would have been excluded as a language problem had Spanish not been offered in those two years.

Replication with Additional Data

To provide a baseline for evaluating the impact of church attendance, we will first examine the pattern of change in happiness among women and men in the GSS sample from 1972 to 2008. It is appropriate first to present this pattern graphically to give the reader a visual summary of the changes in happiness over the period studied. Figure 7-1 presents the trends in mean happiness score from 1972 to 2008 for women compared to men. The means are weighted as described above and so are adjusted for the various measurement issues discussed earlier.

With the exception of the addition of the 2008 GSS data, the numbers displayed in Figure 7-1 appear to coincide precisely with those constructed by Stevenson and Wolfers (2009: 197). For women, the general trend begins

---

[1] Stevenson and Wolfers provide on their personal websites the Stata code for this adjustment. I updated this code to Stata version 11 and used it to adjust the data. Unless indicated otherwise, these adjusted data are used throughout. A researcher might consider dropping the cases for the two problematic years rather than applying the adjustment procedure, but because this study is intended as a replication of Stevenson and Wolfers' research, I wanted to maintain as much comparability with their procedures as possible. Furthermore, the authors' adjustments appear sound, and it would be unfortunate to lose two years of the time series unnecessarily. Nevertheless, I made several tests in which I excluded the years 1972 and 1985 and found that while many of the coefficients declined very slightly, the results were consistent with the adjusted dataset including all years.

7 | Impact of Church Attendance on the Decline in Female Happiness

Figure 7-1: Change in Happiness among U.S. Women and Men, 1972–2008

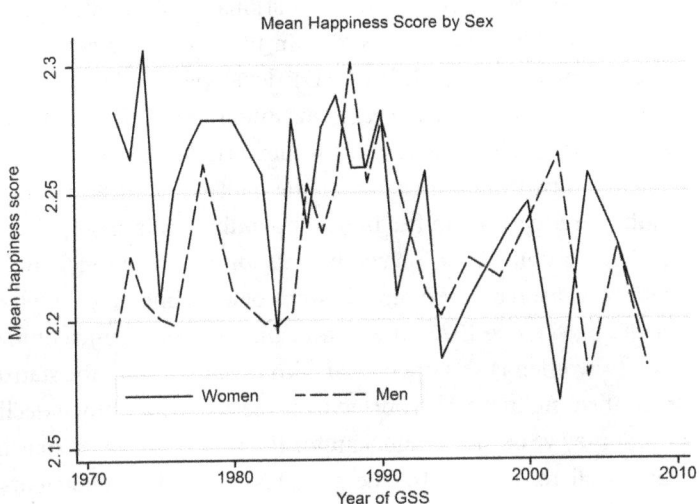

Source: Data from GSS, 1972–2008. Sample weighted as described in text.

at a high level of general happiness, considerably above the level for men, but drops toward the end of the first decade of the survey. The variation over the following years reflects much the same pattern as that for the men and ends in 2008 close to its lowest level in the series. For men, the trend begins low and climbs to its highest point in 1988, in the middle of the series. From there, it decreases in an irregular pattern until, by the end of the series, it reaches a level near its series low, a level nearly identical to that for women. The entire period appears to have begun, therefore, with a clear advantage in happiness for women but ended with a marked decline in women's happiness to a level approximately equal to that of men.

To examine the change in happiness more precisely, I followed Stevenson and Wolfers in constructing two time-trend variables, where female_time = female × (year − 1972)/100 and male_time = male × (year − 1972)/100. These two time variables along with a dummy variable for sex (female) become the principal independent variables in an ordered probit regression in which the standard errors are clustered by year of the survey. In addition to the simple model, I constructed a model that controls for the exogenous variables of age, race, and nativity and a model that controls for these exogenous variables plus a series of socioeconomic variables, including marital status, number of children, religion, region, employment status, real income, and educational attainment. Because of its wide acceptance in studies of religion in the United States, I used the religious traditions variable (RELTRAD) developed by Steensland and colleagues (2000) in place of the religious affiliation indicator employed by Stevenson and Wolfers. The results for these models are shown in Table 7-1. For readability, the coefficients for the controls are not included in the table; they are reported in full in the appendix to this article.

The ordered probit regression coefficients for all three models are consistent with Stevenson and Wolfers' findings of a decline in female happiness over the years since 1972. The significant negative coefficient for the time trend for women is sustained even with the addition of the statistical controls, confirming that self-reported happiness among women declined during the survey years. The coefficient for the time trend for men is non-significant in all three models. The significant positive coefficients for the female dummy variable in all three ordered probit models indicate a higher level of general happiness overall for women than for men.

While the trend in women's happiness is statistically significant, its substantive significance should also be explored. Stevenson and Wolfers offer assistance here by comparing the magnitude of the decline in women's happiness relative to men's happiness to the impact of a factor that is well known to produce changes in self-reported happiness: unemployment. Basing their comparison on an earlier study conducted by Wolfers (2003), they estimate that "the relative decline in the subjective well-being of US women over the past 35 years is roughly comparable to the effects of an 8½ percentage point rise in unemployment rates" (Stevenson and Wolfers 2009: 201). Substituting the coefficients displayed in Table 7-1 would reduce that estimate only slightly (to 8 percent). The change in happiness brought on by, for example, a rise in unemployment from 4 to 12 percent, is likely to be of considerable substantive significance and suggests that the decline in happiness among women displayed by these data is worthy of interest.

The Impact of Church Attendance on Self-Reported Happiness

Having replicated the findings of Stevenson and Wolfers with the 1972–2008 GSS, we now turn to an examination of the relevance of

7 | Impact of Church Attendance on the Decline in Female Happiness

Table 7-1: Trends in Happiness, United States, 1972–2008, GSS

Dependent variable: "Taken all together, how would you say things are these days—would you say that you are very happy, pretty happy, or not too happy?"

Regression Coefficients	Ordered Probit (1)	Ordered Probit (2)	Ordered Probit (3)
Time trend for women	−0.318**	−0.268**	−0.259*
	0.091	0.098	0.114
Time trend for men	0.018	0.052	0.162
	0.087	0.088	0.111
Female indicator	0.091**	0.095**	0.173**
	0.021	0.022	0.027
Control Variables			
Age, race, foreign-born		✓	✓
Socioeconomic controls			✓

Note: N = 42,401 for models with full controls. GSS data cover the years 1972–2008. Robust standard errors are in italics, clustered by year. Exogenous control variables include indicators for ten-year age groups, for race (white, Black, other), and for nativity (foreign-born = 1). Socioeconomic controls include the natural log of real family income, the natural log of real family income squared, and indicators for marital status (married, widowed, divorced, separated, never married), number of children, religious tradition (Black Protestant, evangelical Protestant, Mainline Protestant, Catholic, Jewish, other, unaffiliated), region of residence (nine geographical regions), employment status (full-time, part-time, temporary layoff, unemployed, retired, in school, at home, other), and highest degree attained.
* $p < 0.05$; ** $p < 0.01$.

church attendance for this trend. As we stated above, the general hypothesis guiding this research is that the decline in female happiness over the past three and a half decades is in part a result of the drop in regular church attendance. More specifically, the research hypothesis is that when church attendance is statistically controlled for, the negative trend in female happiness should decrease in strength or disappear altogether.

For this hypothesis to be tenable, we ought first to have some assurance that (1) church attendance is positively associated with general happiness and (2) the frequency of attendance has declined over the past thirty-six years. In addition to the works cited earlier, the dataset indicates that both these criteria are met.

In the GSS, church attendance is measured with the question "How often do you attend religious services?" The question offers nine possible responses, from "never" to "more than once a week." To make the analysis less cumbersome, I will usually use a recoded version of the variable, collapsed into four responses: less than once a year, once to several times a year, one to three times per month, and every week or more. As one can see from the distribution of this variable (broken down by sex) displayed in Table 7-2, the recoded variable yields four approximately equal-sized groups.

It is worth noting that Table 7-2 shows, as expected, that women are more likely than men to attend church regularly. The table indicates that 32 percent of women report that they attend church at least every week compared to 23 percent for men. Adding to this category the next level of attendance, we see that church attendance is important enough to women that 55 percent of them report attending at least once a month compared to 43 percent for men.

A positive association of church attendance with happiness is illustrated in Table 7-3. For this table, the sample is again weighted to adjust for the variation over time in the original measurement of general happiness

Table 7-2: Church Attendance by Sex, GSS, 1972–2008

Church Attendance					
Respondent's Sex	Less Than Once a Year	Once to Several Times a Year	One to Three Times per Month	Every Week or More	Total
Male	28.3%	29.0%	20.0%	22.6%	100.0%
					22,720
Female	20.8%	23.9%	23.0%	32.3%	100.0%
					28,777
Total	24.1%	26.2%	21.7%	28.0%	100.0%
					51,497

Source: GSS 1972–2008. Unweighted sample. Black oversamples and Spanish-only interviews excluded. $\chi^2(3) = 928.6$, $p < 0.001$; gamma = 0.1955, asymptotic standard error (A.S.E.) = 0.006.

Table 7-3: General Happiness by Church Attendance, Women and Men

Church Attendance	General Happiness, Women				General Happiness, Men			
	Not Too Happy	Pretty Happy	Very Happy	Total	Not Too Happy	Pretty Happy	Very Happy	Total
Less than once a year	14.8%	56.2%	29.1%	100.0% 5,336	14.8%	59.8%	25.5%	100.0% 5,585
Once or several times a year	11.4%	57.9%	30.7%	100.0% 6,302	11.2%	59.2%	29.6%	100.0% 6,014
1–3 times a month	9.9%	56.6%	33.6%	100.0% 5,963	9.0%	55.1%	35.9%	100.0% 4,197
Every week or more	8.4%	48.7%	42.9%	100.0% 8,620	7.1%	49.1%	43.8%	100.0% 4,904
Total	10.8%	54.2%	35.0%	100.0% 26,221	10.7%	56.1%	33.1%	100.0% 20,700

Source: GSS 1972–2008. Weighted sample. Women's table: $\chi^2(6) = 447.2$, $p < 0.001$; gamma = 0.17, A.S.E. = 0.008; Men's table: $\chi^2(6) = 522.9$, $p < 0.001$; gamma = 0.21, A.S.E. = 0.009.

and the oversampling of Blacks. The row percentages in the table show a significant positive relationship between frequency of church attendance and general happiness for both sexes. Among women, 43 percent of those who attend church at least weekly report being very happy. The percentage claiming to be very happy drops with each decrement in church attendance, reaching its lowest level of 29 percent for women who attend church less than once a year. Likewise, we see that 8 percent of women who attend church weekly or more report being not too happy. This percentage who are not too happy reaches nearly 15 percent for women who rarely or never attend church.

The men in the sample display a similar pattern, with 44 percent of those with the highest attendance claiming to be very happy compared to just 26 percent of those at the lowest attendance level. Just 7 percent of men who attend church weekly report being not too happy compared to 15 percent for men who attend less than once a year. The relationship between church attendance and general happiness appears to be slightly stronger for men than for women (for men, gamma = 0.21; for women, gamma = 0.17).

Church attendance is, of course, not the only measure of religion associated with happiness, but further analysis of these data indicates that it is an especially salient factor. For example, frequency of prayer is a religious variable that might be expected to affect happiness positively. Measured by the GSS variable PRAY, it has a small positive but significant association with happiness (Spearman $R = 0.07$) and a large positive relationship with church attendance (Spearman $R = 0.52$).[2] To test the relative impact of prayer and church attendance on happiness, I performed a series of ordered probit regressions of happiness on prayer and church attendance, controlling for religious tradition (RELTRAD). For comparability of the coefficients, I standardized the values of PRAY and ATTEND (naming the new variables "Z_PRAY" and "Z_ATTEND").

In the regression of happiness on Z_PRAY alone (with RELTRAD as a control), the coefficient for Z_PRAY was statistically significant, with $\beta_{Z\_PRAY} = 0.088$ (standard error [S.E.] = 0.009, $p < 0.001$). However, when I added Z_ATTEND to Z_PRAY in the regression, the coefficient for Z_PRAY dropped to a very small and nonsignificant value of $\beta_{Z\_PRAY} = 0.002$

---

[2] I reversed the original GSS coding of PRAY so that higher values indicate more frequent prayer.

(S. E. = 0.010, p = 0.839). When I reversed this process, in a regression of happiness on Z_ATTEND (with RELTRAD as a control), the coefficient for Z_ATTEND was much larger at β_{Z_ATTEND} = 0.174 (S.E. = 0.006, $p <$ 0.001). In this case, however, when Z_PRAY was added to the regression, the coefficient for Z_ATTEND remained virtually unchanged at β_{Z_ATTEND} = 0.176 (S. E. = 0.010, $p <$ 0.001).

What these results suggest is that church attendance captures virtually all the association between prayer and happiness but has an additional impact as well. If we take the frequency of prayer as a proxy for spiritual activity, then we might say that church attendance captures most of the positive association between spiritual activity and happiness but that there is something more involved in the link between church attendance and happiness than spirituality. That "something more" is very likely to be the social or communal aspect of regular church attendance. The coefficients above may even give us a basis for a rough approximation of the relative impact of the spiritual and social aspects of church attendance on happiness. The original coefficient for Z_PRAY is about half the size of the coefficient for Z_ATTEND when Z_ATTEND is added to the regression model, suggesting that the spiritual and communal aspects of church attendance are roughly equal in their impact on happiness.

A note of caution is worth being injected here, for what these data demonstrate is simply an association between church attendance and happiness, not a causal relationship. As in so much social research, what we find satisfying are causal hypotheses, but our research designs often give us little basis for specifying the direction or presence of such linkages among our measured variables. I will return to this issue in the discussion section.

The next step is to examine the change in church attendance over the thirty-six years of the GSS. Comparisons between measures of church attendance using interviews and measures based on self-report questionnaires or time-use diaries suggest that questions asked directly by an interviewer tend to elicit higher frequencies of attendance than do the other two techniques (Presser and Stinson 1998). Interviews are subject to a social desirability bias that leads respondents to inflate their reports of behaviors that are evaluated positively by their peers. As a result, the GSS might overstate the frequency of church attendance.

With time-series data on church attendance, however, we also encounter an issue with the stability of measurement over time. If the rate of misreporting changes over time, not only will the average level of attendance be in error, but the trend itself also may be misleading. Unfortunately, unlike the measurement of general happiness discussed earlier, no clear adjustment procedure presents itself. What we can do, however, is to examine the trend in church attendance derived from the GSS data to see whether it is comparable to the results of studies that use methodologies that are less prone to social desirability bias.

Figure 7-2 presents the trends in church attendance by sex derived from the GSS data from 1972–2008. For this figure, I followed Presser and Chaves (2007) in recoding the original nine-point scale to approximate the probability of attending church during the week.[3] The y-axis gives an estimate of the mean probability that respondents would attend church during the week of the interview. Multiplied by 100, these probabilities can be interpreted as the estimated percentage of people attending church during the week.

Both sexes show a statistically significant decline in church attendance over the period of study ($p < 0.001$).[4] However, this trend is more steeply negative for women than for men, a difference that is visible in a careful inspection of Figure 7-2 and confirmed by a postestimation test of the difference between the coefficients for the male and female time trends on probability of attendance ($\chi^2(1) = 4.07, p = 0.044$).

Comparing the trends depicted in Figure 7-2 with research using techniques that are less subject to social desirability bias, we find that the overall level of attendance may be inflated in the GSS data but the trends appear to be compatible. Using time-use diaries as their data source, Presser and Stinson (1998) report a decline from 42 percent attending church in 1965 to 26 percent attending in 1994. This would be a linear decline of 0.55 percent per year. Our GSS data series does not begin until 1972, but it marks a decline from 48 percent (men and women combined) in 1972 to 39 percent in 1994, for a linear decline of 0.41 percent per year. In a later study using time-use diaries, Presser and Chaves (2007) report that after 1994, weekly church attendance stabilized at about

---

[3] The recoding scheme is as follows: several times a week = 0.99, every week = 0.99, nearly every week = 0.85, two to three times a month = 0.58, about once a month = 0.23, several times a year = 0.05, about once or twice a year = 0.02, less than once a year = 0.01, and never = 0.

[4] An ordered probit regression of estimated probability of church attendance on the female and male time trends yielded the following coefficients: $\beta_{female} \times$ time = -0.815 (S.E. = 0.122); $\beta_{male} \times$ time = -0.666 (S.E. = 0.099).

7 | Impact of Church Attendance on the Decline in Female Happiness

Figure 7-2: Estimates of the Probability of Church Attendance during the Week, by Sex

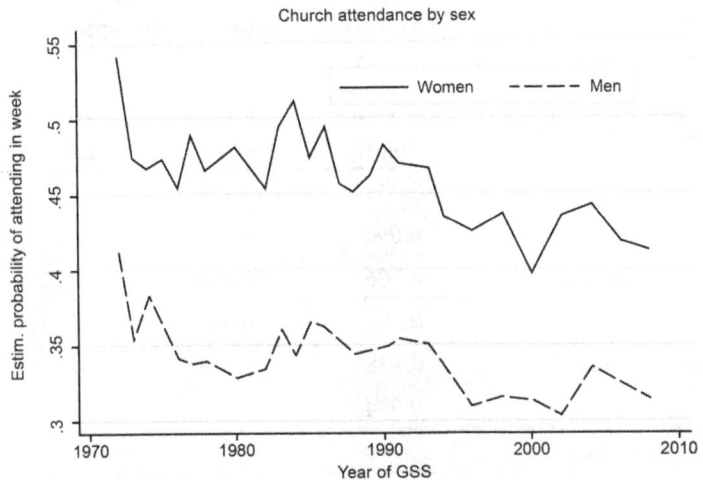

Source: Data from GSS, 1972–2008. Estimated probabilities based on a recoding of the responses to the question "How often do you attend religious services?" See footnote 3 for code definitions.

27–28 percent. Our GSS data series from 1994 forward (men and women combined) indicates that weekly attendance remained between 36 and 39 percent. Thus the GSS series gives estimates of church attendance that are higher than those from time-use diaries but displays trends that are reasonably similar.

Results

To test whether changes in church attendance can account for the decline in happiness among women, I added this variable to the previously constructed probit regressions as three dummy variables, with the lowest attendance level ("less than once a year") as the base. Level 1 of church attendance refers to the response "once to several times a year," level 2 to "one to three times per month," and level 3 to "every week or more." I also tested for interaction between attendance and sex by including interaction factors between the female indicator and the three highest levels of church attendance. The resulting interaction coefficients help to identify whether there are differences for

Table 7-4: Trends in Happiness with Church Attendance as Added Control

Dependent variable: "Taken all together, how would you say things are these days—would you say that you are very happy, pretty happy, or not too happy?"

Regression Coefficients	Ordered Probit (1)	Ordered Probit (2)	Ordered Probit (3)
Time trend for women	−0.231*	−0.156	−0.174
	0.096	0.104	0.118
Time trend for men	0.106	0.154	0.229*
	0.097	0.095	0.117
Female indicator	0.128**	0.119**	0.204**
	0.034	0.035	0.043
Church Attendance			
Attendance level 1	0.141**	0.158**	0.111**
(1 to several times a year)	0.018	0.019	0.021
Attendance level 2	0.294**	0.331**	0.251**
(1 to 3 times a month)	0.024	0.025	0.026
Attendance level 3	0.479**	0.487**	0.379**
(every week or more)	0.027	0.028	0.027
Interaction			
Attendance level 1 by female	−0.056	−0.055	−0.058
	0.031	0.031	0.040
Attendance level 2 by female	−0.128**	−0.107**	−0.108*
	0.037	0.037	0.043
Attendance level 3 by female	−0.114**	−0.094**	−0.068
	0.032	0.033	0.036

(*continued*)

7 | Impact of Church Attendance on the Decline in Female Happiness

Table 7-4: Trends in Happiness with Church Attendance as Added Control (*continued*)

Regression Coefficients	Ordered Probit (1)	Ordered Probit (2)	Ordered Probit (3)
Control Variables			
Age, race, foreign-born		✓	✓
Socioeconomic controls			✓

Note: N = 42,079 for models with full controls. GSS data cover the years 1972–2008. Robust standard errors are in italics, clustered by year. See the note in Table 7-1 for descriptions of controls.
* $p < 0.05$; ** $p < 0.01$.

males and females in the impact of church attendance on happiness. Table 7-4 presents the results of this analysis. (Again, the coefficients are reported in full in the appendix.)

Column 1 in Table 7-4 reports the ordered probit regression coefficients for the model without controls. The first coefficient listed is for the time trend for women, and here we should note that it declines from the value we saw in Table 7-1 (from −0.318 to −0.231), but it remains significant at $p < 0.05$. However, with the addition of the exogenous controls (column 2), the coefficient declines below significance and remains nonsignificant with the addition of the socioeconomic controls (column 3). Let us review the rest of the table before returning to this finding.

The coefficients in the three models for the time trend for men are all positive and larger than they were in Table 7-1, but they remain statistically nonsignificant for two of the models. Only the model with full controls yields a marginally significant ($p = 0.050$) positive coefficient for the time trend for men. The addition of church attendance to the regression analysis therefore appears to lend only a small amount of support for the presence of a positive trend in general happiness for men. The female dummy variable, however, yields significant positive coefficients for all three models, indicating that even when we control for church attendance, women report higher levels of general happiness than men do.

The dummy variables for the three highest levels of church attendance all show significant positive coefficients on general happiness for all three models tested. Furthermore, as the level of attendance rises, the predicted level of happiness increases. Postestimation tests indicate that these increments in the coefficients are statistically significant at $p < 0.001$. Each increase in level of church attendance is associated with a higher level of general happiness.

Interaction effects between levels 2 and 3 of church attendance and the female dummy variable show significant negative coefficients, indicating that the increments in happiness for these two higher levels of attendance (one to three times a month and weekly or more often) are not as strong for females as for males. Nevertheless, postestimation tests indicate that even when the interaction is taken into account, each increment in attendance is significantly associated with an increase in happiness for women as well as for men ($p < 0.001$).

The key finding from Table 7-4 is the weakness in the negative trend in female happiness when we control for church attendance, a finding that supports the hypothesis that church attendance has played a role in the decline of female happiness. This weakness is especially clear when the control variables are included in the regression, for here the time trend for females fails to reach statistical significance. What this suggests is that the drop in church attendance accounts, at least in part, for the observed decline in female happiness from 1972 to 2008.

However, the fact that the coefficient for the time trend for women remains statistically significant in the model without controls prompts us to look more carefully at the impact of church attendance on the trend in happiness for women. While we know that controlling for church attendance reduces the size and significance of the regression coefficient for the time trend for women, we do not know whether this reduction occurs at all levels of church attendance. In other words, there may be interaction between the time trend and church attendance such that there is a significant trend in general happiness at some levels of attendance.

To test for this interaction, Table 7-5 presents the original ordered probit regression model separately for each of the four levels of church attendance. In all four models displayed in Table 7-5, all exogenous and socioeconomic controls used in the earlier regression models are included. (Once more, the coefficients are reported in full in the appendix.)

Of the four coefficients for the time trend for women, only the one for the lowest attendance level—those who attend church less than once a year—is statistically significant. At −0.446, this negative coefficient is substantially stronger than the comparable coefficient of −0.259 from the fully controlled model for all women in Table 7-1. This suggests that for

7 | Impact of Church Attendance on the Decline in Female Happiness

Table 7-5: Trends in Happiness for Each of Four Levels of Church Attendance

Dependent variable: "Taken all together, how would you say things are these days—would you say that you are very happy, pretty happy, or not too happy?"

Regression Coefficients	Ordered Probit for Attendance Level 0 — Less Than Once a Year	Ordered Probit for Attendance Level 1 — One to Several Times a Year	Ordered Probit for Attendance Level 2 — One to Three Times a Month	Ordered Probit for Attendance Level 3 — Weekly or More
Time trend for women	−0.446* *0.189*	0.113 *0.216*	−0.286 *0.222*	−0.217 *0.196*
Time trend for men	0.308 *0.165*	0.264* *0.122*	0.095 *0.198*	0.144 *0.228*
Female indicator	0.298** *0.066*	0.121** *0.045*	0.091 *0.065*	0.097* *0.049*
Control Variables				
Age, race, foreign-born	✓	✓	✓	✓
Socioeconomic controls	✓	✓	✓	✓

Note: $N = 9{,}975$ for attendance level 0; $N = 11{,}211$ for attendance level 1; $N = 9{,}154$ for attendance level 2; $N = 11{,}739$ for attendance level 3. GSS data cover the years 1972–2008. Robust standard errors are in italics, clustered by year. See the note in Table 7-1 for descriptions of controls.
* $p < 0.05$; ** $p < 0.01$.

women, church attendance interacts with the time trend in general happiness; only women who attended church rarely or not at all display a significant decline in happiness over the thirty-six-year period.

All the coefficients for the time trend for men are positive, although only one—for those who attend church one to several times a year—was significant. However, it is important to note that for the group at the lowest level of church attendance, the difference in the trends for males and females is the largest that we find in this study ($\chi^2(1) = 7.37$, $p = 0.0066$). The difference in time trends for this group ($-0.446 - 0.308 = 0.754$) is nearly twice the size of the difference in the time trends reported in Table 7-1. Thus for those who attend church rarely or not at all, the decline in happiness among women is greatest both absolutely and relative to men.

Finally, in three of the four attendance groups, the female dummy variable maintains the significant positive sign that we saw in the earlier tables. This indicates that except for those who attend church one to three times a month, we can say that women had higher levels of general happiness than men throughout the period studied. However, this advantage for women appears to be strongest in the lowest attendance group. For those who attend church more regularly, being female appears to grant less of a bonus in happiness than for those who rarely or never attend church.

Discussion

The results presented above reveal two means by which church attendance appears to have influenced the decline in women's happiness in the United States over the past three and half decades. The first of these, which could be called the direct effect, is a direct consequence of the decline in church attendance with its beneficial effects on happiness. If we assume that the positive association between regular church attendance and general happiness indicates that church attendance is a behavior that augments general happiness, then a reduction in attendance would be expected to reduce that happiness. In other words, the shift over time to lower attendance, a behavior that is associated with decreased general happiness, explains in part the decline in women's happiness from 1972 to 2008.

The second means that the analysis reveals might be called a protective effect. If one supposes that the changes that our society has experienced over the past few decades have had a net detrimental impact on women's happiness, the analysis supports the conclusion that it is women who attend church who have been less susceptible to that impact. The decline in female happiness over the period studied appears to have been experienced most significantly by women who attend church rarely or not at all.

The reduction in the ordered probit regression coefficient for the time trend for women when church attendance was entered into the analysis (Table 7-4) illustrates the first of these two means. Without controls, the coefficient was reduced in size but remained statistically significant; with controls, the coefficients dropped to nonsignificance. The decline or disappearance of a statistical association when one controls for an intervening variable usually indicates that the intervening variable provides an interpretation of the original relationship (Rosenberg 1968). Here, church attendance is the intervening variable, and it interprets for us, in part, the process by which women experienced a decline in their level of general happiness over the past thirty-six years.

It does this only in part, however, for as Table 7-5 demonstrates, the time trend for women appears to remain statistically significant for one of the four major church attendance groups: those who rarely or never attend church. When we reexamine the original ordered probit regression separately for each of the four attendance groups, we find that although three of them maintained the negative sign found in the original table, only one sustained statistical significance. Furthermore, it was among these least-frequent attendees that the decline in happiness for women relative to men was greatest. The results therefore allow us to specify the subpopulation of women who experienced most dramatically the negative trend in general happiness: The women who attended church less than once a year displayed the greatest (and only statistically significant) decline in happiness over the three and half decades covered by the study.

In spite of the fact that church attendance declined for men as well as for women, the men exhibited no decline in happiness over the period studied. In fact, the signs of all the coefficients for the time trends for men are positive, and two are statistically significant. As Stevenson and Wolfers (2009) found, it was women and not men who exhibited a significant decline in self-reported happiness over those thirty-six years.

A question that arises with this finding is why, if church attendance is positively associated with happiness (apparently even more strongly for men than for women), the decline in attendance experienced by both sexes did not lead to a drop in happiness for men. Possible answers are suggested both by the analysis above and by other sources. First, estimations of the decline in church attendance show that women appear to have experienced a steeper decline in attendance over the past few decades than men have. If church attendance is a significant support for a positive sense of well-being, then the fact that women experienced a greater decline in attendance would lead us to expect a greater decline in their happiness.

Commonly observed sex differences in social behavior could also account for the different trend in happiness of women and men. Eagly (2000) summarizes these differences by citing the tendency of women to be drawn to more communal activities while men tend to engage in more agentic behaviors. When one considers the content of the activities associated with church attendance, they appear to be more closely identified with communal rather than agentic behavior and therefore might be expected to serve more immediately the psychological needs of women than of men. Finally, although role expectations for both men and women have changed over the past few decades, it could be argued that they have changed more dramatically for women. In the context of a greater sense of social disruption, perhaps women benefited more than men from the stabilizing influence of regular church attendance.

Although the purpose of the present study is to investigate the impact of church attendance on the decline in women's happiness, it is important to acknowledge that there are many factors that influence happiness. Nevertheless, even if we concentrate on the influence of one factor, caution needs to be exercised in speaking of causal relationships that are tested with time series data, such as have been used in this analysis. Ideally, the investigator would like to have full experimental control over his treatment groups, something that social scientists cannot hope to have for many of the variables they seek to examine. As good a source of data as the GSS is, the samples for each year of the survey do not even comprise the same individuals, although the GSS is now using panel designs for some of its samples. In these circumstances, if we wish to offer intellectually satisfying explanations of social phenomena, our best approach is to subject the statistical associations that we uncover to critical analysis with both statistical controls that check for spuriousness and sound theoretical reasoning.

For example, the positive association that has been found in other research between happiness and being married can be interpreted with either variable posited as the cause. On one hand, being married may increase the happiness of married couples; on the other hand, those who are happy may be more attractive as mates and therefore more likely to marry (Stevenson and Wolfers 2009). However, Baumeister and Leary (1995) observe that the studies that give evidence about the direction of causality have favored the former interpretation.

In the introductory section of this article, I presented theoretical reasons for positing church attendance as the cause of happiness: to the extent to which it provides a transcendent meaning to life and opportunities to form close personal ties, regular church attendance ought to increase a person's sense of well-being and satisfaction with life. In other circumstances, the causal direction may be reversed. For instance, an individual's unhappiness or depression may inhibit his or her desire to engage socially, or the person's cheerless disposition may lead others to discourage his or her attendance. In the absence of means to test this causal hypothesis more rigorously, it is probably most reasonable to assume that the relationship between church attendance and happiness is bidirectional.

Finally, another limitation of the study resides in the conceptualization of happiness underlying the measurement used here and in other studies. St. Augustine (1983) tells us that to be happy, one must possess what one desires, but he adds that possessing what one desires, if that object is hurtful, cannot be called happiness. If we claim to be happy when we desire and obtain what is an apparent good but not a real good, can we truly be called happy? These are philosophical questions that cannot be solved by survey research, but they remind us that measures such as self-reported happiness must be interpreted with caution. We ought, after all, to be concerned with the true good of people and not merely with their subjective evaluation. Nevertheless, regarding the positive impact of church attendance on happiness, St. Augustine would not be surprised at our findings, for he taught that mankind's chief good is God, and "the happy life exists when that which is man's chief good is both loved and possessed."

References

Augustine. 1983. "De Moribus Ecclesiae Catholicae." Translated by Richard Stothert. In *A Select Library of the Nicene and Post-Nicene Fathers*, volume 4: *St. Augustine: The Writings against the Manichaeans and against the Donatists*, edited by Philip Schaff, 41–63. Grand Rapids: Eerdmans.

Baumeister, Roy F., and Mark R. Leary. 1995. "The Need to Belong: Desire for Interpersonal Attachments as a Fundamental Human Motivation." *Psychological Bulletin* 117: 497–529.

Blau, Francine D. 1998. "Trends in the Well-Being of American Women, 1970–1995." *Journal of Economic Literature* 36: 112–65.

Davis, James A., and Tom W. Smith. 2009. "General Social Surveys, 1972–2008." Machine-readable data file. Chicago: National Opinion Research Center [producer]. Storrs, CT: Roper Center for Public Opinion Research, University of Connecticut [distributor].

Diener, Ed. 2000. "Subjective Well-Being: The Science of Happiness and a Proposal for a National Index." *American Psychologist* 55: 34–43.

Durkheim, Emile. 1951. *Suicide: A Study of Sociology*, translated by John A. Spaulding and George Simpson. New York: Free Press.

Eagly, Alice H. 2000. "Gender, Sex, and Culture: Sex Differences and Gender Differences." In *Encyclopedia of Psychology*, volume 2, edited by Alan E. Kazdin, 436–42. Washington, DC: American Psychological Association, Oxford University Press.

Freeman, Catherine E. 2004. *Trends in Educational Equity of Girls and Women: 2004* NCES 2005-016. Washington, DC: National Center for Education Statistics.

Green, Morgan, and Marta Elliott. 2010. "Religion, Health, and Psychological Well-Being." *Journal of Religion & Health* 49: 149–63.

Lee, Marlene A., and Mark Mather. 2008. "U.S. Labor Force Trends." *Population Bulletin* 63: 3–16.

Lewis, Christopher A., and Sharon M. Cruise. 2006. "Religion and Happiness: Consensus, Contradictions, Comments and Concerns." *Mental Health, Religion & Culture* 9: 213–25.

Miller, Alan S., and Takashi Nakamura. 1996. "On the Stability of Church Attendance Patterns during a Time of Demographic Change, 1965–1988." *Journal for the Scientific Study of Religion* 35: 275–84.

Presser, Stanley, and Mark Chaves. 2007. "Is Religious Service Attendance Declining?" *Journal for the Scientific Study of Religion* 46: 417–23.

Presser, Stanley, and Linda Stinson. 1998. "Data Collection Mode and Social Desirability Bias in Self-Reported Religious Attendance." *American Sociological Review* 63: 137–45.

Putnam, Robert D. 2000. *Bowling Alone: The Collapse and Revival of American Community*. New York: Simon & Schuster.

Rosenberg, Morris. 1968. *The Logic of Survey Analysis*. New York: Basic Books.

Smith, Tom W. 1985. "Unhappiness on the 1985 GSS: Confounding Change and Context." GSS Methodological Report No. 34. Chicago: National Opinion Research Center, University of Chicago.

Smith, Tom W. 1990. "Timely Artifacts: A Review of Measurement Variation in the 1972–1989 GSS." Methodological Report No. 56. Chicago: National Opinion Research Center, University of Chicago.

Snyder, Thomas D., Sally A. Dillow, and Charlene M. Hoffman. 2009. *Digest of Education Statistics 2008*. NCES 2009-020. Washington, DC: U.S. Department of Education. Institute of Education Sciences, National Center for Education Statistics.

Soares, J. J. F., G. Grossi, and Ö. Sundin. 2007. "Burnout among Women: Associations with Demographic/Socio-Economic, Work, Life-Style and Health Factors." *Archives of Women's Mental Health* 10: 61–71.
Stark, Rodney, and Jared Meier. 2008. "Faith and Happiness." *Review of Religious Research* 50: 120–25.
Stark, Rodney, and Buster G. Smith. 2010. "Conversion to Latin American Protestantism and the Case for Religious Motivation." *Interdisciplinary Journal for Research on Religion* 6: 1–17.
Steensland, Brian, Jerry Z. Park, Mark D. Regnerus, Lynn D. Robinson, W. Bradford Wilcox, and Robert D. Woodberry. 2000. "The Measure of American Religion: Toward Improving the State of the Art." *Social Forces* 79: 291–318.
Stevenson, Betsey, and Justin Wolfers. 2008. "Happiness Inequality in the United States." *Journal of Legal Studies* 37(S2): S33–S79.
Stevenson, Betsey, and Justin Wolfers. 2009. "The Paradox of Declining Female Happiness." *American Economic Journal: Economic Policy* 1: 190–225.
Wolfers, Justin. 2003. "Is Business Cycle Volatility Costly? Evidence from Surveys of Subjective Well-Being." *International Finance* 6: 1–26.

Appendix: Probit Tables with All Coefficients Included

Table 7-1A: Trends in Happiness, United States, 1972–2008, GSS; Ordered Probit Results for All Variables

Dependent variable: "Taken all together, how would you say things are these days—would you say that you are very happy, pretty happy, or not too happy?"

Independent Variable	Ordered Probit Model 1				Ordered Probit Model 2				Ordered Probit Model 3			
	Coef.	Std. Err.	z	P>|z|	Coef.	Std. Err.	z	P>|z|	Coef.	Std. Err.	z	P>|z|
Female_time	−0.318	0.091	−3.5	0.000	−0.268	0.098	−2.72	0.006	−0.259	0.114	−2.26	0.024
Male_time	0.018	0.087	0.21	0.837	0.052	0.088	0.59	0.554	0.162	0.111	1.47	0.143
Female	0.091	0.021	4.27	0.000	0.095	0.022	4.38	0.000	0.173	0.027	6.44	0.000
Race (base = white)												
Black					−0.401	0.023	−17.66	0.000	−0.246	0.044	−5.6	0.000
Other					−0.119	0.041	−2.87	0.004	−0.033	0.046	−0.72	0.469
Age (base = 18–29)												
30–39					0.101	0.018	5.57	0.000	−0.057	0.023	−2.47	0.013
40–49					0.081	0.016	5.1	0.000	−0.112	0.027	−4.15	0.000
50–59					0.107	0.023	4.75	0.000	−0.065	0.033	−1.98	0.047
60–69					0.200	0.022	9.25	0.000	0.118	0.036	3.26	0.001
70–79					0.183	0.023	7.97	0.000	0.233	0.045	5.13	0.000
80 and above					0.067	0.042	1.59	0.112	0.253	0.072	3.54	0.000
Foreign					−0.042	0.015	−2.69	0.007	−0.172	0.022	−7.81	0.000
Marital (base = married)												
Widowed									−0.561	0.025	−22.72	0.000
Divorced									−0.479	0.019	−25.73	0.000
Separated									−0.643	0.035	−18.54	0.000
Never marr.									−0.397	0.034	−11.69	0.000
Region (base = E. N. Cen.)												
N. Eng.									0.065	0.033	2.01	0.045
Mid Atl.									−0.046	0.021	−2.18	0.029
W. N. Cen.									0.055	0.021	2.64	0.008
S. Atl.									0.073	0.021	3.48	0.001
E. So. Cen.									0.134	0.023	5.71	0.000
W. So. Cen.									0.076	0.024	3.15	0.002
Mtn.										0.024	1.79	0.074

(continued)

Table 7-1A: Trends in Happiness, United States, 1972–2008, GSS; Ordered Probit Results for All Variables (*continued*)

Independent Variable	Ordered Probit Model 1			Ordered Probit Model 2			Ordered Probit Model 3		
	Coef.	Std. Err.	z	$P > |z|$	Coef.	Std. Err.	z	$P > |z|$	Coef.	Std. Err.	z	$P > |z|$
Pacif.									0.005	0.019	0.28	0.779
Reltrad (base = Ev. Prot.)												
Blk. Prot.									0.004	0.051	0.08	0.940
Mainline Prot.									0.010	0.017	0.61	0.544
Cath.									-0.059	0.016	-3.62	0.000
Jewish									-0.179	0.065	-2.74	0.006
Other									0.005	0.051	0.1	0.918
Unaffil.									-0.135	0.022	-6.2	0.000
Wrkstat (base = full-time)												
Wrk. part-time									-0.036	0.020	-1.79	0.073
Temp. not wrk.									-0.091	0.037	-2.48	0.013
Unempl.									-0.394	0.046	-8.62	0.000
Retired									0.029	0.031	0.93	0.353
School									0.134	0.036	3.76	0.000
Keep house									-0.033	0.025	-1.31	0.190
Other									-0.257	0.060	-4.3	0.000
Nat. log. Realinc									-0.453	0.079	-5.73	0.000
Nat. log. Realinc squared									0.031	0.004	7.7	0.000
Degree (base = h.s.)												
Less than h.s.									-0.077	0.018	-4.15	0.000
Jun. col.									0.068	0.030	2.28	0.023
Bachelor's									0.090	0.023	3.99	0.000
Graduate									0.101	0.029	3.49	0.000
Children (base = 0)												
1									-0.106	0.014	-7.45	0.000
2									-0.073	0.017	-4.37	0.000
3									-0.082	0.023	-3.56	0.000
4									-0.054	0.028	-1.92	0.055
5									-0.075	0.031	-2.4	0.016

Table 7-4A: Trends in Happiness with Church Attendance as Added Control; Results for All Variables

Dependent variable: "Taken all together, how would you say things are these days—would you say that you are very happy, pretty happy, or not too happy?"

Independent Variable	Ordered Probit Model 1				Ordered Probit Model 2				Ordered Probit Model 3			
	Coef.	Std. Err.	z	P > |z|	Coef.	Std. Err.	z	P > |z|	Coef.	Std. Err.	z	P > |z|
Female_time	−0.231	0.096	−2.4	0.016	−0.156	0.104	−1.51	0.132	−0.174	0.118	−1.47	0.141
Male_time	0.106	0.097	1.09	0.275	0.154	0.095	1.62	0.104	0.229	0.117	1.96	0.050
Female	0.128	0.034	3.79	0.000	0.119	0.035	3.37	0.001	0.204	0.043	4.78	0.000
Attend (base = never)												
1 to several times/yr.	0.141	0.018	7.74	0.000	0.158	0.019	8.26	0.000	0.111	0.021	5.22	0.000
1–3 times/month	0.294	0.024	12.08	0.000	0.331	0.025	13.35	0.000	0.251	0.026	9.76	0.000
Every wk. or more	0.479	0.027	17.49	0.000	0.487	0.028	17.51	0.000	0.379	0.027	14.07	0.000
Fem. by att4 interaction												

(*continued*)

Table 7-4A: Trends in Happiness with Church Attendance as Added Control; Results for All Variables (*continued*)

Independent Variable	Ordered Probit Model 1				Ordered Probit Model 2				Ordered Probit Model 3			
	Coef.	Std. Err.	z	P>|z|	Coef.	Std. Err.	z	P>|z|	Coef.	Std. Err.	z	P>|z|
Fem. by lev. 1 attend.	−0.056	0.031	−1.82	0.068	−0.055	0.031	−1.77	0.077	−0.058	0.040	−1.46	0.144
Fem. by lev. 2 attend.	−0.128	0.037	−3.49	0.000	−0.107	0.037	−2.86	0.004	−0.108	0.043	−2.55	0.011
Fem. by lev. 3 attend.	−0.114	0.032	−3.57	0.000	−0.094	0.033	−2.82	0.005	−0.068	0.036	−1.9	0.057
Race (base = white)												
Black					−0.445	0.022	−20.45	0.000	−0.284	0.044	−6.53	0.000
Other					−0.129	0.046	−2.83	0.005	−0.055	0.049	−1.13	0.257
Age (base = 18–29)												
30–39					0.080	0.018	4.5	0.000	−0.063	0.023	−2.77	0.006
40–49					0.045	0.016	2.76	0.006	−0.129	0.026	−4.92	0.000
50–59					0.064	0.023	2.8	0.005	−0.087	0.032	−2.74	0.006

(*continued*)

Table 7-4A: Trends in Happiness with Church Attendance as Added Control; Results for All Variables (*continued*)

Independent Variable	Ordered Probit Model 1				Ordered Probit Model 2				Ordered Probit Model 3			
	Coef.	Std. Err.	z	P > |z|	Coef.	Std. Err.	z	P > |z|	Coef.	Std. Err.	z	P > |z|
60–69					0.141	0.022	6.49	0.000	0.081	0.035	2.32	0.020
70–79					0.116	0.024	4.84	0.000	0.180	0.045	4.02	0.000
80 and above					0.020	0.041	0.49	0.626	0.206	0.071	2.91	0.004
Foreign					−0.069	0.018	−3.84	0.000	−0.186	0.024	−7.63	0.000
Marital (base = married)												
Widowed									−0.560	0.024	−23.22	0.000
Divorced									−0.445	0.019	−23.79	0.000
Separated									−0.621	0.034	−18.47	0.000
Never marr.									−0.383	0.033	−11.5	0.000
Region (base = E. N. Cen.)												
N. Eng.									0.082	0.033	2.46	0.014
Mid Atl.									−0.038	0.022	−1.73	0.083

(*continued*)

Table 7-4A: Trends in Happiness with Church Attendance as Added Control; Results for All Variables (*continued*)

Independent Variable	Ordered Probit Model 1			Ordered Probit Model 2			Ordered Probit Model 3		
	Coef.	Std. Err.	z	$P > |z|$	Coef.	Std. Err.	z	$P > |z|$	Coef.	Std. Err.	z	$P > |z|$
W. N. Cen.									0.044	0.020	2.18	0.029
S. Atl.									0.069	0.021	3.27	0.001
E. So. Cen.									0.103	0.023	4.41	0.000
W. So. Cen.									0.057	0.025	2.32	0.020
Mtn.									0.053	0.025	2.17	0.030
Pacif.									0.033	0.019	1.74	0.081
Reltrad (base = Ev. Prot.)												
Blk. Prot.									0.087	0.045	1.92	0.055
Mainline Prot.									0.081	0.018	4.52	0.000
Cath.									0.115	0.020	5.79	0.000
Jewish									−0.027	0.064	−0.41	0.680
Other									0.032	0.047	0.69	0.491

(*continued*)

Table 7-4A: Trends in Happiness with Church Attendance as Added Control; Results for All Variables (*continued*)

Independent Variable	Ordered Probit Model 1				Ordered Probit Model 2				Ordered Probit Model 3			
	Coef.	Std. Err.	z	P>|z|	Coef.	Std. Err.	z	P>|z|	Coef.	Std. Err.	z	P>|z|
Unaffil.									0.017	0.021	0.83	0.408
Wrkstat (base = full-time)												
Wrk. part-time									−0.057	0.020	−2.77	0.006
Temp. not wrk.									−0.081	0.037	−2.2	0.028
Unempl.									−0.384	0.044	−8.7	0.000
Retired									0.031	0.032	0.96	0.335
School									0.098	0.036	2.69	0.007
Keep house									−0.038	0.024	−1.56	0.119
Other									−0.252	0.061	−4.15	0.000
Nat. log. Realinc									−0.488	0.081	−6	0.000

(*continued*)

Table 7-4A: Trends in Happiness with Church Attendance as Added Control; Results for All Variables (*continued*)

Independent Variable	Ordered Probit Model 1				Ordered Probit Model 2				Ordered Probit Model 3			
	Coef.	Std. Err.	z	P>|z|	Coef.	Std. Err.	z	P>|z|	Coef.	Std. Err.	z	P>|z|
Nat. log. Realinc squared									0.032	0.004	7.86	0.000
Degree (base = h.s.)												
Less than h.s.									−0.055	0.018	−3.03	0.002
Jun. col.									0.054	0.030	1.79	0.074
Bachelor's									0.060	0.022	2.69	0.007
Graduate									0.071	0.029	2.45	0.014
Children (base = 0)												
1									−0.105	0.016	−6.57	0.000
2									−0.087	0.017	−5.16	0.000
3									−0.101	0.023	−4.35	0.000
4									−0.071	0.028	−2.56	0.010
5									−0.096	0.030	−3.17	0.002

Table 7-5A: Trends in Happiness for Each of Four Levels of Church Attendance; Results for All Variables

Dependent variable: "Taken all together, how would you say things are these days—would you say that you are very happy, pretty happy, or not too happy?"

Independent Variable	Ordered Probit for "Less Than Once a Year"			Ordered Probit for "One to Several Times a Year"			Ordered Probit for "One to Three Times a Month"			Ordered Probit for "Weekly or More"		
	Coef.	Std. Err.	P > |z|	Coef.	Std. Err.	P > |z|	Coef.	Std. Err.	P > |z|	Coef.	Std. Err.	P > |z|
Female_time	−0.446	0.189	0.018	0.113	0.216	0.602	−0.286	0.222	0.198	−0.217	0.196	0.267
Male_time	0.308	0.165	0.061	0.264	0.122	0.030	0.095	0.198	0.631	0.144	0.228	0.530
Female	0.298	0.066	0.000	0.121	0.045	0.007	0.091	0.065	0.158	0.097	0.049	0.049
Race (base = white)												
Black	−0.272	0.095	0.004	−0.259	0.064	0.000	−0.355	0.076	0.000	−0.279	0.054	0.000
Other	−0.032	0.050	0.526	0.017	0.074	0.819	0.041	0.070	0.562	−0.213	0.070	0.002
Age (base = 18–29)												
30–39	−0.111	0.038	0.004	0.017	0.034	0.613	−0.068	0.041	0.097	0.112	0.046	0.014
40–49	−0.186	0.041	0.000	−0.060	0.040	0.136	−0.170	0.041	0.000	0.004	0.044	0.933
50–59	−0.142	0.053	0.007	0.004	0.052	0.939	−0.090	0.059	0.127	−0.003	0.037	0.942
60–69	−0.048	0.068	0.474	0.123	0.066	0.060	0.142	0.070	0.044	0.196	0.040	0.000

(continued)

Table 7-5A: Trends in Happiness for Each of Four Levels of Church Attendance; Results for All Variables (*continued*)

Independent Variable	Ordered Probit for "Less Than Once a Year"			Ordered Probit for "One to Several Times a Year"			Ordered Probit for "One to Three Times a Month"			Ordered Probit for "Weekly or More"		
	Coef.	Std. Err.	P>|z|	Coef.	Std. Err.	P>|z|	Coef.	Std. Err.	P>|z|	Coef.	Std. Err.	P>|z|
70–79	0.092	0.093	0.321	0.197	0.097	0.042	0.261	0.087	0.003	0.278	0.064	0.000
80 and above	0.167	0.099	0.093	0.293	0.122	0.017	0.261	0.134	0.052	0.261	0.100	0.009
Foreign	−0.354	0.031	0.000	−0.265	0.041	0.000	−0.340	0.045	0.000	0.169	0.039	0.000
Marital (base = married)												
Widowed	−0.589	0.065	0.000	−0.573	0.059	0.000	−0.570	0.067	0.000	−0.536	0.042	0.000
Divorced	−0.428	0.043	0.000	−0.463	0.043	0.000	−0.432	0.046	0.000	−0.466	0.058	0.000
Separated	−0.571	0.068	0.000	−0.589	0.074	0.000	−0.650	0.069	0.000	−0.696	0.101	0.000
Never marr.	−0.421	0.034	0.000	−0.318	0.044	0.000	−0.390	0.046	0.000	−0.401	0.053	0.000
Region (base = E. N. Cen.)												
N. Eng.	0.038	0.053	0.478	0.087	0.062	0.158	−0.097	0.078	0.216	0.134	0.055	0.014
Mid Atl.	−0.118	0.049	0.017	−0.053	0.032	0.105	−0.137	0.052	0.008	0.000	0.041	0.997

(*continued*)

Table 7-5A: Trends in Happiness for Each of Four Levels of Church Attendance; Results for All Variables (*continued*)

Independent Variable	Ordered Probit for "Less Than Once a Year"			Ordered Probit for "One to Several Times a Year"			Ordered Probit for "One to Three Times a Month"			Ordered Probit for "Weekly or More"		
	Coef.	Std. Err.	$P > \lvert z \rvert$	Coef.	Std. Err.	$P > \lvert z \rvert$	Coef.	Std. Err.	$P > \lvert z \rvert$	Coef.	Std. Err.	$P > \lvert z \rvert$
W. N. Cen.	−0.019	0.033	0.573	−0.007	0.050	0.880	−0.120	0.051	0.018	0.082	0.039	0.038
S. Atl.	0.000	0.042	0.993	0.032	0.044	0.473	−0.032	0.051	0.532	0.101	0.043	0.018
E. So. Cen.	−0.010	0.038	0.786	0.149	0.069	0.032	−0.074	0.069	0.283	0.169	0.038	0.000
W. So. Cen.	−0.005	0.053	0.928	0.028	0.054	0.607	−0.094	0.056	0.094	0.105	0.050	0.037
Mtn.	0.050	0.047	0.289	0.004	0.047	0.927	−0.025	0.078	0.745	0.038	0.058	0.515
Pacif.	0.023	0.049	0.640	0.010	0.038	0.800	−0.099	0.066	0.131	0.062	0.051	0.227
Reltrad (base = Ev. Prot.)												
Blk. Prot.	0.120	0.123	0.328	−0.041	0.082	0.614	0.060	0.080	0.450	0.161	0.069	0.020
Mainline Prot.	0.065	0.041	0.111	−0.016	0.029	0.574	−0.028	0.036	0.443	0.186	0.032	0.000
Cath.	0.098	0.046	0.035	0.089	0.037	0.016	−0.080	0.041	0.052	0.162	0.035	0.000
Jewish	0.010	0.038	0.788	−0.051	0.073	0.491	−0.017	0.106	0.876	−0.050	0.185	0.788
Other	−0.133	0.112	0.236	−0.045	0.096	0.639	−0.066	0.120	0.582	0.133	0.063	0.035

(*continued*)

Table 7-5A: Trends in Happiness for Each of Four Levels of Church Attendance; Results for All Variables (*continued*)

Independent Variable	Ordered Probit for "Less Than Once a Year"			Ordered Probit for "One to Several Times a Year"			Ordered Probit for "One to Three Times a Month"			Ordered Probit for "Weekly or More"		
	Coef.	Std. Err.	$P>|z|$	Coef.	Std. Err.	$P>|z|$	Coef.	Std. Err.	$P>|z|$	Coef.	Std. Err.	$P>|z|$
Unaffil.	−0.063	0.105	0.547	−0.145	0.036	0.000	−0.020	0.048	0.668	0.152	0.049	0.002
Wrkstat (base = full-time)												
Wrk. part-time	−0.106	0.046	0.020	−0.090	0.042	0.032	−0.054	0.039	0.167	0.008	0.040	0.845
Temp. not wrk.	0.045	0.084	0.592	−0.211	0.063	0.001	−0.107	0.090	0.231	−0.040	0.099	0.690
Unempl.	−0.384	0.060	0.000	−0.429	0.074	0.000	−0.305	0.107	0.005	−0.415	0.106	0.000
Retired	0.083	0.051	0.103	0.061	0.074	0.411	0.046	0.061	0.450	−0.005	0.053	0.922
School	0.087	0.079	0.270	0.207	0.054	0.000	−0.041	0.096	0.672	0.119	0.074	0.110
Keep house	−0.126	0.042	0.003	−0.075	0.041	0.068	0.003	0.047	0.942	0.015	0.040	0.705
Other	−0.246	0.127	0.053	−0.300	0.104	0.004	−0.214	0.138	0.120	−0.250	0.098	0.010
Nat. log. Realinc	−0.530	0.131	0.000	−0.495	0.143	0.001	−0.426	0.143	0.003	−0.532	0.135	0.000
Nat. log. Realinc squared	0.035	0.007	0.000	0.033	0.008	0.000	0.030	0.008	0.000	0.034	0.007	0.000

(*continued*)

Table 7-5A: Trends in Happiness for Each of Four Levels of Church Attendance; Results for All Variables (*continued*)

Independent Variable	Ordered Probit for "Less Than Once a Year"			Ordered Probit for "One to Several Times a Year"			Ordered Probit for "One to Three Times a Month"			Ordered Probit for "Weekly or More"		
	Coef.	Std. Err.	P > |z|	Coef.	Std. Err.	P > |z|	Coef.	Std. Err.	P > |z|	Coef.	Std. Err.	P > |z|
Degree (base = h.s.)												
Less than h.s.	−0.014	0.037	0.703	−0.053	0.041	0.201	−0.104	0.044	0.019	−0.066	0.039	0.089
Jun. col.	−0.032	0.052	0.537	0.032	0.050	0.522	0.134	0.067	0.047	0.067	0.072	0.355
Bachelor's	0.026	0.045	0.570	0.098	0.043	0.023	0.064	0.032	0.046	0.059	0.040	0.142
Graduate	0.176	0.067	0.008	0.079	0.052	0.129	0.041	0.073	0.575	0.026	0.058	0.646
Children (base = 0)												
1	−0.063	0.032	0.050	−0.135	0.038	0.000	0.189	0.027	0.000	0.070	0.042	0.098
2	−0.032	0.028	0.255	−0.068	0.030	0.021	0.022	0.038	0.562	0.018	0.031	0.563
3	−0.122	0.055	0.027	−0.145	0.044	0.001	0.078	0.040	0.054	0.021	0.037	0.566
4	−0.028	0.071	0.693	−0.118	0.055	0.030	0.095	0.055	0.083	0.021	0.037	0.574
5	−0.162	0.062	0.009	−0.020	0.074	0.791	0.051	0.053	0.338	−0.001	0.039	0.977

8

The Socioeconomic Contribution of Religion to American Society

An Empirical Analysis

Brian J. Grim | Melissa E. Grim

Religion is an active force in the public, professional, and personal lives of many in the United States. Safeguards for religious freedom—including the First Amendment principles of having no established religion and protecting free religious practice—have helped to produce a dynamic religious marketplace, including the ability of each person to have a religion, change religions, or have no religion at all.

A solid body of research has explored the social contributions of religion, which range from increasing civic participation to ministering to spiritual, physical, emotional, economic, and other life needs. Some studies have looked at the social benefits of congregations (Ammerman 2001; Cnaan, Wineburg, and Boddie 1999; and Chaves 1999), including some that have attempted to quantify the social and volunteering benefits that congregations provide to communities (Tirrito and Cascio 2003). Other studies have looked at the role of local religious groups in promoting education and civic engagement (e.g., Regnerus 2001; Muller and Ellison 2001). Studies have also considered how religious participation and programs help decrease crime and deviance (Bainbridge 1989; Hummer et al. 1999; Lester 1987) as well as promote mental health (Johnson, Tompkins, and Webb 2002; Fagan 2006). And yet other studies have looked at how involvement in organized religion improves government stability and economic growth, with the primary mechanism being increased social capital and positive civic networks provided through congregational activities (also see Putnam 2000; Fukuyama 2001; Schwadel 2002; and Zak and Knack 2001).

A recent Supreme Court amicus brief (Picarello et al. 2016) also catalogues a broad body of research specifically on the positive contributions of faith-based organizations to the health and welfare of hundreds of millions of Americans. These include charities such as the Lutheran Services in America, which cares for six million people annually, or about one in every fifty persons in the United States, and Catholic hospitals, which care for one in six U.S. hospital patients. The amicus brief also summarizes studies where faith-based organizations have been found to outperform public counterparts. For instance:

> Faith-based elementary and secondary schools make a distinctive contribution to the education of the Nation's children that public schools have been unable to match. In 2015, the combined average SAT score for students from religious schools was 1596 points, or 134 points higher than the average score of 1462 for public school students. [And s]tudents in religious schools are safer than students in public schools, as measured by fewer instances of violent crime and bullying. A higher percentage of students in religious schools report feeling safe from attack or harm in school compared to their public school peers. (20)

Of course, not every religious organization or group has the same level of impact, and not all of the impact is positive. Indeed, there are high-profile cases where people in religious authority or acting in the name of religion have engaged in destructive activities. These negative impacts range from such things as the abuse of children by some clergy (Cafardi 2008), cases of fraud (De Sanctis 2015), and places of worship becoming recruitment sites for violent extremism (Neumann 2008), all of which detract from the other positive values of religious institutions. Of course, such serious ills affect a wide variety of institutions ranging from major public universities (Moushey and Dvorchak 2013), to publicly traded companies (Gitlow 2005), to online public chatrooms (Erelle 2015). And, while negative news makes news, both sides are important to understand clearly.

Recent studies, such as Numrich and Wedam (2015), provide a more nuanced analysis of the community impact of congregations. In their study of fifteen congregations in the Chicago area—including Catholic parishes, Protestant churches, Jewish synagogues, Muslim mosques, and a Hindu temple—they concluded that religion has a significant role in shaping postindustrial cities, although the impact varies from congregation to congregation. They also provide a helpful framework for analysis of the different types and levels of impact.

In a separate quantitative study on the effect of shutting down a congregation in an inner city, Kinney and Combs (2016) found that this precedes and contributes to the socioeconomic collapse of the community in which the congregation was located. Specifically, their study found that declines in neighborhood viability were significantly related to the closure of congregations characterized by *bridging social capital*, i.e., congregations that connected heterogeneous groups and bridged diversity.

Understanding the socioeconomic value of religion to American society is especially important in the present era characterized by disaffiliation from organized religion. The Pew Research Center study 'Nones' on the Rise,[1] for instance, reports that the number of Americans who are religiously unaffiliated now stands at one-fifth the adult population, while a third of the adults under thirty are unaffiliated. Of the total unaffiliated, nearly 6 percent of the U.S. population identifies as atheist or agnostic, while 14 percent claim no particular religious affiliation. The Pew study found that a majority of the religiously unaffiliated say that they are ambivalent toward religious institutions and some express negative views of religious organizations. For instance, Pew found that a majority of the religiously unaffiliated think that religious organizations are too focused on such things as money and power, and on rules and politics.

At the same time, the Pew study also found that seven in ten religiously affiliated people believe that congregations and religious institutions contributed some or a great deal to solving social problems. However, only 45 percent of the religiously unaffiliated expressed the same. People who identified their religion as "nothing in particular" were evenly split on whether religious institutions were instrumental in solving social problems, while 63 percent of atheists and agnostics said that religious institutions contributed not much or nothing at all to solving social problems.

Given the division of opinion on religion's contribution to American society, this present study seeks to shed light on the topic by making an estimate of religion's socioeconomic value to society. Indeed, we should know if the decline in religion is likely to have negative economic consequences.

In what follows, we provide three estimates of the value of faith to U.S. society. The most conservative estimate takes into account only the

---

1 See http://www.pewforum.org/2012/10/09/nones-on-the-rise/.

revenues of faith-based organizations falling into several sectors: education, healthcare, local congregational activities, charities, media, and food. Our second estimate takes into account the fair market value of congregational social services. This mid-range estimate includes a review of nationally representative survey data on the activities of congregations across multiple faith traditions. It also recognizes the contribution of businesses with religious roots. We then provide a third higher-end estimate based on the annual household incomes of America's religiously affiliated population.

Etimate 1: Revenues of Faith-Based Organizations

This study's conservative estimate of the value of the religious sector to the U.S. economy is based primarily on the *revenues* of religious organizations. We specifically look at the revenues of several main religion sectors: educational institutions, healthcare networks, congregational activities, charitable social services, media, and food. For this economic valuation, we use the most recent year of data available.

Schools: Data on Educational Institutions

We estimate the value of religiously affiliated education to American society by multiplying the numbers of students attending faith-based institutions of higher education, faith-based high school, and faith-based elementary schools by the average cost for each of these three levels of education. For this, we need to know the number of students attending the schools and the average cost of tuition.

Higher Education. Enrollment data for 2011–2012 are available from the National Center for Education Statistics (NCES) and the Institution of Education Sciences (IES).[2] These sources also provide tuition costs for most of the religiously affiliated institutions of higher education, including colleges, universities, theological schools, and seminaries. The totals are summarized in Table 8-1.[3]

---

2   See https://nces.ed.gov/ and http://ies.ed.gov/.
3   In the NCES and IES data there are 1,974,045 students for whom their institution's tuition costs are reported, adding to a total of $45,405,156,773, with an average of $23,001 per student. However, the total number of students enrolled in faith-based higher education according to NCES and IES is 2,033,875, meaning that 59,830 students are without reported tuition data. Applying the known average to these 59,830 students, the total estimated tuition revenues for faith-based institutions of higher education is $46,781,311,080.

8 | The Socioeconomic Contribution of Religion to American Society

Table 8-1: Annual Tuition Payments to Faith-Based Higher Educational Institutions (Estimate)

	Tuition Payments
Total students in faith-based higher ed.	2,033,875
Average tuition/student	$23,001
Total	**$46,781,311,080**

Source: National Center for Education Statistics (NCES) and the Institution of Education Sciences (IES). Data for the cohort entering in 2008. Figures may not total due to rounding of decimals.

Table 8-2: Annual Tuition Payments to Faith-Based Elementary Schools (Estimate)

	Tuition Payments
Elementary students	2,579,858
Average tuition/student	$5,847
Total	**$15,084,427,145**

Source: Number of students from U.S. Department of Education, National Center for Education Statistics NCES, Private School Universe Survey (PSS), 2011–2012; average tuition based on data for Catholic schools from the National Catholic Education Association and used as a proxy for other faith-based schools. Figures may not total due to rounding of decimals.

Elementary and High School Education. The number of students enrolled in faith-based elementary and high schools is available from the U.S. Department of Education, National Center for Education Statistics NCES, Private School Universe Survey (PSS), 2011–2012. However, unlike for higher education, there is no central source for tuition costs at religiously affiliated elementary and high schools. So, we use as a proxy the reported costs of Catholic schools, which account for more than 40 percent of all such faith-based schools.[4] Tables 8-2 and 8-3 summarize faith-based elementary and high school enrollments and estimated revenues.

---

4 While this study does not make cost comparisons between faith-based education and public school education, the National Catholic Educational Association estimates that Catholic schools provide almost $22 billion dollars a year savings for the nation based on a comparison with the costs of public school education as reported by the National Center for Education Statistics.

Table 8-3: Annual Tuition Payments to Faith-Based Secondary Schools (Estimate)

	Tuition Payments
Secondary students	1,025,180
Average tuition/student	$11,790
Total	**$12,086,872,652**

Source: Number of students from U.S. Department of Education, National Center for Education Statistics NCES, Private School Universe Survey (PSS), 2011–2012; average tuition based on data for Catholic schools from the National Catholic Education Association and used as a proxy for other faith-based schools. Figures may not total due to rounding of decimals.

By using tuition revenue, this study arrives at a conservative estimate of the annual value of religiously affiliated education. It is conservative because it neither includes other revenue streams such as donations and grants, nor does it include a valuation of the outreach and public service impacts of religiously affiliated educational institutions. Note that any revenues from congregational education programs such as vocational training and preschools are not counted here.

Data on Health Providers

We estimate the value of religiously affiliated healthcare to American society by adding up the actual annual revenue reported by the largest faith-based healthcare networks in the U.S. Only hospitals and health systems with an active religious affiliation (not just in name) are included, based on their self-descriptions. The health networks included are faith-based networks among the one hundred top-grossing U.S. hospitals and the one hundred top integrated health systems.[5] Revenues were obtained from the reports of the individual health organizations, as shown in Table 8-4.

This is also a conservative estimate because we are neither taking into account all religiously affiliated healthcare providers (we have only identified the largest networks) nor are we estimating the health benefits a

---

[5] These lists are available at Becker's Hospital Review http://www.beckershospitalreview.com/. For Catholic hospital data, we use the overall figure from the Catholic Health Association of the United States.

8 | The Socioeconomic Contribution of Religion to American Society

Table 8-4: Annual Operating Revenues to Major Faith-Based Health Care Systems (Estimate, $Billions)

Health Care Systems	Annual Revenue
Catholic Health Providers	$108.0
Adventist Health System (Florida)	$7.6
Advocate Health Care (Oak Brook, IL)	$5.2
Methodist Hospital (San Antonio)	$5.1
Baptist Medical Center (San Antonio)	$4.5
The Methodist Hospital (Houston)	$4.2
Texas Health Resources (Arlington, TX)	$3.8
Methodist University Hospital (Memphis)	$3.8
Baptist Hospital of Miami	$3.3
Adventist Health (CA)	$3.3
Riverside Methodist Hospital (Columbus, Ohio)	$3.1
Baptist Medical Center Jacksonville (FL)	$2.8
Baptist Health South Florida (Coral Gables)	$2.2
Baptist Memorial Health Care Corp (Memphis)	$1.9
Baptist Healthcare Systems (KY)	$1.6
Baylor Health Care System (Dallas, TX)	$0.5
Total	**$161.0**

Source: Becker's Hospital Review and individual health care system reports; for Catholic hospital data, we use the overall figure from the Catholic Health Association of the United States.
Revenues for 2014. Figures may not total due to rounding of decimals.

substantial body of research has shown to be associated with religious participation.[6] For instance, one rough estimate puts the health savings value of religious participation at $115.5 billion (Stark 2012: 166).

6   Koenig, King, and Carson (2011) in the second edition of Oxford's *Handbook of Religion and Health* note that there have been many thousands of scientific studies on the positive and negative associations between religion and health. For accessible discussions of the benefits, see *The Healing Power of Faith: How Belief and Prayer Can Help You Triumph over Disease* (Koenig and McConnell 1999) and *God, Faith, and Health: Exploring the Spirituality-Healing Connection* (Levin 2001).

Data on Congregational Activities

To estimate the finances and activities of U.S. congregations, we used two nationally representative data sources that included data on multiple faith traditions running the gamut from Adventists to Zoroastrians.

To quantify U.S. congregational finances and activities, we used the National Congregations Study cumulative dataset (1998, 2006–07, 2012) archived at the Association of Religion Data Archives.[7] The National Congregations Study "fills a void in the sociological study of congregations by providing . . . data that can be used to draw a nationally aggregate picture of congregations" (Chaves et al. 1999: 460). The 2012 NCS also includes an oversample of Hispanic congregations.

In order to scale the results to actual dollar and numeric figures, we used the 2010 Religious Congregations and Membership Study (RCMS) conducted by representatives of the Association of Statisticians of American Religious Bodies (ASARB).[8] RCMS 2010 provides data on the number of congregations, members, adherents, and attendees for the 236 religious bodies and denominations participating in the study. Study participants included 217 Christian denominations, associations, or communions (including Latter-day Saints, Messianic Jews, and some Unitarian/Universalist groups); counts of Jain, Shinto, Sikh, Tao, and National Spiritualist Association congregations, and counts of congregations and individuals for Bahá'í, three Buddhist groupings, four Hindu groupings, four Jewish groupings, Muslims, and Zoroastrians. The study also went to special efforts to identify and include data from several religious bodies which have not traditionally participated or have been underrepresented in similar past studies, including improved coverage of predominantly African American religious

---

[7] See http://www.thearda.com/Archive/Files/Descriptions/NCSIII.asp. The data were gathered as part of the General Social Survey (GSS) interviews. But instead of a sample of individuals, these interviews were of a nationally representative sample of congregations via a 50-minute interview with one key informant, usually a clergyperson, from each congregation. The GSS is a face-to-face interview conducted by experienced and well-trained interviewers; in 1998, 2006–2007, and 2012, interviewers were instructed to glean from respondents as much locational information about their congregations as possible. The 1998 and 2012 NCS data were collected by the same interviewers who collected data from GSS respondents; in 2006–2007, some of the data were also collected by phone-bank interviewers.

[8] See http://www.rcms2010.org/ and http://www.thearda.com/rcms2010/.

8 | The Socioeconomic Contribution of Religion to American Society

bodies. The 236 groups surveyed have among them 344,894 congregations and 150,686,156 adherents.[9]

Combining these two sets of data makes it possible, for instance, to estimate the finances for U.S. congregations nationwide as well as the number of congregations engaging in certain activities and ministries. For instance, among the 4071 congregations surveyed in the 2012 National Congregations Study, the average annual income from all sources was $242,910 per congregation (Table 8-5, data point 1). Of this, $216,143 comes from individuals' donations, dues, or contributions (Table 8-5, data point 2). Multiplying this figure by the 344,894 congregations identified by the RCMS study produces an estimated annual income from individual donations for U.S. congregations of $74.5 billion ($74,546,330,721).

As a way to check the plausibility of this figure, we can compare it with the overall sum donated by individuals to religion in 2012. According to the Giving USA foundation, American individuals donated a total of $101.5 billion to religious organizations.[10] Thus, the $74.5 billion estimate (three-quarters of the total) seems plausible considering that religious congregations tend to encourage their members to channel their giving through their local congregation. The total income of $83.8 billion (Table 8-5, data point 1) takes into account other revenue sources including endowments and grants.

Charities

There are thousands of religious charities carrying out the work of hundreds of faith traditions in the United States. Because a central database on the revenues and activities of all of these organizations was not readily available to us, we gathered data on the revenue of charities by identifying the largest faith-based charities in the U.S. from the overall list of the fifty largest U.S. charities. Of these, twenty are faith-based, ranging from the American Jewish Joint Distribution Committee to Lutheran Services in America. The total revenues of these organizations are readily available, as shown in Table 8-6.

We also confirmed that the organizations have a religious element as part of their self-description. For some, the religious element may be deemphasized or not highlighted prominently. The Young Men's Christian

---

9 For more information on the RCMS 2010 study and its methodology, see http://www.rcms2010.org.

10 See http://money.cnn.com/2013/06/21/pf/charitable-donations/.

(text continues on page 220 below)

Table 8-5: Nationally Representative Data on Activities of U.S. Congregations (Multiple Faiths), ordered by amount or frequency of occurrence

Italicized data points indicate activities of congregations across multiple faith traditions that provide for civic life and social cohesion above and beyond providing for the spiritual lives of congregants.

Data point	Income and Spending	Avg. per congregation*	Total amount across 344,894 congregations*
1	Congregation's Annual Income	$242,910	$83,778,191,193
2	Amount of Income from Individual's Donations, Dues, Contributions	$216,143	$74,546,330,721
3	*Total Money Spent on Social Programs 2012*	$26,781	$9,236,699,335
4	*Total Money Spent on Social Programs 2006*	$9,190	$3,169,472,392
5	*Total Money Spent on Social Programs 1998*	$6,880	$2,372,839,680
6	Amount Given to Other Religious Organizations	$2,997	$1,033,799,071
7	*Government Grants, Contracts, Fees for Social Service Projects*	$732	$252,327,899
8	*Amount Received from Foundations, Businesses, United Way*	$354	$122,137,312

Sources: Questions are from the National Congregations Study (NCS) cumulative dataset (1998, 2006–07, 2012) archived at the Association of Religion Data Archive; overall total of congregations from the Religious Congregations and Membership Study (RCMS) conducted by representatives of the Association of Statisticians of American Religious Bodies (ASARB). Data points are for the cumulative average across the years of the NCS, where available. Where not, the most recent year of data is prioritized.

For this study we weighted the data by WTA3CNGD to have results representing the average congregation's perspective.

* Dollar figures and total numbers are reported in detail based on calculations from the dataset; the actual precision is less, but is 95% likely to be within the survey's margin of error of +/−3%. Figures may not total due to rounding of decimals.

8 | The Socioeconomic Contribution of Religion to American Society

Table 8-6: Annual Operating Revenues of Major Faith-Based Charities (Estimate, $Billions)

Charities	Annual Revenue
Lutheran Services in America	$21.0
YMCA USA	$6.6
Catholic Charities	$4.5
Salvation Army	$4.1
Habitat for Humanity	$1.7
Food for the Poor	$1.0
World Vision	$1.0
Boy Scouts of America	$0.9
Compassion International	$0.7
Catholic Relief Services	$0.6
Campus Crusade for Christ	$0.5
Catholic Medical Mission Board	$0.5
Samaritan's Purse	$0.5
Feed the Children	$0.5
American Jewish Joint Distribution Committee	$0.4
Map International	$0.3
Operation Blessing International Relief & Development	$0.3
Cross International (not affiliated with the Red Cross)	$0.3
Total	**$45.3**

Source: Faith-based charities identified by their self-description from a list of the fifty largest U.S. charities on the Forbes top charities list: http://www.forbes.com/top-charities/list/. Revenues for 2014. Figures do not total due to rounding of decimals.

Association, commonly known as the Y.M.C.A., and more recently being branded just as the Y, still has a clear statement of a religious mission on the bottom of each webpage: "The YMCA is a nonprofit organization whose mission is to put Christian principles into practice through programs that build healthy spirit, mind and body for all."[11]

The Boy Scouts of America, on the other hand, is not affiliated with a single faith tradition, but clearly states that being reverent is one of its core values: "Reverent: A Scout is reverent toward God. He is faithful in his religious duties. He respects the beliefs of others."[12] The Boy Scouts also have a special focus on faith and religion, with special resources for Methodists, Baptists, Catholics, Muslims, Judaism and Latter-day Saints (Mormons).[13] They even have Awards/badges for knowledge in all these and many other faiths, including Hinduism, Sikhism, the Baha'i faith, etc.[14] Moreover, scout troops can also be affiliated with a church or faith group. Indeed, nearly twice as many boys belong to religiously affiliated scout troops (1.58 million) as belong to troops with no religious affiliation (0.85 million).[15]

Media

Data on the religious media industry in the United States are hard to come by. Those data that are offered online are largely unsourced and difficult to verify. For instance, one online report suggests that Christian media alone accounts for some $3.6 billion (Gaille 2013). Another better-sourced estimate from several years ago (Einstein 2008) puts the figures for the entire market at nearly double Gaille's figure:

> In 2003, research estimates put the market for religious publishing and products at $6.8 billion and growing at a rate of nearly 5 percent annually. This market is subdivided into three categories: books (the largest segment, with $3.5 billion in sales and a 7 percent growth rate); stationary/giftware/merchandise (sales at $1.4 billion and a 4.5 percent

---

11 See bottom of this page: http://www.ymca.net/.
12 See http://www.scouting.org/FILESTORE/marketing/pdf/02-882.pdf, page 28.
13 See http://www.scouting.org/home/marketing/current%20initiatives/faith.aspx on the faiths initiative, and here for the Mormon resources http://www.scouting.org/about/factsheets/operating_orgs/latter-day_saints.aspx. (The links in notes 13–15 are no longer active.)
14 See http://bsaseabase.org/home/awards/religiousawards/chart.aspx.
15 See http://www.scouting.org/About/FactSheets/operating_orgs.aspx.

growth rate); and audio/video/software ($1.4 billion in sales and flat) (Einstein 2008: 6).

For this study, we only included data that were reasonably available, reliable, and plausible (Table 8-7). Therefore, the data likely represent what we suspect is a significant undercount. But we do find some support for a more conservative figure than Gaille's or Einstein's. For instance, while Einstein cited an estimate of $3.5 billion in religious book sales, Nielson, a leading global information and measurement company, estimated that in 2014 more than 52 million religious book titles were sold in the U.S. (Nielson 2015). Given that the average price for a book falls between $6 and $28,[16] depending on the type, the total would be somewhere between $0.3 billion (if every book was a mass market paperback) and $1.5 billion (if every book was an adult-level hardback). Given that hardbacks represent about 25 percent of the overall market,[17] we concluded that a $554 million estimate by Statista for religious book sales, as shown in Table 8-7, to be more plausible than the higher figures cited in other sources.[18]

In addition to religious book sales, we identified revenue data for two other media market sectors: (a) two large media networks (CBN and EWTN); and (b) Christian/gospel album sales.

Many denominations have media branches, but we were suspicious that reporting those revenues might double count congregational revenue, which, through various cooperative and denominational programs, may be channeled centrally to support denominational media initiatives.

Food

We do not count sales of food (or other items such as gifts) for religion-based holidays, such as Christmas. If we did, this would have a dramatic impact. According to estimates, Christmas purchases in the United States' retail industry in 2013 added to more than $3 trillion, or about 19.2 percent of total retail sales, and resulted in hiring an extra 768,000 employees to handle the holiday rush.[19] We do not include these sales because they

16 See http://tln.lib.mi.us/dept/technical-services/acq/files/AverageBookPrices2014 .pdf (link no longer active).
17 See http://www.publishersweekly.com/pw/by-topic/industry-news/bookselling/ article/64170-e-books-remain-third.html.
18 See http://www.statista.com/statistics/251467/religious-books-sales-revenue-in-the -us/.
19 See http://www.statista.com/topics/991/us-christmas-season/.

Table 8-7: Revenues of Faith-Based Media (Estimate, $Billions)

Media Sector	Annual Revenue
Religious Book Sales	$0.55
Christian Broadcasting Network (CBN)	$0.29
EWTN	$0.05
Christian/Gospel Album sales	$0.02
Total	**$0.90**

Sources: Book and album sales, Statista; CBN, Forbes; EWTN, Charity Navigator. Revenues for 2014. Figures do not total due to rounding of decimals.

Table 8-8: Traditional Kosher and Halal Food Sales (Estimate, $Billions)

Food Sector	Annual Revenue
Kosher (Jewish)	$12.5
Halal (Muslim)	$1.9
Total	**$14.4**

Source: Kosher: Lubicom (2014), "Kosher Statistics." Halal: Canadian Government (2011), "Global Pathfinder Report: Halal Food Trends." Figures may not total due to rounding of decimals.

are not primarily based on the actions of organized faith-based groups, but primarily involve the purchasing actions of individuals.

We do, however, include revenues for traditional kosher and halal foods because both of these require the direct actions of religious authorities to certify compliance with religious dietary edicts. As shown in Table 8-8, revenue for the kosher food sector is estimated to be $12.5 billion based on sales of traditional kosher products in the United States. We use this figure rather than the estimated revenues of more than $300 billion when all products certified as kosher are counted to remain conservative with the estimate.[20] Though relatively smaller, the halal food market in the United States was estimated to be $1.9 billion in 2010.[21]

20 See http://www.star-k.org/articles/articles/getting-certified/advantagekosher-certification/1373/the-global-demand-for-kosher/ and http://www.lubicom.com/kosher/statistics/.
21 See https://www.gov.mb.ca/agriculture/market-prices-and-statistics/food-and-value-added-agriculture-statistics/pubs/halal_market_pathfinder_en.pdf, page 4.

8 | The Socioeconomic Contribution of Religion to American Society

This conservative estimate puts the economic contribution of the religion sector to U.S. society at about $378 billion annually. As shown in Table 8-9, this falls into several main sectors: health care ($161.0 billion), local congregational activities ($83.8 billion), education ($74.0 billion), charities ($44.3 billion), media ($0.9 billion), and food ($14.4 billion). As noted above, we deducted the estimated funds directed from congregations to outside religious organizations (see Table 8-5, data point 5) from the total in Table 8-9 to avoid possible double counting.

The data on local congregations show that they provide a significant level of community and social services beyond those provided through religious organizations set up to specifically provide health care, education and charity. As shown in Table 8-5 (data point 2), congregations spent an estimated $9.2 billion on social programs in 2012, the bulk of which came from donations of individual congregants. Indeed, congregations rely overwhelmingly on donations rather than government grants, fees, and other outside sources for their work. Specifically, out of an estimated annual revenue of nearly $84 billion, congregations received only an estimated $0.38 billion from government grants, fees, and other outside sources (Table 8-5, sum of data points 7 and 8). That's less than half a percent.

Table 8-9: Annual Revenue of U.S. Religious Organizations (Estimate, $Billions)

Sector	Revenue	% of Total
Healthcare Networks	$161.0	42.5%
Congregations	$83.8	22.1%
*giving to other religious organizations**	−$1.0	−0.3%
Educational Institutions	$74.0	19.6%
Charities	$45.3	12.0%
Media	$0.9	0.2%
Food (traditional kosher and halal)	$14.4	3.8%
Total	**$378.3**	**100.0%**

Source: The Socioeconomic Contribution of Religion to American Society: An Empirical Analysis

* The estimated funds directed from congregations to outside religious organizations (see Table 8-5, data point 5) are deducted from the total to avoid possible double counting. Figures do not total due to rounding of decimals.

Table 8-10: Total Money Spent on Social Programs ($Billions)

Year	Original $	In 2012 dollars
2012	$9.24	$9.24
2006	$3.17	$3.63
1998	$2.37	$3.32

Sources: Based on analysis of the National Congregations Study (NCS) cumulative dataset (1998, 2006–2007, 2012) archived at the Association of Religion Data Archive, and the Religious Congregations and Membership Study (RCMS) conducted by representatives of the Association of Statisticians of American Religious Bodies (ASARB).

In terms of money spent on social service programs, there is evidence that congregations are increasing their work in this area. As shown in Table 8-10, when controlling for inflation, congregational spending on social programs is 2.5 times higher in 2012 ($9.24 billion) than in 2006 ($3.63 billion) and 2.8 times higher than in 1998 ($3.32 billion).

Estimate 2: Adding in a Valuation of Congregational Social Services, Charitable Halo Effects, and the Economic Contribution of Businesses with Religious Roots

The research of Cnaan et al. (1999), Cnaan et al. (2006), Cnaan et al. (2013), and Cnaan (2015), describes the process by which religious congregations have positive impacts on communities. They argue that communities socially and economically benefit from the *halo effect* of having the stable, attractive force of a congregation in a community, providing a center for education, childcare, social events, charity, and job training, among other functions. Part of this contribution includes that congregations also provide a sizeable number of jobs. Most congregations have full-time or part-time paid staff ranging from pastors and music directors to maintenance and operational staff. For instance, there are paid youth ministers in more than an estimated 124,000 congregations nationwide (see below, Table 8-11, data point 52).

Cnaan and colleagues also catalogue other halo effects ranging from being a magnet attracting visitors for such things as performances, lectures, and weddings (and the local spending made related to these events), to using the green space around congregational buildings for recreation and repose, to attracting people to view a congregation's architecture and art. Looking at the combined data from the National Congregations Study

8 | The Socioeconomic Contribution of Religion to American Society

and the RCMS (described above), we can see that such halo magnet effects are perhaps surprisingly common, with an estimated 116,919 congregations nationwide reporting that they attract visitors to view their architecture and art (Table 8-11, data point 57). By comparison, there are only 35,144 museums in the United States, according to a 2014 estimate by the Institute of Museum and Library Services (IMLS).[22] This means that museum-worthy, visitor-attracting places of worship outnumber America's museums by more than 3.3 times.

The combined National Congregations Study and RCMS data also allows us to see how many congregations do certain social ministries, such as have groups to provide support for persons with HIV-AIDS (Table 8-11, data point 89). The data show that 7.5 percent of congregations report having groups, meetings, classes, or events specifically focused on providing support, such as food, housing, personal items, or pastoral care to persons living with HIV-AIDS. That means that 25,867 congregations are engaged in some form of active ministry to help people living with HIV-AIDS. In terms of the portion of the U.S. population living with HIV infection, this could be considered a higher percentage than expected. Currently, according to the CDC, 1.2 million people live with HIV, or 0.4 percent of the U.S. population.[23] Of course, these ministries do not reach all HIV positive people, but numerically, this is the equivalent of one congregational HIV-AIDS ministry for every 46 people who are HIV positive.

Table 8-11 repeats from Table 8-5 the income and spending data of congregations from the National Congregations Study (NCS) scaled to actual dollar and numeric figures by using the 2010 Religious Congregations and Membership Study (RCMS). However, Table 8-11 greatly expands the data in order to provide a wealth of additional congregational information including estimates of numbers of people involved in classes and programs and types of activities that minister to the social needs of communities (identified in the table by italics). This list is illustrative, not exhaustive.[24] The data in Table 8-11 show the types of social and community

---

22 IMLS is the U.S. agency that is the primary source of federal funding for the nation's museums and libraries. See https://www.imls.gov/news-events/news-releases/government-doubles-official-estimate-there-are-35000-active-museums-us.
23 See https://www.aids.gov/hiv-aids-basics/hiv-aids-101/statistics/.
24 The full list of questions included in the three waves of the National Congregations Study with weighted frequencies can be found here: http://www.thearda.com/Archive/Files/Codebooks/NCSIII_CB.asp.

Table 8-11: Nationally Representative Data on Activities of U.S. Congregations (Multiple Faiths), ordered by amount or frequency of occurrence

Italicized data points indicate activities of congregations across multiple faith traditions that provide for civic life and social cohesion above and beyond providing for the spiritual lives of congregants.

Data point	Income and Spending	Avg. per Congregation*	Total Amount across 344,894 Congregations*
1	Congregation's Annual Income	$242,910	$83,778,191,193
2	Amount of Income from Individual's Donations, Dues, Contributions	$216,143	$74,546,330,721
3	*Total Money Spent on Social Programs 2012*	*$26,781*	*$9,236,699,335*
4	*Total Money Spent on Social Programs 2006*	*$9,190*	*$3,169,472,392*
5	*Total Money Spent on Social Programs 1998*	*$6,880*	*$2,372,839,680*
6	Amount Given to Other Religious Organizations	$2,997	$1,033,799,071
7	Government Grants, Contracts, Fees for Social Service Projects	$732	$252,327,899
8	Amount Received from Foundations, Businesses, United Way	$354	$122,137,312
	Numbers of People Involved in Classes and Programs	**Avg. per Congregation**	**Total People, Groups, or Programs**
9	Number of Adults Attending Weekly Religious Classes	35.6	12,271,329
10	Number of Children 12 and Under Attending Weekly Religious Classes	34.2	11,802,273
11	*Number of Congregants That Volunteered, Social Service Programs*	*22.2*	*7,646,300*
12	Number of Members Receiving Help from Congregation	17.6	6,077,032
13	Number of Teens Attending Weekly Religious Classes	15.3	5,259,634
14	Number of Adult Volunteers	15.1	5,197,553
15	Number of Religious Education Classes Meeting Once a Month or More	6.9	2,362,524
16	*Number of Social Service Programs Sponsored*	*4.7*	*1,621,002*
17	Number of Regular Choir, Musical Performance Groups	1.6	562,177

(continued)

8 | The Socioeconomic Contribution of Religion to American Society

Table 8-11: Nationally Representative Data on Activities of U.S. Congregations (Multiple Faiths), ordered by amount or frequency of occurrence (*continued*)

Data point	Income and Spending	Avg. per Congregation*	Total Amount across 344,894 Congregations*
	Congregational Activities	Share of all Congregations	Total # of Congregations
18	Groups for Musical, Theatrical Performance (not choirs)	93.0%	320,751
19	Recruiting Volunteers for Outside Projects	92.8%	320,062
20	Worship Service Advertised Volunteer Opportunities	92.8%	320,062
21	Religious Clergy Has Higher Education	89.8%	309,715
22	Congregation Had a Visiting Speaker	81.0%	279,364
23	Congregants Greet during Service	80.2%	276,605
24	Congregation Followed up with Visitors	78.7%	271,432
25	Congregation Collaborates on 4 Most Important Social Programs	74.5%	256,946
26	Congregation Groups Meet Monthly for Religious, Social, Recreational Activity	74.3%	256,256
27	Congregation Has Filed for 501(c)(3) Status	72.0%	248,324
28	Groups for Cleaning, and Building Maintenance	71.2%	245,565
29	Joint Worship Service with Another Congregation	68.2%	235,218
30	Visiting Speaking Clergy from Another Congregation	66.0%	227,630
31	Members Serve on Committees, Attended Meetings	64.5%	222,457
32	Worship Service Had Play Production	63.4%	218,663
33	Congregation Has Teen Camps, Retreats, Conferences	63.3%	218,318
34	Congregation Has Organized Youth Group	62.2%	214,524
35	Group for Socializing, Fellowship	61.6%	212,455
36	Facilities Accommodate the Disabled	56.0%	193,141
37	Congregation Owns Copyrighted Music	51.1%	176,241
38	Worship Building Used for Non Congregational Purposes	50.0%	172,447

(*continued*)

Table 8-11: Nationally Representative Data on Activities of U.S. Congregations (Multiple Faiths), ordered by amount or frequency of occurrence (*continued*)

Data point	Income and Spending	Avg. per Congregation*	Total Amount across 344,894 Congregations*
	Congregational Activities	Share of all Congregations	Total # of Congregations
39	Congregation Has Teens Plan, Present Non-Worship Service Events	49.9%	172,102
40	Worship Service Has Focus on Children	48.3%	166,584
41	Groups to Plan or Conduct Community Needs	47.7%	164,514
42	Congregation Placed Paid Add in Newspaper	44.8%	154,513
43	Group that Serves, Volunteers with People of Another Faith	42.7%	147,270
44	Groups to Attend Musical, Theatrical Outside Events	41.9%	144,511
45	Avg. Number of Adult Congregants Participating in Leadership Role	40.6%	140,165
46	Worship Service Has Teen Participation	39.9%	137,613
47	Groups to Train New Religious Education Teachers	39.6%	136,578
48	Groups to Discuss Parenting Issues	39.2%	135,198
49	Groups to Encourage Volunteer Activity	38.7%	133,474
50	Groups for People Struggling with Drug, Alcohol Abuse	37.6%	129,680
51	Groups for Couples on Enriching, Improving Their Marriages	36.2%	124,852
52	Congregation's Youth Minister Is Paid	36.0%	124,162
53	Worship Service Had Hired Singers, Musicians	35.9%	123,817
54	Group Specifically for Women	35.8%	123,472
55	Clergy Holds Multiple Jobs	35.8%	123,472
56	Groups to Help Unemployed People	35.0%	120,713
57	Visitors Come to View Building's Architecture, Artwork	33.9%	116,919
58	Group Travels in U.S. to Help the Needy	32.4%	111,746
59	Groups for Physical Healing	32.4%	111,746
60	Activities to Promote Physical Fitness	29.1%	100,364
61	Activities to Support Military Veterans and Their Families	27.3%	94,156

(*continued*)

Table 8-11: Nationally Representative Data on Activities of U.S. Congregations (Multiple Faiths), ordered by amount or frequency of occurrence (*continued*)

Data point	Income and Spending	Avg. per Congregation*	Total Amount across 344,894 Congregations*
	Congregational Activities	**Share of all Congregations**	**Total # of Congregations**
62	Groups to Teach Personal Finance Management	26.5%	91,397
63	Congregation Conducted, Used Survey of Community	25.6%	88,293
64	Congregation Has Health Focused Programs	24.8%	85,534
65	Groups to Discuss, Learn about a Different Religion	23.9%	82,430
66	Groups for People with Mental Illness	22.9%	78,981
67	Congregation Has Teens Serve on Governing Boards	22.4%	77,256
68	Group for Food	19.7%	67,944
69	Congregation Affiliated with Community Organizing Group	19.2%	66,220
70	Program: Home Building, Repair, Maintenance	18.1%	62,426
71	Program: Providing Clothing, Blankets, Rummage Sales	17.3%	59,667
72	Groups to Discuss Peoples' Problems, Concerns with Work	17.1%	58,977
73	Groups to Discuss Societal Race Relations	16.3%	56,218
74	Groups for Self-Help, Such as AA	16.2%	55,873
75	Worship Building Used for Non-congregational Rehearsals, Performances	16.0%	55,183
76	Congregation Started, Planted New Congregation	15.4%	53,114
77	Number of Paid Employees Spent More Than 25% on Social Service Projects	14.0%	48,285
78	Group for Helping the Needy	13.9%	47,940
79	Program: Non-religious Education	13.6%	46,906
80	Groups to Encourage People to Register to Vote	12.7%	43,802
81	Group for Senior Citizens	12.2%	42,077
82	Program: Homeless or Transient	11.8%	40,697
83	Group for Fine or Performing Arts	10.8%	37,249

(*continued*)

Table 8-11: Nationally Representative Data on Activities of U.S. Congregations (Multiple Faiths), ordered by amount or frequency of occurrence (*continued*)

Data point	Income and Spending	Avg. per Congregation*	Total Amount across 344,894 Congregations*
	Congregational Activities	Share of all Congregations	Total # of Congregations
84	Shares Worship Building with Other Congregations	9.7%	33,455
85	Groups to Offer Services to Immigrants	9.5%	32,765
86	Group for Fundraising	8.7%	30,006
87	Groups Meet to Prevent Transmission of HIV, AIDS	8.6%	29,661
88	Donates to Organizations That Primarily Help People with HIV, AIDS	7.6%	26,212
89	Groups Provide Support to Persons with HIV, AIDS	7.5%	25,867
90	Groups Meet to Raise Awareness of HIV, AIDS	7.4%	25,522
91	Established Separate Nonprofit Org. to Conduct Human Services, Outreach	7.4%	25,522
92	Groups to Discuss Pollution, Environmental Issues	7.4%	25,522
93	Worship Building Used for Noncongregational Art Exhibits	5.6%	19,314
94	Congregations with Elementary or High Schools	5.4%	18,624
95	Program: Disaster Relief	5.3%	18,279
96	Programs to Serve Persons with HIV, AIDS	5.3%	18,279
97	Program for Cleaning Highways or Parks	5.2%	17,934
98	Group for Vacation, Summer Bible Schools	5.0%	17,245
99	Groups to Teach Congregants English	4.8%	16,555
100	Program: Substance Abuse	4.4%	15,175
101	Group for Couples, Marriage Preparation Classes	4.0%	13,796
102	Group for Visiting Shut-ins, Incarcerated Individuals	3.5%	12,071
103	Program: Habitat for Humanity	3.2%	11,037
104	Group for Bingo, Cards, Game Playing	3.2%	11,037

(*continued*)

8 | The Socioeconomic Contribution of Religion to American Society

Table 8-11: Nationally Representative Data on Activities of U.S. Congregations (Multiple Faiths), ordered by amount or frequency of occurrence *(continued)*

Data point	Income and Spending	Avg. per Congregation*	Total Amount across 344,894 Congregations*
	Congregational Activities	**Share of all Congregations**	**Total # of Congregations**
105	*Group for Festivals, Bazaars, Craft Fairs, or Other Celebrations*	3.1%	10,692
106	*Joint Worship Service with Jewish Congregation*	3.1%	10,692
107	*Program Serves Victims of Rape, Domestic Violence*	2.1%	7,243
108	*Group for Sewing*	2.1%	7,243
109	*Group for Dealing with the Loss of a Loved One*	2.0%	6,898
110	*Program: Prisoners, People in Trouble with the Law and Their Families*	2.0%	6,898
111	*% of Adult Congregants Who Moved to the US in Past 5 Years*	2.0%	6,898
112	*Group for Racial/Ethnic relations*	1.6%	5,518
113	*Joint Worship Service with Muslims*	1.5%	5,173
114	*Group for Helping People with Substance Abuse Problems*	1.2%	4,139
115	*Program: St. Vincent de Paul*	0.5%	1,724

Sources: Questions are from the National Congregations Study (NCS) cumulative dataset (1998, 2006–2007, 2012) archived at the Association of Religion Data Archive; overall total of congregations from the Religious Congregations and Membership Study (RCMS) conducted by representatives of the Association of Statisticians of American Religious Bodies (ASARB).

Data points are for the cumulative average across the years of the NCS, where available. Where not, the most recent year of data is prioritized.

For this study we weighted the data by WTA3CNGD to have results representing the average congregation's perspective.

* Dollar figures and total numbers are reported in detail based on calculations from the dataset; the actual precision is less, but is 95% likely to be within the survey's margin of error of +/−3%. Figures may not total due to rounding of decimals.

impact that Cnaan and colleagues have taken into account when estimating the value provided by congregations to a community. To provide a ballpark estimate of the real value of such halo effects nationally is possible by drawing on Cnaan's most recent work (2015), which is described in the section after the table. Indeed, these data provide context and support for this study's second estimate of faith's socioeconomic contribution to American society by giving an overview of the types of activities that congregations do beyond worship services, many of which contribute to a robust civic society. These include some specifically religion-related activities such as religious education classes, but they also include a large number of community activities ranging from recruiting volunteers for outside projects (data point 19) to activities to support military and their families (data point 61). This information sheds light on the social contributions resulting from revenues of religious congregations.

In addition, congregations provide community and social services by fielding an estimated 7.6 million volunteers in social service programs (data point 11). These activities and the volunteers that run them tend to be collaborative endeavors with other groups in society, promoting social cohesion through broader civic engagement beyond the congregations' doors. Indeed, nearly three in four congregations, or almost 257,000 congregations nationwide, engage in collaboration with other groups and organizations on social programs (data point 25). In fact, almost all congregations (93 percent) recruit volunteers for outside projects (data point 19).

Valuation of Congregations: A Summary

Cnaan (2015) reports on the estimated economic value to communities of ninety congregations in three cities: Philadelphia (forty), Chicago (thirty), and Fort Worth (twenty). His team interviewed clergy (or other leaders) and program directors (where needed) to collect data on six ways congregations provide value to the communities in which they are located.

First, Cnaan's study estimated the value of the positive individual impact provided by a congregation's leaders who provide support to individuals, couples, and families. These include activities that (a) promote health and well-being, (b) mitigate negative costs such as legal troubles or lost productivity, (c) increase benefits to the local communities, including employment, which also includes paying employment taxes, and (d) investment in family and children. As Cnaan notes, such activities are

8 | The Socioeconomic Contribution of Religion to American Society   233

associated with decreased drug and alcohol abuse, divorce, domestic violence, and other personal problems. Second, the study estimated the direct spending of congregations that contribute to the local economy, including buying goods and services, employing local residents, and using local vendors. Third, the study estimated the "Magnet Effect," including the value of hosting weddings, funerals, artistic performances, and other events, such as lectures, that draw out-of-town visitors. These Magnet Effects are tangible activities, such as visitors spending money at local restaurants and other small businesses. Fourth, Cnaan's study estimated the value of schools and daycare centers associated with congregations. Fifth, the study estimated the value of "Open Space," i.e., a congregation's outdoor space often provides a garden and other features that contribute not only to increasing community aesthetics and lowering stormwater runoff treatment costs, but also of recreational and leisure possibilities. And sixth, the study estimated the invisible safety net provide by congregations, including the volunteer and in-kind support that augments the city's network of social services.

The study found that for the ninety congregations from Chicago, Fort Worth, and Philadelphia, the average distribution of contributions was as follows:

- ☐ Individual Impact (37.9%)
- ☐ Education (21.8%)
- ☐ Direct Spending (20%)
- ☐ Magnet Effect (16.7%)
- ☐ Invisible Safety Net (3.5%)
- ☐ Open Space (0.1%)

The Cnaan study did not find significant differences between the results for the congregations in Chicago, Fort Worth, or Philadelphia, reporting similar overall average contributions to their local economy. While the limitation of the study is that it focused only on urban congregations, there is some indication from the results that they match the national profile of congregations. For instance, the Cnaan study found that on average the number of different social programs per congregation was 4.73. This is almost identical to the findings from the National Congregations Study (NCS), which was 4.7 social service programs (Table 8-11, data point 16).

Applying the Methodology to a National Valuation

Applying the above findings to a national estimate, we begin by taking the cash revenues of congregations as roughly the equivalent of the direct spending of congregations. This is appropriate because, as the norm, congregations pretty much spend what comes in.[25] Taking, then, $83,778,191,193 (Table 8-11, data point 1) as the direct spending of congregations nationwide, which we assume based on Cnaan's study to be 20 percent of the total value of congregational activities, we can then allot the other 80 percent proportionally (as shown in Figure 8-1): Individual Impact (37.9 percent), $158.8 billion; Education (21.8 percent), $91.3 billion; Magnet Effect (16.7 percent), $70.0 billion; Invisible Safety Net (3.5 percent), $14.7 billion; Open Space (0.1 percent), $0.4 billion; Total (100 percent), $418.9 billion. Using this approach, we come up with a more realistic value of the multifaceted services provided by congregations, including education ranging from preschool and schools to seminars and conferences to job and marriage courses.

The Halo Effect: An Adjustment for Charities

In addition, a separate study by Partners for Sacred Places and McClanahan Associates Inc. (2015) quantified the Halo Effect of the Salvation Army's Kroc Centers, and found that the total economic benefit to the communities where the charitable work was carried out was about 2.1 times the annual budget of the programs. So, applying this same ratio to the revenues of faith-based charities adds an additional $49.8 billion to the value estimate (as shown in Table 8-13). We believe this corrects what we consider an undervaluation in the first estimate, which only counted revenues of faith-based charities.

Businesses with Religious Roots

In 2014, a landmark decision by the United States Supreme Court determined that the closely held for-profit corporation Hobby Lobby is exempt from a law that its owners religiously object to, as long as there is a less restrictive means of furthering the law's interest. That ruling was the first time the Supreme Court recognized a for-profit business's claim of religious belief. While the ruling was limited to closely held corporations, it sets up the situation where the boundaries of faith and business are clearly not absolute. It is therefore reasonable in any valuation of the role of faith

---

25 See "How Churches Spend Their Money," *Christianity Today*, August 28, 2014.

8 | The Socioeconomic Contribution of Religion to American Society

Figure 8-1: Religious Congregations' Value to U.S. Society
($418.9 billion, annually)

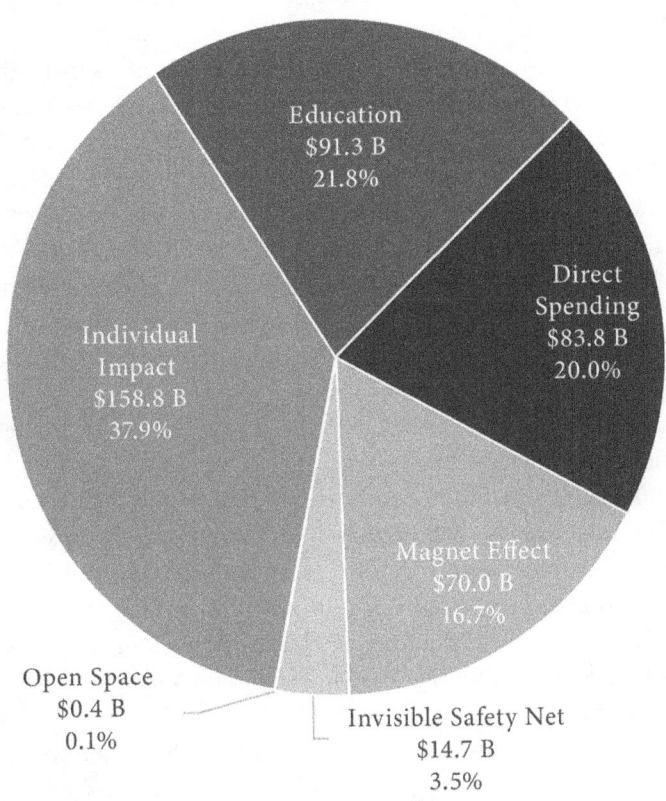

(Figures may not total due to rounding of decimals.)
Source: Brian J. Grim and Melissa E. Grim, "The Socioeconomic Contribution of Religion to American Society," *Interdisciplinary Journal of Research on Religion* (2016)

to the U.S. economy to recognize businesses that have religious roots. This expands our purview beyond companies that have a specific religious purpose, such as producing traditional halal or kosher foods, to companies that have religion as a part of their corporate culture or founding.

To identify such companies, this second estimate includes companies identified recently as having religious roots (see Table 8-12). For instance, Deseret News recently identified twenty companies with religious roots, and CNN produced a list of religious companies besides Chick-fil-A.[26] Also, the recent book by Oxford University business professor Theodore Malloch (2015) produced a global list of such faith-inspired companies. Not all of these would identify specifically as being faith-based. But faith is part of the founding and operating ethos. Malloch notes that although the commercial success of Walmart is well known, "less well known are Walmart's connections to the distinct religious world of northwest Arkansas and rural America . . . [and its] corporate culture and how specific executives incorporated religious culture into their managerial philosophy" (2015: 82).[27] For a full discussion of the religious roots of Walmart, see Moreton (2009). Likewise, although the Marriott hotels are not religiously run, John Willard Marriott, a member of The Church of Jesus Christ of Latter-day Saints, founded the chain and supplied many of the rooms with not only the Bible but The Book of Mormon.

Some other companies listed in Table 8-12, however, have a more overt religious identity. Tyson Foods company, founded by John Tyson, provides 120 office chaplains for employees, ministering to the personal and spiritual needs regardless of the employee's faith or non-faith, as the case may be. The Deseret News story notes that Tyson speaks openly about the company's aspiration to honor God and be a faith-friendly company. Also, as a further indication of the company's faith-orientation, Tyson recently financed the launch of the Tyson Center for Faith and Spirituality in the Workplace at the University of Arkansas.

One business in Table 8-12 is overtly religious. The Knights of Columbus is a Catholic fraternal organization.[28] Since the Knights' founding in 1882—by passing the hat for widows and orphans—their mission has been to "protect families from the financial ruin caused by the death of the breadwinner." To fulfill that mission today, the Knights employ more than 1,400 people to operate their faith-based insurance and retirement program with over $99 billion of insurance in force. Not only do the Knights provide a safety net for their members, they also provide jobs, charity

---

26 See: https://www.deseret.com/2013/8/5/20545110/20-companies-with-religious-roots and http://religion.blogs.cnn.com/2012/07/24/7-religious-companies-besides-chick-fil-a/.

27 Malloch (2015) in *Practical Wisdom in Management: Business across Spiritual Traditions*, also identified a wide range of faith-inspired businesses from various religious and belief systems.

28 See: https://www.kofc.org/uns/en/insurance/index.html.

8 | The Socioeconomic Contribution of Religion to American Society

Table 8-12: Religion-Based Companies (Estimate, $Billions, 2014)

Food Sector	Annual Revenue
Walmart, U.S.	$279.4
Tyson Foods	$37.6
Tom's of Maine	$15.0
Whole Foods Market	$14.2
Kosher Food Industry, U.S.	$12.5
Amway	$11.8
Marriott, North America	$8.3
JetBlue	$5.8
Chick-fil-A	$5.8
Alaska Airlines	$5.4
Mary Kay	$4.0
Forever 21	$3.8
Hobby Lobby	$3.7
ServiceMaster	$2.5
Knights of Columbus	$2.1
Herman Miller	$2.1
Halal Food Industry, U.S.	$1.9
Timberland	$1.7
Interstate Batteries	$1.5
Carl's Jr.	$1.3
In-N-Out Burger	$0.8
Curves	$0.5
Anschutz Entertainment Group	$0.3
eHarmony	$0.3
Habitat for Humanity	$0.3
Covenant Transportation	$0.1
Trijicon	$0.1
Total	**$422.7**

Sources: Religious roots identified by one of the following: Deseret News, "20 Companies with Religious Roots"; CNN, "Religious Companies besides Chick-fil-A"; Halal and Kosher marketing reports; *Practical Wisdom in Management: Business across Spiritual Traditions*, Theodore Roosevelt Malloch (Greenleaf Publishing, 2015). 2014 revenues from company annual reports or Forbes. (Figures do not total due to rounding of decimals.)

work, and avenues for social involvement and networking, all of which are direct socioeconomic contributions to American society. The Knights of Columbus currently has more than 15,100 councils and 1.9 million members throughout the United States, Canada, the Philippines, Mexico, Poland, the Dominican Republic, Puerto Rico, Panama, the Bahamas, the Virgin Islands, Cuba, Guatemala, Guam, Saipan, Lithuania, Ukraine, and South Korea. Indeed, such an organization shows how difficult it is to draw a precise theoretical and at times legal line between business activities (such as insurance) and charitable activities (such as caring for widows and orphans).

Finally, our second estimate of the socioeconomic contribution of religion to American society, which is summarized in Table 8-13, includes one other oft-mentioned religion-related business—major films with an overtly religious theme, many of which are promoted heavily by religious groups themselves. In 2014, the reference year for this study, there were four such blockbusters, with combined domestic U.S. revenues of nearly half a billion dollars: "Son of God" (20th Century Fox, February 2014); "Heaven Is for Real" (Sony Pictures, April 2014); "Noah" (Regency Enterprises, November 2014); and "Exodus" (20th Century Fox, December 2014). While $409 million in combined domestic revenue is not a large amount relative to other categories, the advertising and promotion of the films, and their ongoing viewership through streaming and/or DVDs, makes them an example of how religion crosses the boundaries between business and culture within American society.

Table 8-13 presents what we consider to be a better estimate than the first estimate of the economic contribution of religion to American society. As shown in the table, faith-based healthcare networks contribute $161 billion annually, or 13.9 percent of the total contribution of religion to the U.S. economy. Congregations contribute about $327 billion annually (28.2 percent), plus an additional $91.3 billion if schools and daycare are taken into account (together making 36.1 percent of the total). Higher education adds another $46.8 billion annually (4 percent), but as with healthcare, this is likely an undercount as well because it only takes into account tuitions. Charities add another $95.2 billion annually (8.2 percent). And finally, the business sector contributes $438 billion annually, slightly more than a third of the total (37.8 percent).

As shown in Table 8-13, these add up to $1,159.2 billion dollars, or about $1.2 trillion.

8 | The Socioeconomic Contribution of Religion to American Society

Table 8-13: Annual Socioeconomic Contribution of Religious Organizations to U.S. Society (Estimate, $Billions)

Sector	Revenue	% of Total
Healthcare Networks	$161.0	13.9%
Congregations:	**$326.5**	**28.2%**
Direct Spending	$83.8	7.2%
Giving to Other Religious Organizations	$(1.0)	-0.1%
Individual Impact	$158.8	13.7%
Magnet Effect	$70.0	6.0%
Invisible Safety Net	$14.7	1.3%
Open Space	$0.4	0.0%
Education:	**$138.1**	**11.9%**
Higher Education	$46.8	4.0%
Schools and Daycare	$91.3	7.9%
Charities:	**$95.2**	**8.2%**
Charities' Revenues	$45.3	3.9%
Charities' Halo Effect (estimate)	$49.8	4.3%
Business:	**$438.4**	**37.8%**
Religious Media	$0.9	0.1%
Religion-Themed Films	$0.4	0.0%
Food (traditional kosher and halal)	$14.4	1.2%
Businesses with Religious Backgrounds	$422.7	36.5%
Total	$1,159.2	100.0%

Figures may not total due to rounding of decimals.
Source: Brian J. Grim and Melissa E. Grim, "The Socioeconomic Contribution of Religion to American Society," *Interdisciplinary Journal of Research on Religion* (2016)

Estimate 3: The Revenues of Religiously Affiliated Americans

The third estimate of this study recognizes that many, if not most people of faith, aim to conduct their affairs (to some extent, however imperfectly) guided by and inspired by their religious ideals. In a recent Atlantic article by Jared Keller (2015) and an earlier Harvard Business Review article by Charles Handy (2001), there is a keen sense that the tie between religion and the American spirit put forth in the nineteenth century by Alexis de Tocqueville (1945 [1835]), a French observer of American life, is still alive and well. Referencing Australian author Robert Hughes, Handy notes:

> The Puritans saw themselves as successors to Moses, leading their people to a promised land and starting a new phase of history. That vision still holds today. On the back of every one-dollar bill are the words *novus ordo seclorum*—"a new order of the ages." John Winthrop, their leader, famously preached a sermon in mid-Atlantic in which he spoke of creating a "city upon a hill" where "the eyes of all people are upon us." Hughes argues that the Puritans' values infect the great bulk of Americans to this day. They implanted the American work ethic, as well as the tenacious primacy of religion in American life, equaled only by the Muslim world. In no other country would presidential candidates feel it electorally desirable to proclaim their religious beliefs.

To the extent that religious ethics and ethos pervade how Americans approach work and life, it could be argued that religion's socioeconomic contribution to American society is incalculably large. Perhaps one way to count its value is to take into account the incomes of religiously affiliated people. This is not so different than a similar methodology used in a recent study conducted for the World Economic Forum's Global Agenda Council on the Role of Faith (Grim and Connor 2015). That study connected self-identified religious affiliation with economic environments around the world, seeking to examine how different religious groups will grow both in population and economic power in terms of gross domestic product (GDP) under their control.

Similar to the methodology used in that study, our upper-end estimate of the contribution of religion to American society is based on the estimated annual income of people of faith. For a ballpark estimate, we simply take the share of the adult U.S. population that is religiously affiliated (77.2 percent, according to Pew Research) and multiply that by the median household income, as shown in Table 8-14. Given that Pew Research indicates that a higher share of religiously unaffiliated people are in the highest income categories,[29] the $4.8 trillion estimate, or the equivalent of nearly a third of the country's gross domestic product (GDP), is most likely an upper-end estimate. Our intent in providing this estimate, however, is not

---

29 See: http://www.pewforum.org/2015/05/12/chapter-3-demographic-profiles-of-religious-groups/pr_15-05-12_rls_chapter3-04/.

Table 8-14: Income of Religiously Affiliated (77.2% of population)

	Household Income	Annual Revenue
Households in U.S. (116,211,092)	$53,482	$6,215,736,442,344
Affiliated Households (89,714,963)	$53,482	$4,798,135,652,450
Unaffiliated Households (26,498,129)	$53,482	$1,417,187,908,854

Sources: Pew Research http://www.pewforum.org/2015/05/12/americas-changing-religious-landscape/ and U.S. Census Bureau for Number & median income of households: http://www.census.gov/quickfacts/table/HSD410214/00 (Figures may not total due to rounding of decimals.)

to achieve exact precision, but to offer another plausible way to take into account the contribution of religion to the American economy.

Discussion and Conclusion

The faith sector is undoubtedly a significant component of the overall American economy, impacting and involving the lives of the majority of the U.S. population. We conclude that our first estimate of the economic contribution of religion to the U.S. society ($378 billion annually) is conservative and an undervaluation because it focuses on revenues rather than on the value of the goods and services provided by religious organizations.

We believe that our second estimate of $1.2 trillion is a more reasonable estimate because it takes into account both the value of the services provided by religious organizations and the impact religion has on a number of important American businesses.

Our third estimate takes into account the energetic religious spirit identified by Tocqueville that motivated the public at large toward civic participation and economic vibrancy. Certainly the legacy of such things as the Protestant Work Ethic and Catholic Social Teaching, to name just two, continue to animate many millions of Americans in their work and life. We offer the third estimate of some $4.8 trillion, not as a preferred estimate, but rather as an upper-end estimate that takes these personal and social religious dynamics into account.

There are several important limitations of this study. First, it does not take into account the value of financial or physical assets of religious groups. Second, it does not account for the negative impacts that occur in some religious communities, including, as mentioned above, such things as the abuse of children by some clergy, cases of fraud, and the possibility of being recruitment sites for violent extremism. Obviously, such actions detract from the positive contributions made by religious institutions and adherents in the same way that they harm society in any context in which they occur—in homes, schools, businesses, and friendship networks, as well as in civic, trade, political, and governmental institutions. The most important limitation of this study is that the estimate of the fair market value of the goods and services provided by religious organizations is based on the proposition that the findings from Cnaan's and related halo effect studies can be extrapolated up to the national level. Our estimate the contribution of faith-based healthcare networks ($161 billion annually) is likely also an underestimate because it only counts revenues.

Despite these limitations, we believe that the data and estimates discussed in this article will be a useful starting point for further studies of the socioeconomic contributions of religion to the United States and perhaps other countries as well. Future studies might fruitfully focus on at least six areas.

- ☐ First, future studies might consider refining, improving, and tracking changes over time in annual revenues of religious organizations.
- ☐ Second, additional inquiry into the value of religion-related assets, such as endowments and property, would help to show the economic potential and capital that make many of the social services discussed above possible.
- ☐ Third, it would be helpful to improve estimates of the fair market value of goods and services provided by religious organizations, such as additional fieldwork to estimate halo effects in diverse settings and varied organizational contexts.
- ☐ Fourth, careful cost-benefit analyses of faith-based programs versus public programs would be useful in evaluating religious programs relative to similar non-religious programs.
- ☐ Fifth, more frequent nationally representative surveys of congregations would allow trends and activities to be better understood and tracked.
- ☐ And sixth, a more detailed valuation of faith-based healthcare contributions is needed, including viewing their impact relative to non-faith-based healthcare systems.

The data are clear. Religion is a highly significant sector of the American economy. Religion provides purpose-driven institutional and economic contributions to health, education, social cohesion, social services, media, food, and business itself. Perhaps most significantly, religion helps set Americans free to do good by harnessing the power of millions of volunteers from nearly 345,000 diverse congregations present in every corner of the country's urban and rural landscape.

References

Ammerman, Nancy T. 2001. *Doing Good in American Communities: Congregations and Service Organizations Working Together*. Hartford, CT: Hartford Institute for Religion Research, Hartford Seminary.

Bainbridge, William Sims. 1989. "The Religious Ecology of Deviance." *American Sociological Review* 54: 288–95.

Cafardi, Nicholas P. 2008. *Before Dallas: The U.S. Bishops' Response to Clergy Sexual Abuse of Children*. New York: Paulist Press.

Canadian Government. 2011. "Global Pathfinder Report: Halal Food Trends." Available at https://www.gov.mb.ca/agriculture/market-prices-and-statistics/food-and-value-added-agriculture-statistics/pubs/halal_market_pathfinder_en.pdf.

Chaves, Mark. 1999. "Religious Congregations and Welfare Reform: Who Will Take Advantage of Charitable Choice?" *American Sociological Review* 64: 836–46.

Chaves, Mark, Mary Ellen Konieczny, Kraig Beyerlein, and Emily Barman. 1999. "The National Congregations Study: Background, Methods, and Selected Results." *Journal for the Scientific Study of Religion* 38: 458–76.

Cnaan, Ram A. 2015. "Measuring Social Valuation: The Case of Local Religious Congregations." Presented at the G20 Interfaith Summit 2015, Istanbul, Turkey, November 17. Available at http://www.iclrs.org/content/events/116/2707.pdf.

Cnaan, Ram A., Stephanie C. Boddie, Charlene C. McGrew, and Jennifer J. Kang. 2006. *The Other Philadelphia Story: How Local Congregations Support Quality of Life in Urban America*. Philadelphia: University of Pennsylvania Press.

Cnaan, Ram A., Tuome Forrest, Joseph Carlsmith, and Kelsey Karsh. 2013. "If You Don't Count It, It Doesn't Count: A Pilot Study of Valuing Urban Congregations." *Journal of Management, Spirituality and Religion* 10: 3–36.

Cnaan, Ram A., with Robert J. Wineburg and Stephanie C. Boddie. 1999. *The Newer Deal: Social Work and Religion in Partnership*. New York: Columbia University Press.

De Sanctis, Fausto Martin. 2015. *Churches, Temples, and Financial Crimes: A Judicial Perspective of the Abuse of Faith*. New York: Springer.

Einstein, Mara. 2008. *Brands of Faith: Marketing Religion in a Commercial Age*. London: Routledge.

Erelle, Anna. 2015. *In the Skin of a Jihadist: Inside Islamic State's Recruitment Networks*. London: HarperCollins.

Fagan, Patrick F. 2006. "Why Religion Matters Even More: The Impact of Religious Practice on Social Stability." Washington, DC: The Heritage Foundation.

Fukuyama, Francis. 2001. "Social Capital, Civil Society, and Development." *Third World Quarterly* 22: 7–20.

Gaille, Brandon. 2013. "11 Christian Music Industry Statistics and Trends," November 10, 2013. Available online at http://brandongaille.com/11-christian-music-industry-statistics-and-trends/.

Gitlow, Abraham L. 2005. *Corruption in Corporate America: Who Is Responsible? Who Will Protect the Public Interest?* Lanham, MD: University Press of America.

Grim, Brian J., and Phillip Connor. 2015. "Changing Religion, Changing Economies: Future Global Religious and Economic Growth." Research prepared for the Global Agenda Council on the Role of Faith. Available at https://religiousfreedomandbusiness.org/wp-content/uploads/2015/10/Changing-religion-Changing-economies-Religious-Freedom-Business-Foundation-October-21-2015.pdf.

Handy, Charles. 2001. "Tocqueville Revisited: The Meaning of American Prosperity." *Harvard Business Review*, January issue. Available at https://hbr.org/2001/01/tocqueville-revisited-the-meaning-of-american-prosperity.

Hummer, Robert A., Richard G. Rogers, Charles B. Nam, and Christopher G. Ellison. 1999. "Religious Involvement and U.S. Adult Mortality." *Demography* 36: 273–85.

Johnson, Byron R., Ralph Brett Tompkins, and Derek Webb. 2002. "Objective Hope—Assessing the Effectiveness of Faith-Based Organizations: A Systematic Review of the Literature." New York: Manhattan Institute for Policy Research, Center for Research on Religion and Urban Civil Society.

Keller, Jared. 2015. "What Makes Americans So Optimistic? Why the U.S. Tends to Look on the Bright Side." *The Atlantic*, March 25. Available at http://www.theatlantic.com/politics/archive/2015/03/the-american-ethic-and-the-spirit-of-optimism/388538/.

Kinney, Nancy T., and Todd Bryan Combs. 2016. "Changes in Religious Ecology and Socioeconomic Correlates for Neighborhoods in a Metropolitan Region." *Journal of Urban Affairs* 38: 409–28.

Koenig, Harold, Dana King, and Verna B. Carson. 2012. *Oxford's Handbook of Religion and Health*. 2nd ed. Oxford: Oxford University Press.

Koenig, Harold, and Malcolm McConnell. 1999. *The Healing Power of Faith: How Belief and Prayer Can Help You Triumph over Disease*. New York: Touchstone.

Lester, David. 1987. "Religiosity and Personal Violence: A Regional Analysis of Suicide and Homicide Rates." *The Journal of Social Psychology* 127: 685–86.

Levin, Jeff. 2001. *God, Faith, and Health: Exploring the Spirituality-Healing Connection*. New York: John Wiley & Sons.

Lubicom. 2014. "Kosher Statistics." New York: Lubicom Marketing Consultants. Available online at http://www.lubicom.com/kosher/statistics/.

Malloch, Theodore Roosevelt. 2015. *Practical Wisdom in Management: Business across Spiritual Traditions*. Sheffield, UK: Greenleaf Publishing.

Moreton, Bethany. 2009. *To Serve God and Wal-Mart: The Making of Christian Free Enterprise*. Cambridge, MA: Harvard University Press.

Moushey, Bill, and Robert Dvorchak. 2013. *Game Over: Jerry Sandusky, Penn State, and the Culture of Silence*. New York: HarperCollins.

Muller, Chandra, and Christopher G. Ellison. 2001. "Religious Involvement, Social Capital, and Adolescents' Academic Progress: Evidence from the National Education Longitudinal Study of 1988." *Sociological Forces* 34: 155–83.

Neumann, Peter R. 2008. *Joining Al-Qaeda: Jihadist Recruitment in Europe*. London: The International Institute for Strategic Studies.

Nielsen Company, The. 2015. "Focusing on Our Strengths: Insights into the Christian Book Market." Available online at www.nielsen.com/us/en/insights/reports/2015/focusing-on-our-strengths-insights-into-the-christian-book-market.html.

Numrich, Paul D., and Elfriede Wedam. 2015. *Religion and Community in the New Urban America*. New York: Oxford University Press.

Partners for Sacred Places and McClanahan Associates, Inc. 2015. "The Economic Halo Effect of The Salvation Army Ray & Joan Kroc Corps Community Centers." A report to The Salvation Army, May 2015.

Picarello, Anthony R., Jr., Jeffrey Hunter Moon, Michael F. Moses, and United States Conference of Catholic Bishops. 2016. "Brief *Amicus Curiae* of United States Conference of Catholic Bishops; Institutional Religious Freedom Alliance; World Vision, Inc.; Catholic Relief Services; Family Research Council; Association of Catholic Colleges and Universities; Thomas More Society; and the Cardinal Newman Society in Support of Petitioners and Supporting Reversal." Available online at http://www.scotusblog.com/wp-content/uploads/2016/01/Zubik-USCCB-brief.pdf.

Putnam, Robert. 2000 [1990]. *Bowling Alone: The Collapse and Revival of American Community*. New York: Simon & Schuster.

Regnerus, Mark D. 2001. "Making the Grade: The Influence of Religion upon the Academic Performance of Youth in Disadvantaged Communities." Philadelphia: University of Pennsylvania, Center for Research on Religion and Urban Civil Society Report No. 3 44: 394–413.

Schwadel, Philip. 2002. "Testing the Promise of the Churches: Income Inequality in the Opportunity to Learn Civic Skills in Christian Congregations." *Journal for the Scientific Study of Religion* 41: 565–75.

Stark, Rodney. 2012. *America's Blessings: How Religion Benefits Everyone, Including Atheists*. West Conshohocken, PA: Templeton Press.

Tirrito, Terry, and Toni Cascio. 2003. *Religious Organizations and Community Services: A Social Work Perspective*. New York: Springer.

Tocqueville, Alexis de. 1945 [1835]. *Democracy in America*, vol. 1. New York: Vintage.

Zak, Paul J., and Stephen Knack. 2001. "Trust and Growth." *The Economic Journal* 111: 295–321.

III
Addressing Social Problems

A mounting body of evidence documents the significant link between the effects of religious belief and practice on a host of salutary outcomes for diverse societies. For example, a number of scholars find a relationship between religion and democratic governance, civility, women's rights, economic development, innovation, literacy, healthcare, and prosocial behavior.[1] For example, the conventional wisdom that Western success depended upon overcoming religious barriers to progress is debunked in Rodney Stark's important book, *The Victory of Reason: How Christianity Led to Freedom, Capitalism, and Western Success*. In this book Stark advances a revolutionary and controversial idea—that Christianity and its related institutions are directly responsible for the most significant intellectual, political, scientific, and economic breakthroughs of the past millennium. In a counternarrative, Stark asserts that the very source of reason, logic, freedom, and progress is Christian theology.[2]

---

1 Johnson, Byron R. 2011. *More God, Less Crime: Why Religion Matters and How It Could Matter More*. West Conshohocken, PA: Templeton Press. Reimer, William D. 2016. *Revisiting "Toronto the Good": Violence, Religion and Culture in a Late-Victorian City*. Winnipeg, MB: Gerhard & Co. Stark, Rodney. 1996. *The Rise of Christianity*. Princeton, NJ: Princeton University Press. Stark, Rodney. 2001. *One True God: Historical Consequences of Monotheism*. Princeton, NJ: Princeton University Press. Stark, Rodney. 2006. *The Victory of Reason: How Christianity Led to Freedom, Capitalism, and Western Success*. New York: Random House. Stark, Rodney. 2012. *America's Blessings: How Religion Benefits Everyone, Including Atheists*. West Conshohocken, PA: Templeton Press.
2 Stark 2006; 2012.

Recent scholarship offers support for Stark's claims. For example, based on global data, Brian Grim finds that "the presence of religious freedom in a country mathematically correlates with the longevity of democracy" as well as civil and political liberty, women's income, freedom of press, lower infant mortality, and economic freedom.[3] Moreover, Grim and Finke found a statistically significant relationship between the degree of regulation of religion and the levels of religious intolerance and persecution in a society.[4] Stated differently, religious freedom contributes to civility in society, while the restriction of religious freedom generates religious violence.

Robert Woodberry has spent many years studying why some nations develop stable representative democracies—in which citizens enjoy the rights to vote, speak, and assemble freely—while neighboring countries suffer authoritarian rulers and internal conflict. Woodberry has also investigated why public health and economic growth can differ dramatically from one country to another, even among countries that share similar geography, cultural background, and natural resources. Woodberry's research stands in direct contrast to the assumptions that many have held about the work of foreign Protestant missionaries.[5] Woodberry's landmark publication demonstrated that areas where Protestant missionaries had a significant presence in the past are on average more economically developed today, with comparatively better health, lower infant mortality, lower corruption, greater literacy, higher educational attainment (especially for women), and more likely to have robust membership in nongovernmental associations.

Not unlike missionaries, faith-based organizations have for many decades provided social services and programs that address some of the most pressing social problems in America. This is why President George W. Bush signed an executive order in January of 2001, creating the White House Office of Faith-Based and Community Initiatives and similar offices within five federal agencies. The goal was to eliminate

---

3   Grim, Brian J. 2008. "Religious Freedom: God for What Ails Us?" *Review of Faith & International Affairs* 6: 3–7.
4   Grim, Brian J., and Roger Finke. 2006. "International Religion Indexes: Government Regulation, Government Favoritism, and Social Regulation of Religion." *Interdisciplinary Journal for Research on Religion* 2: 1–40.
5   Woodberry, Robert D. 2012. "The Missionary Roots of Liberal Democracy." *American Political Science Review* 106: 244–74.

government barriers inhibiting partnerships with faith-based and grassroots charities and to strengthen the work of America's faith-motivated people in addressing difficult social problems. And though the title of the faith-based initiative would slightly change, President Barack Obama retained the office during his administration.

Though largely unrecognized, a dramatic increase in the extent and prevalence of public-private, sacred-secular partnerships emerged in communities across the country. Indeed, many state and local governments continue to collaborate with faith-based organizations in an unprecedented and concerted effort to attack need in America.[6] But beyond this bipartisan support, what do we know about the reach, capacity, and efficacy of these faith-based efforts to achieve important civic goals and outcomes?

To answer this question, I brought together top scholars from political science, sociology, philosophy, law, criminology, medicine, psychiatry, and education to write about the state of faith-based efforts to address various social problems.[7] In sum, the report provides evidence for as well as important insights into how faith-based efforts are making strides in addressing difficult-to-solve social problems. This research describes strategic and creative ways policy-makers and faith-motivated workers can think more intentionally about collaborative and effective approaches to various social ills, including homelessness, domestic violence, drug and alcohol addiction, disaster relief, prisoner reentry, and HIV/AIDS in Africa. Based on historic and contemporary data, it is accurate to argue that religion and religious freedom have been working and continue to work diligently and often successfully in addressing diverse social problems. The following chapters provide important insights to this often overlooked contribution that religion continues to make in society.

As policy-makers consider strategies to reduce various social problems, such deliberations should consider the role of religion and religious institutions in implementing, developing, and sustaining multifaceted approaches. From after-school programs for disadvantaged youth to public-private partnerships that bring together secular and sacred groups

---

6 Hein, Jay F. 2013. *The Quiet Revolution: An Active Faith That Transforms Lives And Communities*. New York: Waterfall Press.
7 Johnson, Byron R. 2008. *Not by Faith or Government Alone: Rethinking the Role of Faith-Based Organizations*. Special Report, Institute for Studies of Religion, Baylor University.

to tackle social problems like suicide, drug abuse, or crime, it is apparent that any effective strategy will be needlessly incomplete unless the power of religion and religious communities, and the networks of social support found within them, are integrally involved. Indeed, a better understanding of the mechanisms associated with prosocial behavior will assist in the development of future prevention and intervention strategies. Unraveling the role of religiosity, religious institutions and congregations, and the ways in which they promote prosocial behavior should be a priority for academic researchers as well as for federal and private sources of funding. The chapters in this section shed light on many of these timely issues.

9

Religion, Intact Families, and the Achievement Gap

William H. Jeynes

Over the last four decades, one of the most persistent debates in education has been on how to close the achievement gap between white students on the one hand and Black and Hispanic students on the other (Green 2001; Simpson 1981). This achievement gap exists in virtually every measure of educational progress, including standardized tests, GPA, the dropout rate, and the extent to which students are left back a grade (Conciatore 1990; Gordon 1976; Green et al. 2000; So and Chan 1984). The United States was founded on the principle of equality. As a result, Americans tend to feel uncomfortable when unequal results emerge, and American educators have frequently tried to reduce those inequalities (Green 2001; Osborne 1999).

The intractable nature of the difference in academic outcomes that exists between students of certain races of color and white students and those of low versus high socioeconomic status has been of considerable concern to educators and the American public (Rayburn and Hayes 1975; Roscigno 1998). Ronald Roach (2001: 377) recently asserted that "in the academic and think tank world, pondering achievement gap remedies takes center stage." Given the persistence of this gap, the government has launched a plethora of initiatives designed to eradicate it (Green et al. 2000; Jones 1984; Rumberger and Willms 1992). These initiatives include Head Start, the school lunch program, President Clinton's national standards program, a host of affirmative action programs, No Child Left Behind, and various other programs. Moreover, copious private programs have been initiated by various academics, research institutes, foundations, and other organizations (Navarro and Natalicio 1999; Ross, Smith, and Casey 1999; Slavin and Madden 2001; Trent 1997). These efforts have focused on multicultural teaching, attempting to raise students' self-esteem, parental involvement, requiring school uniforms, community partnerships, and so forth (Henderson 1975; Slavin and Madden 2001; Vail 1996).

Of all the inequalities that exist in the American education system, researchers have probably tried to address racial inequality more than any other (Haycock 2001; Orfield et al. 2000). And while there was a period during the 1980s when the achievement gap did show some reduction, which some social scientists credit to the Back to Basics movement (Green 2001; Haycock and Jerald 2002; Jerald and Haycock 2002), it remains adamantly wide even to this day (Cross and Slater 2000; Haycock 2001; Hedges and Nowell, 1999; Lindjord 1998; Orfield et al. 2000; Slater 1999). Although researchers and educators acknowledge that an achievement gap exists, social scientists differ widely in their suggestions about how to bridge the gap. One such solution includes religious commitment of students.

Increasingly, particularly over the last two decades, social scientists have examined the influence of religious commitment, religious schools, and family structure on the educational outcomes of students of color (Jeynes 1999, 2003a). Various studies using a variety of analytic approaches, including meta-analyses, nationwide datasets, and qualitative techniques, have found a consistent positive relationship between variables such as religious commitment, Christian schooling, and intact parental family structure and school success (Jeynes 2002a). These trends exist not only for American students generally, but specifically for students of color (Jeynes 1999, 2003a). For example, students of color who are religious (defined by both intrinsic and extrinsic measures) outperform their counterparts who are less religious (Jeynes 1999, 2003a). Minority students attending Christian or other religious schools achieve at higher rates scholastically than do their counterparts at public schools, even when the study has adjusted for socioeconomic status (Jeynes 2002b). Finally, students of color from intact families excel at higher levels in school than do students from less traditional family structures (Jeynes 1999, 2003a).

Although religiosity, attending religious schools, and being raised in an intact family have ameliorative influences on scholastic outcomes for minority students, research results only suggest the possibility that these factors reduce the achievement gap. Given that these three factors are also associated with improved grades and scores for white students, it is conceivable that these factors could benefit white children more than children of color. In this scenario, these factors could actually benefit young people overall but exacerbate the achievement gap. Therefore, it is important to assess not only the effects of these factors on the educational outcomes of children of color, but also their effect on the achievement gap.

The possibility that Christian and other religious schools could serve to reduce the achievement gap appears consistent with the religious emphasis on providing succor for the downtrodden. When one looks at some of the poorest sections of U.S. and European cities, the vast majority of the shelters that minister to the poor are religious. While some secularists talk of the need to give to the poor, it is usually religious people who are the ones reaching the poor in the trenches of homelessness and poverty (Deck, Tarango, and Matovina 1995; Greenway 1992; Henry and Hancock 1979; Nicholls and Wood 1996; Perkins 1995). Considering the strong impact that religious and family variables have on people's lives, there has been a puzzling dearth of studies examining the influence of these factors on the achievement gap (Jeynes 1999, 2001, 2003a). The need for the research presented in this article is particularly noteworthy (Jeynes 1999, 2003a) for three reasons.

The first reason is the debate surrounding the idea of school choice plans that include private schools. If attending religious schools improves the educational outlook for low-socioeconomic-status (low-SES) children, this enhances the argument in favor of including private schools in a school choice system. However, if attending private religious schools does not improve these children's academic results, then the argument in favor of a choice program that would permit them to attend private religious schools is substantially weakened. Nevertheless, one should note that there are other nonacademic reasons why school choice may be laudable. The second reason is that educators, parents, and sociologists need added insight into how to raise the accomplishments and aspirations of low-SES students (Jeynes 2003a, 2003b, 2005b). The third reason is the importance of ascertaining whether public school educators can benefit by examining the religious school model (Hudolin 1994). To the extent to which low-SES children perform better in religious schools, this strengthens the argument that public school educators can learn from some of the practices of religious schools (Bryk, Lee, and Holland 1993; LePore and Warren 1997; McEwen, Knipe, and Gallagher 1997). Bryk, Lee, and Holland (1993) and other researchers note that many theorists do not favor school choice but still assert that educators can learn from the religious school model (Schmidt 1988). Other social scientists contend that religious schools do not do a better job than their public school counterparts in educating low-SES children (Noell 1982; Willms 1985). Given this disparity of perceptions, it is important to resolve this issue.

Moreover, Kozol (1991) and other researchers assert that low-SES children represent the children it is most crucial for the U.S. educational system to reach. These researchers argue that low-SES children consistently trail high-SES children in educational outcomes (Ogbu 1992). Consequently, it is crucial to uncover what works in raising these children's school achievement (Ogbu 1992). Perhaps almost as important as the answers to the above questions is that if religious students, religious schools, and intact families do have a positive impact on achievement, it is important to determine some of the reasons why. In this way, social scientists can maximize the benefits of learning from these influences to broaden their impact in the educational arena.

Methods and Data Sources

To assess the extent to which religious commitment, religious schools, and family factors could influence achievement, two types of statistical analysis were undertaken. The first type of analysis involved using an esteemed nationwide sample (the National Education Longitudinal Survey, abbreviated NELS88) of 24,599 students from 1,052 schools that was representative of the nation's student population. The second analysis involved completing a meta-analysis. A meta-analysis statistically combines all the relevant existing studies on a given subject to determine the aggregated results of said research (Hedges and Cooper 1994).

From the nationwide sample (NELS), a broad list of variables was examined, including the effects of religious commitment, religious schools, and family structure.

Religious Commitment

Whether a student was classified as "very religious" depended on whether each student described herself or himself as all of the following: (1) very religious, (2) actively involved in a religious youth group, and (3) attending church at least three or four times a month.

9 | Religion, Intact Families, and the Achievement Gap

School and Student Identifying Variables

In addition to distinguishing between religious and nonreligious schools, various school variables were measured, including assessments of (1) school atmosphere, (2) racial harmony, (3) level of school discipline, (4) school violence, and (5) amount of homework done. Achievement tests in mathematics, reading, science, and social studies (history, civics, and geography) were also given to the students. Additional academic measures included assessments of whether a child had been left back a grade and whether the child had taken the basic core set of courses identified by the National Association of Educational Progress (NAEP). This basics program consisted of four years of English courses, three years of social studies courses, three years of science courses, three years of math courses, two years of foreign language courses, and half a year of computer science courses. Measures of socioeconomic status, race, and gender were also taken.

Family Structure Variable

Students were distinguished on the basis of whether they were living in an intact family. A total of 398 Black and Hispanic adolescents were defined as coming from backgrounds in which the student was highly religious and from an intact family.

Low-SES versus High-SES Analyses

Two sets of analyses were completed to examine the achievement gap between low-SES and higher-SES students. The first involved comparing low-SES religious school and public school students via SES quartiles in the NELS. The second involved a meta-analysis of the existing studies that compared the academic outcomes of low-SES students attending religious schools to those of low-SES students in public schools. The analysis was based on a literature search in twenty-five databases in which more than sixty studies were found that examined the relationship between religious schools and academic outcomes. Of these, thirteen specifically examined the effects of low-SES students attending religious schools on academic outcomes; those thirteen studies are synthesized in this report. Measures of academic achievement included both standardized and nonstandardized measures.

Results

According to the findings, students of low socioeconomic status and students of color especially benefit from attending religious schools.

Examination of the NELS Dataset

The results of the NELS dataset analysis indicate that (1) children in the lowest SES quartile who attend religious schools achieve at higher levels than do children in the lowest SES quartile who attend public schools and (2) children in the lowest SES quartile benefit from attending religious schools more than do students in the other SES quartiles. Low-SES students attending religious schools outperformed their counterparts in public schools on both standardized and nonstandardized measures. Among the standardized tests, the religious school students' scores varied from 7.8 percent higher for the Test Composite to 5.4 percent higher for the Science test. The religious school advantage was even greater for the nonstandardized Basic Core measure, at 8.2 percent higher.

The results listed in Table 9-1 show how the religious school advantage differs by SES quartile in the student sample. For all the academic achievement measures examined, students from the lowest SES quartile showed the greatest academic benefit, as measured by percentage gain from attending religious schools compared to their counterparts in public schools. This advantage was greater than that experienced by students in the other three socioeconomic quartiles. The increase for students in the lowest quartile was 3.0 percent higher than the increase for students in the highest quartile for the Test Composite and Basic Core classes and was at least 2.0 percent higher in every academic category. The religious school advantage was inversely related to the student's socioeconomic quartile. For all measures, students from the lowest SES quartile benefited the most from attending religious schools, followed by the second-lowest quartile, and so on, the high-SES quartile students benefiting the least from attending religious schools.

When we examine the racial achievement gap, the effects of religious schools are similar to the pattern found for SES. Table 9-2 indicates that the standardized test scores of African American and Latino students varied from 8.3 percent higher than those of their public school counterparts for Math, Social Studies, and Test Composite to 6.0 percent higher for Science. When SES and gender were controlled for, the standardized test scores of African American and Latino students varied from 5.2 percent higher than their public school counterparts for the Social Studies test to 2.0 percent higher for the Science test. For all the academic measures, whether SES was controlled for or not, African American and Latino students benefited more than whites did from attending religious schools. For the

Table 9-1: Effects (in Percentage Score Increases) on the Academic Achievement of Twelfth-Grade Children by SES Quartile (NELS Dataset: $N = 20,706$)

	Lowest SES Quartile	Second-Lowest SES Quartile	Second-Highest SES Quartile	Highest SES Quartile
Reading Achievement	7.6%	6.8%	5.8%	5.2%
Math Achievement	7.0%	6.2%	5.6%	5.0%
Social Studies Achievement	6.8%	5.8%	5.2%	4.6%
Science Achievement	5.4%	4.0%	3.4%	3.2%
Test Composite	7.8%	6.6%	5.4%	4.8%
Left Back	5.8%	5.0%	4.4%	3.8%
Basic Core	8.2%	6.6%	5.8%	5.2%

standardized tests, African American and Latino students gained 2.5 percent more than white students for the Social Studies test and 1.8 percent more for the Science test. When SES was controlled for, African American and Latino students gained 1.8 percent more than white students for the Social Studies test and 0.8 percent more for the Science test.

Meta-Analysis

The meta-analysis indicated that low-SES students benefit more than moderate-SES and high-SES students do from attending religious schools. These results held across all the standardized and nonstandardized measures. The difference in the advantage, measured in standard deviation units, was largest for the Basic Core set of courses (2.7 percent) and least for Math test and being left back a grade (1.7 percent). These differences are similar to those found by using the NELS dataset. As indicated in Table 9-3, the meta-analysis showed an advantage of 5.1 percent in favor of low-SES students attending religious schools over their counterparts in public schools. The religious school student advantage was somewhat higher for

Table 9-2: Effects (in Percentage Score Increases) on the Academic Achievement of Twelfth-Grade Children by Race (NELS Dataset: N = 20,706)

	Considering SES and Gender		Not Considering SES and Gender	
	African American and Latino	White	African American and Latino	White
Reading Achievement	8.2%	6.0%	4.6%	3.4%
Math Achievement	8.3%	6.0%	4.2%	3.0%
Social Studies Achievement	8.3%	5.8%	5.2%	3.4%
Science Achievement	6.0%	4.2%	2.0%	1.2%
Test Composite	8.3%	6.0%	4.8%	3.8%
Left Back	5.1%	3.7%	3.0%	2.0%
Basic Core	8.3%	6.5%	3.4%	3.0%

standardized tests (5.3 percent) than for nonstandardized measures (4.8 percent). This trend also held for the high school level, where the religious school advantages for standardized tests and nonstandardized measures were 5.7 percent and 5.0 percent, respectively. At the middle school level, this pattern did not hold. In this case, the religious school advantages were both 5.2 percent. Another pattern that emerged was that the effect sizes for overall achievement for middle school (5.2 percent) and high school (5.4 percent) were greater than those for elementary school (3.1 percent).

These results suggest that the advantage for attending religious schools is greater at higher grades, that is, at the middle school and high school levels. One might interpret these findings as indicating that religious schools do a particularly good job of aiding high school and middle school students. However, another possible explanation is that, at least for the students who begin attending religious schools at a young age, the

9 | Religion, Intact Families, and the Achievement Gap

Table 9-3: Meta-Analysis Advantage for Low-SES Children Attending Religious Schools versus Their Counterparts in Public Schools by Level of Schooling

	Combined Standardized and Nonstandardized Results	Standardized Test Results	Nonstandardized Results
All Levels of Schooling Combined	5.1%	5.3%	4.8%
High School Level	5.4%	5.7%	5.0%
Middle School Level	5.2%	5.2%	5.2%
Elementary School Level	3.1%	3.1%	N.A.*

* N.A. = Not applicable.

larger effect sizes may simply be a reflection of giving sufficient time for the religious school advantage to be manifested.

Additional Thoughts Based on the Results

The results of this study support the argument that attending religious schools is associated with higher levels of academic achievement among low-SES students. The studies from which this meta-analysis drew generally took into consideration gender, race, and various other factors, including parental involvement and the extent to which a school's program was demanding. One intriguing finding is that the effect sizes tended to be smaller for the meta-analysis than for the analysis examining the NELS dataset. One of the primary reasons for this difference is that a number of the studies that were included in the meta-analysis controlled for variables such as parental involvement and the extent to which the school had a demanding curriculum, which a number of researchers assert are some of the very reasons why students at religious schools perform better than their counterparts in public schools (Coleman 1988; Coleman and Hoffer 1987). In undertaking the NELS analysis, given that the goal was to determine whether and how much low-SES children benefited from attending religious schools, controlling for some the very factors that provide explanations for that advantage seemed unwise. Another reason for the difference in overall results is that the NELS analysis included only high school students, who tended to benefit more than younger students from attending religious schools.

Why Attending Religious Schools Reduces the Achievement Gap

Although it is apparent that religious schools reduce socioeconomic and racial achievement gaps, the question that emerges is about what features of religious schools help to explain the alleviating of these achievement gaps. Social scientists commonly propound three reasons to explain the achievement gap.

First, they believe that the culture of the religious schools contributes to the abating of the gap (Gaziel 1997). Some social scientists argue that to the extent to which this is true, religious schools do a better job of helping disadvantaged students (Coleman 1988; Coleman, Hoffer, and Kilgore 1982; Gaziel 1997; Marsch 1991; Morris 1994). In terms of the outward manifestations of this culture, theorists note several differences that can be objectively measured by using the NELS dataset. Some social scientists believe that the religious school advantage is due to the school atmosphere (Lee and Bryk 1986; Morris 1994). Another possibility is that religious schools require students to do more homework (Mentzer 1988). Other researchers believe that religious schools are less likely to have violence or threats of violence, which can often serve as major distractions for students trying to learn (Hudolin 1994; Irvine and Foster 1996). Still other social scientists believe that a higher level of racial harmony exists at religious schools because of the common thread of faith and Christian brotherhood (Irvine and Foster 1996). Finally, some social scientists believe that religious schools are likely to have modes of discipline that make them more prone to success (Morris 1994; Sander 1996).

A second factor, family factors or a broader sense of what Coleman described as "social capital," results from both family-based and community-based sources (Coleman 1988; Coleman and Hoffer 1987). Educators, sociologists, and psychologists have been quick to point out that religious people are more likely to remain in intact families, become engaged in their children's education, and provide an upbringing and community that encourage an atmosphere of morality and self-discipline (Jeynes 2005a, 2006, 2007).

Finally, a third possible factor is the fact that religious schools promote Christian, Jewish, or other forms of devotion (Irvine and Foster 1996). This, in turn, yields positive effects.

Each of these three factors is explained further in the following sections.

Culture of the School

The first factor to which social scientists point in helping to explain the religious school student advantage is school culture. This study sought to statistically examine many aspects of school culture. First, the study focused on five aspects of school culture: (1) school atmosphere, (2) racial harmony, (3) level of school discipline, (4) school violence, and (5) amount of homework done. The results demonstrate that religious schools outperform nonreligious schools in all of the five school trait categories and in nearly all of the individual questions that make up those categories. Table 9-4 shows the effects of attending a religious school for all the individual questions under each school trait category. In the first column, data are adjusted for SES, race, gender, and whether or not the school was in an urban setting; in the second column, data are adjusted only for race and gender. All of the differences are listed in standard deviation units, a procedure that is important for effectively comparing different measures because different assessments have different grading units and the scores vary to different degrees. Presenting the results in a standardized form makes it possible to compare the results of different tests more fairly and accurately. The effects for racial harmony and school atmosphere, on average, showed the largest advantage for the religious schools.

When data are adjusted for race and gender but not for SES and for whether the school was in an urban setting, the results were as follows. The regression coefficient for fewer racial/ethnic fights occurring at religious schools was 0.56. The regression coefficient for students being friendly with other racial groups was 0.20. The effects for the school atmosphere category were 0.26 for school spirit and 0.30 for teachers being interested in the students. Statistical analysis indicated that there was less than a 1 in 10,000 possibility that each of these results emerged by chance or coincidence. The effects for school violence were also noteworthy but varied considerably

Table 9-4: Effects (in Standard Deviation Units) of Religious Schools versus Nonreligious Schools on the Five School Variables for the Twelfth Grade (1992) (N = 18,726)

	Results Controlling for Gender and Race	Results Controlling for SES, Urban Setting, Gender, and Race
School Atmosphere Variables:		
School Spirit	0.26****	0.30****
Teachers Interested	0.30****	0.18****
Racial Harmony Variables:		
Friendly	0.20****	0.13****
Racial Fights	0.56****	0.57****
Discipline Variables:		
Disruptions	0.17****	0.11***
Ignore Cheating	−0.05	0.01
Offered Drugs	0.13****	0.20****
Violence Variables:		
Many Gangs	0.54****	0.66****
Threaten to Hurt	0.10***	0.11**
Fights	0.06*	0.03
Homework	0.14****	0.05**

*$p < .05$; **$p < .01$; ***$p < .001$; ****$p < .0001$.

depending on the question. The effect for whether there were many gangs showed a regression coefficient of 0.54 for attending a religious school, meaning that there were fewer gangs in religious schools. This result, based on statistical analysis, also had just a 1 in 10,000 possibility of occurring by chance or coincidence. The regression was smallest in this category for getting into a physical fight at school: 0.06. Going to a religious school also meant that students generally did more homework; the regression coefficient in this case was 0.14. The effects for school discipline were generally the smallest of the five categories. In fact, one of the three questions in this category, whether teachers ignore student cheating, yielded near zero

9 | Religion, Intact Families, and the Achievement Gap

Table 9-5: Rank Order of Learning Habits in Which Religious School Students Enjoy the Largest Advantage over Public School Students and Learning Habits Most Closely Associated with High Academic Achievement

	Largest Advantage for Religious Students Not Considering SES Factors	Largest Advantage for Religious Students Considering SES Factors	Greatest Influence on Math Achievement Not Considering SES Factors	Greatest Influence on Reading Achievement Considering SES Factors
First-Largest Effect	Taking harder Courses	Diligence	Taking harder courses	Taking harder courses
Second-Largest Effect	Diligence	Taking harder courses	Diligence	Diligence
Third-Largest Effect	Work habits	Work habits	Paying attention	Work habits
Fourth-Largest Effect	Work handed in on time	Work handed in on time	Work habits	Paying attention
Fifth-Largest Effect	Paying attention	Paying attention	Less absenteeism	Less absenteeism

effects. The effects for disruptions that impede learning and drugs offered to the students at school yielded effects of 0.17 and 0.13, respectively.

When data were adjusted for SES and for whether a school was in an urban setting in addition to race and gender factors, the results showed a similar pattern, the regression coefficient rising for whether there were gangs (0.66), racial fights (0.57), and a school spirit (0.30). Some regression coefficients decreased, including whether teachers were interested in students (0.18), whether the school was racially friendly (0.13), and whether the students did more homework (0.05).

When one examines the effects of learning habits on achievement, the results are quite intriguing. The results indicate that the three learning habits in which religious students enjoy the greatest advantage over their public school counterparts are the learning habits that are most strongly related to academic achievement. That is, taking harder courses, diligence, and overall work habits were the learning habits in which religious school students enjoyed their largest advantage over public school students.

Family, Social Capital, and Religious Commitment

A second reason that social scientists frequently cite for the achievement gap being narrower in religious schools is the fact that Christian and other religious schools emphasize the role of parental involvement more than is commonly found in public schools (Coleman 1988; Coleman and Hoffer 1987; Jeynes 2002b). Research also indicates that highly religious couples are more likely to remain married than are less religious couples and that intact families on average have children with considerably higher levels of achievement than do nonintact families (Jeynes 2002a; Sullivan 2001). Coleman (1988) and his colleagues assert that these two facts enable religious school students to possess, on average, a higher level of social capital than their public school counterparts have. He believes that social capital represents the degree to which certain key members of a society invest their time, energy, wisdom, and knowledge in an individual or institution.

According to Coleman and other social scientists, given that Christian and other religious school students are more likely to have had parents, teachers, churches, and other factors invest in them, they are more likely to excel academically. Religious school students are more likely to have involved parents, caring teachers, and other factors that have shown to be positively associated with high academic outcomes (Coleman and Hoffer 1987; Jeynes 2002c). One might ask why religious schools are more likely to be correlated with parental involvement and caring teachers. Coleman avers that religious and public schools have very different orientations that result in religious school students eventually being endowed with higher levels of social capital. He asserts that the orientation of the public schools is one that "sees schools as society's instrument for releasing a child from the blinders imposed by accident of birth into this family or that family. Schools have been designed to open broad horizons to the child, transcending the limitations of the parents." By contrast, the religious school orientation "sees a school as the extension of the family, reinforcing the family's values" (Coleman and Hoffer 1987: 3).

A third factor that social scientists frequently use to help explain the smaller achievement gap in religious schools is that Christian, Jewish, and similar schools encourage religious commitment among their students. Especially since the Supreme Court decisions of 1962 and 1963 removing prayer and Bible reading from the public schools, religious commitment has not been encouraged in public schools (Blanshard 1963; Jeynes 2005a; Kliebard 1969; Murray 1982).

There are a number of reasons why religious commitment could have a positive impact on academic outcomes that could ultimately reduce the achievement gap. The first of these reasons, and historically probably the most acknowledged, deals with a religious work ethic. This is often referred to as the "Protestant work ethic." Recent research, however, indicates that it may extend beyond the Protestant sphere to other religious groups. For example, Mentzer (1988) has found that Catholics in the United States possess a strong work ethic. Research in the social sciences has consistently indicated the existence of a religious work ethic (Furnham 1987; Gerhards 1996; Giorgi and Marsh 1990; Mudrack 1992).

A second reason why religious commitment could positively affect academic outcomes stems from the finding of some studies that suggest that religious people are more likely to have an internal locus of control (Jackson and Coursey 1988; Shrauger and Silverman 1971). Educational researchers have found a rather consistent relationship between having an internal locus of control and performing well in school (Garner and Cole 1986; Johnson 1992).

A third reason to think that there might be a correlation between religious commitment and academic outcomes emerges from the tendency for religious people to avoid behaviors that are typically regarded as undisciplined and harmful to educational achievement. A number of studies indicate that religiously committed teens are less likely to become involved in drug and alcohol abuse (Bahr, Hawks, and Wang 1993; Brownfield and Sorenson 1991; Nylander, Tung, and Xu 1996). Other studies indicate that religiously committed teens are less likely to engage in sexual behavior or become pregnant while they are still teenagers (Beck, Cole, and Hammond 1991; Holman and Harding 1996; Miller and Olson 1988).

When one combines the third reason given for the reduced achievement gap, religious commitment, with at least a portion of the family/social capital component of the second reason given for the reduced gap, that is, family structure, an amazing result emerges: the achievement gap disappears.

Table 9-6 indicates that when the data are adjusted for SES and gender, Black and Hispanic adolescents who are religious and from intact families do just as well academically as white students. In Table 9-6, the academic indicator favors African American and Latino students if the result is listed as a positive number and favors white students if it is a negative number. One can see that once one controls for SES and gender, the achievement gap essentially evaporates for all the standardized test measures except in Science. Moreover, religious African American and Latino students from intact families are actually less likely to be left back a grade and are more likely to take the Basic Core set of courses, as prescribed by the NAEP, than are white students. Even if one does not factor in SES (see the last column of Table 9-6), the achievement gap is quite small when religious African American and Latino students from intact families are compared with white students.

The results suggest that the achievement gap might not be quite as indefatigable and pervasive as many people believe. Given the number of efforts social scientists have launched to reduce the achievement gap, the fact that the combination of personal religious commitment and coming from an intact family eliminates the gap for African American and Latino students is nothing short of magnificent. Various other comparisons of religious and nonreligious schools not only indicate that Christian and other religious schools reduce the achievement gap, but also indicate some of the most likely reasons why this is the case.

These findings concerning the reduction and even elimination of the achievement gap are especially noteworthy when we consider that schools have been inundated with programs designed to reduce the gap that have had only marginal success (Green 2001; Haycock 2001). Showing that factors as simple as religious commitment, religious schools, and family structure can reduce or eliminate the gap may inspire educators and social scientists to encourage policies that are supportive of faith and the family so that the gap can be narrowed significantly.

Policy Implications

The results of this research have vital implications for educational policy in assessing whether school choice programs that include private schools should be initiated and determining whether educators in the public

9 | Religion, Intact Families, and the Achievement Gap

Table 9-6: Effects (in Standard Deviation Units) on Academic Achievement for Twelfth-Grade (1992) Black and Hispanic Children from a "More Traditional" Background versus White Children, Using the SES Model (N = 24,599)

Academic Measure	Achievement Gap Controlling for Gender and SES	Achievement Gap Controlling for Gender but Not SES
Standardized measures		
Math	0.4%	–0.8%
Reading	–0.4%	–1.5%
Science	–2.4%	–3.6%
Social Studies	0.0%	–1.5%
Composite	0.0%	–1.3%
Other measures		
Left Back[a]	2.0%	1.1%
Basic Core[a]	6.2%	5.6%

[a] Logistic regression.

schools may have something to learn from certain aspects of how religious schools are run.

Determining Whether School Choice Programs Should Be Initiated

A primary reason why school choice attracts so much attention is the belief that it will produce an overall improvement in school quality. The late Milton Friedman (1994) epitomized this view when he stated, "Choice produces competition. Competition produces quality." This assertion gains some credence when one examines the results of this study suggesting that students in religious schools outperform their counterparts in nonreligious schools.

Although many social scientists acknowledge the educational advantage that religious schools enjoy, a significant number of them wonder whether school choice is an attractive option. The reasons that are given are as follows. Opponents of choice question whether such a program would really yield the level of competition that its supporters claim. These opponents contend that for the competition level to increase, there would need to be a large number of students willing to leave their current schools and participate in school choice programs. In reality, although the current evidence is limited, those few places that practice school choice programs have low student participation rates. Minnesota's public school choice system, for example, has about forty thousand students participating out of more than eight hundred thousand students statewide (Colopy and Tarr 1994). The participation rate in Britain's school program, which includes both public and private schools, is only about 15 percent (Gewirtz, Ball, and Bowe 1995; Woods, Bagley, and Glatter 1998).

Nevertheless, to the extent to which religious schools promote parental involvement, religious commitment, and an overall more disciplined lifestyle, all of which relate to positive academic and social outcomes, it becomes very difficult to argue against allowing choice without sounding insular and self-serving (Lieberman 1993; Moe 2001). After all, even with low school choice participation rates, if the participant students of color are benefiting and the academic gap is reduced, it once again appears illogical and potentially racially oppressive and discriminatory to deny minority students the right to more fully reach their potential via a school choice system.

Determining Whether Educators in the Public Schools May Have Something to Learn from Religious Schools

A number of social scientists believe that it is crucial that public school educators learn from the example set by religious schools. The findings of this study support this view. The results indicate not only that students in religious schools outperform their counterparts in nonreligious schools on virtually every measure of academic achievement, but also that in religious schools, the academic gaps are reduced that commonly exist between low-SES and high-SES students as well as those between Black and Hispanic students and white students. Especially because reducing these gaps is one of the primary aims of educators, it is logical that if religious schools have learned to produce these outcomes, they have something to teach the secular educational community. Many public school educators have tried for years to reduce these seemingly unalterable academic gaps. If religious educators have developed a strategy that causes the gaps to shrink, public school educators would be wise to seriously examine the religious school model.

The primary area that public school educators are imitating is the character education emphasis of Christian and other religious schools (Bryk, Lee, and Holland 1993; Halstead and Lewicka 1998; McEwen, Knipe, and Gallagher 1997). Before 1963, character education was a major part of public school education. After state-approved prayer and Bible reading were removed from the public schools, character education ceased to be a major emphasis in many public schools (Haynes 1999; Miller 1998). Immediately in 1963, there was an ostensible decrease in most major academic achievement measures and a sudden increase in adolescent crime (U.S. Department of Education 2000; U.S. Department of Justice 1993). From 1963 to 1980, average scores on the Stanford Achievement Test, the California Achievement Test, the Scholastic Achievement Test, and the Iowa Test of Education Development, among others, decreased more than at any time in the history of these tests (Harnischfeger and Wiley 1975; U.S. Department of Education 2000). Concurrently, most measures of juvenile crime and delinquent behavior rose 300–700 percent (U.S. Department of Health and Human Services 1992; U.S. Department of Justice 1993). Social scientists differ in the extent to which they believe the absence of character education in the public schools contributed to these trends (Brunsma and Rockquemore 1998). Nevertheless, in the eyes of many educators, character education is important in the development of the self-discipline necessary to perform well in school and avoid harmful behavior (Edwards 2000; Ryan and Bohlin 1998; Smagorinsky 2000).

Maintaining high academic standards is a second area in which social scientists believe that public educators can learn from religious schools. Mentzer (1988) states that religious schools frequently require more homework. Hoffer (1997) and Bryk, Lee, and Holland (1993) observe that religious schools encourage students to take college preparation courses more than one usually finds in public schools. Research evidence suggests that disadvantaged children, in particular, benefit from this emphasis on demanding educational standards (Coleman 1988; Coleman, Hoffer, and Kilgore 1982; Gaziel 1997). Social scientists suggest that there may be myriad other areas in which public schools can apply the religious school rubric. These include some of the variables that were addressed in this analysis, such as ways in which Christian and religious schools increase racial harmony and reduce school fighting (Irvine and Foster 1996).

However, before one gets too excited about the potential of public school educators learning from private school educators, one caveat is in order: some social scientists believe that this is very difficult if not impossible. Gaziel (1997) believes that the achievement gap between religious and public schools can be explained by a difference in school culture. To the extent to which this is true, it might be difficult for public schools to replicate the results that often emerge in religious schools. Carbonaro (1999) and Hallinan and Kubitschek (1999) suggest that the religious school culture that includes an emphasis on family values and personal morality plays a large role in explaining why religious school students do so well academically. Given that public school educators might not place an emphasis on these same areas, this limits the degree to which public schools can benefit from the strengths of the religious school system.

Although educators are frequently divided over the merits of school choice, there is a growing consensus that public schools can benefit by imitating some of the strengths of the religious school model. There may be limitations on just what qualities can be imitated, but the increased emphasis on character education, high academic standards, and parental involvement can be imitated (Barber 1984; Hyde 1990; Schmidt 1988). There is also a growing awareness that public schools should not inhibit religious freedom but should allow it just as they do the other freedoms guaranteed by the Constitution.

The results of this study indicate that religious education is a vibrant part of the education system in the United States. It should inspire researchers to examine more closely specifically why students who attend religious schools outperform their counterparts in nonreligious schools. It also supports the notion that including religious schools in a system of school choice conceivably could improve the overall quality of the U.S. education system. It would seem beneficial to further examine why students from religious schools outperform students in public schools.

References

Bahr, Stephen J., Ricky D. Hawks, and Gabe Wang. 1993. "Family and Religious Influences on Adolescent Substance Abuse." *Youth and Society* 24: 443–65.

Barber, Lucie. 1984. "Clues for Religious Education." *Religious Education* 79: 66–75.

Beck, Scott H., Bettie S. Cole, and Judith A. Hammond. 1991. "Religious Heritage and Premarital Sex: Evidence from a National Sample of Adults." *Journal for the Scientific Study of Religion* 30: 173–80.

Blanshard, Paul. 1963. *Religion and the Schools*. Boston: Beacon Press.

Brownfield, David, and Ann Marie Sorenson. 1991. "Religion and Drug Use among Adolescents: A Social Support Conceptualization and Interpretation." *Deviant Behavior* 12: 259–76.

Brunsma, David L., and Kerry A. Rockquemore. 1998. "Effects of School Uniforms on Attendance, Behavior Problems, Substance Use, and Academic Achievement." *Journal of Educational Research* 92: 53–62.

Bryk, Anthony, Valerie E. Lee, and Peter B. Holland. 1993. *Catholic Schools and the Common Good*. Cambridge, MA: Harvard University Press.

Carbonara, William J. 1999. "Opening the Debate on Closure and School Outcomes: Comment on Morgan and Sørensen." *American Sociological Review* 64: 682–86.

Coleman, James S. 1988. "'Social Capital' and Schools: One Reason for Higher Private School Achievement." *Education Digest* 53: 6–9.

Coleman, James S., and Thomas Hoffer. 1987. *Public and Private High Schools: The Impact of Communities*. New York: Basic Books.

Coleman, James, Thomas Hoffer, and Sally Kilgore. 1982. *High School Achievement: Public, Catholic, and Private Schools Compared*. New York: Basic Books.

Colopy, Kelly W., and Hope Tarr. 1994. *Minnesota's Public School Options*. Washington, DC: Policy Studies Associates.

Conciatore, Jacqueline. 1990. "Nation's Report Card Shows Little Progress: Black Students Close Gap." *Black Issues in Higher Education* 6: 30–31.

Cooper, Harris, and Larry V. Hedges, eds. 1994. *The Handbook of Research Synthesis*. New York: Russell Sage Foundation.

Cross, Theodore, and Robert Bruce Slater. 2000. "The Alarming Decline in the Academic Performance of African-American Men." *Journal of Blacks in Higher Education* 27: 82–87.

Deck, Allan Figueroa, Yolanda Tarango, and Timothy M. Matovina. 1995. *Perspectivas: Hispanic Ministry*. Kansas City, MO: Sheed and Ward.

Edwards, Clifford H. 2000. "The Moral Dimensions of Teaching and Classroom Discipline." *American Secondary Education* 28: 20–25.

Friedman, M. 1994. Commentary on the *Nightly Business Report* (2 August).

Furnham, Adrian. 1987. "Predicting Protestant Work Ethic Beliefs." *European Journal of Personality* 1: 93–106.

Garner, C. William, and Ernest G. Cole. 1986. "The Achievement of Students in Low-SES Settings: An Investigation of the Relationship between Locus of Control and Field Dependence." *Urban Education* 21: 189–206.

Gaziel, Haim H. 1997. "Impact of School Culture on Effectiveness of Secondary Schools with Disadvantaged Students." *Journal of Educational Research* 90: 310–18.

Gerhards, J. 1996. "Religion and the Spirit of Capitalism: A Comparison of Attitudes toward Work and the Economic Order in the USA and Spain." *Berliner Journal für Soziologie* 6: 541–49.

Gewirtz, Sharon, Stephen J. Ball, and Richard Bowe. 1995. *Markets, Choice, and Equity in Education*. Buckingham, UK: Open University.

Giorgi, Liana, and Catherine Marsh. 1990. "The Protestant Work Ethic as a Cultural Phenomenon." *European Journal of Social Psychology* 20: 499–517.

Gordon, Margaret T. 1976. "A Different View of the IQ-Achievement Gap." *Sociology of Education* 49: 4–11.

Green, Laura R., Katherine Blasik, Kristen Hartshorn, and Elizabeth Shatten-Jones. 2000. "Closing the Achievement Gap in Science: A Program to Encourage Minority and Female Students to Participate and Succeed." *ERS Spectrum* 18: 3–13.

Green, R. Stephen. 2001. "Closing the Achievement Gap: Lessons Learned and Challenges Ahead." *Teaching and Change* 8: 215–24.

Greenway, Roger S. 1992. *Discipling the City: A Comprehensive Approach to Urban Mission*. Grand Rapids: Baker.

Hallinan, Maureen T., and Warren N. Kubitschek. 1999. "Conceptualizing and Measuring School and Social Networks: Comment on Morgan and Sørensen." *American Sociological Review* 64: 687–93.

Halstead, J. Mark, and Katarzyna Lewicka. 1998. "Should Homosexuality Be Taught as an Acceptable Alternative Lifestyle? A Muslim Perspective." *Cambridge Journal of Education* 28: 49–64.

Harnischfeger, Annegret, and David E. Wiley. 1975. *Achievement Test Score Decline: Do We Need to Worry?* Chicago: CEMREL.

Haycock, Kati. 2001. "Closing the Achievement Gap." *Educational Leadership* 58: 6–11.

Haycock, Kati, and Craig Jerald. 2002. "Closing the Achievement Gap." *Principal* 82: 20–23.

Haynes, Charles. 1999. "Religion in the Public Schools." *School Administrator* 56: 6–10.

Hedges, Larry V., and Amy Nowell. 1999. "Changes in the Black-White Gap in Achievement Test Scores." *Sociology of Education* 72: 111–35.

Henderson, Ronald D. 1975. "School Climate in White and Black Elementary Schools: A Comparative Study." *Urban Education* 9: 380–99.

Henry, Carl F. H., and Robert Lincoln Hancock. 1979. *The Ministry of Development in Evangelical Perspective: A Symposium on the Social and Spiritual Mandate*. Pasadena, CA: William Carey Library.

Hoffer, Thomas B. 1997. "High School Graduation Requirements: Effects on Dropping Out and Student Achievement." *Teachers College Record* 98: 584–607.

Holman, Thomas B., and John R. Harding. 1996. "The Teaching of Nonmarital Sexual Abstinence and Members' Sexual Attitudes and Behaviors: The Case of the Latter-Day Saints." *Review of Religious Research* 38: 51–60.

Hudolin-Gabin, Janet. 1994. "Lessons from Catholic Schools: Promoting Quality in Chicago's Public Schools." *Educational Forum* 58: 282–88.

Hyde, Kenneth Edwin. 1990. *Religion in Childhood and Adolescence: A Comprehensive Review of the Research*. Birmingham, AL: Religious Education Press.

Irvine, Jacqueline Jordan, and Michèle Foster, eds. 1996. *Growing up African American in Catholic Schools*. New York: Teachers College.

Jackson, Laurence E., and Robert D. Coursey. 1988. "The Relationship of God Control and Internal Locus of Control to Intrinsic Religious Motivation, Coping and Purpose in Life. *Journal for the Scientific Study of Religion* 27: 399–410.

Jerald, Craig, and Kati Haycock. 2002. "Closing the Gap." *School Administrator* 59: 16–22.

Jeynes, William. 1999. "The Effects of Religious Commitment on the Academic Achievement of Black and Hispanic Children." *Urban Education* 34: 458–79.

Jeynes, William. 2001. "Religious Commitment and Adolescent Behavior." *Journal of Interdisciplinary Studies* 23: 31–50.

Jeynes, William. 2002a. *Divorce, Family Structure, and the Academic Success of Children*. Binghamton, NY: Haworth Press.

Jeynes, William. 2002b. "Educational Policy and the Effects of Attending a Religious School on the Academic Achievement of Children. *Educational Policy* 16: 406–24.

Jeynes, William. 2002c. Why Religious Schools Positively Impact the Academic Achievement of Children. *International Journal of Education and Religion* 3: 16–32.

Jeynes, William. 2003a. "The Effects of Black and Hispanic Twelfth Graders Living in Intact Families and Being Religious on Their Academic Achievement." *Urban Education* 38: 35–57.

Jeynes, William. 2003b. *Religion, Education, and Academic Success*. Greenwich, CT: Information Age Press.

Jeynes, William. 2005a. "Effects of Parental Involvement and Family Structure on the Academic Achievement of Adolescents." *Marriage and Family Review* 37: 99–117.

Jeynes, William. 2005b. "The Impact of Religious Schools on the Academic Achievement of Low-SES Students." *Journal of Empirical Theology* 18: 22–40.

Jeynes, William. 2006. "Adolescent Religious Commitment and Their Consumption of Marijuana, Cocaine, and Alcohol." *Journal of Health and Social Policy* 21: 1–20.

Jeynes, William. 2007. *American Educational History: School, Society, and the Common Good*. Thousand Oaks, CA: Sage.

Johnson, Sylvia T. 1992. "Extra-School Factors in Achievement, Attainment, and Aspiration among Junior and Senior High School-Age African American Youth." *Journal of Negro Education* 61: 99–119.

Jones, Lyle V. 1984. "White-Black Achievement Differences: The Narrowing Gap." *American Psychologist* 39: 1207–13.

Kliebard, Herbert M. 1969. *Religion and Education in America*. Scranton, PA: International Textbook Company.

Kozol, Jonathan. 1991. *Savage Inequalities*. New York: Crown Publishers.

Lee, Valerie E., and Anthony S. Bryk. 1986. "Effects of Single-Sex Secondary Schools on Student Achievement and Attitudes. *Journal of Educational Psychology* 78: 381–95.

LePore, Paul C., and John Robert Warren. 1997. "A Comparison of Single-Sex and Coeducational Catholic Secondary Schooling: Evidence from the National

Educational Longitudinal Study of 1988." *American Educational Research Journal* 34: 485–511.

Lieberman, Myron. 1993. *Public Education: An Autopsy.* Cambridge, MA: Harvard University Press.

Lindjord, Denise. 1998. "A Nation Divided: Study Highlights the Economic and Racial Gap among Families Is Wide and Growing Wider." *Journal of Early Education and Family Review* 5: 6–7.

Marsh, Herbert W. 1991. "Public, Catholic Single-Sex, and Catholic Coeducational High Schools: Their Effects on Achievement, Affect, and Behaviors." *American Journal of Education* 99: 320–56.

McEwen, Alex, Damian Knipe, and Tony Gallagher. 1997. "The Impact of Single-Sex and Coeducational Schooling on Participation and Achievement in Science: A 10-Year Perspective." *Research in Science and Technological Education* 15: 223–33.

Mentzer, Marc S. 1988. "Religion and Achievement Motivation in the United States: A Structural Analysis." *Sociological Focus* 21: 307–16.

Miller, Brent C., and Terrance D. Olson. 1988. "Sexual Attitudes and Behavior of High School Students in Relation to Background and Contextual Factors." *Journal of Sex Research* 24: 194–200.

Miller, W. R. 1998. "Researching the Spiritual Dimensions of Alcohol and Other Drug Problems." *Addiction* 93: 979–90.

Moe, Terry M. 2001. *School Vouchers and the American Public.* Washington, DC: Brookings Institution.

Morris, Andrew B. 1994. "The Academic Performance of Catholic Schools." *School Organization* 14: 81–89.

Mudrack, Peter E. 1992. "'Work' or 'Leisure': The Protestant Work Ethic and Participation in an Employee Fitness Program." *Journal of Organizational Behavior* 13: 81–88.

Murray, William J. 1982. *My Life without God.* Nashville, TN: Nelson.

Navarro, M. Susana, and Diana S. Natalicio. 1999. "Closing the Achievement Gap in El Paso: A Collaboration for K-16 Renewal." *Phi Delta Kappan* 80: 597–601.

Nicholls, Bruce J., and Beulah Wood. 1996. *Sharing Good News with the Poor.* Grand Rapids: Baker.

Noell, Jay. 1982. "Public and Catholic Schools: A Reanalysis of 'Public and Private Schools.'" *Sociology of Education* 55: 123–32.

Nylander, A. B., Y. Tung, and X Xu. 1996. "The Effect of Religion on Adolescent Drug Use in America: An Assessment of Change, 1976–1992." Paper presented at the annual meeting of the American Sociological Association.

Ogbu, John U. 1992. "Adaptation to Minority Status and Impact on School Success." *Theory into Practice* 31: 287–95.

Orfield, G., R. D. Kahlenberg, E. W. Gordon, F. Genessee, P. D. Slocumb, and R. K. Payne. 2000. "The New Diversity." *Principal* 79: 6–32.

Osborne, Jason W. 1999. "Unraveling Underachievement among African American Boys from an Identification with the Academics Perspective." *Journal of Negro Education* 68: 555–65.

Perkins, John M. 1995. *Restoring At-Risk Communities: Doing It Together and Doing It Right*. Grand Rapids: Baker.

Rayburn, Wendell G., and Edward J. Hayes. 1975. "Compensatory Education: Effective or Ineffective?" *Journal of Counseling Psychology* 22: 523–28.

Roach, Ronald. 2001. "In the Academic and Think-Tank World, Pondering Achievement-Gap Remedies Takes Center Stage." *Black Issues in Higher Education* 18: 26–27.

Roscigno, Vincent J. 1998. "Race and the Reproduction of Educational Disadvantage." *Social Forces* 76: 1033–61.

Ross, Steven M., Lana J. Smith, and Jason P. Casey. 1999. "'Bridging the Gap': The Effects of the Success For All Program on Elementary School Reading Achievement as a Function of Student Ethnicity and Ability Level." *School Effectiveness and School Improvement* 10: 129–50.

Rumberger, Russell W., and J. Douglas Willms. 1992. "The Impact of Racial and Ethnic Segregation on the Achievement Gap in California High Schools." *Educational Evaluation and Policy Analysis* 14: 377–96.

Ryan, Kevin, and Karen E. Bohlin. 1998. *Building Character in Schools: Practical Ways to Bring Moral Instruction to Life*. San Francisco: Jossey-Bass.

Sander, William. 1996. "Catholic Grade Schools and Academic Achievement." *Journal of Human Resources* 31: 540–48.

Schmidt, P. F. 1988. "Moral Values of Adolescents: Public versus Christian Schools." *Journal of Psychology and Christianity* 7: 50–54.

Shrauger, J. Sidney, and Ronald E. Silverman. 1971. "The Relationship of Religious Background and Participation to Locus of Control." *Journal for the Scientific Study of Religion* 10: 11–16.

Simpson, Carl. 1981. "Classroom Organization and the Gap between Minority and Non-minority Student Performance Levels." *Educational Research Quarterly* 6: 43–53.

Slater, Robert Bruce. 1999. "Ranking the States by the Black-White Scoring Gap." *Journal of Blacks in Higher Education* 26: 105–10.

Slavin, Robert E., and Nancy A. Madden. 2001. "Reducing the Gap: Success for All and the Achievement of African American and Latino Students." Paper presented at the annual meeting of the American Educational Research Association, Seattle, WA.

Smagorinsky, Peter. 2000. "Reflecting on Character through Literary Themes." *English Journal* 89: 64–69.

So, Alvin Y., and Kenyon S. Chan. 1984. "What Matters? The Relative Impact of Language Background and Socioeconomic Status on Reading Achievement." *NABE: The Journal for the National Association for Bilingual Education* 8: 27–41.

Sullivan, K. 2001. "Understanding the Relationship between Religiosity and Marriage: An Investigation of the Immediate and Longitudinal Effects of Religiosity on Newlywed Couples." *Journal of Family Psychology* 15: 610–26.

Trent, William T. 1997. "Why the Gap between Black and White Performance in School? A Report on the Effects of Race on Student Achievement in the St. Louis Public Schools." *Journal of Negro Education* 66: 320–29.

U.S. Department of Education. 2000. *Digest of Education Statistics, 1999.* Washington, DC: U.S. Department of Education.

U.S. Department of Health and Human Services. 1992. *Statistical Abstract of the United States.* Washington, DC: U.S. Department of Health and Human Services.

U.S. Department of Justice. 1993. *Age-Specific Arrest Rate and Race-Specific Arrest Rates for Selected Offenses, 1965–1992.* Washington, DC: U.S. Department of Justice.

Vail, Kathleen. 1996. "Tornado from Texas." *Executive Educator* 18: 16–18.

Willms, J. Douglas. 1985. "Catholic-School Effects on Academic Achievement: New Evidence from the High School and Beyond Follow-up." *Sociology of Education* 58: 98–114.

Woods, Philip A., Carl Bagley, and Ron Glatter. 1998. *School Choice and Competition: Markets in the Public Interest?* London: Routledge.

10

Religion and Academic Achievement among Adolescents

Benjamin McKune | John P. Hoffmann

The term *religiosity* refers to various aspects of religious devotion, activity, and belief. Previous research has focused mostly on the effects of religiosity among adults, yet its effect on adolescent behaviors has also earned significant attention. Much of this attention has addressed delinquency and other forms of deviant behavior, such as drug use and premarital sexual activity; few studies have assessed the association between religiosity and academic achievement. Given the effects that academic achievement during adolescence can have on future educational attainment, occupational success, and socioeconomic status, it is unfortunate that more research has not addressed this area. The few studies that have addressed the topic show that adolescents' church participation is positively associated with their own educational expectations, which expectations then lead to higher math and reading scores on standardized tests (Regnerus 2000; Regnerus, Smith, and Fritsch 2003). In addition, the religious involvement of adolescents in tenth grade is consistently and positively associated with subsequent academic achievement (Muller and Ellison 2001). This association holds for African American and Latino youths (Brown and Gary 1991; Jeynes 2002; Sikkink and Hernandez 2003) and for both urban and nonurban students (Jeynes 2003).

Some researchers have suggested that the relationship between religiosity and academic outcomes is spurious and can be explained by variations in family income. In this view, adolescents who live with affluent parents are more likely to be religious and to have more academic success. This alleged relationship has been refuted, however, by research that has examined broader measures of academic achievement, family income, and neighborhood income levels (Regnerus, Smith, and Fritsch 2003).

Other research has suggested that the relationship between academic performance and religious commitment can be explained by whether or not a student attends a private religious school. This line of research contends that private religious schools are more likely to have religiously committed students and that these schools promote self-discipline, moral training, and high standards (Bryk, Lee, and Holland 1993; Coleman, Hoffer, and Kilgore 1982). However, subsequent research has demonstrated that the relationship between academic achievement and religious commitment remains virtually unaffected when the type of school (whether private religious or not) is taken into account (Jeynes 2003).

There is, nonetheless, evidence that fundamentalist affiliation and belief have a significant negative influence on educational attainment (Darnell and Sherkat 1997). Proponents of this position claim that many fundamentalist Christians and Evangelicals are suspicious of the usefulness of secular education because it serves to undermine both secular and divine authority by promoting "humanism and denigrating faith" (Darnell and Sherkat 1997: 307). However, Beyerlein and Smith (2004) have demonstrated that the negative association between fundamentalist beliefs and educational attainment does not persist when thorough measures of religious beliefs and a sufficient number of Protestant denominations are examined.

A more compelling argument is that the effect of religiosity on academic achievement can be explained by variations in family capital and community capital (Muller and Ellison 2001). The evidence that family social capital positively influences academic achievement is persuasive (e.g., Parcel and Dufur 2001). Moreover, students who come from favorable family and community backgrounds not only are more likely to earn better grades, but also tend to be more religious. Muller and Ellison (2001), in a comprehensive assessment of this view, found that the effects of religiosity on students' educational expectations, time spent on homework, number of mathematics courses taken, and probability of graduation are partially mediated by family capital and community capital.

Nevertheless, Muller and Ellison's (2001) analysis had several shortcomings that raise questions about their results. First, their measures of family and community capital were limited. For example, the measure of family social capital was based on questions about the following three issues: (1) what parents expected of their children, (2) how often parents discussed school with their children, and (3) how often parents and children discussed things that were studied in class. Although these were solid elementary measures of family capital, Muller and Ellison looked simply at how involved a parent was in the child's education and not at the overall quality of the relationship between parent and child (Coleman 1988). Muller and Ellison's measure of community capital was also limited. They used questions that asked about (1) how well the parents knew their teens' friends' parents and (2) how much the adolescents' peer group valued academic success. It is clear that these were assessments of peer associations rather than of community capital.

Second, Muller and Ellison's operationalization of religious involvement was not sufficient. They assessed religious involvement on the basis of three questions about (1) frequency of religious attendance, (2) participation in religious activities, and (3) whether or not students considered themselves to be religious. These give a truncated view of religiosity; other variables such as prayer or views of scripture were not available in their dataset.[1] Moreover, this measurement scheme provides only a limited picture, since it ignored the issue of parents' religiosity. Yet it is clear that adolescents' religiosity is affected in a large degree by their parents' religiosity in that religious parents provide an environment that socializes adolescents to family norms and practices. Research demonstrates that parents' religiosity has a direct effect on their children's religiosity (Myers 1996; Regnerus, Smith, and Smith 2004).

There are other reasons for presuming that religiosity ought to have an effect on academic achievement regardless of family and community social capital. First, religious involvement provides opportunities for youths to gain skills that help them to succeed in school, such as discipline, respect for authority, and a tendency to take responsibility for their own actions (Jeynes 2003). Similarly, religious institutions, in the main, "largely reinforce traditional paths to success" (Regnerus 2000: 364). Religious involvement also provides a context in which students can develop social contacts that help them in their education, and it puts them in

---

[1] In their study, Muller and Ellison (2001) use the National Educational Longitudinal Study dataset, which includes limited measures of religiosity.

contact with religious leaders and youth group coordinators, who often serve as positive role models (Gardner 2004). Religious involvement also deters involvement in deviant activities. Students who spend more time in religious activities tend to spend less time involved in deviant activities (Johnson et al. 2000), and this pattern might foster conventional behaviors such as working on school projects, doing homework, seeing education as a worthwhile pursuit, and avoiding deviant peer networks.

In addition, religion has a causal influence on the morals and actions of adolescents that is not entirely reducible to nonreligious explanations involving social control, solidarity, deterrence, or other social phenomena (Nonnemaker, McNeely, and Blum 2006). Indeed, "there is something particularly religious in religion, which is not reducible to nonreligious explanations" (Smith 2003: 19). Perceived relationships with the divine exert "pro-social influences in the lives of youth not by happenstance or generic social process, but precisely as an outcome of American religions' particular theological, moral, and spiritual commitments" (Smith 2003: 20). These observations about academic achievement and adolescent religiosity lead to our first hypothesis:

> *Hypothesis 1*: Religiosity and academic achievement are associated even when adjusting for the effects of family and community social capital.

A recent study helps to illuminate some additional ways in which religiosity might promote academic achievement among adolescents. Although this study focused on delinquency, the consistent negative association between delinquency and academic achievement suggests that its results could also inform studies of the latter outcome (Maguin and Loeber 1996; McGloin, Pratt, and Maahs 2004). Pearce and Haynie (2004) demonstrated that higher levels of mother *and* child religiosity by themselves had modest attenuating effects on delinquency. Nonetheless, their key finding was that the concordance between parent religiosity and child religiosity was negatively associated with delinquency. This occurred regardless of whether the concordance favored religiosity or irreligiosity. In particular, they found that mother-child religious homogamy was as strongly and as consistently associated with subsequent delinquency or lack thereof as was an adolescent's own religiosity.

One might be tempted to assume that the connection between parent-child religious homogamy and positive adolescent outcomes was the result of an improvement in the quality of the parent-child relationship.

However, the negative relationship between religious homogamy and delinquency was shown to hold even when dimensions of family well-being were taken into account (Pearce and Haynie 2004).

In our analysis, we drew on Muller and Ellison's (2001) model as a baseline, but we utilized more complete measures of religiosity, family capital, and community capital than those used in their study. We also considered the model of religious homogamy to further explore the association between religiosity, social capital, and academic achievement. In addition, we examined change in academic achievement over time to ensure the reliability of our findings and to carefully specify the temporal nature of religion and academic achievement.

> *Hypothesis 2*: Religious homogamy between parents and children is positively related to increasing levels of academic achievement among adolescents, even after adjusting for the effects of family and community social capital.

Data and Measures

We examined the hypothesis with data for two years from the National Longitudinal Study of Adolescent Health (Add Health). These data were collected in the 1994–1995 and 1995–1996 academic years and included information from approximately twenty thousand adolescents in grades 7 through 12. The students were asked a number of questions about their background, general health, schoolwork, community, home life, social relationships, and religious beliefs and practices. Their parents were asked a number of questions about relationships with their children and their community, family, and religious lives. After omitting adolescents who did not participate in Wave 2 of the study (because they were in twelfth grade in Wave 1 and then graduated, because they dropped out of school between Wave 1 and Wave 2, or because they were otherwise unavailable) and adolescents whose parents had not participated in the study, we were left with a subsample of approximately fourteen thousand adolescents. Further, after removing cases representing respondents who did not respond to the complete battery of questions regarding grades, religiosity, family and community social capital, and demographic characteristics, we were left with an analytic subsample of 8,051. Approximately four thousand cases were lost because of the large amount of missing data on the variable that measured family income. A major drawback of the data could be that they disproportionately exclude those at the bottom of the socioeconomic strata, who are more likely to drop out of school and are more reluctant to report their income.[2]

The outcome variable, academic achievement in the 1995–1996 school year, was gauged by students' self-reported grades in mathematics, science, history/social sciences, and English/language arts. The possible responses were "A," "B," "C," and "D or lower." The variables were recoded to a scale ranging from 0 to 3, where higher scores indicated that students had reported receiving a higher grade. The means of the four variables were used to create an overall measure of academic achievement. The scale had a Cronbach's α score of 0.75. Although some research has recommended the use of standardized scores to assess academic achievement (or ability), several studies have indicated that the reliability of self-reported grades is high and that this is generally a valid assessment of differences in academic achievement among adolescents. Moreover, students' self-reported grades were strongly associated with other objective academic outcomes across groups, such as test scores (Anaya 1999; Pace, Barahona, and Kaplan 1985; Pike 1995, 1996). However, the Add Health dataset did not include test scores, so we could not determine the validity of this claim in this study.

The first independent variable that we included in the model, academic achievement in the 1994–1995 school year, was measured in the same way as academic achievement in the 1995–1996 school year. The scale had a Cronbach's α of 0.75. By including Wave 1 academic achievement in the statistical model, we assessed changes over time in academic achievement and specified more clearly the association between the predictor variables and the outcome variable.

We assessed various aspects of religiosity on the basis of questions that inquired (1) how often the student attended religious services, (2) how important religion was to the student, (3) how often the student prayed, and (4) whether or not the student agreed that the sacred scriptures of his or her religion were the work of God and were completely without mistake. Although recent research suggests that public and private religiosity could have different effects on adolescent outcomes (Nonnemaker, McNeely, and Blum 2003), we chose to combine these four measures of religiosity into one scale for three main reasons. First, the only other aspect of

---

[2] Indeed, we found that while families in which neither parent has more than a high school education constitute only 33.0 percent of our sample, they make up 41.6 percent of those who refused to report their income.

public religiosity that could be included in the scale besides frequency of religious service attendance was how often the adolescent attended youth groups. However, not all congregations provided youth groups for their adolescent members. Second, to make the adolescent religiosity scale directly comparable to the parent religiosity scale, the measure of youth group attendance had to be dropped from the analysis, since there was no equivalent measure of religiosity in the parent survey. Third, a factor analysis revealed that the four remaining measures of religiosity loaded onto a single factor, with component matrix coefficients of 0.750, 0.822, 0.772, and 0.537 for church attendance, the importance of religion, the frequency of prayer, and biblical inerrancy, respectively. The scale had a Cronbach's α of 0.67. When the variable measuring public religiosity was removed from the scale, the overall scale Cronbach's α was reduced to 0.58.

The first two variables of the religiosity scale—religious service attendance and importance of religion—ranged from 1 to 4 but were recoded to a scale that ranged from 0 to 3, where higher numbers were indicative of higher levels of religiosity. This was to make the measures consistent, so a student who reported no religious behavior or beliefs had a score of 0 on the scale. The third variable, frequency of prayer, was measured on a scale from 1 to 5 but was recoded to a scale of 0 to 3, where the responses "at least once a month" and "less than once a month" were combined (moreover, few respondents selected these options). The final religion variable was a dichotomous variable that was recoded so that a score of 3 indicated that a student believed that the sacred scriptures of his or her religion were the work of God and were completely without mistake and a score of 0 indicated that the student did not hold this belief. Students who reported belonging to a religion that had no sacred scriptures were assigned a score of 2.4, which was the average score reported by students who belonged to religions that had sacred scriptures. The mean of the four variables was then used as the measure of religiosity. We used the same items, with identical coding procedures, to measure parental religiosity. The resulting scale for parents had a Cronbach's α of 0.86.[3]

---

3 As a test of validity, we tried creating the religiosity scale by means of a factor analysis. We also tried recoding the scriptural inerrancy and frequency of prayer variables in different ways before creating the scale. In each case, the resulting scale was highly and significantly associated with the scale that we used in our analysis, indicating that different coding strategies did not change the nature of the latent variable being measured.

We also included a product term in the model, consisting of the child religiosity scale multiplied by the parent religiosity scale. This allowed us to examine the relationship between parent religiosity and child religiosity and allowed a direct test of the question of parent-child religious homogamy. Previous research has indicated a strong interaction between parent religiosity and child religiosity. Therefore we believed that the inclusion of this product term in the model would account for the interaction between parent religiosity and child religiosity and would avoid specification error in the form of omitted variable bias. Along the same lines, the inclusion of the product term offered a more accurate estimation of the relationship between the dependent and independent variables, and it explained more of the variation in the dependent variable. Although it might have been feasible to examine the absolute value of religious heterogeneity between parent and child, we believed that it was more instructive to examine whether the religious homogamy score was positive or negative, to determine whether the parent or the child was more religious. Hence the product term approach was used.

We also examined family social capital and community social capital. The term *social capital* in general refers to the resources that one gains from various networks of relationships. In this context, family social capital refers to the resources that the adolescent gains from his or her relationship with his or her parents. Family social capital is distinguished from family financial capital (the family's income or wealth) and human capital (the cognitive environment that parents provide for their children). According to Coleman (1988: 110), family social capital can be measured by examining "the strength of the relations between parents and children." Therefore the variables that we used to gauge family social capital came from a scale developed by Ward and Laughlin (2003). This was based on eighteen questions that asked respondents about issues such as how close they felt to their mother or mother figure, how much they felt their mother cared about them, how close they felt to their father or father figure, how much they felt their father cared about them, and whether they talked to their mother or father about school. (See Appendix A for a complete list of questions about family social capital.) The variables were coded so that all were on a scale from 0 to 4, where a higher score indicated a higher level of family social capital. The mean of the eighteen variables was used to create the measure of family social capital (Cronbach's $\alpha = 0.80$).

Community social capital refers to resources that one gains from relationships with members of the local community. To gauge this issue, we examined variables that measured the quality of adolescents' relationships in the community and adolescents' and parents' perception of the overall cohesiveness of the local community (Ward and Laughlin 2003). We used six questions that were asked of the adolescents and eleven questions that were asked of their parents. The questions that were asked of adolescents included how happy they were overall living in their neighborhood, how happy or unhappy they would be if they had to move from their neighborhood, and how many people they knew in their neighborhood; the questions that were asked of parents included whether they lived in their current neighborhood because there was less crime there than in other neighborhoods, whether they lived in their neighborhood because it was closer to their relatives or friends, and whether they lived in their neighborhood because the schools were better there than in other neighborhoods. (See Appendix A for a complete list of questions about community social capital.) All the variables were coded so that higher values indicated greater community capital. The mean of the seventeen items was then used to assess community social capital (Cronbach's $\alpha = 0.69$).

We also incorporated several control variables into our model, including parental education, sex, race/ethnicity, family structure, family income, religious denominational group, urbanity, and grade level. Parental education was measured on a nine-point scale on which higher values indicated higher levels of education. If both parents reported their education, we used the highest level reported. The race/ethnicity categories included white, Black, Hispanic, Asian/ Pacific Islander, Native American, and other. Total family income was measured in thousands of dollars per year. Family structure included two-parent families, single-parent families, stepfamilies, and other families (cf. Jeynes 2007). Consistent with recent studies of religious affiliation, religious preference categories included Mainline Protestant, Evangelical, Black Protestant, Catholic, and other (Steensland et al. 2000).[4] Urbanity was measured by three dummy

---

4 Because previous research shows a strong correlation between an Evangelical religious affiliation and a belief in scriptural inerrancy (one of the control variables), a cross-tabulation was run to ensure that the two variables were not measuring the same thing. The percentages of members of Evangelical, Mainline Protestant, Black Protestant, Catholic, and other religious groups who believed in the inerrancy of their sacred scripture(s) were 91 percent, 74 percent, 87 percent, 70 percent, and 74 percent, respectively, suggesting that variation in scriptural literalism exists within the Evangelical religious affiliation.

variables: rural, suburban, and urban. Grade level was measured by using a continuous variable ranging from 7 to 12.

Because the students' self-reported grades closely followed a normal distribution,[5] we used ordinary least squares regression to examine the empirical model. However, we adjusted for the multistage, clustered sampling design of Add Health, using software that allowed for poststratification adjustment and weighting. Hence the standard errors in the regression model were corrected for the sampling design.

Results

To assess the first hypothesis, we first estimated a linear regression model in which academic achievement was the dependent variable and religiosity was the independent variable (as well as the control variables that we previously mentioned). Given the cross-lagged panel design, this model examined the effects of student religiosity on changes in self-reported grades. The results are shown in Table 10-1.

The results showed that religiosity had a significant positive relationship with changes in self-reported grades. Next, we added family and community social capital to the model (see Table 10-2). Although the unstandardized coefficient for religiosity remained positive, it decreased from 0.025 to 0.020, and the p-value increased from 0.045 to 0.106. These results failed to support the first hypothesis, which was that student religiosity and academic achievement would be significantly related, even when controlling for family and community social capital.

To test the second hypothesis in an elementary fashion, we regressed grades during Wave 2 on the following variables: Wave 1 grades, adolescent religiosity, parent religiosity, and a religiosity product term (adolescent religiosity × parent religiosity). We also included several control variables to determine whether these results depended on parents' education, student gender, race/ethnicity, religious group, grade level, or urbanity. This model examined the effects of religiosity on changes in self-reported grades. Table 10-3 provides the results of this model.

The significant religiosity product term indicated that the highest grades were reported by adolescents whose religiosity scores were concordant

---

5 A kurtosis statistic of −0.654 reveals that the variable has a slightly flat distribution that is nevertheless within normal limits. In addition, a skewness statistic of −0.251 (with a mean of 1.79 and a standard deviation of 0.76) indicates an acceptable deviation from the normal curve.

Table 10-1: Regression Coefficients for Religiosity Predicting Academic Achievement (Partial Model), Add Health, 1994–1996

Variable	Unstandardized Coefficient	Standard Error	p-Value
Intercept	0.388	0.069	<0.001
Grades—Wave 1	0.606	0.012	<0.001
Student religiosity	0.025	0.012	0.045

Adjusted R^2 = .441.
Note: The model controls for the effects of parental education, gender, race/ethnicity, religious group, family structure, grade level, and urbanity.

Table 10-2: Regression Coefficients for Religiosity Predicting Academic Achievement (Full Model), Add Health, 1994–1996

Variable	Unstandardized Coefficient	Standard Error	p-Value
Intercept	0.282	0.080	0.001
Grades—Wave 1	0.601	0.013	<0.001
Student religiosity	0.020	0.012	0.106
Family capital	0.054	0.013	<0.001
Community capital	−0.022	0.027	0.410

Adjusted R^2 = .443.
Note: The model controls for the effects of parental education, gender, race/ethnicity, religious group, family structure, grade level, and urbanity.

with their parents' scores; the lowest occurred among those whose religiosity scores were most discrepant. The religiosity coefficients were only modestly attenuated by the inclusion of the control variables, with a product term that continued to be significantly different from 0.

Table 10-4 shows the results of the model after including not only the control variables, but also family and community capital. Recall that earlier research suggested that these sources of social capital partially mediate the effects of religiosity on academic achievement. However, our results failed to support these findings. Rather, even though family social capital

Table 10-3: Religious Homogamy and Academic Achievement (Partial Model), Add Health, 1994–1996

Variable	Unstandardized Coefficient	Standard Error	p-Value
Intercept	0.579	0.101	<0.001
Grades—Wave 1	0.607	0.013	<0.001
Parent religiosity	−0.073	0.037	0.051
Student religiosity	−0.073	0.039	0.064
Religiosity product term	0.044	0.017	0.010

Adjusted R^2 = .445.
Note: The model controls for the effects of parental education, gender, race/ethnicity, religious group, family structure, grade level, and urbanity.

Table 10-4: Religious Homogamy and Academic Achievement (Full Model), Add Health, 1994–1996

Variable	Unstandardized Coefficient	Standard Error	p-Value
Intercept	0.477	0.109	<0.001
Grades—Wave 1	0.603	0.013	<0.001
Parent religiosity	−0.069	0.037	0.062
Student religiosity	−0.078	0.039	0.048
Religiosity product term	0.044	0.017	0.011
Family capital	0.048	0.015	0.001
Community capital	−0.017	0.029	0.555

Adjusted R^2 = .466.
Note: The model controls for the effects of parental education, gender, race/ethnicity, religious group, family structure, grade level, and urbanity.

had the expected positive association with self-reported grades, the religiosity effects remained at roughly the same levels as in the previous model.[6]

To understand more fully the association between religiosity and academic achievement, we computed predicted scores based on variations in parental and adolescent religiosity. Figure 10-1 shows the predicted scores that corresponded to low (one or more standard deviations below the mean), medium (at the mean), and high (one or more standard deviations above the mean) levels of religiosity. These results showed that the highest expected grades occurred when there was correspondence between religiosity scores, whether on the high or the low end. The lowest expected grades occurred when there was a discrepancy between the religiosity of parents and that of their adolescent children. This supported Pearce and Haynie's (2004) result but extended it to academic achievement.

Discussion

The results appear to provide evidence against the first hypothesis, which is that student religiosity and academic achievement are related even when controlling for family and community social capital. However, the results do provide support for the second hypothesis: that the association between religiosity and academic achievement depends on the concordance or discordance of religious involvement between adolescents and their parents. Moreover, this association is not mediated by variations in family or community social capital. In fact, although family capital has a strong and consistent positive association with academic achievement (cf. McNeal 1999), its effects are relatively independent of the effects of religiosity. Additional analyses using the Add Health data indicate a positive association between family capital and religiosity among parents and adolescents, but this association does not affect the direct effects of religious homogamy on academic achievement.

The results also suggest that Pearce and Haynie's (2004) model of religious homogamy among parents and adolescents provides an interesting

---

6 Since some previous research suggests that the results may vary depending on religious group affiliation (Darnell and Sherkat 1997), we also estimated differences by denominational group (e.g., Evangelical, Mainline Protestant). However, we found no consistent patterns. For example, the results applied as much to Evangelical families as to the whole sample. We also examined whether discrepancies in the child and parent reports of affiliation mattered, but we determined that they did not.

Figure 10-1: Predicted Average Grades, by Parent and Adolescent Religiosity

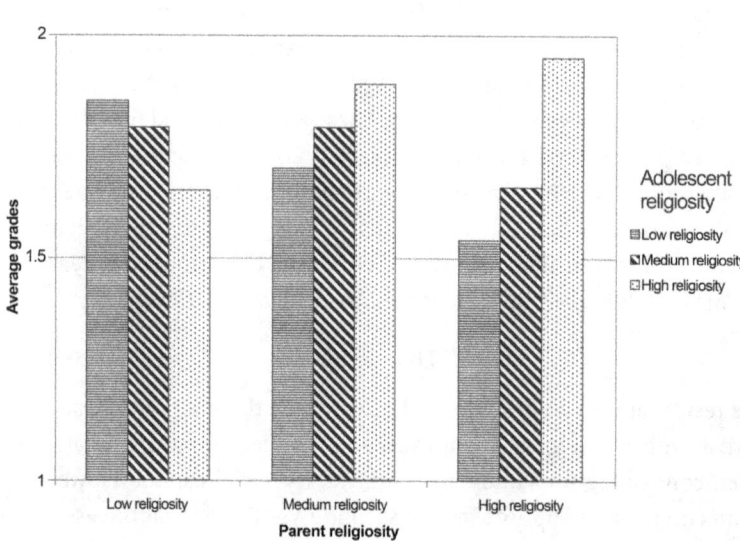

explanation not only for delinquency, but also for prosocial outcomes such as school success. As they speculate, "religious similarity may be important because it brings about the type of parent-child closure described in social control and differential association theories, and perhaps this closure is necessary to provide adolescent religiosity its protective power through dimensions such as moral order, learned competencies, and social and organizational ties" (Pearce and Haynie 2004: 1567). Consistent with these findings, Carbonaro (1998) identifies a positive association between parent-child closure and academic achievement that holds even when controlling for social and background characteristics.

However, it is also possible that religious homogamy provides a form of social capital that general measures of family relations or family involvement fail to assess. For example, religious homogamy could indicate additional resources available to adolescents, such as trusting relationships and a network of positive peer and adult ties. These arguments are attractive explanations because both networks of positive ties and trusting relationships have been shown to be related to higher levels of academic achievement (Bank, Slavings, and Biddle 1990; Goddard 2003). Networks of positive ties "provide opportunities for the exchange of information that can facilitate outcomes desirable to group members" (Goddard 2003: 60). Trusting relationships make the open exchange of information more likely and give group members the confidence that other members are dependable and competent (Goddard 2003). Unfortunately, we were not able to examine trusting relationships and peer networks directly, owing to the design of the study.[7]

Another explanation is that low levels of religious homogamy between parents and children may cause stress and strain, which then lead to lower academic outcomes. Some studies show that strain is more likely to occur in parent-child dyads in which there is a low level of agreement on values, attitudes, and religious beliefs. It is important to note that mental strain and disagreement still occur in relationships that are characterized by high levels of social integration (Pruchno, Burant, and Peters 1994). In addition, it has been demonstrated that higher levels of stress and strain are associated with poorer academic performance for both white and minority students (Smedley, Myers, and Harrell 1993). It is also notable that the only part of our model in which increased religious homogamy does not follow the expected pattern of heightened academic achievement is in the medium parental religiosity category, in which discrepancies between parent religiosity and child religiosity are less pronounced and the relationship is less likely to be strained.

In general, then, religiosity by itself does not necessarily benefit adolescents. Rather, it is the similarity of religious practices and beliefs between parent and child that most profoundly affects academic achievement and perhaps even other prosocial behaviors. We recommend that future

---

[7] To gather peer network data, the designers of Add Health asked each student to name his or her five best male friends and five best female friends. The students were then asked a few questions about each of these friends. We did not use these data for three main reasons: First, because the five questions relating to peer relationships could be answered only by checking a box or leaving it blank, we were unable to determine whether students who did not check the box intended to give a negative response, skipped the question, did not know the answer, or refused to answer the question altogether. Second, many respondents did not have five friends of each sex and therefore could not be directly compared to those who did. Third, it is possible that many respondents had more than five friends of either given gender who had a significant effect on their behavior.

research on adolescent religiosity consider how parent-child concordance or discordance of beliefs and practices affects various positive and negative outcomes.

Conclusion

Although the convergence of our results with previous research offers persuasive evidence of the effects of religious homogamy on adolescent behavior, additional research is needed to validate these results. Moreover, future research should consider additional forms of social capital, such as school capital and resources, as well as networks of affiliations among adolescents (Parcel and Dufur 2001). Research should also consider additional academic outcomes, such as high school graduation, college attendance, dropping out of school, and educational expectations or aspirations. Furthermore, it is not clear whether these results generalize to different gender or racial/ethnic groups. The role of family income should also be considered in more detail, since the Add Health data are plagued with missing value problems on this key variable. Other aspects of the family, such as family structure, as well as whether the models generalize across gender and racial subgroups, should also be considered in future research (Jeynes 2007). Finally, although community capital does not have significant effects in the model, neighborhood-level characteristics might affect how religiosity or family capital is channeled into academic success.

The present study, however, contributes to the current literature in several respects. First, in analyzing the relationship between religiosity and academic achievement among adolescents, it uses more complete measures of family capital, community capital, and religiosity than have been used in the past. Second, the analysis examines changes in academic achievement over time both to examine the temporal nature of academic achievement and to ensure the reliability of the results. Third, we demonstrate that the relationship between religiosity and academic achievement is significantly attenuated when more thorough measures of family and community social capital are taken into account. Fourth, we examine and lend credence to Pearce and Haynie's (2004) study on the association between parent-child religious homogamy and delinquency by examining how adolescent academic achievement relates to intergenerational religious dynamics between parents and children. Consistent with Pearce and Haynie's conclusions, we find a positive association between academic achievement and parent-child religious homogamy.

However, we also find that this relationship cannot be explained entirely by including measures of family and community social capital, which examine the quality of the parent-child relationship as well as the resources available to students at home and in the community. Therefore other factors that involve the religious climate of the home and relationships among parents and children should be explored in greater detail.

References

Anaya, Guadalupe. 1999. "College Impact on Student Learning: Comparing the Use of Self-Reported Gains, Standardized Test Scores, and College Grades." *Research in Higher Education* 40: 499–526.

Bank, Barbara J., Ricky L. Slavings, and Bruce J. Biddle. 1990. "Effects of Peer, Faculty, and Parental Influence on Students' Persistence." *Sociology of Education* 63: 208–25.

Beyerlein, Kraig K., and Christian Smith. 2004. "Specifying the Impact of Conservative Protestantism on the Perceived Value of a College Education." *Journal for the Scientific Study of Religion* 43: 505–18.

Brown, Diane R., and Lawrence E. Gary. 1991. "Religious Socialization and Educational Attainment among African Americans: An Empirical Assessment." *Journal of Negro Education* 60: 411–26.

Bryk, Anthony, Valerie E. Lee, and Peter B. Holland. 1993. *Catholic Schools and the Common Good*. Cambridge, MA: Harvard University Press.

Carbonaro, William J. 1998. "A Little Help from My Friend's Parents: Intergenerational Closure and Educational Outcomes." *Sociology of Education* 71: 295–313.

Coleman, James S. 1988. "Social Capital and the Creation of Human Capital." *American Journal of Sociology* 94: 95–120.

Coleman, James S., Thomas Hoffer, and Sally Kilgore. 1982. *High School Achievement: Public, Catholic, and Private Schools Compared*. New York: Basic Books.

Darnell, Alfred, and Darren E. Sherkat. 1997. "The Impact of Protestant Fundamentalism on Educational Attainment." *American Sociological Review* 62: 306–15.

Gardner, Nancy Augustine. 2004. *Does Religious Participation Help Keep Adolescents in School?* Washington, DC: American Youth Policy Forum. Available at https://www.aypf.org/wp-content/uploads/2014/07/Religious-Participation-Gardner-final.pdf.

Goddard, Roger D. 2003. "Relational Networks, Social Trust, and Norms: A Social Capital Perspective on Students' Chances of Academic Success." *Educational Evaluation and Policy Analysis* 25: 58–77.

Jeynes, William H. 2002. "A Meta-Analysis of the Effects of Attending Religious Schools and Religiosity on Black and Hispanic Academic Achievement." *Education and Urban Society* 35: 27–49.

Jeynes, William H. 2003. "The Effects of Religious Commitment on Academic Achievement of Urban and Other Children." *Education and Urban Society* 36: 44–62.

Jeynes, William H. 2007. "Religion, Intact Families, and the Achievement Gap." *Interdisciplinary Journal for Research on Religion* 3: 1–24.

Johnson, Byron R., Spencer De Li, David B. Larson, and Michael McCullough. 2000. "A Systematic Review of the Religiosity and Delinquency Literature: A Research Note." *Journal of Contemporary Criminal Justice* 16: 32–52.

Maguin, Eugene, and Rolf Loeber. 1996. "Academic Performance and Delinquency." *Crime and Justice: An Annual Review of Research* 20: 145–264.

McGloin, Jean Marie, Travis C. Pratt, and Jeff Maahs. 2004. "Rethinking the IQ-Delinquency Relationship: A Longitudinal Analysis of Multiple Theoretical Models." *Justice Quarterly* 21: 603–35.

McNeal, Ralph B. 1999. "Parental Involvement as Social Capital: Differential Effectiveness on Science Achievement, Truancy, and Dropping Out." *Social Forces* 78: 117–44.

Muller, Chandra, and Christopher G. Ellison. 2001. "Religious Involvement, Social Capital, and Adolescents' Academic Progress: Evidence from the National Longitudinal Study of 1988." *Sociological Focus* 34: 155–83.

Myers, Scott M. 1996. "An Interactive Model of Religiosity Inheritance: The Importance of Family Context." *American Sociological Review* 61: 858–66.

Nonnemaker, James, Clea McNeely, and Robert Blum. 2003. "Public and Private Domains of Religiosity and Adolescent Health Risk Behaviors: Evidence from the National Longitudinal Study of Adolescent Health." *Social Science & Medicine* 57: 2049–54.

Nonnemaker, James, Clea McNeely, and Robert Blum. 2006. "Public and Private Domains of Religiosity and Adolescent Smoking Transitions." *Social Science & Medicine* 62: 3084–95.

Pace, C. Robert, Doris Barahona, and David Kaplan. 1985. *The Credibility of Student Self-Reports*. Report of the Center for the Study of Evaluation. Los Angeles: University of California.

Parcel, Toby L., and Mikaela J. Dufur. 2001. "Capital at Home and at School: Effects on Student Achievement." *Social Forces* 79: 881–911.

Pearce, Lisa D., and Dana L. Haynie. 2004. "Intergenerational Religious Dynamics and Adolescent Delinquency." *Social Forces* 82: 1553–72.

Pike, Gary R. 1995. "The Relationship between Self-Reports of College Experiences and Achievement Test Scores." *Research in Higher Education* 36: 1–22.

Pike, Gary R. 1996. "Limitations of Using Students' Self-Reports of Academic Development as Proxies for Traditional Achievement Measures." *Research in Higher Education* 37: 89–114.

Pruchno, Rachel, Christopher Burant, and Norah D. Peters. 1994. "Family Mental Health: Marital and Parent-Child Consensus as Predictors." *Journal of Marriage and the Family* 56: 747–58.

Regnerus, Mark. 2000. "Shaping Schooling Success: Religious Socialization and Educational Outcomes in Urban Public Schools." *Journal for the Scientific Study of Religion* 39: 363–70.

Regnerus, Mark, Christian Smith, and Melissa Fritsch. 2003. *Religion in the Lives of American Adolescents: A Review of the Literature*. Report of the National Study of Youth and Religion. Chapel Hill: University of North Carolina. Available at https://youthandreligion.nd.edu/assets/102506/religion_in_the_lives_of_american_adolescents_a_review_of_the_literature.pdf.

Regnerus, Mark, Christian Smith, and Brad Smith. 2004. "Social Context in the Development of Adolescent Religiosity." *Applied Developmental Science* 8: 27–38.

Sikkink, David, and Edwin I. Hernandez. 2003. *Religion Matters: Predicting Schooling Success among Latino Youth*. Report of the Institute for Latino Studies. Notre Dame, IN: University of Notre Dame.

Smedley, Brian D., Hector F. Myers, and Shelly P. Harrell. 1993. "Minority-Status Stresses and the College Adjustment of Ethnic Minority Freshmen." *Journal of Higher Education* 64: 434–52.

Smith, Christian. 2003. "Theorizing Religious Effects among American Adolescents." *Journal for the Scientific Study of Religion* 42: 17–30.

Steensland, Brian, Jerry Z. Park, Mark D. Regnerus, Lynn D. Robinson, W. Bradford Wilcox, and Robert D. Woodberry. 2000. "The Measure of American Religion: Toward Improving the State of the Art." *Social Forces* 79: 291–318.

Ward, Catherine L., and James E. Laughlin. 2003. "Social Contexts, Age and Juvenile Delinquency: A Community Perspective." *Journal of Child and Adolescent Mental Health* 15: 13–26.

Appendix A: Items Used in Family and Community Capital Scales

FAMILY SOCIAL CAPITAL

(1) How close do you feel to your mother (or mother figure)?

(2) How much do you feel your mother cares about you?

(3) How close do you feel to your father (or father figure)?

(4) How much do you feel your father cares about you?

(5) How warm or loving is your mother toward you most of the time?

(6) How satisfied are you with your relationship with your mother?

(7) How warm or loving is your father toward you most of the time?

(8) How satisfied are you with your relationship with your father?

(9) How much do you feel your parents care about you?

(10) How much do you feel your family understands you?

(11) How much do you feel your family pays attention to you?

(12) How much has your mother encouraged you to be independent?

(13) Have you talked to your mother about schoolwork or grades?

(14) Has your mother worked with you on a school project?

(15) Have you talked with your mother about what you were doing in school?

(16) Have you talked to your father about schoolwork or grades?

(17) Has your father worked with you on a school project?

(18) Have you talked with your father about what you were doing in school?

COMMUNITY SOCIAL CAPITAL

Student Responses:

(1) How happy are you overall living in your neighborhood?

(2) How happy or unhappy would you be if you had to move away from your neighborhood?

(3) How many of the people in your neighborhood do you know?

(4) Have you stopped to talk with someone on the street in your neighborhood in the last month?

(5) Do you think that people in the neighborhood look out for each other?

(6) Do you usually feel safe in your neighborhood?

Parent Responses:
"Do you live in this neighborhood because . . ."

(1) There is less crime there than there is in other neighborhoods?

(2) There is less drug use and other illegal activities there than there is in other neighborhoods?

(3) You are closer to your relatives or friends?

(4) The schools are better there than they are in other neighborhoods?

(5) There are children who are the same age as your children?

(6) You or your spouse was born in this neighborhood?

(7) How much would you like to move away from this neighborhood?

(8) How large a problem is litter or trash on the streets and sidewalks?

(9) How large a problem are drug dealers and drug users in your neighborhood?

(10) Would you tell a neighbor if you saw that neighbor's child getting in trouble?

(11) Would your neighbors tell you if they saw your child getting in trouble?

11

The Faith Factor and Prisoner Reentry[1]

Byron R. Johnson

As long as prisons have existed, prisoners have had difficulty in transitioning back into society. In the United States, the process of reintegrating ex-prisoners into society has been a problem in need of a solution for many decades. What is different now is the sheer number of prisoners returning to American communities each year (Osborne and Solomon 2006). What has been referred to as an unprecedented and disturbing development is now beginning to be recognized for what it is not: a temporary trend. Between 1980 and 2006, the U.S. prison population increased by 467 percent (from 319,598 to 1,492,973), and the parole population increased by 362 percent (from 220,438 to 798,202) (U.S. Department of Justice 2006). The inevitable increase in the number of prisoners returning to communities across the country has created a national debate about how best to handle what has become known as the prisoner reentry crisis, one of the most challenging dilemmas in correctional history (Travis 2005).

A number of well-known correctional programs have been implemented over the years to help manage the difficult adjustment period when prisoners transition back into society. Halfway houses, community

---

1 This article is based on a paper prepared for *Innovations in Effective Compassion: Compendium on Research, Outcomes, and Evaluation of Faith-Based and Community Initiatives*, published by the U.S. Department of Health and Human Services, Office of the Secretary for Planning and Evaluation in June 2008.

corrections, intensive supervision, and community reintegration programs represent but a few of the various post-release efforts designed to make prisoner reentry into society less difficult for ex-prisoners while ensuring public safety (Petersilia 2003). But despite corrections expenditures that are now in excess of $60 billion annually, the likelihood that a former prisoner will succeed in the community has not improved (Bauer 2002). Indeed, about two-thirds of all offenders who leave prison are rearrested within three years of their release (Langan and Levin 2002). Growing caseloads have made effective case management by parole officers increasingly difficult. A by-product is increasing occupational stress on parole officers (Finn and Kuck 2003). As a result of these conditions, there is increasing concern that the number of ex-prisoners returning to society could pose a major threat to public safety. Even though the problems faced by ex-prisoners returning to society are readily identifiable, public efforts to address these reentry and aftercare problems have been limited (Travis and Visher 2005). The question is not whether this is true but why it is true.

In general, policymakers are reluctant to support correctional policies that endorse or appear to favor offender treatment, job training, and counseling for ex-prisoners and their families in the community. Such efforts can be interpreted as taking a "soft on crime" approach. Even though one might argue that a prisoner reentry plan that includes such programs has the potential to reduce recidivism significantly and thus improve public safety, few policymakers have been willing to publicly defend such programs. Not surprisingly, law-and-order crime policies have consistently trumped those that favor offender treatment models (Cullen 2002).

Furthermore, the lack of a comprehensive governmental response to prisoner reentry is influenced by money. Creating new offender treatment and support programs in prisons as well as in communities would place a significant financial burden on correctional budgets that many Americans already regard as too high. In an era of finite resources and ever-tightening budgets, efforts to significantly expand existing educational, vocational, and counseling programs in prisons and communities have not received serious consideration.

However, it is both unrealistic and unfair to lay the sole responsibility of comprehensive prisoner reentry at the feet of government. Though often overlooked, the role of religion, religious volunteers, religious programs, and faith-based organizations in the criminal justice system has been a constant in U.S. history. This oversight is unfortunate, since numerous theoretical perspectives, published research, and common sense suggest that communities of faith have the potential to be powerful partners to the government in developing a comprehensive prisoner reentry plan. The following section reviews research documenting the role of religion in prisons and prisoner reentry and research connecting religion to crime reduction and prosocial behavior and thus provides a basis for the inclusion of a faith-based approach to prisoner reentry.

The Relevance of Religion in Prisons and Prisoner Reentry

Religion and Prisons

The evolution of the U.S. correctional system has been accompanied by the constant influence of religion and religious workers. Terms such as *corrections, penitentiary, reformation, restoration,* and *solitary confinement* can be traced to religious origins (see, for example, McGowen 1995; Peters 1995). The role of religion in prisons not only is important in a historical sense, but also continues to be prominent and pervasive in correctional institutions. Faith-motivated volunteers in prisons are as likely to be involved in life-skills training or instruction in GED programs as they are to conduct Bible studies or lead worship services. In this way, religious volunteers have played and continue to play a vital role in the vast majority of American correctional institutions. Indeed, besides work, education, or vocational training, religious activities attract more participants than any other type of personal enhancement program offered inside a prison.[2]

There are many ways in which religion might be consequential for prisoners and ex-prisoners. However, where correctional decision makers and policy stakeholders are concerned, the overriding issue is whether an intervention reduces recidivism. In the mid-1990s, Prison Fellowship (PF), a nonprofit religious ministry to prisoners, commissioned research to determine the effects of faith-based interventions on prisoner recidivism. Utilizing a quasi-experimental design, the study examined the influence of religious programs on prisoner adjustment (i.e., institutional infractions or rule violations) and recidivism rates (i.e., post-release arrests) in two matched groups of inmates from four adult prisons in New

2   This conclusion is based on data from face-to-face interviews with 13,986 inmates in 1991 and published by the Bureau of Justice Statistics. Similar surveys were conducted in 1974, 1979, and 1986.

York State.[3] One group had participated in programs sponsored by PF; the second group had no involvement with PF programs. Researchers found that after controlling for level of involvement in PF-sponsored programs, inmates who were most active in Bible studies were significantly less likely to be arrested during the one-year follow-up period (Johnson, Larson, and Pitts 1997). A second study, conducted with an additional seven years of follow-up data, documented that after the sample was divided into groups of high and low levels of participation in Bible studies, high participants were less likely to be rearrested at two and three years post-release (Johnson 2004). The study concluded that more research is necessary to determine how religion might be related to offender rehabilitation, inmate adjustment, and prisoner reentry. This small but growing body of research indicates that participation in religious programs and activities can contribute to positive adjustment while the inmate is in prison as well as reducing the likelihood of recidivism following release from prison (see, for example, Johnson 2003, 2004).

From Bible Studies to Faith-Based Prison Programs

An overarching implication of this relatively new body of research is that religious volunteers and faith-based programs have the potential to play a significant role in how we think about prison management, safety, and offender rehabilitation. For example, preliminary research suggests that faith-based dormitories and housing units have the potential to significantly counter the negative and often debilitating prison culture that permeates so many American correctional institutions (see, for example, Clear and Sumter 2002; Johnson 2003).

A six-year evaluation of a faith-based prison program called the InnerChange Freedom Initiative (IFI)[4] found that inmates who completed the program were significantly less likely than a matched group of offenders[5]

---

3 On the basis of a multivariate matched sampling method, seven variables most strongly predicted members of the PF groups: age, race, religious denomination, county of residence, military discharge, minimum sentence, and security classification.
4 Founded in 1997, the InnerChange Freedom Initiative is operated by Prison Fellowship Ministries at the Carole Vance Unit, outside of Houston, Texas.
5 The comparison group was matched with IFI participants on race, age, offense type, and salient factor risk score (a correctional assessment tool that is used in most prisons to help predict the level of risk that prisoners pose to correctional authorities).

to be rearrested (17 percent versus 35 percent) or reincarcerated (8 percent versus 20 percent) during a two-year follow-up period (Johnson 2003). The study revealed a stark contrast between the areas of the prison that are controlled by the faith-based program and the areas that house prisoners from the general population. The general population was typified by the presence of a distinct prison code of behavior that often condoned rule breaking and other inappropriate behaviors. Not surprisingly, traditional prison culture often works to undermine the very premises on which a rehabilitation model is based.[6]

In contrast, the faith-based side of the prison was typified by educational classes, study, work, worship services, little free time, and the absence of television sets. Furthermore, the faith-based program enjoyed an atmosphere that promoted forgiveness, honesty, and personal accountability. Efforts such as IFI and Kairos, another faith-based prison program, are designed to discourage antisocial and destructive behavior and to encourage transparency, contrition, and spiritual transformation, all of which run counter to the pervasive prison code. Preliminary research lends support to the notion that faith-based units can create an environment that is conducive to effective treatment and to rehabilitation programs more generally (Johnson 2003). In this way, faith-based interventions have the potential to enhance the achievement of a secular goal and civic good: lower recidivism.

Faith-Based Prisoner Reentry: Shortcomings and Potential

As important as volunteer work within correctional facilities might be, it does not diminish the fact that reentry and aftercare tend to be largely overlooked by most religious volunteers and organizations. Compared to reentry, prison ministry is a much easier task to pursue and a safe service opportunity in what many consider to be an unsafe environment. Prisoners often appreciate the attention they receive from the outside world, and these exchanges tend to be overwhelmingly positive and nonthreatening for volunteers. Prison ministry, therefore, can be found in many U.S. congregations and among the thousands of religious volunteers who

---

6   The subculture of prisons has been an ongoing topic of sociological and criminological inquiry. Donald Clemmer (1958) coined the term *prisonization*, a process whereby inmates become socialized into prison culture. Assumptions of prisonization are that inmates internalize prison culture and that their subsequent behavior is a reflection of this internalization.

visit prisons every day. Likewise, faith-based organizations disproportionately opt for in-prison ministry rather than out-of-prison services because reentry and aftercare are anything but easy or safe. For example, Prison Fellowship Ministries (PF), the largest faith-based prison ministry in the United States, has always recognized that reentry and aftercare are vitally important, but PF's efforts have been only marginally involved in these areas. This oversight was recently acknowledged by PF president Mark Early, at a White House "Compassion in Action" Roundtable event on prisoner reentry in March 2007, when he stated an intention to remedy the imbalance by significantly expanding the organization's aftercare emphasis.

While the disproportionate emphasis on volunteerism in prisons rather than on aftercare in communities is undeniable, it would be inaccurate to suggest that faith-based prisoner reentry programs are nonexistent. Unfortunately, it is unclear how many faith-based reentry programs are in operation, though it is likely that they exist in many of the communities where prisons are located. Faith-based prisoner reentry programs tend to be small, isolated, and in need of coordination as well as evaluation.

Is There a Link between Religion and Crime Reduction?

Systematic reviews and one meta-analysis of religion and crime literature have provided evidence that religious commitment and involvement are linked to reductions in delinquent behavior and deviant activities (Baier and Wright 2001; Johnson, Tompkins, and Webb 2006).[7] Recent evidence suggests that such effects persist even if there is not a strong prevailing social

---

7   Baier and Wright reviewed a total of sixty published studies and found that (1) religious beliefs and behaviors exert a moderate deterrent effect on individuals' criminal behavior and (2) conceptual and methodological approaches account for some of the inconsistencies in the research literature. In a second review, Johnson and colleagues reviewed 151 studies that examined the relationship between religiosity and drug use ($N = 54$) or alcohol use ($N = 97$) and abuse. The vast majority of these studies demonstrated that participation in religious activities is associated with less of a tendency to use or abuse drugs (87 percent) or alcohol (94 percent). These findings held regardless of the population under study (i.e., children, adolescents, and adult populations) or whether the research was conducted prospectively or retrospectively. In this same study, Johnson and colleagues reviewed forty-six published studies that examined the relationship between religiosity and delinquency. Seventy-eight percent of these studies reported that reductions in delinquency and criminal acts were associated with higher levels of religious activity and involvement.

control against delinquent behavior in the surrounding community. For example, several studies found that young Black males from poverty tracts in Boston, Chicago, and Philadelphia were much less likely to be involved in crime and delinquent behavior if they regularly attended church (Freeman 1986; Johnson et al. 2000b). Similarly, research has found that highly religious low-income youths from high-crime areas are less likely to use drugs than are less religious youths in these same disadvantaged communities. Furthermore, these highly religious teens from crime "hot spots" were also less likely to use drugs than were less religious teens from middle-class suburban communities or "good places" (Jang and Johnson 2001). There is also evidence that religious involvement can lower the risks of a broad range of delinquent behaviors, including both minor and serious forms of criminal behavior (Evans et al. 1996). Research also shows that religious involvement might have a cumulative effect throughout adolescence and might significantly lessen the risk of later adult criminality (Johnson et al. 2001). Studies find that religion can be used as a tool to help prevent high-risk urban youths from engaging in delinquent behavior (Johnson et al. 2000a, 2001). For example, African American churches appear to play a key role in reducing crime among Black youths from urban communities (Johnson et al. 2000a). It is precisely to these communities of disadvantage that many ex-prisoners will be returning.

There are many theoretical perspectives that help to explain why and how religious beliefs and practices can influence behavior. To review these would be beyond the scope of this article, but in sum, it is safe to say that religious involvement helps some people to learn prosocial behavior (i.e., actions that emphasize concern for other people's welfare). These prosocial skills can instill a greater sense of empathy toward others and thus lessen the likelihood of committing acts that harm others (Johnson et al. 2000a). Similarly, once individuals become involved in deviant behavior, it is possible that participation in religious activities can help to steer them back to a course of less deviant behavior and away from potential career criminal paths (Johnson 2009). An important study by Evans and colleagues (1995) found that religion, as indicated by religious activities, reduced the likelihood of adult criminality as measured by a broad range of criminal acts. The relationship persisted even after secular controls were added to the model. Furthermore, the finding did not depend on social or religious contexts.

In sum, religiosity is now beginning to be acknowledged not only as a key protective factor that buffers or protects from harmful outcomes, but also as a variable that can promote prosocial behavior (Johnson 2007). If congregations can be viewed as institutions dedicated to improving the plight of at-risk populations, faith- and community-based organizations could represent key factors in helping ex-prisoners transition to society.

Harnessing Human and Spiritual Capital through Intermediaries

President George W. Bush signed an executive order in January 2001 establishing the White House Office of Faith-Based & Community Initiatives.[8] Over the next several years, Centers of Faith-Based and Community Initiatives were created in eleven federal agencies through a series of executive orders.[9] In his executive orders and speeches on the initiative, President Bush acknowledged the long tradition of faith-based and community organizations helping Americans, especially those who confront serious disadvantages. The president was also convinced that the federal government had not been a very good partner to the faith- and community-based groups that have been working to target serious social problems. Furthermore, he believed that the federal government had made it difficult for faith-based and community groups to compete for funds on an equal standing with secular nonprofit service providers for far too long. The 2001 White House report *An Unlevel Playing Field* systematically reviewed federal funding and identified the barriers that stand in the way of effective government partnerships with faith- and community-based organizations (White House Office of Faith-Based and Community Initiatives 2001). For example, the report found that the Office of Justice Programs at the U.S. Department of Justice estimated that in fiscal 2001, it would award about 0.3 percent of total discretionary grant funds ($1.9 million of $626.7 million) to faith-based organizations and 7.5 percent ($47.2 million) to community-based providers.

---

8   Executive Order 13199 created the White House Office of Faith-Based & Community Initiatives on January 29, 2001.

9   Executive Order 13198 created five Centers for Faith-Based & Community Initiatives on January 29, 2001; Executive Order 13280 created two Centers for Faith-Based and Community Initiatives on December 12, 2002; Executive Order 13279 requires equal protection for faith-based and community organizations as of December 12, 2002; Executive Order 13342 created three new Centers for Faith-Based & Community Initiatives at the Departments of Commerce and Veterans Affairs and the Small Business Administration on June 1, 2004; and Executive Order 13397 created a new Center for Faith-Based & Community Initiatives at the Department of Homeland Security on March 7, 2006.

Since 2001, considerable progress has been made in overcoming obstacles (for example, before 2001, references to faith-based groups were virtually absent from federal funding announcements covering social service delivery or demonstration projects) that have prevented faith-based and community organizations from seeking grants to build capacity and thereby strengthen outreach to underserved populations, including prisoners and ex-prisoners. Since 2001, conferences for faith- and community-based groups have been offered in all regions of the United States to identify and explain the federal funding processes. Indeed, no American president has devoted more funding, resources, and attention to the plight of ex-prisoners and their families than has George W. Bush. First as a governor and then as president, he has consistently favored public-private partnerships whose mission is to assist offenders, prisoners, ex-prisoners, and their children. Although the president has indicated that the government has a very clear role to play when it comes to prisoner reentry, he has been equally firm in asserting that government is not equipped to provide the mentoring, care, and social supports that are essential for any effective and holistic plan for prisoner reentry.

Stated differently, government cannot effectively address the prisoner reentry crisis by itself. The alternative is also true: faith-based organizations and individuals cannot effectively address the prisoner reentry problem by themselves. In fact, sacred and secular partnerships represent our best hope for developing an effective prisoner reentry strategy.

In the concluding chapter of their book *Prisoner Reentry and Crime in America*, Jeremy Travis and Christy Visher (2005) ask two important questions:

> Is it possible to imagine a world in which the agencies of the justice system—corrections, police, courts, and parole—work together with other public and private institutions—housing providers, workforce development agencies, drug treatment providers, foster care agencies, and churches and other faith institutions—to systematically reduce the risk of failure around the time of reentry? . . . What would such a strategy look like? (255–56)

As a result of President Bush's belief in the role of intermediaries as well as his interest in prisoner reentry, two major prisoner reentry initiatives are now beginning to give us some preliminary answers to these questions. A third and related initiative, commonly referred to as the Second Chance

Act, was passed by Congress three years after first being introduced, and the president signed it into law in April 2008. Intended to reduce repeat offenses and to improve former prisoners' chances for success in the community, the Recidivism Reduction and Second Chance Act authorized $165 million annually over two years to support mentoring programs, substance abuse treatment, literacy classes, job training, and other assistance intended to help ex-offenders pursue productive, crime-free lives after their sentences are up. The bill authorized grant funding for fiscal years 2009 and 2010 for state and local governments to launch or continue programs to improve ex-offenders' return to society. It also allocated competitive grants to faith-based and community nonprofits to offer programs that link ex-offenders with mentors or that help them seek and keep jobs. The bill included elements of the Bush Administration's Prisoner Reentry Initiative (PRI), launched in 2004, which connects ex-offenders with religious and secular nonprofits for mentoring and other programs to help them make a successful transition to community life.

Ready4Work

In 2003, the U.S. Department of Labor launched Ready4Work, a three-year pilot program to address the needs of ex-prisoners through faith-based and community-based organizations. Ready4Work emphasized on-the-job training, job placement, case management, mentoring, and other aftercare services. Community and faith-based organizations were selected to provide services to adult ex-offenders in eleven cities.[10]

Ready4Work purposely targeted participants who had a high probability of recidivism;[11] ex-prisoners in Ready4Work had extensive criminal

---

10 The eleven sites were City of Memphis Second Chance Ex-Felon Program (Memphis, TN); Allen Temple Housing & Economic Development Corporation (Oakland, CA); East of the River Clergy, Police & Community Partnership (Washington, DC); Exodus Transitional Community (East Harlem, NY); Holy Cathedral/Word of Hope Ministries (Milwaukee, WI); Operation New Hope (Jacksonville, FL); SAFER Foundation (Chicago, IL); Search for Common Ground (Philadelphia, PA); Union Rescue Mission (Los Angeles, CA); Wheeler Avenue Baptist Church & the InnerChange Freedom Initiative (Houston, TX); and America Works Detroit (Detroit, MI).

11 Participant eligibility for Ready4Work was determined on the basis of three factors: age of the ex-offender, presenting offense, and length of time before or after release. Ex-prisoners between the ages of eighteen and thirty-four years who had most recently been incarcerated for a nonviolent felony offense and were no more than ninety days pre-release or post-release were eligible to enroll in the program.

histories, and half had previously been arrested five or more times (Farley and Hackman 2006). Once individuals entered the program, they were eligible for services lasting up to one year. Participants were also matched with mentors in one-to-one and/or group mentoring relationships. Job placement specialists helped participants to find jobs, and case managers continued to provide assistance after participants became employed.

The Ready4Work pilot ended in 2006, and results indicate that a total of 4,482 former prisoners enrolled in Ready4Work. Of these ex-prisoners, 97 percent received case management services, 86 percent received employment services, and 63 percent received mentoring services. Ready4Work sites placed 2,543 participants (57 percent) into jobs; 63 percent retained jobs for three consecutive months after placement (Farley and Hackman 2006).

Public/Private Ventures (PPV), an action-based research, public policy, and program development organization, oversaw the Ready4Work demonstration project as an intermediary. PPV reported that only 2.5 percent of Ready4Work participants were reincarcerated within six months and that 6.9 percent had been reincarcerated at the one-year post-release mark. Although this was not a randomized design, the findings are impressive.

Over 60 percent of Ready4Work participants received mentoring as part of their services. We already knew that mentoring matters for youths; this study demonstrated that mentoring affected outcomes for Ready4Work participants. Ready4Work participants who met with a mentor remained in the program longer, were twice as likely to obtain a job, and were more likely to stay employed than were participants who did not meet with a mentor (Farley and McClanahan 2007). PPV researchers conclude that "while mentoring alone is not enough, supportive relationships—which can be fostered through mentoring programs—should be considered a core component of any reentry strategy" (McClanahan 2007).

Ready4Work gives us an important preliminary snapshot of what is possible when an intermediary brings together public and private entities to address prisoner reentry in a comprehensive and coordinated strategy. Early results from Ready4Work support the notion that a comprehensive prisoner reentry plan is possible and that it can be accomplished without a massive expansion of the existing criminal justice system. As far as federal projects go, the Ready4Work initiative in eleven cities represents a major demonstration project. Additionally, Ready4Work has helped to highlight the work of faith- and community-based groups that are addressing prisoner reentry, such as Exodus Transitional Community in New York and Word of Hope Ministries in Milwaukee or the Safer Foundation of Chicago.

The President's Prisoner Reentry Initiative

The Prisoner Reentry Initiative (PRI), which President Bush announced in 2004, grew out of the U.S. Department of Labor's Ready4Work project. PRI was designed to further test the proposition that prisoner reentry could be effectively accomplished by a comprehensive strategy that is designed to draw heavily from partnerships with community and faith-based groups. The PRI helps to connect former prisoners with faith-motivated groups as well as secular community-based organizations that are willing to help ex-prisoners locate employment and stay out of trouble by following prosocial paths. Currently, thirty PRI grantees across the country are providing mentoring, employment, and other transitional services to thousands of ex-inmates.

PRI sites began serving program participants in the spring of 2006, and the results, like those of Ready4Work, have been promising. It is important to note, however, that these early outcomes are very preliminary and are not based on a randomized design with strict controls. A total of 10,361 PRI participants had been enrolled as of November 2007, and about 6,000 participants have been placed in jobs. Participants' one-year post-release recidivism rate is currently 20 percent. These early findings are positive.

As can be seen in Figure 11-1, nine of the thirty PRI grants went to faith-based organizations. Twenty-one grants went to community-based organizations, and all but three of these secular organizations report working with faith-based organizations. Indeed, collaborations with faith-based organizations appear to be important for faith-based as well as community-based PRI recipients. These alliances confirm the premise that sacred and secular partnerships can be essential in establishing a network of social supports necessary for comprehensive and coordinated prisoner reentry.

Keys to a Comprehensive and Scalable Prisoner Reentry Plan

Any prisoner reentry plan that is comprehensive and can achieve a large scale will require new people as well as programs that do not currently exist in most jurisdictions. It is unlikely that governments will or can provide these programs. Faith- and community-based groups represent a crucial piece of the reentry puzzle that has yet to be integrated in a systematic

Figure 11-1: Prisoner Reentry Initiative (PRI) Grants

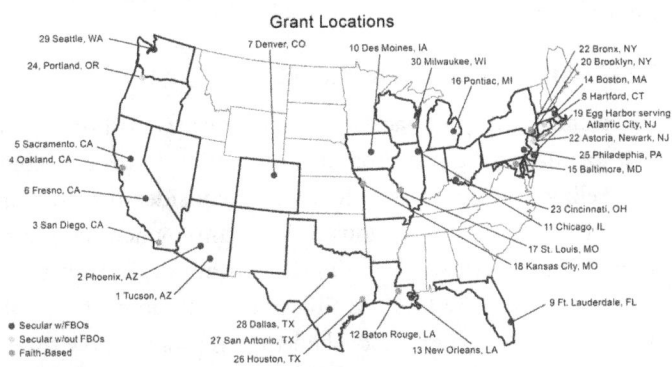

fashion. A comprehensive prisoner reentry plan will be sustainable only if partnerships between sacred and secular as well as national and community groups are encouraged rather than discouraged. A healthy atmosphere of mutual respect must replace the suspicion that still too often typifies relations between public and private organizations and between secular and religious groups that nonetheless have similar social service missions. This represents another way in which intermediaries can be strategic in building bridges and alliances to address social problems.

For example, religious individuals and faith-based groups need to recognize that ongoing training regarding correctional issues is something to be coveted rather than merely tolerated. Religious volunteers should be required to undergo basic training regarding custodial and security issues before being allowed to do volunteer work. Furthermore, ongoing training for religious volunteers should be endorsed as well as widely promoted by faith-based organizations. This is especially true for faith-motivated volunteers who are interested in mentoring prisoners and ex-prisoners.

Faith-based groups need to understand that accountability, assessment, and evaluation of their efforts—which will surely follow if these groups partner with government—are extremely useful tools. Overstating program effectiveness without empirical evidence has often been a problem for religious volunteers and faith-based organizations. If their efforts are to be taken seriously, religious volunteers must understand that faith-based programs, like others, must be evaluated objectively. This kind of accountability will go a long way toward improving relationships with other private and public groups whose confidence faith-based groups need in a comprehensive and coordinated response to prisoner reentry.

The Role of Volunteerism in Prisoner Reentry

An effective and positive impact on prisoner reentry will require a paradigm shift for many religious programs. Instead of leading a Bible study in prison, religious volunteers will need to consider developing strategies to improve, for example, housing and employment conditions for ex-offenders who are already living in the community as well as for prisoners who will eventually be returning home. The importance of mentoring relationships that are established in prison and carry over to the community cannot be overemphasized. Research confirms that mentoring matters—not just for children, but also for adults. The problem is that there is a severe shortage of mentors, especially for prisoners and ex-prisoners. This is precisely why communities of faith, America's most volunteer-rich organizations, are uniquely positioned to assist (see, for example, Cornwell and Harrison 2004; Musick and Wilson 2007). However, faith communities have not been approached in any meaningful way on a national scale to provide these mentors. Another possibility is having properly trained volunteers to specifically assist parole and other community corrections personnel. Ultimately, a comprehensive prisoner reentry plan will require very large numbers of committed and trained volunteers and partners as well as a willingness to connect them, along with their varied networks of social and spiritual support, to correctional, governmental, and secular entities that are committed to prisoner reentry and aftercare. Without a comprehensive approach that coordinates public and private, secular and sacred partnerships, the lack of effective prisoner reentry support will remain a national emergency. There is great promise if government and faith-based groups collaborate in meaningful partnerships to successfully address prisoner reentry problems.

We know that lack of housing, employment, transportation, counseling, and mentoring are substantial obstacles that make the transition from prison to society difficult for ex-prisoners. Obviously, tackling these problems will call for a great deal of new human and financial resources as well as the participation of key community leaders. Thus, any comprehensive strategy for confronting the problems of prisoner reentry will require an infusion of an unprecedented number of new volunteers who have or can develop strategic alliances focused on each of the problems ex-prisoners encounter. But where will these new volunteers and resources come from?

Organizations such as Big Brothers Big Sisters of America (BBBSA), the largest mentoring organization in the world, have developed immensely successful strategies for recruiting mentors. In the last eight or nine years alone, BBBSA has more than doubled the number of children served (Big Brothers Big Sisters of America 2005). Along with many other grantees, BBBSA has led the Mentoring Children of Prisoners (MCP) efforts nationally, in a partnership program known as Amachi. It took BBBSA ninety-five years to make 120,000 matches; there are currently 250 MCPs in forty-eight states partnering with over 6,000 churches to serve more than 100,000 children (Amachi 2008). Conversations with Rev. Dr. W. Wilson Goode, who has directed the amazing growth of Amachi, reveal the foundational role of congregations in recruiting mentors. The Amachi experience confirms that when people are asked to volunteer, many will do just that (Musick and Wilson 2007). A comprehensive plan for prisoner reentry that draws heavily on volunteers will need to develop strategies for recruiting mentors, although this effort will certainly look different from the BBBSA and Amachi models.

The vast majority of the many thousands of correctional volunteers tend to come from religious congregations. No source is more volunteer-rich than are America's houses of worship (Musick and Wilson 2007), and there are approximately 361,000 congregations in the United States (American Church Lists 2008). Religious congregations not only mobilize volunteer labor for the church itself, but also are feeder systems for many other nonprofit and volunteer organizations. Furthermore, religious volunteers do not necessarily choose between volunteering for the church and volunteering for a secular organization; many do both (Clain and Zech 1999; Cornwell and Harrison 2004). Surveys have consistently found a positive association between religious affiliation and attendance and charitable behavior in terms of both financial giving and volunteering (Brooks 2006; Independent Sector 2002). Harvard University scholar Robert Putnam and his colleagues in the Saguaro Seminar echoed this finding when they observed:

> Houses of worship build and sustain more social capital—and social capital of more varied forms—than any other type of institution in America. Churches, synagogues, mosques and other houses of worship

provide a vibrant institutional base for civic good works and a training ground for civic entrepreneurs. Roughly speaking, nearly half of America's stock of social capital is religious or religiously affiliated, whether measured by association memberships, philanthropy, or volunteering (Putnam et al. 2001: 54).

Research confirms that volunteers will respond if they are approached with the right message, but it is not enough simply to attract large numbers of volunteers. The coordination and mobilization of volunteers and organizations are equally important.

The Role of the Intermediary in Prisoner Reentry

As was discussed above, developing a truly comprehensive prisoner reentry plan is difficult because there are so many different challenges that complicate an ex-prisoner's effort to make a successful transition back into society. Focusing on housing without giving proper consideration to employment is a recipe for failure. Likewise, concentrating on transportation without planning for mentoring and other social supports is likely to be unsuccessful. Any comprehensive prisoner reentry plan must be able to coordinate all the major obstacles to successful reentry. Ready4Work and the PRI have provided a very preliminary and positive glimpse of a multifaceted reentry plan that owes much to the contribution of an intermediary organization to coordinate such efforts. In the case of Ready-4Work, Public/Private Ventures is overseeing the demonstration project as a national intermediary. PRI has utilized a different approach by funding community- and faith-based organizations to serve as local intermediaries coordinating reentry efforts (see Figure 11-1).

But what exactly is an intermediary, and what roles do intermediaries play? Meredith Honig (2004) offers a helpful definition of an intermediary:

> Intermediaries are organizations that occupy the space in between at least two other parties. Intermediary organizations primarily function to mediate or to manage change in both those parties. Intermediary organizations operate independently of these two parties and provide distinct value beyond what the parties alone would be able to develop or to amass by themselves. At the same time, intermediary organizations depend on those parties to perform their essential functions. (65–87)

In recent years, the federal government has begun to utilize intermediaries to help faith- and community-based organizations build capacity, strengthen programs, and improve the delivery of social services. Perhaps the best recent example is the Compassion Capital Fund, established by Congress in 2002, which provides funds to be distributed by the U.S. Department of Health and Human Services to intermediary organizations across the country to provide training, technical, and financial assistance to faith- and community-based organizations.

The role of faith- and community-based intermediaries in social service provision is still relatively new and underdeveloped. This is unfortunate, since intermediary organizations could be the most important underutilized element in building successful prisoner reentry models that incorporate working with volunteers, especially volunteers from religious congregations. Intermediaries can be a bridge between ex-prisoners and the many social service providers and various governmental agencies. Intermediaries can coordinate reentry efforts of community- and faith-based organizations, volunteers, social services, mentors, and parole officers. Additionally, intermediaries can serve in many important ways by providing management and oversight to groups and organizations; technical assistance to agencies, groups, and ministries; and ongoing training to strengthen capacity and sustainability.

Without this kind of assistance, there is a strong likelihood that small grassroots groups will ultimately fail (McKinsey & Company 2001). According to Mike Doyle, Executive Director of the Cornerstone Assistance Network, a faith-based intermediary organization in Fort Worth, Texas, failure to develop a sound organization will cause even successful programming to suffer if not to surrender to financial and reporting pressures. Intermediaries can play a key role in coordinating the efforts of fragmented community and faith-based organizations (Fink and Branch 2005). Too often, these small groups operate in relative isolation from each other and, as a result, are not able to build or sustain capacity. Influential and well-networked intermediaries are well positioned to coordinate resources locally and beyond. Organizations such as the United Way provide an example of how organizations, through targeted mission statements, can have a substantial and scalable influence.[12]

Intermediaries are essential to a comprehensive and coordinated prisoner reentry plan that can recruit a large number of skilled and trained

---

12 The United Way is a national network of more than 1,300 locally governed organizations that work to create lasting positive changes in communities.

volunteers while developing private and public partnerships to confront key reentry and aftercare problems.

Finally, intermediaries can interact with governmental entities while drawing on the substantial human capital of volunteers as well as the social and spiritual capital of individuals and organizations in the private sector. The Compassion Capital Fund, the Faith and Community Technical Support Project, the Latino Coalition for Faith and Community Initiatives, and Nueva Esperanza provide but a few examples of the unique role intermediaries can play at local and national levels.

Conclusion

Because prisoner reentry is a problem facing communities all across the United States, the goal of any plan should be to establish a model that not only is effective in a particular area, but also can be effective on a larger scale in multiple communities. It is one thing to have isolated local success; it is quite another to succeed at a statewide level. For example, although not a prisoner reentry program, Amachi Texas is a unique public-private partnership that was designed to reach a statewide scale.[13] What has been missing until recently is a prisoner reentry model or template that links all the nonnegotiable elements of reentry together in a way that can be replicated and sustained in cost-effective ways in local communities, in regions, or statewide. We need a plan in which coordination and collaboration are central, the goals of the reentry model are realistically achievable, the specific elements of the plan are replicable in any community, and the plan is affordable and does not add new costs to already overburdened correctional budgets.

The role of the government in reentry and aftercare is important, even central, but it should not be all-encompassing. The criminal justice system should be viewed as a key partner among other public and private partners collaborating with the many reentry initiatives that are being led in the community and coordinated through intermediaries. Ready4Work and PRI provide initial evidence that sacred and secular groups as well

---

13 Amachi Texas, a joint initiative between the Office of the Governor, the Texas Department of Criminal Justice, the Texas Workforce Commission, OneStar Foundation, and Big Brothers Big Sisters of Texas, was launched in 2005. The program helps children of prisoners by working in communities throughout Texas via mentoring relationships. The Amachi Texas initiative is currently the subject of a three-year evaluation that incorporates a randomized controlled study.

as national and community government institutions can work together to address comprehensive prisoner reentry in a scalable way. To replicate these experiences, the federal and state governments need to continue to welcome and accommodate religious and community-based volunteers and groups. Additionally, faith- and community-based intermediaries will have to bring much-needed expertise in coordinating and training volunteers as well as organizations in the areas of employment, housing, education, and counseling. In this way, sacred and secular partnerships can play a catalytic role in a truly comprehensive and scalable approach to prisoner reentry.

References

Amachi. 2008. *Amachi: People of Faith Mentoring Children of Promise*. Retrieved from www.amachimentoring.org.

American Church Lists. 2008. Now available at https://lists.nextmark.com.

Baier, Colin J., and Bradley R. E. Wright. 2001. "If You Love Me Keep My Commandments: A Meta-analysis of the Effects of Religion on Crime." *Journal of Research in Crime and Delinquency* 38: 3–21.

Bauer, Lynn. 2002. *Justice Expenditure and Employment in the United States*. Washington, DC: U.S. Department of Justice, Bureau of Justice Statistics.

Big Brothers Big Sisters of America. 2005. *Big Brothers Big Sisters of America Expands Relationship with Kintera*.

Brooks, Arthur C. 2006. *Who Really Cares? The Surprising Truth about Compassionate Conservatism*. New York: Basic Books.

Clain, Suzanne Heller, and Charles E. Zech. 1999. "A Household Production Analysis of Religious and Charitable Activity." *American Journal of Economics and Sociology* 58: 923–46.

Clear, Todd R., and Melvina T. Sumter. 2002. "Prisoners, Prison, and Religion: Religion and Adjustment to Prison." *Journal of Offender Rehabilitation* 35: 127–59.

Clemmer, Donald. 1958. *The Prison Community*. New York: Holt, Rinehart and Winston.

Cornwell, Benjamin, and Jill Ann Harrison. 2004. "Union Members and Voluntary Associations: Membership Overlap as a Case of Organizational Embeddedness." *American Sociological Review* 69: 862–81.

Cullen, Francis. 2002. "Rehabilitation and Treatment Programs." In *Crime: Public Policies for Crime Control*, edited by James Q. Wilson and Joan Petersilia, 253–89. Oakland, CA: ICS Press.

Evans, T. David, Francis T. Cullen, Velmer S. Burton Jr., R. Gregory Dunaway, Gary L. Payne, and Sesha R. Kethineni. 1996. "Religion, Social Bonds, and Delinquency." *Deviant Behavior* 17: 43–70.

Evans, T. David, Francis T. Cullen, R. Gregory Dunaway, and Velmer S. Burton Jr. 1995. "Religion and Crime Reexamined: The Impact of Religion, Secular Controls, and Social Ecology on Adult Criminality." *Criminology* 33: 195–224.

Farley, Chelsea, and Sandra Hackman. 2006. *Ready4Work in Brief—Interim Outcomes are In: Recidivism at Half the National Average.* Philadelphia: Public/Private Ventures.

Farley, Chelsea, and Wendy S. McClanahan. 2007. *Ready4Work In Brief—Update on Outcomes: Reentry May Be Critical for States, Cities.* Philadelphia: Public/Private Ventures.

Fink, Barbara, and Alvia Y. Branch. 2005. *Promising Practices for Improving the Capacity of Faith- and Community-Based Organization.* Philadelphia: Branch Associates and Abt Associates.

Finn, Peter, and Sarah Kuck. 2003. *Addressing Probation and Parole Officer Stress.* Final Report to the National Institute of Justice. Washington, DC: U.S. Department of Justice, National Criminal Justice Reference Service. https://nij.ojp.gov/library/publications/addressing-probation-and-parole-officer-stress-final-report.

Freeman, Richard B. 1986. "Who Escapes? The Relation of Churchgoing and Other Background Factors to the Socioeconomic Performance of Black Male Youths from Inner-City Poverty Tracts." In *The Black Youth Employment Crisis*, edited by Richard B. Freeman and Harry J. Holzer, 353–76. Chicago: University of Chicago Press.

Honig, Meredith I. 2004. "The New Middle Management: Intermediary Organizations in Education Policy Implementation." *Educational Evaluation and Policy Analysis* 26: 65–87.

Independent Sector. 2002. *Giving and Volunteering in the United States, 2001: Findings from a National Survey.* Washington, DC: Independent Sector.

Jang, Sung Joon, and Byron R. Johnson. 2001. "Neighborhood Disorder, Individual Religiosity, and Adolescent Drug Use: A Test of Multilevel Hypotheses." *Criminology* 39: 501–35.

Johnson, Byron. 2003. *The InnerChange Freedom Initiative: A Preliminary Evaluation of a Faith-Based Prison Program.* ISR Report. Waco, TX: Baylor University, Institute for Studies of Religion.

Johnson, Byron. 2004. "Religious Program and Recidivism among Former Inmates in Prison Fellowship Programs: A Long-Term Follow-Up Study." *Justice Quarterly* 21: 329–54.

Johnson, Byron. 2007. "A Tale of Two Religious Effects: Evidence for the Protective and Prosocial Impact of Organic Religion." In *Authoritative Communities: The Scientific Case for Nurturing the Whole Child*, edited by Kathleen Kline, 187–226. New York: Springer.

Johnson, Byron. 2009. "The Role of Religious Institutions in Responding to Crime and Delinquency." In *The Oxford Handbook of the Sociology of Religion*, edited by Peter B. Clarke, 1463–89. Oxford: Oxford University Press.

Johnson, Byron R., Sung Joon Jang, David B. Larson, and Spencer De Li. 2001. "Does Adolescent Religious Commitment Matter? A Reexamination of the Effects of Religiosity on Delinquency." *Journal of Research in Crime and Delinquency* 38: 22–44.

Johnson, Byron R., Sung Joon Jang, Spencer De Li, and David Larson. 2000a. "The 'Invisible Institution' and Black Youth Crime: The Church as an Agency of Local Social Control." *Journal of Youth and Adolescence* 29: 479–98.

Johnson, Byron R., David B. Larson, Spencer De Li, and Sung Joon Jang. 2000b. "Escaping from the Crime of Inner-Cities: Church Attendance and Religious Salience among Disadvantaged Youth." *Justice Quarterly* 17: 701–15.

Johnson, Byron R., David B. Larson, and Timothy C. Pitts. 1997. "Religious Programming, Institutional Adjustment and Recidivism among Former Inmates in Prison Fellowship Programs." *Justice Quarterly* 14: 145–66.

Johnson, Byron R., with Ralph Brett Tompkins and Derek Webb. 2006. *Objective Hope Assessing the Effectiveness of Faith-Based Organizations: A Review of the Literature*. ISR Report. Waco, TX: Baylor University, Institute for Studies of Religion.

Langan, Patrick A., and David J. Levin. 2002. *Recidivism of Prisoners Released in 1994*. NCJ 193427. Washington, DC: U.S. Department of Justice, Bureau of Justice Statistics.

McClanahan, Wendy S. 2007. *P/PV Preview: Mentoring Ex-Prisoners in the Ready-4Work Reentry Initiative*. Philadelphia: Public/Private Ventures.

McGowen, Randall. 1995. "The Well-Ordered Prison: England, 1780–1865." In *The Oxford History of the Prison: The Practice of Punishment in Western Society*, edited by Norval Morris and David J. Rothman, 71–99. New York: Oxford University Press.

McKinsey & Company. 2001. *Effective Capacity Building in Nonprofit Organizations*, published for Venture Philanthropy Partners, 27–32. Haryana, India: McKinsey & Company.

Musick, M., and J. Wilson. 2007. *Volunteers: A Social Profile*. Bloomington: Indiana University Press.

Osborne, Jenny, and Amy Solomon. 2006. *Jail and Reentry Roundtable Initiative*. Washington, DC: Urban Institute.

Peters, Edward M. 1995. "Prison before the Prison: The Ancient and Medieval Worlds." In *The Oxford History of the Prison: The Practice of Punishment in Western Society*, edited by Norval Morris and David J. Rothman, 3–43. New York: Oxford University Press.

Petersilia, Joan. 2003. *When Prisoners Come Home: Parole and Prisoner Reentry*. New York: Oxford University Press.

Putnam, Robert D. 2001. *Better Together: Report of the Saguaro Seminar*. Cambridge, MA: Harvard University, John F. Kennedy School of Government.

Travis, Jeremy. 2005. *But They All Come Back: Facing the Challenges of Prisoner Reentry*. Washington, DC: Urban Institute Press.

Travis, Jeremy, and Christy Visher, eds. 2005. *Prisoner Reentry and Crime in America*. Cambridge: Cambridge University Press.

U.S. Department of Justice. 2006. *Adults on Probation, in Jail or Prison, and Parole*. Sourcebook of Criminal Justice Online. Table 6.1. Available at http://www.albany.edu/sourcebook/pdf/t612006.pdf.

White House Office of Faith-Based and Community Initiatives. 2001. *Unlevel Playing Field: Barriers to Participation by Faith-Based and Community Organizations in Federal Social Service Programs*. https://georgewbush-whitehouse.archives.gov/news/releases/2001/08/unlevelfield.html.

12

Does Change in Teenage Religiosity Predict Change in Marijuana Use over Time?[1]

Scott A. Desmond | George Kikuchi | Kristen Budd

Only a limited number of studies have used longitudinal data to examine the relationship between religiosity and delinquency or substance use (for a few exceptions, see Giordano et al. 2008; Jang, Bader, and Johnson 2008; Jang and Johnson 2010; Petts 2009; Ulmer et al. 2010). Instead, research on religiosity has relied heavily on cross-sectional designs. For instance, a recent systematic review, which included more than one hundred studies on religiosity and substance use, revealed that four out of five studies published between 1997 and 2006 were cross-sectional (Chitwood, Weiss, and Leukefeld 2008). Similarly, an earlier review of research on religiosity and delinquency found that thirty-five out of forty studies were cross-sectional (Byron Johnson et al. 2000). In addition to the overabundance of cross-sectional studies, many longitudinal studies consist of only two waves of data separated by a year. Therefore many of the existing longitudinal studies of religiosity and substance use have covered very short periods of time.

Because there have been few longitudinal studies of religiosity and substance use, we know little about the long-term effects of adolescent

---

[1] This research uses data from the National Youth Survey (NYS). The NYS data were made available, in part, by the Inter-university Consortium for Political and Social Research (ICPSR). The data were originally collected by Delbert Elliott. Neither the collector of the original data nor the consortium bears any responsibility for the analyses or interpretations presented here.

religiosity on substance use or about how changes in religiosity influence changes in delinquency over the life course. Previous research indicates that religious behaviors and attitudes do change, especially as adolescents make the transition to young adulthood (Desmond, Morgan, and Kikuchi 2010; Uecker, Regnerus, and Vaaler 2007). Among adolescents who attend religious services at least once a month, almost 70 percent attend less often when they become young adults (Uecker, Regnerus, and Vaaler 2007). Furthermore, 20 percent of adolescents report that religion is less important when they become young adults (Uecker, Regnerus, and Vaaler 2007). Although such studies have shown that religious behaviors and attitudes, especially religious service attendance, change significantly from adolescence to young adulthood, few studies have examined how changes in religiosity over an extended period of time influence substance use.

Jang, Bader, and Johnson (2008: 771–72) contend that "previous studies of religious effects on drug use have been mostly nondevelopmental, despite the increasing emphasis on life course perspectives within criminology over the last 20 years" (see also Giordano et al. 2008). Jang, Bader, and Johnson (2008: 772) additionally argue that childhood religiosity can "result in cumulative advantages that build throughout the life course." Using three waves of data from the National Survey of Children, they also found that children who were reared in religious households were more likely than other children to be religious and to remain religious into adulthood. Children's religiosity was also positively related to protective factors, such as attachment to parents and school, and negatively related to risk factors, such as associating with delinquent peers and low self-control. Ultimately, children who were raised by religious parents were less likely to use drugs in adolescence and young adulthood. Therefore childhood religiosity results in advantages, such as strong parental attachment and higher self-control, which gradually accumulate through adolescence and continue into adulthood.

To address some of the limitations of previous research, we use growth curve modeling to examine how adolescent religiosity influences marijuana use across five waves (1978–1987) of the National Youth Survey (NYS), a longitudinal study of adolescents living in the United States. After determining how patterns of marijuana use change from adolescence to young adulthood, we attempt to address the following research questions. First, does adolescent religiosity predict long-term trajectories of marijuana use? To answer this question, we examine the relationship between adolescent religiosity, measured at Wave III of the NYS, and patterns of marijuana use from Wave III to Wave VII. Second, do changes in religiosity predict changes in marijuana use over time? For the second question, we model the effect of changes in religiosity from Wave III to Wave VII of the NYS on changes in marijuana use during the same time period.

Theoretical Background and Literature Review

Previous research consistently shows that religious youths are less likely than nonreligious youths to engage in delinquency and/or substance use (Baier and Wright 2001; Chitwood, Weiss, and Leukefeld 2008; Byron Johnson et al. 2000). Several different theories have been used to study the relationship between religiosity and delinquency and substance use, including social bonding theory (Bahr, Hawks, and Wang 1993; Cretacci 2003), social learning theory (Bahr, Hawks, and Wang 1993; Marcos, Bahr, and Johnson 1986), strain theory (Jang and Johnson 2005; Matthew Johnson and Morris 2008; Wills, Yaeger, and Sandy 2003), and low self-control theory (Geyer and Baumeister 2005; Welch, Tittle, and Grasmick 2006).

Social Bonding Theory

Social bonding theory assumes that individuals are self-serving and will act in ways that provide the greatest benefit to themselves (Hirschi 1969). Because of this hedonistic view of human nature, Hirschi (1969: 10) argued that criminologists need to explain "why people obey the rules" rather than why they commit crimes. According to Hirschi (1969), adolescents refrain from substance use when they develop a bond to social institutions, such as family and school. In contrast, when adolescents do not have a strong social bond, they are free to engage in substance use.

According to Hirschi (1969), the social bond consists of four elements: attachment, commitment, involvement, and belief. Attachment is the emotional bond adolescents have with others, including parents, teachers, and peers (Hirschi 1969). When adolescents do not care about the expectations of other people, they are more likely to engage in substance use. Commitment is the investment individuals have in society or social institutions and the amount of risk involved in using illegal substances (Hirschi 1969). Adolescents who lack commitment are more likely to engage in substance use because they have nothing to lose. Involvement refers to adolescents' participation in conventional activities (Hirschi 1969). Heavy involvement in legitimate activities leaves no time for substance use.

The last element, belief, refers to the extent to which individuals think they should obey the law (Hirschi 1969: 23–26). Adolescents who do not believe in the rules of society, or who do not believe that a particular behavior is wrong, are more likely to break those rules than are adolescents who believe that the rules should be followed.

When discussing the elements of the social bond, Hirschi (1969) emphasized the family and school. Scholars argue that religiosity is an additional element of the social bond that can influence both initiation into and desistance from delinquency and substance use (Adamczyk and Palmer 2008; Chu 2007; Longest and Vaisey 2008). Like attachment, commitment, involvement, and belief, religious behaviors and attitudes can prevent substance use. The other elements of the social bond may also be influenced by religiosity. For example, adolescent religiosity is significantly related to parental attachment (Smith and Denton 2005). Commitment can be reinforced by religious institutions, which often foster a cognitive orientation toward the future. Involvement in religious activities, including church attendance and religious youth groups, absorbs time that might otherwise be used for recreational substance use. Finally, religiosity enhances conventional moral beliefs, which then reduce delinquency (Byron Johnson et al. 2001). Thus religiosity, in conjunction with attachment, commitment, involvement, and belief, can play an important role in preventing substance use.

Social Learning Theory

The relationship between religiosity and substance use has also been investigated within the framework of social learning theory (Akers 1973). Social learning theory extends Sutherland's (1947) differential association theory by reframing and broadening the scope of how substance use is learned. In essence, "social learning theory offers an explanation of crime and deviance which embraces variables that operate both to motivate and control criminal behavior; both to promote and undermine conformity" (Akers and Sellers 2004: 85). Based in behavioral psychology, social learning theory argues that the social environment that individuals interact with and learn from is the most important source of reinforcement for behavior.

According to social learning theory, substance use is learned through four distinct processes: differential association, definitions, imitation, and differential reinforcement (Akers and Sellers 2004). Differential association, or whom people interact with, forms the foundation for how people learn to behave and whether or not their behavior will be law-abiding or law-violating (Akers and Sellers 2004). Through interaction with other people, adolescents learn how they define themselves, others, and particular behaviors. Definitions include personal beliefs, such as morals or ethics, and the meaning people attach to specific behaviors, such as smoking marijuana (Akers and Sellers 2004). Imitation occurs when individuals act in certain ways after observing the same or similar behaviors (Akers and Sellers 2004). Behavior might or might not be imitated, depending on the people being observed, their behavior, and whether there are visible consequences (Vold, Bernard, and Snipes 2002). Finally, with differential reinforcement, individuals act according to their perception of the rewards and/or punishments that follow their behavior (Akers and Sellers 2004). Overall, learning to use substances begins by associating with people who have definitions that are favorable to violating the law. Substance use can then be modeled and imitated. For individuals who begin to use substances, rewards and punishments will determine whether or not their substance use continues.

Religious socialization and exposure to religious activities have the potential to influence differential association, definitions, differential reinforcement, and imitation. As a result of participation in religious activities, adolescents may become differentially associated with other religious people who do not engage in substance use and are more likely to express attitudes against such behaviors. As a result of their exposure to nonusers, religious youths are more likely to learn definitions that clearly define substance use as wrong or undesirable. In addition, religiosity may offer differential reinforcement in the form of rewards for not using drugs or alcohol, such as a prized place in the afterlife, or punishments, such as penance. As Baier and Wright (2001: 4) argue, "religion deters individual-level criminal behavior through the threat of supernatural sanctions and promotes normative behavior through the promise of supernatural reward." Finally, religious youths are likely to model and imitate the "virtuous" behaviors of other religious individuals.

General Strain Theory

According to general strain theory, there are three types of strain (Agnew 1992). First, following Merton (1938), strain is caused by a failure to achieve positively valued goals, such as wealth, respect, and autonomy.

Second, strain can result when individuals lose something they value, such as a friend or family member (Agnew 1992). Third, strain occurs when individuals are treated in a negative manner by others, such as being bullied at school (Agnew 1992). In short, the more strain adolescents feel, the more likely they are to turn to substance use. This does not mean, however, that all strain will lead to substance use. Many factors, such as coping skills, social support, and association with substance-using peers, can influence how people cope with strain.

Several studies have found that religiosity can reduce the impact of strain on the likelihood of delinquency and substance use (Jang and Johnson 2005; Matthew Johnson and Morris 2008; Wills, Yaeger, and Sandy 2003). Jang and Johnson (2005: 335) found that religiosity had a significant buffering effect on situational distress such that "non- or less religious African Americans are more vulnerable to the deviance-inducing effects of distress than their more religious counterparts." Wills, Yaeger, and Sandy (2003) found that the impact of life stress on adolescent substance use was reduced by high levels of religiosity. Matthew Johnson and Morris (2008) determined that religiosity diminished the impact of stressful school problems on violent and property offenses, although the effects were small.

Low Self-Control Theory

Gottfredson and Hirschi (1990) proposed a general theory to explain individual differences in the propensity to commit delinquent acts and substance use, regardless of age and circumstances. Gottfredson and Hirschi (1990) argued that when individuals have low self-control, they are more likely to engage in substance use. Low self-control results from a lack of proper socialization, primarily ineffective child-rearing. The amount of self-control that is formed during childhood solidifies around age eight and then remains relatively stable throughout life. Gottfredson and Hirschi deduced several dimensions of low self-control. In short, these authors conclude that "people who lack self-control will tend to be impulsive, insensitive, physical (as opposed to mental), risk-taking, short-sighted, and nonverbal, and they will tend therefore to engage in criminal and analogous acts" (Gottfredson and Hirschi 1990: 90). Low self-control has consistently been linked to involvement in a variety of deviant behaviors, although the strength of the relationship appears to be modest (Pratt and Cullen 2000). Not all individuals with low self-control use substances, however, because substance use depends on the available opportunities. That is, even individuals with low self-control might not engage in substance use if the risk of getting caught is high or their access to substances is limited.

Previous research suggests that religious individuals often exhibit greater levels of self-control than nonreligious individuals do (Aziz and Rehman 1996). Therefore adolescents may develop greater self-control as a result of participation in organized religious activities. Put another way, as a result of their religious commitment, individuals may learn to suppress their deviant impulses and to deny the temptation for immediate gratification. In turn, as a result of having greater self-control, adolescents might be less likely to engage in substance use. Although very few studies have examined religiosity and self-control, Welch, Tittle, and Grasmick (2006) found that religiosity was positively related to self-control and that religiosity had a negative effect on projected acts of deviance that was not rendered spurious by self-control.

In summary, many sociological theories of delinquency and substance use, including social bonding theory, social learning theory, general strain theory, and low self-control theory, predict that adolescent religiosity will be negatively related to delinquency and substance use. According to these theoretical perspectives, religious youths should be more likely to have strong social bonds, learn definitions that prohibit substance use, cope with strain in constructive ways, and develop greater self-control. Because few studies have examined how religiosity influences patterns of substance use over the life course, however, we use growth curve modeling to examine the relationship between adolescent religiosity and smoking marijuana, using five waves of the NYS. In doing so, we hope to determine whether adolescent religiosity predicts long-term trajectories of marijuana use. Also, we investigate whether changes in religiosity predict changes in marijuana use over time.

Methods

Sample

The National Youth Survey is a probability sample of households in the continental United States. The original sample was drawn in 1976, and 2,360 youths were eligible for the survey. Of the eligible youths, 1,725 (73 percent) agreed to participate in the study. Five waves of data were collected annually between 1976 and 1980. A sixth and a seventh wave of data were collected in 1983 and 1987, respectively. We use Waves III through VII of the NYS because religion-related items were not included in the first two waves of the survey. At Wave III, the adolescents were between the ages of thirteen and nineteen years. By Wave VII, which was collected nine years later, respondents were twenty-two to twenty-eight years old. Respondent loss over the first seven waves of the NYS was approximately 20 percent, which compares favorably with that of other longitudinal studies (see Menard 2002). On the basis of the first six waves of the NYS, Elliott, Huizinga, and Menard (1989: 3) reported that "loss by age, sex, ethnicity, class, place of residence, and reported delinquency did not substantially influence... the representativeness of the sample." For a more complete description of the NYS sample, see Elliott, Huizinga, and Ageton 1985.[2]

Dependent Variable: Marijuana Use

Although the NYS contains a large number of items that can be used to measure delinquency, for our analysis we focused on marijuana use. For marijuana use, adolescents were asked how many times in the last year they had used marijuana or hashish, measured on a scale that ranged from never to two or three times a day. Because the same item appears in every wave of the NYS, we were able to examine changes in marijuana use over time. We chose to focus on marijuana use for two reasons. First, previous research suggests that religiosity has a stronger effect on victimless crimes, such as marijuana use, than on other types of crimes (Burkett and White 1974; Cochran and Akers 1989).[3] Second, since the peak age for involvement in property offenses and violent offenses is sixteen to eighteen years, very few respondents in later waves of the NYS reported committing these delinquent acts.

---

2 For missing values, we used Full Information Maximum Likelihood (FIML), which is preferable to other methods that are commonly used with missing data, such as listwise deletion, pairwise deletion, and mean substitution (Acock 2005; Enders 2001).

3 Although some researchers have argued that religiosity has a stronger effect on victimless crimes (Burkett and White 1974; Cochran and Akers 1989), such as substance abuse, research on the "antiascetic hypothesis" is mixed. In short, there is a substantial body of research that suggests that religiosity is significantly related to a wide variety of delinquent behaviors, not just victimless crimes (Baier and Wright 2001; Johnson et al. 2000). Nonetheless, the effects of religiosity on other forms of delinquency may be different from the effects on marijuana use.

Religiosity

Unfortunately, no religion-related items were included in the first and second waves of the NYS, and only two religion-related items were included in the third wave. The first of these was "During the past year, how often did you attend church, synagogue, or other religious services?" Church attendance was measured on a scale ranging from 4 = several times a week to 0 = never. The second question was "How important has religion been in your life?" Importance of religion was also measured on a scale ranging from 4 = very important to 0 = not important at all. We combined church attendance and importance of religion to create a measure of adolescent religiosity that ranges from 0 to 8 (mean = 4.4).

For the first part of the analysis, we use religiosity at Wave III to predict trajectories of marijuana use over five waves (Waves III to VII) of the NYS. For the second part of the analysis, we examine the effect of change in religiosity on change in marijuana use. When focusing on change in religiosity, we constructed identical measures of religiosity, combining church attendance and importance of religion, for Waves IV through VII of the NYS. Since we have items that measure religiosity at all five time points, we can determine how adolescent religiosity changes over time and how the changes correlate with adolescents' marijuana use.

Control Variables

Since previous research suggests that sex (Chapple, McQuillan, and Berdahl 2005; Liu and Kaplan 1999), age (Sampson and Laub 1993; Steffensmeier and Streifel 1991), and race (Hawkins 2003; Matsueda and Heimer 1987) are significantly related to delinquency and substance use, we controlled for the effects of these variables in our analysis. Sex was coded as a dichotomous variable (1 = male, 0 = female). Age is an interval-level variable that ranges from thirteen to nineteen years for our sample. Because the NYS does not include many Asian, Hispanic, or Native American youths, race was coded 1 = non-white and 0 = white.

In addition to basic demographic characteristics, previous research suggests that family structure and process are significantly related to delinquency and substance use (Cernkovich and Giordano 1987; Laub and Sampson 1988), so we included a measure of family structure and family attachment in our models. For family structure, adolescents who were living with both biological parents were coded as 1, and all other family structures were coded as 0. Family attachment was measured by using an index of five agree/disagree items ($\alpha = 0.810$): "I feel like an outsider with my family" (reversed), "My family is willing to listen if I have a problem," "Sometimes I feel lonely when I'm with my family" (reversed), "I feel close to my family," and "My family doesn't take much interest in my problems" (reversed). Higher scores on the index indicate greater attachment to family.

Peer influences, such as peer attachment and associating with delinquent peers, are strongly related to delinquency and substance use (Warr 2002). Peer attachment was measured by agreement/disagreement with the following statements, which were combined to form an index ($\alpha = 0.754$): "I don't feel that I fit in very well with my friends" (reversed), "My friends don't take much interest in my problems" (reversed), "I feel close to my friends," "My friends are willing to listen if I have a problem," and "Sometimes I feel lonely when I'm with my friends" (reversed). Higher scores on the index indicate greater attachment to peers. To measure association with delinquent peers, adolescents were asked how many of their friends (all, most, some, or none) had used marijuana.

School experiences are also significantly related to delinquency and substance use (Cernkovich and Giordano 1992; Crosnoe 2006), so we controlled for the effects of school attachment and grades. School attachment was measured by agreement/disagreement with the statements "Teachers don't call on me in class, even when I raise my hand" (reversed), "I often feel like nobody at school cares about me" (reversed), "I don't feel as if I really belong at school" (reversed), "Even though there are lots of kids around, I often feel lonely at school" (reversed), and "Teachers don't ask me to work on special classroom projects" (reversed) ($\alpha = 0.664$). Higher scores on the index indicate greater attachment to school. Grades were measured with the item "Which of the following best describes the grades you are getting at school?" Responses ranged from 4 = mostly A's/excellent to 0 = mostly F's/failing.

Finally, previous research suggests that moral beliefs are significantly related to delinquency and substance use (Hannon, DeFronzo, and Prochnow 2001; Mears, Ploeger, and Warr 1998). In general, adolescents who believe that a particular behavior is wrong are less likely to engage in that behavior. To measure the effect of moral beliefs on marijuana use, we used an item that asks adolescents how wrong they think it is for someone to use marijuana (3 = very wrong to 0 = not wrong at all). Descriptive statistics for marijuana use, religiosity, and the control variables are provided in Table 12-1.

12 | Does Change in Teenage Religiosity Predict Change?

Table 12-1: Descriptive Statistics for Marijuana Use, Religiosity, and Control Variables

Variables	Mean	Standard Deviation	Minimum	Maximum
Dependent				
Marijuana use (Wave III)	1.30	2.20	0.00	8.00
Marijuana use (Wave IV)	1.48	2.27	0.00	8.00
Marijuana use (Wave V)	1.61	2.34	0.00	8.00
Marijuana use (Wave VI)	1.54	2.31	0.00	8.00
Marijuana use (Wave VII)	1.25	2.12	0.00	8.00
Religiosity (Wave III)	4.45	2.28	0.00	8.00
Religiosity (Wave IV)	4.20	2.27	0.00	8.00
Religiosity (Wave V)	4.14	2.25	0.00	8.00
Religiosity (Wave VI)	3.81	2.32	0.00	8.00
Religiosity (Wave VII)	3.76	2.26	0.00	8.00
Independent				
Sex[a]	0.53	0.50	0.00	1.00
Age	15.87	1.94	13.00	19.00
Race (Non-white)[a]	0.20	0.40	0.00	1.00
Biological family[a]	0.62	0.48	0.00	1.00
Family attachment	15.24	3.08	0.00	20.00
Peer attachment	15.16	2.60	4.00	20.00
School attachment	14.54	2.63	4.00	20.00
Grade	2.71	0.82	0.00	4.00
Peers marijuana	1.28	1.37	0.00	4.00
Moral marijuana	1.94	1.07	0.00	3.00

[a] For dichotomous variables, means correspond to the proportion of cases.

Analytic Strategy: Latent Growth Curve

We used latent growth curve modeling to analyze the relationship between adolescent religiosity and changes in marijuana use over time. In a latent growth curve framework, researchers are primarily interested in finding the latent factors that are assumed to have given rise to the observed data (Bollen and Curran 2006; Duncan et al. 1999). The basic idea behind the latent growth curve is to estimate regression lines (or curves) for each individual, where a dependent variable is regressed on time. For example, in the current research, for each adolescent in the sample, marijuana use is regressed on time. It is quite possible that such regression lines vary considerably in their functional form across individuals. Some adolescents may show an increase in marijuana use, while others may show stability over time, and still others may show a decrease in marijuana use. The varying regression lines for each individual are then smoothed to produce an unobserved (latent) growth curve that captures the average trend for the adolescents in the sample. It is this unobserved curve that is believed to have given rise to the observed data. While various regression lines based on observed data reflect individual-level patterns, the unobserved (latent) curve represents the group-level trend. In short, a latent growth curve model allows researchers to simultaneously examine the overall trends (the group level trajectory) and individual variability in such trends.[4] Two parameters associated with latent growth curves, mean and variance, are summary measures that represent the overall trend as well as the amount of individual variability.

---

[4] Formally, a latent growth curve model can be considered a multilevel model with two levels (Bollen and Curran 2006). The first-level equation that assesses changes within individuals is $y_{it} = \alpha_i + \beta_i \lambda_t + \varepsilon_{it}$, where y_{it} is marijuana use for individual i at time t and α_i and β_i are an intercept and slope, respectively, that characterize the trajectory pattern for each individual. The subscript i of α and β indicates variation across individuals in their trajectory patterns. The second-level equations that express the intercept and slope are $\alpha_i = \mu_\alpha + \xi_{\alpha_i}$ and $\beta_i = \mu_\beta + \xi_{\beta_i}$, respectively. ξ indicates the deviation from the mean intercept and slope for each individual trajectory pattern. If we substitute α_i and β_i in the first-level equation, the combined model is $y_{it} = (\mu_\alpha + \lambda_t \mu_\beta) + (\xi_{\alpha_i} + \xi_{\beta_i} + \varepsilon_{it})$. The terms in the first set of parentheses reflect a fixed component, while the terms in the second set of parentheses reflect a random component. That is, while the fixed component captures the overall trajectory pattern across individuals, the random component reflects individual variability in trajectory patterns.

Using a latent growth curve is advantageous for the analysis of longitudinal data for several reasons (Bollen and Curran 2006; Duncan et al. 1999). First, a latent growth curve provides summary measures that capture an underlying trajectory that has given rise to a large set of observations. For example, the initial level of marijuana use and the shape and rates of change over time can be analyzed with a latent growth curve. The mean and variance parameters of the latent growth curve indicate the overall trend in marijuana use as well as the extent of individual variability. Second, various functional forms of change over time can be modeled.

For example, changes in marijuana use can be linear (increase or decrease) or quadratic (acceleration or deceleration). Third, covariation between the initial level and rates of change can be examined. For example, adolescents who start with a high level of marijuana use might experience a slower decrease in marijuana use over time than other adolescents do. Finally, both time-invariant and time-variant covariates can be incorporated to explain variability in the initial level of marijuana use and rates of change over time at the individual level. For example, compared to nonreligious adolescents, religious adolescents might have lower levels of marijuana use initially, and they might decrease their marijuana use more rapidly over time.

Results

Unconditional Latent Growth Curve Model

Latent growth curve models allow for the analysis of group-level changes and individual variability in changes simultaneously. In particular, latent growth curve models can be specified via observed data and latent factors. Figure 12-1 depicts an unconditional latent growth curve model for marijuana use. Variables in rectangles represent observed data—the level of marijuana use—at each time point, while latent factors are represented by ovals. By formulating single-direction arrows from the latent factors to the observed data, the model specifies that the latent growth curve factors represent unobserved and underlying trajectories of marijuana use that have given rise to the observed data.

The model in Figure 12-1 has three latent growth curve factors: the intercept, slope, and quadratic components. Furthermore, each factor has two parameter estimates, a mean and variance, which capture the group-level trend and the individual variability in trajectories, respectively. For example, the mean of the intercept represents the estimated mean level

Figure 12-1: Unconditional Latent Growth Curve Model for Marijuana Use

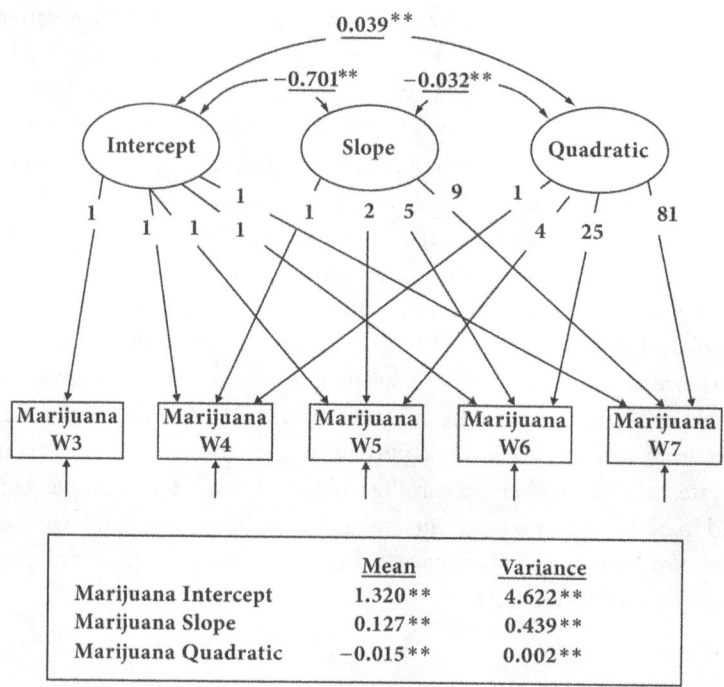

Note: Underlined covariances, as well as means and variances, are estimated parameters. Numbers without underlines were fixed for estimation. Fixed factor loadings represent the passage of time.
* $p < 0.05$. ** $p < 0.01$.

of marijuana use at Wave III, the initial data point. Thus in our data, a statistically significant mean intercept (1.320, $p < 0.01$) indicates that the mean level of marijuana use at Wave III is significantly different from 0. Although the mean captures the average trend for the entire sample, the variance associated with each growth curve parameter indicates the individual variability in trajectories. That is, a statistically significant variance for the intercept (4.622, $p < 0.01$) indicates that the amount of marijuana use at Wave III varied considerably across individuals. Some individuals used marijuana more often than others did.

While the intercept captures the initial level of marijuana use, two additional latent growth curve parameters, slope and quadratic, capture changes in marijuana use across time. In particular, the slope component captures linear change, and the quadratic component captures nonlinear change over time. Like the intercept, the change components of the latent growth curve have mean and variance estimates, which capture the group-level trend and individual variability in the shape of trajectories. The mean slope is positive (0.127, $p < 0.01$), indicating that adolescents increased their level of marijuana use by 0.127 annually on a scale ranging from 0 to 8. A statistically significant variance associated with the slope component (0.439, $p < 0.01$), however, indicates the linear rate of change in marijuana use varied considerably across individuals. Additionally, the mean for the quadratic component was negative (−0.015, $p < 0.01$), indicating that the nonlinear change was downward. That is, on average, people use marijuana less often as they age. A statistically significant variance for the quadratic component (0.002, $p < 0.01$) indicates that the shape and rate of nonlinear change in marijuana use vary significantly across individuals.

The adequacy of latent growth curve models can be examined in two ways. First, predicted mean levels of marijuana use (or model implied means) can be compared with observed means. The predicted means for marijuana use across the five waves of data were 1.32, 1.43, 1.51, 1.57, and 1.21, whereas the observed means for marijuana use were 1.30, 1.48, 1.61, 1.54, and 1.25, respectively. If we compare the predicted and observed means for marijuana use, the predicted means closely follow the observed means, implying the adequacy of the model specification. Second, a series of model fit statistics can also be examined. A comparative fit index (CFI) or a normative fit index (NFI) higher than 0.90, and a root mean square error of approximation (RMSEA) lower than 0.10 are indicative of good model fit (Bollen and Curran 2006; Kline 2005). Following these rules of thumb, we found that our model was an acceptable fit (CFI = 0.996, NFI = 0.995, and RMSEA = 0.055).

In sum, the average trajectory of marijuana use indicated an initial increase and a subsequent decrease. The shape and rate of change, however, significantly varied across individuals. Individual variability in both the initial level and the rate of change in marijuana use indicates that we need to consider characteristics such as adolescent religiosity to account for the variability among individuals.

Conditional Latent Growth Curve Model with Predictors

On the basis of the unconditional latent growth curve model, predictors are included in subsequent analyses to explain individual variability in each growth curve component. The effects of independent variables on marijuana use, in terms of initial levels (intercept), linear change (slope), and nonlinear change (quadratic), are reported in Table 12-2. The coefficients for the initial level of marijuana use show the effects of independent variables, measured at Wave III, on marijuana use, also measured at Wave III. Therefore for the intercept, the coefficients can be interpreted like an OLS regression. For example, sex was positively related to marijuana use, so males had higher initial levels of marijuana use than females. Similarly, peer attachment and peer marijuana use were positively related to the initial level of marijuana use. Therefore adolescents who were more attached to their peers and associated with more peers who smoked marijuana had higher levels of marijuana use. In contrast, adolescents who (1) lived with both biological parents, (2) were attached to their family, (3) had higher grades in school, and (4) believed that marijuana use was wrong had significantly lower initial levels of marijuana use. Of particular interest for our purposes, religious youths also showed significantly lower initial levels of marijuana use. Including predictors in the model reduced the individual variability in initial levels of marijuana use considerably, as indicated by a reduction in the variance associated with the intercept from 4.662 to 1.346. That is, much of the variability in the initial level of marijuana use was explained by predictors that were included in the model.

With respect to the change components, age and religiosity exhibited strong effects on both linear and nonlinear change, while peer marijuana use and moral beliefs about using marijuana affected linear change. The interpretation of the coefficients in a latent growth curve model depends on the baseline model in which no predictors are included. Because the baseline model indicated that adolescents increase their marijuana use over time, both positive and negative coefficients are interpreted with reference to this increase. Age, peer marijuana use, and religiosity were negatively associated with the linear component, indicating that adolescents who (1) were older, (2) had more marijuana-using peers, and (3) exhibited higher religiosity increased their marijuana use more slowly than other adolescents did. Conversely, younger adolescents, youths who had fewer marijuana-using peers, and nonreligious adolescents increased their frequency of marijuana use more rapidly. Moral beliefs about the wrongfulness of marijuana use positively affected the linear component of the growth curve, indicating that adolescents who believed that marijuana use

12 | Does Change in Teenage Religiosity Predict Change?

Table 12-2: Latent Growth Curve Model of Marijuana Use with Predictors

	Intercept	Linear	Quadratic
Coefficient Estimates			
Sex	0.251**	0.079	−0.006
	(0.071)	(0.043)	(0.004)
Age	−0.021	−0.061**	0.004**
	(0.020)	(0.012)	(0.001)
Race	0.029	−0.006	−0.001
	(0.091)	(0.056)	(0.006)
Biological family	−0.165*	0.025	−0.003
	(0.076)	(0.046)	(0.005)
Family attachment	−0.038**	0.007	0.000
	(0.013)	(0.008)	(0.001)
Peer attachment	0.045*	0.016	−0.002
	(0.018)	(0.011)	(0.001)
School attachment	−0.020	−0.007	0.000
	(0.019)	(0.011)	(0.001)
Grade	−0.155**	0.011	−0.002
	(0.046)	(0.028)	(0.003)
Peer Marijuana Use	0.739**	−0.071**	0.000
	(0.037)	(0.022)	(0.002)
Moral beliefs	−0.649**	0.067*	−0.005
	(0.048)	(0.029)	(0.003)
Religiosity	−0.047**	−0.025*	0.002*
	(0.017)	(0.010)	(0.001)
Growth Curve Parameters			
Mean	2.739**	0.825**	−0.046
	(0.431)	(0.261)	(0.026)
Variance	1.346**	0.293**	0.002**
	(0.137)	(0.046)	(0.001)

(continued)

Table 12-2: Latent Growth Curve Model of Marijuana Use with Predictors (*continued*)

	Intercept	Linear	Quadratic
Growth Curve Parameters			
Covariance			
Intercept			
Linear	−0.210** (0.057)		
Quadratic	0.012* (0.005)	−0.022** (0.005)	
Model Fit Statistics			
CFI	0.998		
NFI	0.995		
RMSEA	0.022		

* $p < 0.05$; ** $p < 0.01$.

was wrong at Wave III increased marijuana use more rapidly.[5] A meaningful reduction in the variance of the slope component from 0.439 to 0.293 indicated that predictors included in the growth curve model explained a considerable amount of the individual variability in the rate of linear change in marijuana use over time.

Turning to the growth curve component for nonlinear change in marijuana use over time, we found that only the effects of age and religiosity were statistically significant. Both of these variables were positively

---

[5] Latent growth curve models can sometimes produce results that seem counterintuitive. For example, we found that adolescents who had more marijuana-using peers at Wave III increased their marijuana use more slowly and adolescents who believed that marijuana use was wrong increased marijuana use more rapidly. Effects such as these are most likely the result of a "ceiling effect." For example, adolescents who believe that there is nothing wrong with using marijuana already use marijuana frequently, so there is not much room for them to increase in marijuana use over time (i.e., they are already at the high end of the distribution, so there is a ceiling on how high their marijuana use can get). In contrast, adolescents who believe that using marijuana is wrong at Wave III rarely, if ever, use marijuana. As a result, if adolescents who believe that using marijuana is wrong use marijuana in the future, their increase in marijuana use may appear more rapid because they started at a low level.

associated with the quadratic component (0.004 for age and 0.002 for religiosity), indicating that older adolescents and those with higher religiosity at Wave III were likely to experience a slower nonlinear change in marijuana use over time. Because nonlinear change followed a downward trajectory, these coefficient estimates indicated that older adolescents and those with higher religiosity experienced a slower deceleration (desistance) from marijuana use over time. The variance associated with the quadratic component was small to begin with, so a notable reduction in explained variance was not observed when predictors were included in the model.

The interpretation of latent growth curve models can be facilitated by examining trajectories with typical characteristics (see Figure 12-2). To illustrate the effects of religiosity on the predicted levels of marijuana use over time, controlling for the effects of other independent variables, all independent variables except for religiosity were set to their means. Trajectories of marijuana use for adolescents with religiosity equal to 0, 2, 4, 6, and 8 at Wave III are illustrated in Figure 12-2.

First, religiosity was negatively associated with the initial level of marijuana use, indicating that the higher adolescents' religiosity was, the lower their initial level of marijuana use at Wave III. The coefficient estimate for the linear slope was also negative, indicating that the higher adolescents' religiosity, the smaller their linear increase in marijuana use. Conversely, the lower adolescents' religiosity, the larger their linear increases in marijuana use. In fact, the effect of religiosity on the linear slope was so strong that there was *no apparent increase in marijuana use for the most religious adolescents* (see Figure 12-2). Finally, the coefficient estimate for the quadratic term was positive (0.002), indicating slower nonlinear change for individuals with higher religiosity.

Because the nonlinear change in the data had a downward curvature (the mean associated with the quadratic term was negative), this nonlinear effect can also be called *deceleration*. At first, slower deceleration among highly religious youths might seem counterintuitive. However, these highly religious adolescents were already experiencing a decrease in marijuana use because of the effect of religiosity on the linear change component. That is, although highly religious individuals might not have experienced nonlinear downward change, their levels of marijuana use decreased nonetheless because of religiosity's effect on the linear component of the latent growth curve. Nonreligious adolescents, on the other hand, were more likely to experience this nonlinear deceleration because their levels of marijuana use were high when nonlinear change started to take effect. By the time these nonreligious adolescents reached young adulthood, they had more opportunity to decrease their level of marijuana use.

Dual-Trajectory Latent Growth Curve Model

Our analysis indicated that religiosity was the only variable that had a statistically significant effect on all three growth curve components. That is, adolescents' initial level, linear change, and nonlinear change in marijuana use varied depending on their religiosity. However, our model formulation so far included predictors measured at Wave III. To examine further the dynamic relationship between religiosity and marijuana use, we formulated a dual-trajectory model in which changes in religiosity and changes in marijuana use were analyzed simultaneously (see Figure 12-3). Thus we focus on religiosity as an explicit time-varying predictor. Similar to the previous model formulation, latent growth curve components are depicted in ovals. Our initial analysis of an unconditional growth curve model for religiosity indicated that linear change was the best model. Therefore although the marijuana use trajectory was represented by three components (intercept, slope, and quadratic), the religiosity trajectory was represented by only two components: the intercept and slope.[6]

Figure 12-2: Religiosity and Trajectories of Marijuana Use

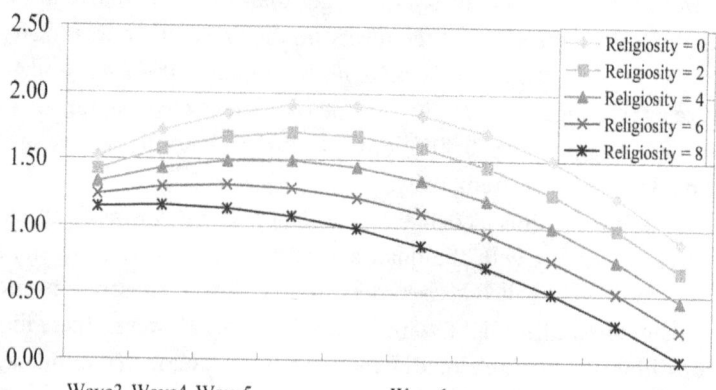

---

6   A series of model specifications was tested for religiosity, including a quadratic latent growth curve component and nonlinear factor loadings. However, the

First of all, each growth curve can be examined by analyzing the mean and variance associated with each growth curve component. For the religiosity trajectory, the mean of the intercept was 4.322 ($p < 0.01$), while the mean of the linear slope was −0.072 ($p < 0.01$). Thus adolescent religiosity at Wave III was, on average, 4.3 (the scale ranges from 0 to 8), and adolescents decreased their religiosity over time. However, there was considerable variability in both the initial level and the rate of change in religiosity over time, as indicated by the statistically significant variances for the intercept (3.394, $p < 0.01$) and slope (0.029, $p < 0.01$) components.

The latent growth curve for marijuana use was similar to the unconditional model depicted in Figure 12-1. All parameters associated with the three latent growth curve components were statistically significant. The average trajectory for marijuana use was found to be a nonlinear curve with an initial increase, followed by a subsequent decrease over time, indicated by the significant positive slope (0.127, $p < 0.01$) and negative quadratic component (−0.015, $p < 0.05$). The initial level, as well as linear and nonlinear rates of change, in marijuana use varied considerably across individuals, as indicated by statistically significant variances for the intercept (4.492, $p < 0.01$), slope (0.402, $p < 0.01$), and quadratic (0.002, $p < 0.01$) components.

In a dual-trajectory model, covariance estimates capture the temporally dynamic association between changes in religiosity and marijuana use over time. First, covariances among growth curve components can be examined for religiosity and marijuana use separately. For example, for the religiosity trajectory, the covariance estimate was negative and statistically significant, indicating that adolescents with higher levels of religiosity at Wave III were more likely to experience a steeper decrease in religiosity over time, compared to those with lower levels of religiosity at Wave III.[7]

---

observed means for religiosity indicated a uniform decrease over time. Because the rate of change diverged from a linear decrease only slightly, it was determined that the nonlinear change in religiosity was negligible. A linear model specification for religiosity is also advantageous for interpretation because of its parsimonious covariance structure. For example, covariances between two quadratic (nonlinear) components in a dual-trajectory model would have been extremely difficult to describe in words.

7   Again the pattern for religiosity is most likely the result of a ceiling effect (see note 4). Adolescents who start at the highest levels of religiosity can only maintain or decrease their religiosity over time, so their decrease appears steeper. In contrast,

Figure 12-3: Dual-Trajectory Model of Religiosity and Marijuana Use

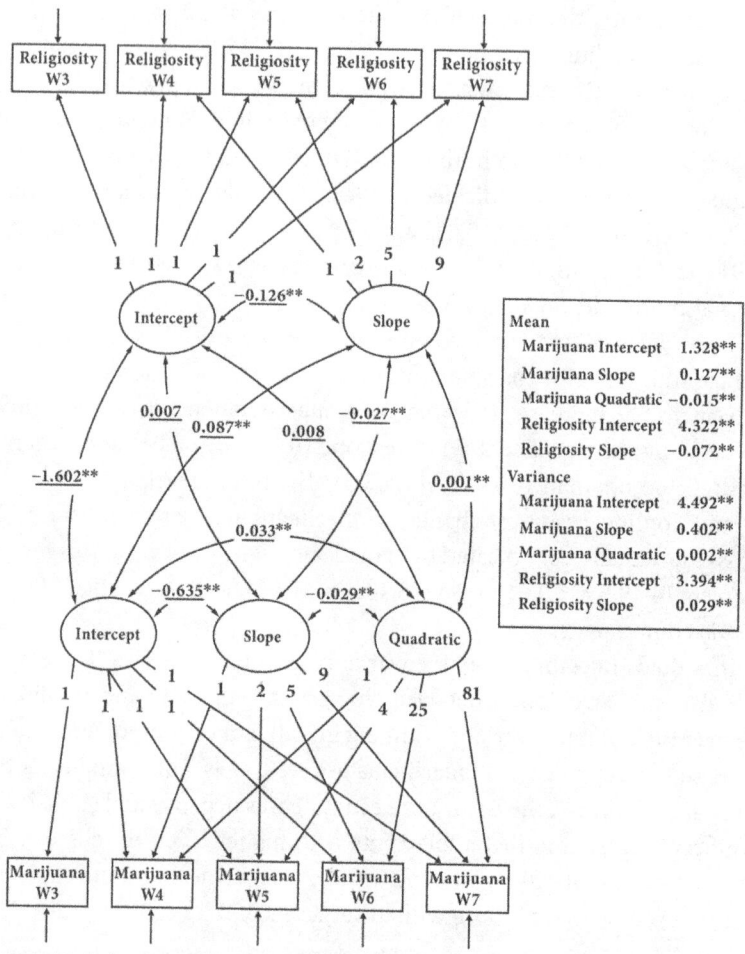

Note: Underlined covariances, as well as means and variances, were estimated parameters. Numbers without underlines were fixed for estimation. Fixed factor loadings represent the passage of time.
* $p < 0.05$. ** $p < 0.01$.

For the marijuana use trajectory, there were negative covariances between the intercept and slope components (−0.635, $p < 0.01$) and between the slope and quadratic components (−0.029, $p < 0.05$). The negative covariance

---

adolescents who start at a low or moderate level of religiosity cannot decrease their religiosity much over time, so their decrease in religiosity appears more gradual.

between the intercept and slope components means that adolescents with higher levels of marijuana use at Wave III were likely to experience less of an increase in marijuana use over time. The negative covariance between the slope and quadratic component means that a large slope value (i.e., a steeper increase in marijuana use) was associated with a smaller value for the quadratic component (i.e., a smaller nonlinear change or a deceleration in marijuana use over time). That is, adolescents who experienced a steeper increase in marijuana use were less likely to desist from using marijuana over time. Finally, the covariance between the intercept and the quadratic component was positive (0.033, $p < 0.01$), indicating that adolescents with higher initial levels of marijuana use at Wave III experienced smaller nonlinear change and were less likely to experience desistance from marijuana use over time.

Additionally, we can examine the covariances among growth curve components across the two trajectories. For example, the covariance between the intercepts for religiosity and marijuana use was negative (-1.602, $p < 0.01$), meaning that adolescents with higher levels of religiosity at Wave III used marijuana less frequently than did those with lower levels of religiosity. Covariances among the intercept for the religiosity growth curve and the slope and quadratic factors for the marijuana use growth curve were not statistically significant (covariance estimates were 0.007 and 0.008, respectively). These findings indicated that the initial level of religiosity at Wave III did not predict changes in marijuana use over time. Rather, change in marijuana use was predicted by change in religiosity, signifying a temporally dynamic association between changes in religiosity and changes in adolescents' delinquent behavior. For example, the negative covariance between the religiosity slope and the marijuana use slope (-0.027, $p < 0.01$) indicated that adolescents whose religiosity trajectory was closer to a flat line (i.e., had less of a decrease) were less likely to experience an increase in marijuana use. That is, adolescents who maintained their high levels of religiosity were less likely to engage in marijuana use over time. A positive covariance between the religiosity slope and the quadratic component for marijuana use (0.001, $p < 0.01$), on the other hand, indicated that adolescents with a larger slope value (a less steep decrease or a flatter trajectory in religiosity) were associated with a larger curvature value (less downward trajectory). That is, adolescents who maintained their religiosity over time were less likely to experience a nonlinear decrease in marijuana use over time.

Variances associated with each growth curve component decreased to some extent when religiosity was considered as a time-varying predictor. Nonetheless, a considerable amount of individual-level variability remained for initial levels, linear change, and nonlinear change over time. In fact, all variances associated with the dual-trajectory model were statistically significant. Hence, a final analysis was performed by including all independent variables as predictors in the dual-trajectory model.

Dual-Trajectory Latent Growth Curve Model with Predictors

Table 12-3 summarizes the results for the dual-trajectory latent growth curve model in which the effects of independent variables on both the marijuana use and religiosity trajectories are taken into account. Looking at the intercept component for the marijuana use growth curve, we see that the results are comparable to the first set of analyses (see Table 12-1). The effects of sex, biological family, family attachment, peer attachment, grades, peer marijuana use, and moral beliefs about marijuana use retained significant effects on the intercept component of the marijuana use trajectory, with the same direction and magnitude, even after we treated religiosity as a time-varying variable. Such results were expected, however, because coefficient estimates on the intercept component are essentially the same as a cross-sectional analysis. Thus allowing religiosity to change over time should not have much effect on other variables predicting the initial level of marijuana use. When the change components for the marijuana use trajectory were examined, several differences were observed. When religiosity was treated as a time-varying predictor, the effect of sex on the linear change in marijuana use became statistically significant. In particular, a positive effect of sex on the linear slope indicated that males, who had higher initial levels of marijuana use than females, increased their levels of marijuana use faster than females did. The effect of moral beliefs about marijuana use on the linear change in marijuana use, on the other hand, became statistically insignificant when religiosity was treated as a time-varying variable.

In the dual-trajectory model with predictors, the effects of independent variables on the religiosity growth curve can also be examined. Sex and peer marijuana use were negatively associated with the initial level of religiosity. Non-white race, greater peer attachment, higher grades, and stronger moral beliefs against marijuana usage were associated with higher initial levels of religiosity. Many independent variables were also associated with changes in religiosity. Sex, peer attachment, and beliefs about marijuana use were negatively associated with the linear slope component of religiosity, indicating that males, adolescents who were less attached to their peers, and youths who believed that marijuana use was wrong experienced steeper decreases in religiosity over time than others did. Older, nonwhite youths with many peers who used marijuana were likely to experience less of a decrease in religiosity over time.

Most important, all covariance estimates among the growth curve parameters for marijuana use and religiosity were statistically significant, except for the covariance between the marijuana use intercept and the religiosity slope and the covariance between the quadratic change in marijuana use and the religiosity slope. These covariances were statistically significant even after controlling for the effects of other independent variables. Thus the dual-trajectory model with predictors further suggests a temporally dynamic relationship between changes in religiosity and marijuana use.

Conclusion

Despite the recent emphasis on longitudinal research, few studies have examined the long-term effects of adolescent religiosity on delinquency. Using latent growth curve modeling, we examined the association between religiosity and marijuana use over time. While a variety of individual characteristics were considered as additional independent variables, the trajectory of marijuana use for adolescents was largely characterized by the adolescents' religiosity. Highly religious adolescents used marijuana less often than others did at the beginning of the marijuana use trajectory. While adolescents, on average, followed an initial increase and subsequent decrease in marijuana use, highly religious adolescents were unlikely to experience an increase in marijuana use over time. Although most adolescents, as they aged, matured out of their illicit activities, if they ever engaged in them, the predicted frequency of marijuana use was always lower for religious adolescents than for nonreligious adolescents. Overall, our results suggest that religiosity is an important variable in predicting the trajectory of marijuana use from adolescence to young adulthood. Religiosity acts as a protective factor that deters youths from marijuana use.

When religiosity was treated as a time-varying predictor, the importance of religiosity in characterizing change in marijuana use over time

Table 12-3: Dual-Trajectory Model of Religiosity and Marijuana Use

	Marijuana Use			Religiosity	
	Intercept	Slope	Quadratic	Intercept	Slope
Coefficient Estimates					
Sex	0.265**	0.087*	−0.006	−0.291**	−0.028*
	(0.071)	(0.043)	(0.004)	(0.100)	(0.012)
Age	−0.024	−0.062**	0.004**	0.019	0.015**
	(0.020)	(0.012)	(0.001)	(0.028)	(0.003)
Race	0.006	−0.016	0.000	0.472**	0.039*
	(0.091)	(0.055)	(0.006)	(0.129)	(0.016)
Biological family	−0.171*	0.022	−0.003	0.148	−0.017
	(0.076)	(0.046)	(0.005)	(0.107)	(0.013)
Family attachment	−0.037**	0.007	0.000	−0.002	0.001
	(0.013)	(0.008)	(0.001)	(0.018)	(0.002)
Peer attachment	0.043*	0.014	−0.002	0.062**	−0.010**
	(0.018)	(0.011)	(0.001)	(0.025)	(0.003)
School attachment	−0.021	−0.007	0.000	0.021	0.005
	(0.019)	(0.011)	(0.001)	(0.026)	(0.003)
Grade	−0.165**	0.007	−0.002	0.260**	−0.014
	(0.046)	(0.028)	(0.003)	(0.065)	(0.008)
Peer marijuana use	0.751**	−0.066**	0.000	−0.217**	0.014*
	(0.037)	(0.022)	(0.002)	(0.052)	(0.006)
Moral beliefs	−0.664**	0.054	−0.004	0.498**	−0.017*
	(0.048)	(0.029)	(0.003)	(0.067)	(0.008)
Growth Curve Parameters					
Mean	2.680**	0.786**	−0.043	1.376*	−0.177*
	(0.432)	(0.262)	(0.026)	(0.607)	(0.075)
Variance	1.353**	0.292**	0.002**	3.080**	0.029**
	(0.137)	(0.046)	(0.001)	(0.143)	(0.006)
Covariance					

(continued)

Table 12-3: Dual-Trajectory Model of Religiosity and Marijuana Use (*continued*)

	Marijuana Use			Religiosity	
	Intercept	Slope	Quadratic	Intercept	Slope
Marijuana intercept	1.000				
Marijuana slope	−0.202** (0.058)	1.000			
Marijuana quadratic	0.011* (0.005)	−0.022** (0.005)	1.000		
Religiosity intercept	−0.169* (0.067)	−0.143** (0.041)	0.014** (0.004)	1.000	
Religiosity slope	0.015 (0.008)	−0.013** (0.005)	0.001 (0.000)	−0.094** (0.016)	1.000
Model Fit Statistics					
CFI	0.994				
NFI	0.989				
RMSEA	0.026				

* $p < 0.05$; ** $p < 0.01$.

was further highlighted. In particular, when religiosity was allowed to change over time in the latent growth curve model, the initial level of religiosity did not predict changes in marijuana use. Rather, changes in marijuana use were significantly related to changes in religiosity. Such associations between changes in religiosity and changes in marijuana use remained even after we controlled for other independent variables.

We believe that our study adds to the growing body of research on the effects of religiosity on substance use. However, like all studies using secondary data, ours is limited by the questions in the NYS. For example, the first two waves of the NYS do not include any measures of religiosity. Although a few religion-related items were added to the third wave of the NYS, the measures of religiosity are still very limited. Therefore while we included both a public (attendance) and a private (importance) measure of religiosity in our analysis, future research should examine the longitudinal effects of additional measures of religiosity on substance use, such as frequency of prayer, images of God, participation in religious youth groups, how religion affects life decisions, and how close adolescents feel to God. Future research should also examine whether or not life course trajectories in substance use differ on the basis of denominational affiliation, given that religious groups differ in terms of how strongly they prohibit substance use (Beeghley, Bock, and Cochran 1990).

In addition to adolescent religiosity, it could be important to measure parents' religiosity, since previous research suggests that parents' religiosity can influence adolescent involvement in delinquency and substance use (Foshee and Hollinger 1996). Regnerus (2003) determined that parents' religiosity was negatively related to female delinquency, but among boys, an increase in parents' religiosity contributed to an increase in delinquency. Pearce and Haynie (2004: 1553) determined that the combination of parents' religiosity and adolescents' religiosity can influence delinquency, such that "when either a mother or child is very religious and the other is not, the child's delinquency increases." Therefore future research should examine the long-term effects on substance use of parents' religiosity and of religious agreement between adolescents and parents. It will be interesting to determine whether religious adolescents who live with religious parents have substance use trajectories that are the same as or similar to those of adolescents who do not live with religious parents.

Along with additional measures of religiosity, future research should examine additional measures of delinquency. Although we found that religiosity has a significant effect on marijuana use, researchers have noted that religion has a stronger effect on "antiascetic" or victimless forms of deviance, such as alcohol and drug use (Burkett and White 1974). Since there is some debate about the types of deviance that religiosity influences, future research should examine other types of delinquency, such as theft and violence. Future research would also do well to examine the long-term effects of religiosity on prosocial behaviors, such as grades and volunteering.

Finally, although growth curve modeling allows for a sophisticated analysis of how adolescent religiosity influences changes in marijuana use over time, researchers still need to specify the mechanisms that account for the effect of religiosity on delinquency. Although we argued that religiosity can influence adolescents' marijuana use by strengthening social bonds, influencing the learning process, helping adolescents to cope with strain, and increasing self-control, our analysis does not enable us to specify which of these processes account for religiosity's effect on trajectories of marijuana use. Therefore future research should focus on specifying the theoretical mechanisms that account for religiosity's long-term effects on delinquency and substance use.

In sum, the results of our study offer several avenues for future research. At the most general level, we recommend that researchers put more emphasis on longitudinal studies using data collected over extended periods of time (i.e., more than two waves separated by a year). Although previous research generally emphasized the contemporaneous effects of religiosity, a small but growing body of research suggests that religiosity could have long-term effects on behavior over the life course (Giordano et al. 2008; Jang, Bader, and Johnson 2008; Petts 2009; Ulmer et al. 2010). Establishing the immediate effects of religiosity on delinquency is a productive approach, but testing longitudinal models to identify the cumulative advantages of religiosity over the life course might be more fruitful.

References

Acock, Alan C. 2005. "Working with Missing Values." *Journal of Marriage and Family* 67: 1012–28.

Adamczyk, Amy, and Ian Palmer. 2008. "Religion and Initiation into Marijuana Use: The Deterring Role of Religious Friends." *Journal of Drug Issues* 38: 717–42.

Agnew, Robert. 1992. "Foundation for a General Strain Theory of Crime and Delinquency." *Criminology* 30: 47–87.

Akers, Ronald L. 1973. *Deviant Behavior: A Social Learning Approach*. Belmont, CA: Wadsworth.

Akers, Ronald L., and Christine S. Sellers. 2004. *Criminological Theories: Introduction, Evaluation, and Application*. Los Angeles: Roxbury.

Aziz, Shagufta, and Ghazala Rehman. 1996. "Self Control and Tolerance among Low and High Religious Groups." *Journal of Personality and Clinical Studies* 12: 83–85.

Bahr, Stephen, Ricky D. Hawks, and Gabe Wang. 1993. "Family and Religious Influences on Adolescent Substance Abuse." *Youth and Society* 24: 443–65.

Baier, Colin J., and Bradley R. E. Wright. 2001. "'If You Love Me, Keep My Commandments': A Meta-Analysis of the Effect of Religion on Crime." *Journal of Research in Crime and Delinquency* 38: 3–21.

Beeghley, Leonard, E. Wilber Bock, and John K. Cochran. 1990. "Religious Change and Alcohol Use: An Application of Reference Group Theory." *Sociological Forum* 5: 261–78.

Bollen, Kenneth A., and Patrick J. Curran. 2006. *Latent Curve Models: A Structural Equation Perspective*. Hoboken, NJ: John Wiley and Sons.

Burkett, Steven R., and Mervin White. 1974. "Hellfire and Delinquency: Another Look." *Journal for the Scientific Study of Religion* 13: 455–62.

Cernkovich, Stephen A., and Peggy C. Giordano. 1987. "Family Relationships and Delinquency." *Criminology* 25: 295–321.

Cernkovich, Stephen A., and Peggy C. Giordano. 1992. "School Bonding, Race, and Delinquency." *Criminology* 30: 261–91.

Chapple, Constance L., Julia A. McQuillan, and Terceira A. Berdahl. 2005. "Gender, Social Bonds, and Delinquency: A Comparison of Boys' and Girls' Models." *Social Science Research* 34: 357–83.

Chitwood, Dale D., Michael L. Weiss, and Carl G. Leukefeld. 2008. "A Systematic Review of Recent Literature on Religiosity and Substance Abuse." *Journal of Drug Issues* 38: 653–88.

Chu, Doris. 2007. "Religiosity and Desistance from Drug Use." *Criminal Justice and Behavior* 34: 661–79.

Cochran, John K., and Ronald L. Akers. 1989. "Beyond Hellfire: An Exploration of the Variable Effects of Religiosity on Adolescent Marijuana and Alcohol Use." *Journal of Research in Crime and Delinquency* 26: 198–225.

Cretacci, Michael A. 2003. "Religion and Social Control: An Application of a Modified Social Bond on Violence." *Criminal Justice Review* 28: 254–77.

Crosnoe, Robert. 2006. "The Connection between Academic Failure and Adolescent Drinking in Secondary School." *Sociology of Education* 79: 1–44.

Desmond, Scott A., Kristopher H. Morgan, and George Kikuchi. 2010. "Religious Development: How (and Why) Does Religiosity Change from Adolescence to Young Adulthood?" *Sociological Perspectives* 53: 247–70.

Duncan, Terry E., Susan C. Duncan, Lisa A. Strycker, Fuzhong Li, and Anthony Alpert. 1999. *An Introduction to Latent Variable Growth Curve Modeling*. Mahwah, NJ: Lawrence Erlbaum Associates.

Enders, Craig K. 2001. "The Performance of the Full Information Maximum Likelihood Estimator in Multiple Regression Models with Missing Data." *Educational and Psychological Measurement* 61: 713–40.

Elliott, Delbert S., David Huizinga, and Suzanne S. Ageton. 1985. *Explaining Delinquency and Drug Use*. Newbury Park, CA: Sage.

Elliott, Delbert S., David Huizinga, and Scott Menard. 1989. *Multiple Problem Youth: Delinquency, Substance Use, and Mental Health Problems*. New York: Springer-Verlag.

Foshee, Vangie A., and Bryan R. Hollinger. 1996. "Maternal Religiosity, Adolescent Social Bonding, and Adolescent Alcohol Use." *Journal of Early Adolescence* 16: 451–68.

Geyer, Anne, and Roy F. Baumeister. 2005. "Religion, Morality, and Self Control." In *Handbook of the Psychology of Religion and Spirituality*, edited by Raymond F. Paloutzian and Crystal L. Park, 412–32. New York: Guilford Press.

Giordano, Peggy C., Monica A. Longmore, Ryan D. Schroeder, and Patrick M. Seffrin. 2008. "A Life-Course Perspective on Spirituality and Desistance from Crime." *Criminology* 46: 99–132.

Gottfredson, Michael R., and Travis Hirschi. 1990. *A General Theory of Crime*. Stanford, CA: Stanford University Press.

Hannon, Lance, James DeFronzo, and Jane Prochnow. 2001. "Moral Commitment and the Effects of Social Influences on Violent Delinquency." *Violence and Victims* 16: 427–39.

Hawkins, Darnell F. 2003. *Violent Crime: Assessing Race and Ethnic Differences*. Cambridge: Cambridge University Press.

Hirschi, Travis. 1969. *Causes of Delinquency*. Berkeley: University of California Press.

Jang, Sung Joon, Christopher D. Bader, and Byron R. Johnson. 2008. "The Cumulative Advantage of Religiosity in Preventing Drug Use." *Journal of Drug Issues* 38: 771–98.

Jang, Sung Joon, and Byron R. Johnson. 2005. "Gender, Religiosity, and Reactions to Strain among African Americans." *Sociological Quarterly* 46: 323–57.

Jang, Sung Joon, and Byron R. Johnson. 2010. "Religion, Race, and Drug Use among American Youth." *Interdisciplinary Journal for Research on Religion* 6: 1–22.

Johnson, Byron, Spencer De Li, David B. Larson, and Michael McCullough. 2000. "A Systematic Review of the Religiosity and Delinquency Literature." *Journal of Contemporary Criminal Justice* 16: 32–52.

Johnson, Byron R., Sung Joon Jang, David B. Larson, and Spencer De Li. 2001. "Does Adolescent Religious Commitment Matter? A Reexamination of the Effect of Religiosity on Delinquency." *Journal of Research in Crime and Delinquency* 38: 22–44.

Johnson, Matthew C., and Robert G. Morris. 2008. "The Moderating Effects of Religiosity on the Relationship between Stressful Life Events and Delinquent Behavior." *Journal of Criminal Justice* 36: 486–93.

Kline, Rex B. 2005. *Principles and Practice of Structural Equation Modeling*. New York: Guilford.

Laub, John H., and Robert J. Sampson. 1988. "Unraveling Families and Delinquency: A Reanalysis of the Gluecks' Data." *Criminology* 26: 355–80.

Liu, Xiaoru, and Howard B. Kaplan. 1999. "Explaining the Gender Difference in Adolescent Delinquent Behavior: A Longitudinal Test of Mediating Mechanisms." *Criminology* 37: 195–215.

Longest, Kyle C., and Stephen Vaisey. 2008. "Control or Conviction: Religion and Adolescent Initiation of Marijuana Use." *Journal of Drug Use* 38: 659–715.

Marcos, Anastasios C., Stephen J. Bahr, and Richard E. Johnson. 1986. "Test of a Bonding/Association Theory of Adolescent Drug Use." *Social Forces* 65: 135–61.

Matsueda, Ross L., and Karen Heimer. 1987. "Race, Family Structure, and Delinquency: A Test of Differential Association and Social Control Theories." *American Sociological Review* 52: 826–40.

Mears, Daniel P., Matthew Ploeger, and Mark Warr. 1998. "Explaining the Gender Gap in Delinquency: Peer Influence and Moral Evaluations of Behavior." *Journal of Research in Crime and Delinquency* 35: 251–66.

Menard, Scott. 2002. *Longitudinal Research*. Thousand Oaks, CA: Sage.

Merton, Robert K. 1938. "Social Structure and Anomie." *American Sociological Review* 3: 672–82.

Pearce, Lisa D., and Dana L. Haynie. 2004. "Intergenerational Religious Dynamics and Adolescent Delinquency." *Social Forces* 82: 1553–72.

Petts, Richard J. 2009. "Family and Religious Characteristics' Influence on Delinquency Trajectories from Adolescence to Young Adulthood." *American Sociological Review* 74: 465–83.

Pratt, Travis C., and Francis T. Cullen. 2000. "The Empirical Status of Gottfredson and Hirschi's General Theory of Crime: A Meta-Analysis." *Criminology* 38: 931–64.

Regnerus, Mark D. 2003. "Linked Lives, Faith, and Behavior: Intergenerational Religious Influence on Adolescent Delinquency." *Journal for the Scientific Study of Religion* 42: 189–203.

Sampson, Robert, and John Laub. 1993. *Crime in the Making: Pathways and Turning Points through Life*. Cambridge, MA: Harvard University Press.

Smith, Christian, and Melinda Lundquist Denton. 2005. *Soul Searching: The Religious and Spiritual Lives of American Teenagers*. New York: Oxford University Press.

Steffensmeier, Darrell, and Cathy Streifel. 1991. "Age, Gender, and Crime across Three Historical Periods: 1935, 1960, and 1985." *Social Forces* 69: 869–94.

Sutherland, Edwin. 1947. *Principles of Criminology*. Philadelphia: Lippincott.

Uecker, Jeremy E., Mark D. Regnerus, and Margaret L. Vaaler. 2007. "Losing My Religion: The Social Sources of Religious Decline in Early Adulthood." *Social Forces* 85: 1667–92.

Ulmer, Jeffrey T., Scott A. Desmond, Sung Joon Jang, and Byron R. Johnson. 2010. "Teenage Religiosity and Changes in Marijuana Use during the Transition to Adulthood." *Interdisciplinary Journal for Research on Religion* 6: 1–19.

Vold, George B., Thomas J. Bernard, and Jeffrey B. Snipes. 2002. *Theoretical Criminology*. 5th ed. New York: Oxford University Press.

Warr, Mark. 2002. *Companions in Crime*. Cambridge: Cambridge University Press.

Welch, Michael, Charles Tittle, and Harold Grasmick. 2006. "Christian Religiosity, Self Control, and Social Conformity." *Social Forces* 84: 1605–23.

Wills, Thomas A., Alison M. Yaeger, and James M. Sandy. 2003. "Buffering Effect of Religiosity for Adolescent Substance Abuse." *Psychology of Addictive Behaviors* 17: 24–31.

13

Religiosity as a Buffer in the Association between Economic Disadvantage and Violence[1]

Cassady Pitt | Alfred DeMaris

To what extent does religiosity protect impoverished youth from engaging in delinquent behavior? Prior research suggests that economic disadvantage is a strong correlate of violent delinquency (Allison et al. 1999; Anderson 1999; Baron 2007; Bearman and Moody 2004; Elliot et al. 1996; Kasarda and Janowitz 1974; Kingston, Huizinga, and Elliott 2009; Messner and South 1986; Sampson, Morenoff, and Earls 1999; Shaw and McKay 1942; Webber 2008). It is not currently well understood, however, whether religiosity could be a protective factor in this association. Theoretically, such a role for religiosity is reasonable. General strain theory (GST) (Agnew 1992, 2001) has provided a foundation for much of the research on strain concepts in the criminological literature by suggesting that there is a positive relationship between economic strain and violent delinquency. Strain theorists suggest, however, that certain

---

[1] This research uses data from Add Health, a program project directed by Kathleen Mullan Harris and designed by J. Richard Udry, Peter S. Bearman, and Kathleen Mullan Harris at the University of North Carolina at Chapel Hill and funded by grant P01-HD31921 from the Eunice Kennedy Shriver National Institute of Child Health and Human Development, with cooperative funding from twenty-three other federal agencies and foundations. Special acknowledgment is due Ronald R. Rindfuss and Barbara Entwisle for assistance in the original design. Information on how to obtain the Add Health data files is available on the Add Health website (http://www.cpc.unc.edu/addhealth). No direct support was received from grant P01-HD31921 for this analysis.

conditioning factors may moderate the relationship between strain and negative outcomes (Agnew 1992, 2001). These conditioning effects presumed to be crime-inhibiting include social control, social support, and social capital.

Religiosity has been alluded to as a possible moderator for the relationship between strain and negative behavior (Jang 2007; Jang and Johnson 2003, 2005; Johnson and Morris 2008; Piquero and Sealock 2004). Religiosity has been identified as a mechanism that helps individuals positively cope with stressful circumstances (Compas et al. 2001; Pargament 1990; Pargament and Saunders 2007) such as those brought about by economic disadvantage. It has been established that adolescents who are religiously oriented are substantially less likely to engage in criminal behavior (Adamczyk 2009; Burkett and White 1974; Cochran 1993; Cretacci 2003; Regnerus 2007; Smith and Denton 2005; Tittle and Welch 1983; Wallace et al. 2007). For this reason, religious adherence may embody both social control and social capital with respect to the relationship between economic disadvantage and violence.

Only a small number of studies (Jang and Johnson 2003, 2005; Johnson and Morris 2008) have assessed the ability of religiosity to serve as a coping mechanism for stress. Religiosity can act as a buffer to strain-induced negative emotions, which by extension may help to deter criminal behavior. Specifically, Jang and Johnson (2003) posit that because the relationship between strain and criminal behavior is predicated upon negative emotions, religiosity may function as a conditioning factor in the aforementioned relationship. Religious individuals are not only less likely to develop negative emotions when faced with strain, they are more likely to have positive coping resources, such as stronger social support systems through family and friends who are also religious (Smith and Denton 2005). Yet previous work has failed to examine directly whether religiosity buffers the relationship between economic disadvantage and violence. Therefore, this study seeks to make a contribution to the GST literature by investigating whether religiosity conditions the association between economic disadvantage and violence among adolescents.

Theoretical Framework

Agnew's General Strain Theory elaborates on traditional macrostructural strain models proposed by Durkheim (2006 [1897]), Merton (1938), and Cloward and Ohlin (1960) via the use of a micro-level social psychology perspective (Agnew 1985, 1992, 1999, 2001). Agnew (1985) introduced a different type of strain, which is the failure to escape from aversive situations or stimuli. Additionally, Agnew included the concept of anger and frustration as negative emotions within his idea of strain. Agnew found that individuals who could not escape from an aversive environment would be more likely to be involved in violent delinquency, aggression, and other forms of negative behavior directly and indirectly through the expression of anger. Agnew concluded that there are three central components to GST: strain, negative emotion, and coping strategies.

According to Agnew's GST (Agnew 1992), crime is committed due to the effects of strain caused by a person's failure to achieve society's positively valued goals, the removal of positively valued stimuli from the individual, and the presentation of negative stimuli in an individual's life. Each of these three types of strain increases an individual's feeling of anger, an emotion that not only increases the desire for revenge but also helps both to justify aggressive behavior and to stimulate individuals to action. In looking specifically at strain and its relationship to adolescent violence, Agnew (1992, 2001) found that economic disadvantage strain is cumulative; that is, economic disadvantage leads to additional stressors such as those within the family context (e.g., domestic violence between parents and child maltreatment) and the formation of criminogenic relationships (e.g., delinquent peers).

Adolescents may cope with the stresses and strains of economic disadvantage when there are strains in their household by forming negative relationships with other violent friends (Haynie and Payne 2006; Heimer 1997). This coping mechanism is most common among adolescents who reside in communities that are stricken with economic disadvantage. As suggested in Anderson's (1999) ethnographic study of inner-city Black youths in Philadelphia, in areas plagued by economic disadvantage, adolescent boys adhere to a "code of the streets" that involves the perception of being tough and the use of violence as necessary to achieve desired goals. Older adolescent peers often teach this code to younger children as a way to navigate the streets. Stewart and Simons (2006) also have shown that the use of street code is prevalent among the disadvantaged and associated with violent offending. Further, Haynie, Silver, and Teasdale (2006) examined neighborhood characteristics as correlates of violence and found that the effect of economic disadvantage on delinquency is mediated by exposure to violent peers.

Economic Disadvantage and Violence

The literature examining the relationship between economic disadvantage and violent delinquency does show an association between the two, but it is important to note that the association often hinges upon how economic disadvantage is measured (Office of the Surgeon General 2001). Empirical research indicating that economic disadvantage is associated with delinquency tends to operationalize economic disadvantage among violent youth in one of three ways: as relative economic deprivation (Baron 2007; Messner and South 1986; Webber 2008), as a socioeconomic (SES) measure that includes an admixture of a parent's educational level, parental income, and/or parental occupational status (Bearman and Moody 2004; Heimer 1997), or as concentrated disadvantage, such as living in poor neighborhoods (Allison et al. 1999; Anderson 1999; Jencks 1992; Krivo and Peterson 1996; Ludwig, Duncan, and Pinkstone 2000; Sampson, Morenoff, and Earls, 1999; Shaw and McKay 1942).

Empirical studies that question the existence of an economic disadvantage-violence relationship tend to use SES as an economic disadvantage indicator (Braithwaite 1981; Johnstone 1978; Tittle 1991; Tittle and Meier 1990; Wright et al. 1999). For example, Tittle and Meier (1991) argue that SES-related measures only show a relationship between SES and delinquency for those individuals who are experiencing the most drastic and severe forms of economic disadvantage. Wright et al. (1999) measured SES through the use of a six-point scale developed by Elley and Irving (1976) that assessed parental occupational status; in addition, their model accounted for parental education achievement and joint income. Wright and colleagues (1999) found that there are certain social-psychological and structure factors associated with high and low SES that both promote and inhibit delinquency via mediation effects. Specifically, the authors found that low SES promoted delinquency when people experienced increased financial strain and aggression but that when low-SES individuals had higher educational and occupational aspirations, their violence was inhibited.

Studies examining the relationship between economic deprivation and delinquency find that economic disadvantage is strongly associated with crime (Baron 2006; Messner and South 1986; Webber 2008). Baron (2006) used measures of relative deprivation in terms of financial goals, financial success, and current financial status on youth delinquency and found a significant relationship between the two. That is, those who are of a lower SES who are also unable to meet certain financial goals of getting out of economic disadvantage are more likely to have children who engage in delinquency. Messner and South (1986) found similar results among white and Black families whose incomes were below $4,000 (the economic disadvantage line for that time period). Both studies indicate that there is a direct relationship between strains of economic disadvantage and delinquency.

There is a significant amount of literature pertaining to the relationship between concentrated disadvantage and violent delinquency (Allison et al. 1999; Anderson 1999; Elliot et al 1996; Kasarda and Janowitz 1974; Kingston, Huizinga, and Elliott 2009; Sampson, Morenoff, and Earls 1999; Shaw and McKay 1942). Shaw and McKay's classic study in 1942 on the geographic distribution of delinquent boys and the manner in which rates of violent delinquency varied from area to area in Chicago has often been used to understand the relationship between concentrated economic disadvantage and juvenile delinquency. Their main findings are that socially disorganized areas contribute to the occurrence of juvenile delinquency when these areas experience low residential stability, and high rates of economic disadvantage, and are racially heterogeneous. That is, much of the research shows that living in a neighborhood that is predominantly poor increases an adolescent's likelihood of engaging in delinquency and especially in violence.

The Conditioning Effect of Religion

The strains associated with economic disadvantage may cause negative coping, such as engaging in violence. But it has been suggested (Agnew 2001; Pargament 1997) that religion may reduce the strain that some adolescents face because it provides connectedness to God, to religious others, and to religious institutions. When attempting to cope with strain, individuals who seek to understand their circumstances from a religious perspective may interpret their suffering as spiritual warfare, punishment by God, or a test meted out by God (Pargament 1999; Pargament and Mahoney 2005; Pargament et al. 1992). Religious coping refers to using the significance and sacredness of religion to regulate emotions, thoughts, and behaviors in the event of a stressful or strained environment (Compas et al. 2001; Pargament 1990, 1997). Thus, coping is an active response to dealing with stress or strain. Likewise, the practice of religious beliefs can also guide the pathway an adolescent chooses to follow. Those who are religious may be less likely to participate in certain behaviors their religion denounces, such as violence.

Religious coping involves a "unique form of motivation" to abstain from certain behaviors, such as violence (Pargament, Magyar-Russell, and Murray-Swank 2005: 669–70). Teens who practice religion are more likely to refrain from engaging in violent crimes because their religion tells them it is wrong and because of their associations with religious others (Smith and Denton 2005). This motivation to abstain from negative behaviors is perpetuated by the support received from the relationships that religion establishes or strengthens, such as support from family, friends, and teachers (Pargament and Maton 2000). This theory is similar in scope to the ideas of Hirschi's social control/bond theory, as adolescents who form strong positive social bonds to parents, peers, and teachers are less likely to be involved in violence (Agnew 1993; Cernkovich and Giordano 1992). Pargament (1997) also suggests that religion is unique because of the unity among those in religious groups. This community provides additional resources for individuals who may not have access to particular means (i.e., social capital) that help them deal with strain (Pargament and Maton 2000).

A contrary perspective on the relationship between religion and strain/stress is that religiosity might actually intensify the positive relationship between economic disadvantage and delinquency. Religious adolescents may perceive that God is punishing them or feel abandoned by God when they are under stressful circumstances. These feelings are examples of negative religious coping (Pargament 1997; Pargament and Mahoney 2005). If religious adolescents feel abandoned by God, they may in turn feel justified in committing acts of violence. Another possible explanation for why religious adolescents engage in violence may be that they do not believe the behavior they are committing is morally wrong (Burkett and Ward 1993; Curry 1996; Desmond et al. 2009; Stark 2001). In many Judeo-Christian religious sects, there are justifications for violence towards another person. For instance, war may justify violence. Juergensmeyer (2003: 94) argues that in some Judeo-Christian and even some other religious sects, violence is justifiable if it is outlined in religious texts as the appropriate punishment for sins or wrongs. In addition, another body of literature suggests that some more fundamentalist sects of Christianity accept that the wife and children need to submit to the authority of the husband or man of the household. Disobedience of this law may result in physical altercations (Gunnoe, Hetherington, and Reiss 1999; Koch and Ramirez 2009). Aside from the religious perspective, it may be the case that there are dissimilar moral or religious beliefs between a child and other members of the household (Ellison, Bartkowski, and Anderson 1999; Pearce and Haynie 2004; Stokes and Regnerus 2009). Religious discord tends to lower the quality of the parent-teen relationship (Stokes and Regnerus 2009) primarily because the strained relationship is directly related to parental attachment and thus neutralizes religious coping as a mechanism of social control. Despite this line of reasoning, the weight of evidence from prior research suggests a more beneficial role of religion vis-à-vis economic disadvantage and delinquency.

Current Study

The picture painted by the current research suggests that there are gaps in our understanding of the relationship between economic disadvantage, violence, and religiosity. Much of the research pertaining to economic disadvantage and violence focuses on why violence occurs rather than why it does not occur. The current investigation hopes to shed further light on these associations.

This study seeks to make two contributions to the field of sociology. First, the findings on the economic disadvantage and violence relationship are inconsistent, which may be a function of how economic disadvantage is operationalized. Earlier studies indicate a direct correlation between the two, and some suggest that the relationship is causal and due to a myriad of social-psychological and structural mediators (Tittle and Meier 1990; Wright et al. 1999). As suggested by some researchers, these differences may also be due to how economic disadvantage is measured (Baron 2006; Ford, Bearman, and Moody 1999; Messner and South 1986).[2] This study therefore attempts to consider multiple dimensions of economic disadvantage by creating a scale comprising the many different aspects of economic disadvantage, such as household income, education level, job or profession, struggling to pay bills, government assistance, and neighborhood economic disadvantage so as to determine better the status of the economic disadvantage-violence relationship.

---

2   While there is literature for both correlation and causation between poverty and violence, we are making an argument for a causal effect of economic disadvantage on violence. To protect against the possibility of reverse causation, we are doing an autoregressive model. In addition, the time ordering of the measures should allow us to claim that we are estimating a causal effect.

Second, this study builds on Pargament's (1992, 1997, 1999, 2005) and Johnson and colleagues' work (Jang 2007; Jang and Johnson 2003, 2005; Johnson and Morris 2008; Piquero and Sealock 2004) on religiosity as a way of coping with negative life events. What is not known at this time is how adolescents use religiosity to cope with negative life events, such as economic disadvantage. Johnson and his colleagues have suggested that religiosity may condition the effects of economic disadvantage on adolescent delinquency. This study's main contribution to this line of research will be to examine whether Johnson and his colleagues were correct in their assumption that religiosity buffers the effect of economic disadvantage strain.

Data and Methods

This study utilizes Waves I and II of the National Longitudinal Study of Adolescent to Adult Health (Add Health), which is a nationally representative sample of U.S. adolescents in grades seven through twelve that was first conducted during the 1994–1995 school year (Bearman, Jones, and Udry 1997). Add Health initially surveyed over 90,000 students from 132 schools in 80 different communities through the use of a school-based clustered sample design. A subset of 20,745 adolescents completed in-home interviews during the Wave I phase that was conducted in 1994 and 1995. A total of 14,396 adolescents completed both an in-home and an in-school survey during Wave I. Wave II data were collected in 1996, in which approximately 71 percent ($N = 14,738$) of the Wave I sample participated. It should be noted that Wave I twelfth-graders who graduated between waves were not included in Wave II. Also, those students with physical disabilities were excluded from Wave II. The cases that had valid data on all variables brought the base sample for this investigation to 10,798. The use of multiple imputation for missing data on all independent variables allowed for an increase of the base sample to 14,091 (Chantala and Tabor 1999).

Measures

Dependent Variable

Violent delinquency was created from eight measures from previous work that asked respondents two different sets of questions (Brookmeyer, Fanti, and Henrich 2006; Demuth and Brown 2004; Fang and Corso 2007; Haynie and Payne 2005; Johnson and Morris 2008; Resnick,

Ireland, and Borowsky 2004).[3] The first four measures asked the respondent, "How often did you (a) engage in a serious physical fight; (b) hurt someone badly enough to need bandages or medical care; (c) use or threaten to use a weapon to get something from someone and; (d) take part in a fight where a group of your friends was against another group?" These four measures were coded on a scale of 0 (for never) to 3 (for 5 or more times). The second set of questions asked the respondent, "In the past 12 months did you (a) pull a knife or gun on someone; (b) shoot or stab someone; (c) carry a weapon to school, and; (d) use a weapon in a fight?" These four measures were coded 0 (for no) and 1 (for yes). The violent delinquency items were standardized because they had different measurement metrics. The eight items were then scaled to create the violent delinquency measure by taking the mean of these scores and multiplying by the number of items present. The scale created from all eight measures had a Cronbach's alpha reliability of 0.75.

Key Independent Variables

Religiosity.
Private religiosity. Private religiosity includes the combination of two variables: religious importance and frequency of prayer. Religious importance is measured by a question that asks, "How important is religion to you?" Responses for this question range from 0 (for not important at all) to 3 (for very important). Frequency of prayer asks the respondent, "How often do you pray?" Responses range from 0 (for never pray) to 4 (for daily prayer or more). Since these two items had differences in measurement metrics, they were standardized. These two items were then scaled by taking the mean of the items and multiplying by two. This scale had a Cronbach's alpha reliability of 0.81.

Public religiosity. Public religiosity was measured by two variables: church or service attendance and involvement in other religious activities (Bible study, choir, youth group, etc.). Church or religious service attendance was measured by asking respondents, "In the past 12 months, how often did you attend such activities?" These responses range from 0 (for never) to 3 (for weekly or more). Participation in other church-related

---

3 The dependent variable is a self-report of frequency of behavioral acts committed. Although subject to recall bias and self-serving under reporting, it is similar to the way in which several such phenomena are measured, e.g. domestic violence and other behaviors.

activities was measured by asking respondents, "Many churches, synagogues, and places of worship have special activities for teenagers, such as youth group, bible classes, or choir. In the last 12 months, how often did you participate in these activities?" Responses for this question ranged from 0 (for never) to 3 (for once a week or more). The two items were combined into a single scale. The scale had a Cronbach's alpha reliability of 0.75. This scale was then centered around the mean.

Born-again. Being a born-again Christian was measured via a single item that asked respondents, "Do you think of yourself as a Born-again Christian?" Responses for this variable were 0 (for no) and 1 (for yes). Being born-again refers to a biblical passage (John 3:1-5) where rebirth is achieved via both water and spiritual baptism. Therefore, identifying as born-again means that the respondent has a strong belief that his or her behavior needs to reflect that of Jesus Christ because it is believed that the spirit of God resides inside the person (Bielo 2004).

Economic Disadvantage Strain Measure. Much of the literature in criminology measures economic disadvantage based on a combination of income, educational level, occupation, welfare or government assistance, and concentrated disadvantage (Allison et al.1999; Anderson 1999; Bearman and Moody 2004; Elliot et al. 1996; Kasarda and Janowitz 1974; Kingston, Huizinga, and Elliott 2009; Sampson, Morenoff, and Earls 1999; Shaw and McKay 1942). It has been argued in family research, however, that economic disadvantage is subjective depending on those contributing to the household income, the household size, and the number of children in the household (Edin and Kissane 2010; Roosa et al. 2005). Therefore, to incorporate the multidimensional aspects of economic disadvantage noted throughout both bodies of literature, the measure that operationalized economic disadvantage was created from many indicators. Each indicator was measured at Wave I and was self-reported by the parents of the adolescent.

To obtain an accurate depiction of actual economic disadvantage for each household, an economic disadvantage threshold measure was created. The economic disadvantage threshold measure includes the size of each household (number of adults and children) and the minimum income that the household would need to be considered above the economic disadvantage line (U.S. Census Bureau 1994). The household size was taken from twenty different questions that asked respondents to indicate the ages of persons in their household. In the Add Health data, responses for household size ranged from 0 to 90. Persons who were eighteen or older were counted as adults, and those seventeen and younger were counted as children. Two separate variables were created from this information so that one variable would measure the total number of adults per household, and the other variable would measure the total number of children per household. Because the data did not ask the respondent to include himself or herself, one was added to the summed number of children.

Household income was derived from a single measure that asked the respondents' parents, "About how much total income, before taxes, did your family receive in 1994? Include your own income, the income of everyone else in your household, and income from welfare benefits, dividends, and all other sources." Responses ranged from $0 to $999,000. The U.S. Census Bureau's 1994 income threshold chart was used to determine the economic disadvantage level threshold for each household by taking the number of adults, the number of children, and the minimum income that household would need to stay above economic disadvantage. These data were used to create a binary economic disadvantage threshold indicator. Households with income at or below the threshold were coded 1 to indicate economic disadvantage, while those with incomes above the threshold were coded 0 to indicate that they were not in economic disadvantage.

To account for more extreme measures of economic disadvantage, a series of questions asking the respondents' parents, "Did you or any member of your household receive . . . ?" were also included in the analyses. These items included some form of state government assistance, such as supplemental security income (SSI), aid to families with dependent children, food stamps, unemployment, welfare, or housing subsidy or public housing. A binary variable was created to indicate if a respondent's household received one or more forms of assistance, with yes coded as 1 and no coded as 0. An additional economic stress measure was included through the use of a single question that asked the respondents' parents, "Did you ever feel you didn't have the money to pay your bills?" This question was also coded as a binary measure (0 = no; 1 = yes).

In alignment with prior research (Bearman and Moody 2004), parents' education and employment status were combined into a scale of family socioeconomic status (fSES). The fSES variable utilizes separate measures of mother's education, father's education, mother's occupation, and father's occupation (each coded as a 5-point scale, from low to high). These four summed scores then range from 1 = low SES to 10 = high SES. This measure was then reverse coded to 1 = high SES to 10 =

low SES so that it would be in the same direction as the other economic disadvantage indicators.

A neighborhood economic disadvantage measure was created using U.S. Census track data that reports the percentage of families below economic disadvantage residing in a given neighborhood. This measure is coded based on the proportions of persons with income in 1989 below the economic disadvantage level in each respondent's neighborhood. Neighborhood economic disadvantage was coded 1 (for 30 percent or more of families living at or below economic disadvantage level in the respondent's neighborhood) and 0 (for 29 percent or fewer of families living at or below economic disadvantage level in the respondent's neighborhood).

All of the aforementioned measures (economic disadvantage threshold, extreme measures of economic disadvantage, fSES, neighborhood economic disadvantage) were then standardized since they had different measurement metrics. Once standardized, these items were then scaled by taking the mean of the items and then multiplying by the number of items. This process created one measure of economic disadvantage, a measure which includes all of the aforementioned dimensions of economic disadvantage.

Controls

Control variables were measured at Wave I and were self-reported. Prior violence was operationalized via violent behavior. This variable was measured the same way as the outcome mentioned earlier. Sociodemographic variables include race, gender, family structure, and age. Race and ethnicity were operationalized by four mutually exclusive racial categories: White, Black, Hispanic/Latino origin, and Other. Three dummy variables were created to model these categories, with white serving as the reference category. *Gender* was coded 1 for females and 0 for males with male as the reference group. *Family structure* variables were used to account for findings in previous literature that single parents are most likely to live in economic disadvantage (Petts 2009). A series of binary measures were created to operationalize family structure and measured whether adolescents live with two biological parents, a stepfamily, a single mother, or a single father. Two-parent biological families served as the reference category. *Age* was calculated as the number of years between birth and the Wave I interview.

Other potentially important controls as outlined by previous literature are family support or coping, parental supervision, and parents' social capital. Family support is a key aspect of adolescent delinquency, as family support provides coping strategies for adolescents when they are dealing with difficulties (Anderson 1999). A five-item index for family social support was created from the following questions: (a) how much do you feel your parent cares about you; (b) your family understands you; (c) your family gives you attention; (d) your family has fun together, and; (e) you desire to leave home. Each of these items was coded 1 (for not at all) to 5 (for very much), with the exception that desire to leave home was reverse coded so that higher numbers indicate less desire to leave home. These five items were then summed, and the scale has a Cronbach's alpha of 0.76.

Parental supervision is important for keeping adolescents' behavior on task and ensuring they are completing their responsibilities (Anderson 1999). Following Demuth and Brown (2004), a parental supervision index was created for use in the current study. The parental supervision index includes seven items concerning family processes. Six of the items were derived from the following questions: (a) how often is your mother home when you leave for school; (b) how often is your mother home when you return from school; (c) how often is your mother home when you go to bed; (d) how often is your father home when you leave for school; (e) how often is your father home when you return from school, and; (f) how often is your father home when you go to bed? These variables ranged from 0 (for never) to 4 (for always). The last item included in the index was taken from the question, "How often each week does at least one of your parents eat with you?" This question was also measured on a metric ranging from 0 (for never) to 4 (for always). These seven items were summed, and the scale has a Cronbach's alpha of 0.79.

In line with Coleman's (1988) social capital description, intergenerational closure was measured with a single item that asked parents the number of their child's friends' parents they had talked to in the previous four weeks. Possible responses ranged from 0 = none to 6 = six or more.

Analytical Strategy

We use Tobit regression to model violence as a function of economic disadvantage and other predictors. Tobit is intended for continuous data that are censored at a certain limiting value (DeMaris 2004), as is the case in this study. That is, our response value is censored at a lower limit of zero.

For measures of self-reported offending in Add Health data, there may be some response measures (e.g., measures of violent delinquency) that are not sensitive enough to pick up lower levels of the construct measuring delinquency (Osgood, Finken, and McMorris 2002). We estimate Tobit regression models using an autoregressive approach. That is, the Wave I measure of the dependent variable was included as a control in all the models. Hence, the regressor effects can be interpreted as effects on the change in delinquency from Wave I to Wave II. First, the economic disadvantage and violence at Wave I variable was entered into the model, followed by the main religion measures (public and private religiosity), the interaction terms of religiosity measures with economic disadvantage, and lastly the control variables.

Additionally, some respondents at Wave I did not stay in school and had dropped out of the study by Wave II. This occurrence can introduce sample-selection bias into the regression estimates if characteristics associated with dropping out of the sample are also predictive of delinquency. We therefore reran our final model using Heckman's (1979) technique that controls for sample selectivity. It turned out that the correlation of errors in the substantive and selection equations in the Heckman model was nonsignificant (not shown). This finding implies that there are no unmeasured factors affecting both the tendency to be included in the sample and the response variable. In other words, no evidence of sample-selection bias was found in the current analyses. Hence, only the Tobit regression analyses are reported in this manuscript (Heckman results are available from the senior author upon request).

Results

Table 13-1 presents the descriptive statistics for all the variables used in the analysis. This table includes respondents from Waves I and II. Adolescent violence was the sum of the standardized items. On average, the mean score of 2.429 suggests that respondents were publicly involved in religiosity on at least a monthly basis. The mean for private religiosity is zero because this measure is the mean of the sum of standardized items. About 27 percent of respondents identify as born-again. The sociodemographic characteristics of this sample indicate that approximately 52 percent of respondents in the sample were female, 54 percent were white, 22 percent were Black, 16 percent were Hispanic/Latino, and 8 percent were from other racial or ethnic classifications. Average age of respondents was 15.275 years old. About 50 percent of the respondents were

Table 13-1: Descriptive Statistics

Variable	Mean	Std. Dev.	Min.	Max.
Violence Wave 2	0.000	5.231	−3.007	44.81
Economic Disadvantage	0.000	5.190	−5.896	24.492
Violence Wave 1	0.000	2.920	−2.926	44.81
Public Religiosity	2.429	2.166	0	6
Private Religiosity	0.000	1.849	−3.935	1.796
Born-Again	0.267	0.442	0	1
Performing Arts	0.331	0.408	0	1
Female	0.510	0.499	0	1
Age	15.275	1.423	11	17
White	0.536	0.499	0	1
Black	0.220	0.419	0	1
Hispanic	0.164	0.369	0	1
Other	0.079	0.273	0	1
Biological Parents	0.495	0.499	0	1
Stepfamilies	0.163	0.369	0	1
Single Mom	0.248	0.432	0	1
Single Dad	0.035	0.183	0	1
Other Parent	0.058	0.234	0	1
Family Support	19.829	3.510	5	25
Parental Supervision	9.943	2.214	0	14
Social Capital	2.076	1.753	0	6

$N = 14,091$

residing with both biological parents, 16 percent were residing in stepfamilies, 25 percent were residing in single-mother households, 4 percent were residing in single-father households, and 6 percent were residing in other family structures.

Multivariate Results: Religiosity as Moderation

Table 13-2 presents the Tobit regression results. Model 1 establishes a baseline for further analysis of the relationship between economic disadvantage and violence by controlling for Wave I violence. When examining the economic disadvantage effect, Model 1 shows that economic disadvantage has a positive and statistically significant effect on violence. Model 2 adds the religiosity dimensions of public religiosity, private religiosity, and born-again religious identification. The second model suggests that public religiosity and born-again status are nonsignificant predictors of violence. Private religiosity is negatively associated with violence at an alpha level of 0.05. Private religiosity is associated with 0.034 less violence. That is to say, the more privately religious the respondent is, the less he or she will engage in violent behavior.

Model 3 adds the interaction effects of each religiosity dimension with economic disadvantage. None of these effects were statistically significant. Model 4 adds the statistical controls of gender, age, race and ethnicity, family structure, family support, parental supervision, and social capital. The results show that economic disadvantage remains a statistically significant and positive predictor of violence in Model 4. The interaction effects become significant once the controls are in the model. The effect of economic disadvantage is 0.121 for those with mean public and private religiosity; it gets stronger by 0.046 with each unit increment in public religiosity and weaker by 0.028 with private religiosity. In addition, being female, older, and having family support will lower the amount of violence perpetrated by respondents. In contrast, being Black, Hispanic, being in a stepfamily, having a single mother, and having some other type of family structure will increase a participant's level of violence.[4]

---

[4] Additional data analyses (not shown) were run with the models for separate measures of prayer, religious importance, church attendance, and involvement in church activities. These results indicated that religious importance and prayer were nonsignificant. Church attendance was negatively related to violence, and religious activities were positively related to violence at 0.05. When the interactions are added in Model 3, however, none are statistically significant. When the control variables are added in Model 4, religious activity involvement and poverty interaction is statistically significant; no other interactions were statistically significant. Items were added together to create the public and private religiosity and the born-again measures to get at different aspects of religiosity and the cumulative effect of being involved in more than one aspect as previous work suggests (Jang 2007; Jang and Johnson 2003, 2005; Johnson and Morris 2008; Pargament 1997, 1999; Pargament and Mahoney 2005; Pargament et al. 1992; Smith and Denton 2005).

Table 13-2: Tobit Regression Coefficient Estimates (Standard Errors) for Models of Economic Disadvantage, Religiosity, and Violence

Predictors	Model 1		Model 2		Model 3		Model 4	
Intercept	-2.687	(0.086)***	-2.493	(0.096)***	-2.499	(0.097)***	-2.365	(0.441)***
Economic Disadvantage	0.051	(0.020)**	0.046	(0.020)*	0.048	(0.025)*	0.121	(0.037)***
Violence Wave 1	0.826	(0.014)***	0.856	(0.015)***	0.856	(0.015)***	0.764	(0.016)***
Public Religiosity			-0.018	(0.019)	-0.039	(0.023)	-0.067	(0.023)**
Private Religiosity			-0.035	(0.017)*	-0.034	(0.016)*	-0.024	(0.018)
Born-Again			-0.079	(0.076)	-0.077	(0.076)	-0.109	(0.084)
Public Religiosity*Economic Disadvantage					0.020	(0.013)	0.047	(0.017)**
Private Religiosity*Economic Disadvantage					-0.009	(0.011)	-0.028	(0.015)+
Born-Again*Economic Disadvantage					0.004	(0.052)	-0.013	(0.073)
Female							-0.957	(0.666)***
Age at Wave 1							-0.203	(0.021)***
Black							0.440	(0.085)***

(continued)

Table 13-2: Tobit Regression Coefficient Estimates (Standard Errors) for Models of Economic Disadvantage, Religiosity, and Violence (*continued*)

Predictors	Model 1	Model 2	Model 3	Model 4
Hispanic				0.382 (0.089)***
Other Race				0.196 (0.340)
Stepfamily				0.196 (0.092)*
Single Mother				0.216 (0.084)**
Single Father				0.466 (0.196)*
Other Family Structure				0.567 (0.153)***
Family Support				−0.078 (0.009)***
Parental Supervision				0.012 (0.016)
Parent Social Capital				0.001 (0.017)
R^2	0.1001	0.1003	0.1006	0.1106

$N = 14{,}091$ respondents; * $p < 0.05$, ** $p < 0.01$, *** $p < 0.001$, + $p < 0.1000$

Discussion and Conclusion

The results of our analyses show that with respect to the relationship between economic disadvantage and violence, economic disadvantage does increase the amount of violence among teens in the sample, net of other factors. Our finding aligns with some of the previous literature pertaining to strain theory on the relationship between economic disadvantage and delinquency (Allison et al. 1999; Anderson 1999; Baron 2006; Braithwaite 1981; Messner and South 1986; Webber 2008). In alignment with this work, we found that economic disadvantage is associated with more violence, net of controls. This finding is not surprising given that the economic disadvantage measure was operationalized to include the multiple dimensions of income disadvantage. This finding is also not surprising when one considers the fact that economic disadvantage is cumulative in nature, insofar as one dimension of economic disadvantage can lead to another (Agnew 2001). Nonetheless, it is important to acknowledge the magnitude of this finding, as there has been much debate over the economic disadvantage-violence relationship in the literature (Braithwaite 1981; Tittle and Meier 1991; Wright et al. 1999).

Results also illustrate that private religiosity moderates the economic disadvantage-violence relationship, meaning that private religiosity acts as a buffer to the relationship between economic disadvantage and violence. That is to say, poorer youth who self-report more private religiosity engage in less violence. While this result was only marginally significant, this relatively weak effect may be due to measurement limitations. It may be the case that the private religiosity measure we employed does incorporate some aspect of one's private relationship with God, but it does not provide enough information about the depth of that relationship. Pargament (1997) argues that individuals who believe their faith to be a sacred, significant, and ongoing connection with God are more likely to cope with stressful situations than someone who may just pray and attend church. This measurement limitation is one of the drawbacks of our study that will be discussed later pertaining to the use of global indicators of religiosity rather than measures which aim at drawing out the strength of how close an individual feels to God (Pargament 1997, 1999; Pargament and Mahoney 2005; Pargament et al. 1992).

Contrary to the expectation put forth in our study, it was also found that public religiosity amplifies the relationship between economic disadvantage and violence. Due to the nature of the data, however, we do not have the measures that would allow us to untangle the dynamics behind this finding. It may simply be the case that the more violent youth are more publicly involved at their churches at the request of their parents or court officials.

Within the social control theory religiosity literature, there is much debate on whether or not religiosity effectively decreases delinquency (Eggebeen and Dew 2009; Hirschi and Stark 1969; Johnson et al. 2001; Tittle and Welch 1983). Scholars who used a single indicator of church attendance did not find much of an impact (Hirschi and Stark 1969) as compared to researchers who used several indicators to capture the multiple dimensions of religiosity (Chu 2007; Cochran et al. 1994; Desmond et al. 2009; Jang and Johnson 2001; Mason and Windle 2002; Wallace et al. 2007). As expected, this line of thought that religiosity is multidimensional supported the previously hypothesized buffering relationship that private religiosity will be more negatively related to delinquency than other dimensions of religiosity.

Study Limitations

There are a few limitations in this study that are worth noting. First, it should be acknowledged that the Add Health dataset is a school-based questionnaire. The school-based design of Add Health creates a potential sample selection bias because it may exclude the most disadvantaged groups of individuals who were incarcerated or dropped out of school for various reasons before the data were collected. Participation of these groups is essential to a study of this nature, and their exclusion may have resulted in conservative estimates of the moderation of religiosity on the association between economic disadvantage and violence. We did attempt to address some of the selection issues via use of the Heckman sample selection correction. This approach was only applied to possible selection that may have occurred between Waves I and II, however, and not prior to data collection.

There are some measurement issues that also need to be addressed. The primary purpose of this study was to assess the moderation of religiosity on the economic disadvantage-violence association. There were a number of shortcomings with regard to the operationalization of religiosity. The most prominent weakness of the religiosity measures employed in this study is the lack of a denominational measure. Research consistently indicates (Burdette et al. 2007) that there is considerable variation across denominations in the adherence to religious prescriptions and proscriptions regarding a litany of delinquent behaviors (e.g. alcohol use and drug use). It is therefore highly plausible that the conditioning effects of religiosity are potentially a result of denominational affiliation. It could also be argued that the moderating effects of religiosity are more likely to be in operation among a religious denomination that is known for its fundamental principles (i.e., evangelical Protestants). While adopting a general classification for religious denomination may appear to be straightforward, there is considerable empirical debate as to the correct classification of individual denominations (Blanchard et al. 2008; Burdette et al. 2007; Steensland et al. 2000) into broader categories based on some dimension of conservatism. The resulting ambiguity from this debate in the empirical religious literature makes classification a difficult task, and based on this lack of consensus within the scientific community (as well as the convoluted coding schemes of religious denomination in the Add Health dataset), a measure of religious denomination was not included in this investigation. Taking this limitation into account, it must be acknowledged that the lack of an indicator of denominational affiliation may have had a deleterious impact on the results of our study.

Our study examined religiosity in terms of more global measures, i.e., church attendance, other church activities, prayer, and religious importance. There is research that suggests that when individuals seek to understand their circumstances from a religious (i.e., godly) perspective, they may interpret their suffering as spiritual warfare, punishment by God, or as a test or trial by God (Pargament 1999; Pargament and Mahoney 2005; Pargament et al. 1992). Estimating these aspects of religiosity was beyond the capabilities of the Add Health dataset. Nevertheless, measuring these more esoteric aspects of religiosity may allow for a greater potential to discover relationships than when more common global measures of religiosity are used. Pargament and colleagues (1992, 1997, 1999, 2005) measure religious coping through a series of indices asking individuals about their relationship with or closeness to God, God's control in situations, responsiveness of God to prayers or meditations, and living a more godly life. Their work suggests that measuring religiousness in this context addresses the individual's inner spirituality and connectedness to God. Unfortunately, global indicators of religiosity were the only types of measures available aside from religious affiliation in the Add Health dataset in Waves I and II.

Despite these limitations, the findings of this study contribute to the augmentation of existing research that assesses the potential moderation effects of religiosity on the economic disadvantage-delinquency relationship. This study extended the line of inquiry established by other researchers (Allport 1971 [1954]; Eggebeen and Dew 2009; Jang and Johnson 2003) through an improvement in the economic disadvantage and religiosity measures used in this investigation. Most specifically, this study contributed to the body of literature in two areas. First, the moderating effect of religiosity does depend on the dimension of religiosity (e.g. public, private, born-again). Our study demonstrates religiosity does condition the association between economic disadvantage and violence. Second, the elaboration of Agnew's strain theory as having potential conditioning factors related to social control is useful in helping to understanding and potentially reducing violence among poor teens.

References

Adamczyk, Amy. 2009. "Understanding the Effects of Personal and School Religiousness on Decision to Abort a Premarital Pregnancy." *Journal of Health and Social Behavior* 50: 180–95.

Agnew, Robert. 1985. "A Revised Strain Theory of Delinquency." *Social Forces* 64: 151–67.

Agnew, Robert. 1992. "Foundation for a General Strain Theory of Crime and Delinquency." *Criminology* 30: 47–87.

Agnew, Robert. 1993. "Why Do They Do It? An Examination of the Intervening Mechanisms between 'Social Control' Variables and Delinquency." *Journal of Research in Crime and Delinquency* 30: 245–66.

Agnew, Robert. 1999. "A General Strain Theory of Community Differences in Crime Rates." *Journal of Research in Crime and Delinquency* 36: 123–55.

Agnew, Robert. 2001. "Building on the Foundations of General Strain Theory: Specifying the Types of Strain." *Journal of Research in Crime and Delinquency* 38: 319–61.

Allison, Kevin W., Isiaah Crawford, Peter E. Leone, Edison Tickett, Alina Perez-Febles, Linda M. Burton, and Ree LeBlanc. 1999. "Adolescent Substance Use: Preliminary Examinations of School and Neighborhood Context." *American Journal of Community Psychology* 27: 111–41.

Allport, Gordon W. 1971 [1954]. *The Individual and His Religion: A Psychological Interpretation*. New York: Macmillan.

Anderson, Elijah. 1999. *Code of the Street: Decency, Violence, and the Moral Life of the Inner City*. New York: Norton.

Baron, Stephen W. 2006. "Street Youth, Strain Theory, and Crime." *Journal of Criminal Justice* 34: 209–23.

Baron, Stephen W. 2007. "Street Youth, Gender, Financial Strain: Exploring Broidy and Agnew's Extension to General Strain Theory." *Deviant Behavior* 28: 273–302.

Bearman, Peter S., Jo Jones, and J. Richard Udry. 1997. *The National Longitudinal Study of Adolescent Health: Research Design*. Available at http://www.cpc.unc.edu/addhealth.

Bearman, Peter, and James Moody. 2004. "Suicide and Friendships among American Adolescents." *American Journal of Public Health* 94: 89–95.

Bielo, James S. 2004. "Walking in the Spirit of Blood: Moral Identity among Born-Again Christians." *Ethnology* 43: 271–89.

Blanchard, Tony C., John P. Bartkowski, Todd L. Matthews, and Kent R. Kerley. 2008. "Faith, Morality, and Mortality: The Ecological Impact of Religion on Population Health." *Social Forces* 86: 1591–1619.

Braithwaite, John. 1981. "The Myth of Social Class and Criminality Reconsidered." *American Sociological Review* 46: 36–57.

Brookmeyer, Kathryn A., Kostas A. Fanti, and Christopher C. Henrich. 2006. "Schools, Parents, and Youth Violence: A Multilevel, Ecological Analysis." *Journal of Clinical Child & Adolescent Psychology* 35: 504–14.

Burdette, Amy M., Christopher G. Ellison, Darren E. Sherkat, and Kurt A. Gore. 2007. "Are There Religious Variations in Marital Infidelity?" *Journal of Family Issues* 28: 134–54.

Burkett, Steven R., and David A. Ward. 1993. "A Note on Perceptual Deterrence, Religiously Based Moral Condemnation, and Social Control." *Criminology* 31: 119–34.

Burkett, Steven R., and Mervin White. 1974. "Hellfire and Delinquency: Another Look." *Journal for the Scientific Study of Religion* 13: 455–62.

Cernkovich, Stephen A. and Peggy C. Giordano. 1992. "School Bonding, Race, and Delinquency." *Criminology* 30: 261–91.

Chantala, Kim, and Joyce Tabor. 1999. "National Longitudinal Study of Adolescent Health: Strategies to Perform a Design-Based Analysis Using the Add Health." Carolina Population Center, University of North Carolina Chapel Hill.

Chu, Doris C. 2007. "Religiousness and Desistance from Drug Use." *Criminal Justice and Behavior* 34: 661–79.

Cloward, R., and L. Ohlin. 1960. *Delinquency and Opportunity*. Glencoe, IL: Free Press.

Cochran, John K. 1993. "The Variable Effects of Religiousness and Denomination on Adolescent Self-Reported Alcohol Use by Beverage Type." *Journal of Drug Issues* 23: 479–91.

Cochran, John K., Peter B. Wood, and Bruce J. Arneklev. 1994. "Is the Religiosity-Delinquency Relationship Spurious? A Test of Arousal and Social Control Theories." *Journal of Research in Crime and Delinquency* 61: 92–123.

Coleman, James S. 1988. "Social Capital in Creation of Human Capital." *The American Journal of Sociology* 94 (Supplemental): S95-S120.

Compas, Bruce E., Jennifer K. Connor-Smith, Heidi Saltzman, Alexandra Harding Thomsen, and Martha E. Wadsworth. 2001. "Coping with Stress in Childhood and Adolescences: Problems, Progress, and Potential in Theory and Research." *Psychological Bulletin* 127: 87-127.

Cretacci, Michael A. 2003. "Religion and Social Control: An Application of Modified Social Bond on Violence." *Criminal Justice Review* 28: 254-77.

Curry, Theodore R. 1996. "Conservative Protestantism and the Perceived Wrongfulness of Crimes: A Research Note." *Criminology* 34: 453-64.

DeMaris, Alfred. 2004. *Regression with Social Data: Modeling Continuous and Limited Response Variables*. Hoboken, NJ: John Wiley & Sons.

Demuth, Stephen, and Susan L. Brown. 2004. "Family Structure, Family Processes, and Adolescent Delinquency: The Significance of Parental Absence versus Parental Gender." *Journal of Research in Crime and Delinquency* 4: 58-81.

Desmond, Scott A., Sara E. Soper, David J. Purpura, and Elizabeth Smith. 2009. "Religiousness, Moral Beliefs, and Delinquency: Does the Effect of Religiousness on Delinquency Depend on Moral Beliefs." *Sociological Spectrum* 29: 51-71.

Durkheim, Emile. 2006 [1897]. *On Suicide*, translated by R. Buss. New York: Penguin.

Edin, Kathryn, and Rebecca Joyce Kissane. 2010. "Economic Disadvantage and the American Family: A Decade in Review." *Journal of Marriage and Family* 72: 460-79.

Eggebeen, David, and Jeffrey Dew. 2009. "The Role of Religion in Adolescence for Family Formation in Young Adulthood." *Journal of Marriage and Family* 71: 108-21.

Elley, Warrick B., and James C. Irving. 1976. "Revised Socio-Economic Index for New Zealand." *New Zealand Journal of Educational Studies* 7: 153-67.

Elliot, Delbert S., William Julius Wilson, David Huizinga, Robert J. Sampson, Amanda Elliott, and Bruce Rankin. 1996. "The Effects of Neighborhood Disadvantage on Adolescent Development." *Journal of Research in Crime and Delinquency* 33: 389-426.

Ellison, Christopher G., John P. Bartkowski, and Kristin L. Anderson. 1999. "Are There Religious Variations in Domestic Violence?" *Journal of Family Issues* 20: 87-113.

Fang, Xiangming, and Phaedra S. Corso. 2007. "Child Maltreatment, Youth Violence, and Intimate Partner Violence: Developmental Relationships." *American Journal of Preventive Medicine* 33: 281-90.

Ford, Carol A., Peter S. Bearman, and James Moody. 1999. "Foregone Health Care among Adolescents." *Journal of American Medical Association* 282: 2227-34.

Gunnoe, Marjorie Lindner, E. Mavis Hetherington, and David Reiss. 1999. "Parental Religiosity, Parenting Style, and Adolescent Social Responsibility." *The Journal of Early Adolescence* 19: 199–225.

Haynie, Dana L., and Danielle C. Payne. 2006. "Race, Friendship Networks, and Violent Delinquency." *Criminology* 44: 775–805.

Haynie, Dana L., Eric Silver, and Brent Teasdale. 2006. "Neighborhood Characteristics, Peer Networks, and Adolescent Violence." *Journal of Quantitative Criminology* 22: 147–69.

Heckman, James J. 1979. "Sample Selection Bias as a Specification Error." *Econometrics* 47: 153–61.

Heimer, Karen. 1997. "Socioeconomic Status, Subculture Definitions, and Violent Delinquency." *Social Forces* 75: 799–833.

Hirschi, Travis, and Rodney Stark. 1969. "Hellfire and Delinquency." *Social Problems* 17: 202–13.

Jang, Sung Joon. 2007. "Gender Differences in Strain, Negative Emotions, and Coping Behaviors: A General Strain Theory Approach." *Justice Quarterly* 24: 523–53.

Jang, Sung Joon, and Byron R. Johnson. 2001. "Neighborhood Disorder, Individual Religiousness, and Adolescent Use of Illicit Drugs: A Test of Multilevel Hypotheses." *Criminology* 39: 109–43.

Jang, Sung Joon, and Byron R. Johnson. 2003. "Strain, Negative Emotions and Deviant Coping among African Americans: A Test of General Strain Theory." *Journal of Quantitative Criminology* 19: 79–105.

Jang, Sun Joon, and Byron R. Johnson. 2005. "Gender, Religiousness, and Reactions to Strain among African Americans." *The Sociological Quarterly* 46: 323–57.

Jencks, Christopher. 1992. *Rethinking Social Policy: Race, Poverty, and the Underclass*. Cambridge, MA: Harvard University Press.

Johnson, Byron R., Sung Joon Jang, David B. Larson, and Spencer De Li. 2001. "Does Adolescent Religious Commitment Matter? A Reexamination of the Effects of Religiousness on Delinquency." *Journal of Research in Crime and Delinquency* 38: 22–44.

Johnson, Matthew C., and Robert G. Morris. 2008. "The Moderating Effects of Religiosity on the Relationship between Stressful Life Events and Delinquent Behavior." *Journal of Criminal Justice* 36: 486–93.

Johnstone, John W. C. 1978. "Social Class, Social Areas, and Delinquency." *Sociology and Social Research* 63: 49–72.

Juergensmeyer, Mark. 2003. *Terror in the Mind of God*. Berkeley: University of California Press.

Kasarda, John D., and Morris Janowitz. 1974. "Community Attachment in Mass Society." *American Sociological Review* 39: 328–39.

Kingston, Beverly, David Huizinga, and Delbert S. Elliott. 2009. "A Test of Social Disorganization Theory in High-Risk Urban Neighborhoods." *Youth & Society* 41: 53–79.

Koch, Jeremy R., and Ignacio Luis Ramirez. 2009. "Religiosity, Christian Fundamentalism, and Intimate Partner Violence." *Review of Religious Research* 51: 402–10.

Krivo, Lauren J., and Ruth D. Peterson. 1996. "The Structural Context of Homicide: Accounting for Racial Differences in Process." *American Sociological Review* 65: 547–59.

Ludwig, Jens, Greg J. Duncan, and Joshua C. Pinkston. 2000. *Neighborhood Effects on Economic Self-Sufficiency: Evidence from a Randomized Housing-Mobility Experiment*. Evanston, IL: Joint Center for Poverty Research.

Mason, W. A., and M. Windle. 2002. "Family, Religious, School, and Peer Influences on Adolescent Alcohol Use." *The Prevention Researcher* 9: 6–7.

Merton, Robert K. 1938. "Social Structure and Anomie." *American Sociological Review* 54: 597–611.

Messner, Steven F., and Scott J. South. 1986. "Economic Deprivation, Opportunity Structure, and Robbery Victimization: Intra- and Interracial Patterns." *Social Forces* 64: 975–91.

Office of the Surgeon General. 2001. "Youth Violence: A Report of the Surgeon General." U.S. Department of Health and Human Services. Retrieved May 1, 2015 from http://www.ncbi.nlm.nih.gov/books/NBK44293/.

Osgood, D. Wayne, Laura L. Finken, and Barbara J. McMorris. 2002. "Analyzing Multiple-Item Measures of Crime and Deviance II: Tobit Regression Analysis of Transformed Scores." *Journal of Quantitative Criminology* 18: 319–47.

Pargament, Kenneth I. 1990. "God Help Me: Toward a Theoretical Framework of Coping for the Psychology of Religion." *Research in the Social Scientific Study of Religion* 2: 195–224.

Pargament, Kenneth I. 1992. "Of Means and Ends: Religion and the Search for Significance." *International Journal for the Psychology of Religion* 2: 201–29.

Pargament, Kenneth I. 1997. *The Psychology of Religion and Coping: Theory, Research, and Practice*. New York: Guilford Press.

Pargament, Kenneth I. 1999. "The Psychology of Religion and Spirituality? Yes and No." *International Journal for the Psychology of Religion* 9: 3–16.

Pargament, Kenneth I., Gina M. Magyar-Russell, and Nichole A. Murray-Swank. 2005. "The Sacred and the Search for Significance: Religion as a Unique Process." *Journal of Social Issues* 61: 665–87.

Pargament, Kenneth I., and Annette Mahoney. 2005. "Sacred Matters: Sanctification as a Vital Topic for Psychology of Religion." *International Journal for the Psychology of Religion* 15: 179–98.

Pargament, Kenneth I., and Kenneth Maton. 2000. "Religion in American Life: A Community Psychology Perspective." In *Handbook of Community*

Psychology, edited by J. Rappaport and E. Seidman, 495–521. New York: Kluwer Academic/Plenum Publishers.

Pargament, Kenneth I., Hannah Olsen, Barbara Reilly, Kathryn Falgout, David S. Ensing, and Kimberly Van Haitsma. 1992. "God Help Me (II): The Relationship of Religious Orientations to Religious Coping with Negative Life Events." *Journal for the Scientific Study of Religion* 31: 504–13.

Pargament, Kenneth I., and S. M. Saunders. 2007. "Introduction to the Special Issue on Spirituality and Psychotherapy." *Journal of Clinical Psychology* 63: 903–8.

Pearce, Lisa D., and Dana L. Haynie. 2004. "Intergenerational Religious Dynamics and Adolescent Delinquency." *Social Forces* 82: 1553–72.

Petts, Richard J. 2009. "Family and Religion Characteristics' Influence on Delinquency Trajectories from Adolescence to Young Adulthood." *American Sociological Review* 74: 465–83.

Piquero, Nichole Leeper, and Miriam D. Sealock. 2004. "Gender and Strain Theory: A Preliminary Test of Broidy and Agnew's Gender/GST Hypothesis." *Justice Quarterly* 21: 125–58.

Regnerus, Mark. 2007. *Forbidden Fruit: Sex and Religion in the Lives of American Teenagers*. New York: Oxford University Press.

Resnick, Michael D., Marjorie Ireland, and Iris Borowsky. 2004. "Youth Violence Perpetration: What Protects? What Predicts? Findings from the National Longitudinal Study of Adolescent Health." *Journal of Adolescent Health* 35: 424e1–424e3.

Roosa, Mark W., Shiying Deng, Rajmi L. Nair, and Ginger Lockhart Burrell. 2005. "Measures for Studying Economic Disadvantage in Family and Child Research." *Journal of Marriage and Family* 67: 971–88.

Sampson, Robert J., Jeffrey D. Morenoff, and Felton Earls. 1999. "Beyond Social Capital: Spatial Dynamics of Collective Efficacy For Children." *American Sociological Review* 64: 633–60.

Shaw, Clifford R., and Henry McKay. 1942. *Juvenile Delinquency and Urban Areas*. Chicago: The University of Chicago Press.

Smith, Christian, and Melinda Lundquist Denton. 2005. *Soul Searching: The Religious and Spiritual Lives of American Teenagers*. New York: Oxford University Press.

Stark, Rodney. 2001. "Gods, Rituals, and the Moral Order." *Journal for the Scientific Study of Religion* 40: 619–36.

Steensland, Brian, Jerry Z. Park, Mark D. Regnerus, Lynn D. Robinson, W. Bradford Wilcox, and Robert D. Woodbury. 2000. "The Measure of American Religion: Toward Improving the State of the Art." *Social Forces* 79: 291–318.

Stewart, Eric A., Christopher J. Schreck, and Ronald L. Simons. 2006. "'I Ain't Gonna Let No One Disrespect Me': Does the Code of the Street Reduce or Increase Violent Victimization among African American Adolescents?" *Journal of Research in Crime and Delinquency* 43: 427–58.

Stokes, Charles, and Mark D. Regnerus. 2009. "When Faith Divides Family: Religious Discord and Adolescent Reports of Parent-Child Relations." *Social Science Research* 38: 155–67.

Tittle, Charles R. 1991. "Specifying the SES/Delinquency Relationship by Characteristics of Context." *Journal of Research in Crime and Delinquency* 28: 430–55.

Tittle, Charles R., and Robert F. Meier. 1990. "Specifying the SES/Delinquency Relationship." *Criminology* 28: 271–99.

Tittle, Charles R., and Michael R. Welch. 1983. "Religiosity and Deviance: Toward a Contingency Theory of Constraining Effects." *Social Forces* 61: 653–82.

U.S. Census Bureau. 1994. Washington, DC. Available at: http://www.census.gov.

Wallace, John M. Jr., Ryoko Yamaguchi, Jerald G. Bachman, Patrick M. O'Malley, John E. Schulenberg, and Lloyd D. Johnston. 2007. "Religiousness and Adolescent Substance Use: The Role of Individual and Contextual Influences." *Social Problems* 54: 308–27.

Webber, C. 2008. "Revaluating Relative Deprivation Theory." *Theoretical Criminology* 11: 97–120.

Wright, Bradley R. Entner, Avshalom Caspi, Terrie E. Moffitt, Richard A. Miech, and Phil A. Silva. 1999. "Reconsidering the Relationship between SES and Delinquency: Causation but Not Correlation." *Criminology* 37: 175–94.

CONTRIBUTORS

Amy Adamczyk is professor of sociology at John Jay College of Criminal Justice and the Programs of Doctoral Study in Sociology and Criminal Justice at The Graduate Center, City University of New York.

Jennifer Bartholomew completed her Ph.D. in 2015 at the Mandel School of Applied Social Sciences, Case Western Reserve University.

Kristen Budd is associate professor in the sociology and gerontology department at Miami University.

Richard M. Clerkin is professor in the Department of Public Administration and Executive Director of the Institute for Nonprofits at North Carolina State University.

Alfred DeMaris is professor emeritus of sociology at Bowling Green State University.

Scott A. Desmond is assistant professor of sociology at Indiana University-Purdue University, Columbus.

Jacob Felson is professor and chair in the Department of Sociology and Criminal Justice at William Paterson University.

Robert L. Fischer is associate professor in the Mandel School of Applied Social Sciences at Case Western Reserve University.

Meredith J. Greif is assistant professor of sociology at Johns Hopkins University.

Brian J. Grim is a non-resident research fellow at Baylor University's Institute for Studies of Religion and president of the Religious Freedom & Business Foundation.

Melissa E. Grim is a Senior Fellow and Project Director at the Religious Freedom & Business Foundation.

John P. Hoffmann is professor and chair of the department of sociology at Brigham Young University.

William H. Jeynes is professor of education at California State University, Long Beach.

Byron R. Johnson is distinguished professor of the social sciences and director of the Institute for Studies of Religion at Baylor University.

George Kikuchi is assistant professor in the Department of Criminology, California State University, Fresno.

Jennifer M. McClure is assistant professor of religion and sociology at Samford University.

Benjamin McKune is a graduate student in sociology at Pennsylvania State University.

Stephen V. Monsma was a senior fellow at the Henry Institute, at Calvin College.

Cassady Pitt is the program director for the bachelor degree program in criminology at the Chicago School of Professional Psychology.

G. Alexander Ross is affiliated with the Institute for Psychological Sciences at Divine Mercy University.

Terry Shoemaker is a doctoral student in religious studies at Arizona State University.

James E. Swiss is affiliated with the Department of Public Administration at North Carolina State University.

Printed in the USA
CPSIA information can be obtained
at www.ICGtesting.com
LVHW040713191023
761536LV00001B/33